DESIGNERS' GUIDES TO THE EUROCODES

# DESIGNERS' GUIDE TO EN 1994-2 EUROCODE 4: DESIGN OF STEEL AND COMPOSITE STRUCTURES

# PART 2: GENERAL RULES AND RULES FOR BRIDGES

# Eurocode Designers' Guide Series

*Designers' Guide to EN 1990. Eurocode: Basis of Structural Design.* H. Gulvanessian, J.-A. Calgaro and M. Holický. 0 7277 3011 8. Published 2002.

*Designers' Guide to EN 1994-1-1. Eurocode 4: Design of Composite Steel and Concrete Structures. Part 1.1: General Rules and Rules for Buildings.* R. P. Johnson and D. Anderson. 0 7277 3151 3. Published 2004.

*Designers' Guide to EN 1997-1. Eurocode 7: Geotechnical Design – General Rules.* R. Frank, C. Bauduin, R. Driscoll, M. Kavvadas, N. Krebs Ovesen, T. Orr and B. Schuppener. 0 7277 3154 8. Published 2004.

*Designers' Guide to EN 1993-1-1. Eurocode 3: Design of Steel Structures. General Rules and Rules for Buildings.* L. Gardner and D. Nethercot. 0 7277 3163 7. Published 2004.

*Designers' Guide to EN 1992-1-1 and EN 1992-1-2. Eurocode 2: Design of Concrete Structures. General Rules and Rules for Buildings and Structural Fire Design.* A.W. Beeby and R. S. Narayanan. 0 7277 3105 X. Published 2005.

*Designers' Guide to EN 1998-1 and EN 1998-5. Eurocode 8: Design of Structures for Earthquake Resistance. General Rules, Seismic Actions, Design Rules for Buildings, Foundations and Retaining Structures.* M. Fardis, E. Carvalho, A. Elnashai, E. Faccioli, P. Pinto and A. Plumier. 0 7277 3348 6. Published 2005.

*Designers' Guide to EN 1995-1-1. Eurocode 5: Design of Timber Structures. Common Rules and for Rules and Buildings.* C. Mettem. 0 7277 3162 9. Forthcoming: 2007 (provisional).

*Designers' Guide to EN 1991-4. Eurocode 1: Actions on Structures. Wind Actions.* N. Cook. 0 7277 3152 1. Forthcoming: 2007 (provisional).

*Designers' Guide to EN 1996. Eurocode 6: Part 1.1: Design of Masonry Structures.* J. Morton. 0 7277 3155 6. Forthcoming: 2007 (provisional).

*Designers' Guide to EN 1991-1-2, 1992-1-2, 1993-1-2 and EN 1994-1-2. Eurocode 1: Actions on Structures. Eurocode 3: Design of Steel Structures. Eurocode 4: Design of Composite Steel and Concrete Structures. Fire Engineering (Actions on Steel and Composite Structures).* Y. Wang, C. Bailey, T. Lennon and D. Moore. 0 7277 3157 2. Forthcoming: 2007 (provisional).

*Designers' Guide to EN 1992-2. Eurocode 2: Design of Concrete Structures. Bridges.* D. Smith and C. Hendy. 0 7277 3159 9. Forthcoming: 2007 (provisional).

*Designers' Guide to EN 1993-2. Eurocode 3: Design of Steel Structures. Bridges.* C. Murphy and C. Hendy. 0 7277 3160 2. Forthcoming: 2007 (provisional).

*Designers' Guide to EN 1991-2, 1991-1-1, 1991-1-3 and 1991-1-5 to 1-7. Eurocode 1: Actions on Structures. Traffic Loads and Other Actions on Bridges.* J.-A. Calgaro, M. Tschumi, H. Gulvanessian and N. Shetty. 0 7277 3156 4. Forthcoming: 2007 (provisional).

*Designers' Guide to EN 1991-1-1, EN 1991-1-3 and 1991-1-5 to 1-7. Eurocode 1: Actions on Structures. General Rules and Actions on Buildings (not Wind).* H. Gulvanessian, J.-A. Calgaro, P. Formichi and G. Harding. 0 7277 3158 0. Forthcoming: 2007 (provisional).

www.eurocodes.co.uk

Books are to be returned on or before
the last date below.

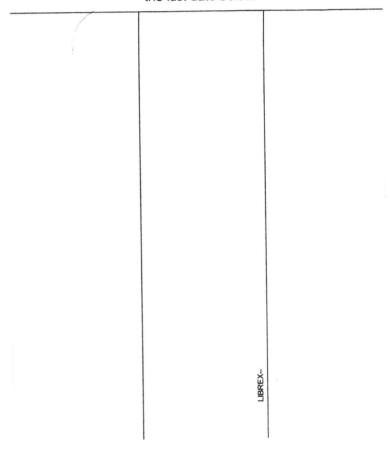

LIBREX–

DESIGNERS' GUIDES TO THE EUROCODES

# DESIGNERS' GUIDE TO EN 1994-2 EUROCODE 4: DESIGN OF STEEL AND COMPOSITE STRUCTURES

# PART 2: GENERAL RULES AND RULES FOR BRIDGES

C. R. HENDY and R. P. JOHNSON

Published by Thomas Telford Publishing, Thomas Telford Ltd, 1 Heron Quay, London E14 4JD
URL: www.thomastelford.com

Distributors for Thomas Telford books are
*USA*: ASCE Press, 1801 Alexander Bell Drive, Reston, VA 20191-4400
*Japan*: Maruzen Co. Ltd, Book Department, 3–10 Nihonbashi 2-chome, Chuo-ku, Tokyo 103
*Australia*: DA Books and Journals, 648 Whitehorse Road, Mitcham 3132, Victoria

First published 2006

---

**Eurocodes Expert**

**Structural Eurocodes offer the opportunity of harmonized design standards for the European construction market and the rest of the world. To achieve this, the construction industry needs to become acquainted with the Eurocodes so that the maximum advantage can be taken of these opportunities**

**Eurocodes Expert is a new ICE and Thomas Telford initiative set up to assist in creating a greater awareness of the impact and implementation of the Eurocodes within the UK construction industry**

**Eurocodes Expert provides a range of products and services to aid and support the transition to Eurocodes. For comprehensive and useful information on the adoption of the Eurocodes and their implementation process please visit our website or email eurocodes@thomastelford.com**

---

A catalogue record for this book is available from the British Library

ISBN: 0 7277 3161 0

This book is published on the understanding that the authors are solely responsible for the statements made and opinions expressed in it and that its publication does not necessarily imply that such statements and/or opinions are or reflect the views or opinions of the publishers. While every effort has been made to ensure that the statements made and the opinions expressed in this publication provide a safe and accurate guide, no liability or responsibility can be accepted in this respect by the authors or publishers.

Typeset by Academic + Technical, Bristol
Printed and bound in Great Britain by MPG Books, Bodmin

# Preface

EN 1994, also known as Eurocode 4 or EC4, is one standard of the Eurocode suite and describes the principles and requirements for safety, serviceability and durability of composite steel and concrete structures. It is subdivided into three parts:

- *Part 1.1: General Rules and Rules for Buildings*
- *Part 1.2: Structural Fire Design*
- *Part 2: General Rules and Rules for Bridges.*

It is used in conjunction with EN 1990, *Basis of Structural Design*; EN 1991, *Actions on Structures*; and the other design Eurocodes.

## Aims and objectives of this guide

The principal aim of this book is to provide the user with guidance on the interpretation and use of EN 1994-2 and to present worked examples. It covers topics that will be encountered in typical steel and concrete composite bridge designs, and explains the relationship between EN 1994-1-1, EN 1994-2 and the other Eurocodes. It refers extensively to EN 1992 (*Design of Concrete Structures*) and EN 1993 (*Design of Steel Structures*), and includes the application of their provisions in composite structures. Further guidance on these and other Eurocodes will be found in other Guides in this series.[1–7] This book also provides background information and references to enable users of Eurocode 4 to understand the origin and objectives of its provisions.

The need to use many Eurocode parts can initially make it a daunting task to locate information in the sequence required for a real design. To assist with this process, flow charts are provided for selected topics. They are not intended to give detailed procedural information for a specific design.

## Layout of this guide

EN 1994-2 has a foreword, nine sections, and an annex. This guide has an introduction which corresponds to the foreword of EN 1994-2, Chapters 1 to 9 which correspond to Sections 1 to 9 of the Eurocode, and Chapter 10 which refers to Annexes A and B of EN 1994-1-1 and covers *Annex C* of EN 1994-2. Commentary on Annexes A and B is given in the Guide by Johnson and Anderson.[5]

The numbering and titles of the sections and second-level clauses in this guide also correspond to those of the clauses of EN 1994-2. Some third-level clauses are also numbered (for example, 1.1.2). This implies correspondence with the sub-clause in EN 1994-2 of the same number. Their titles also correspond. There are extensive references to lower-level clause and paragraph numbers. The first significant reference is in ***bold italic*** type (e.g. ***clause 1.1.1(2)***).

These are in strict numerical sequence throughout the book, to help readers find comments on particular provisions of the code. Some comments on clauses are necessarily out of sequence, but use of the index should enable these to be found.

All cross-references in this guide to sections, clauses, sub-clauses, paragraphs, annexes, figures, tables and expressions of EN 1994-2 are in *italic* type, and do not include 'EN 1994-2'. Italic is also used where text from a clause in EN 1994-2 has been directly reproduced.

Cross-references to, and quotations and expressions from, other Eurocodes are in roman type. Clause references include the EN number; for example, 'clause 3.1.4 of EN 1992-1-1' (a reference in *clause 5.4.2.2(2)*). All other quotations are in roman type. Expressions repeated from EN 1994-2 retain their number. The authors' expressions have numbers prefixed by D (for Designers' Guide); for example, equation (D6.1) in Chapter 6.

Abbreviated terms are sometimes used for parts of Eurocodes (e.g. EC4-1-1 for EN 1994-1-1[8]) and for limit states (e.g. ULS for ultimate limit state).

## Acknowledgements

The first author would like to thank his wife, Wendy, and two boys, Peter Edwin Hendy and Matthew Philip Hendy, for their patience and tolerance of his pleas to finish 'just one more paragraph'. He thanks his employer, Atkins, for providing both facilities and time for the production of this guide, and the members of BSI B525/10 Working Group 2 who provided comment on many of the Eurocode clauses.

The second author is deeply indebted to the other members of the project and editorial teams for Eurocode 4 on which he has worked: David Anderson, Gerhard Hanswille, Bernt Johansson, Basil Kolias, Jean-Paul Lebet, Henri Mathieu, Michel Mele, Joel Raoul, Karl-Heinz Roik and Jan Stark; and also to the Liaison Engineers, National Technical Contacts, and others who prepared national comments. He thanks the University of Warwick for facilities provided for Eurocode work, and, especially, his wife Diana for her unfailing support.

Chris Hendy
Roger Johnson

# Contents

# Introduction

The provisions of EN 1994-2[9] are preceded by a foreword, most of which is common to all Eurocodes. This *Foreword* contains clauses on:

- the background to the Eurocode programme
- the status and field of application of the Eurocodes
- national standards implementing Eurocodes
- links between Eurocodes and harmonized technical specifications for products
- additional information specific to EN 1994-2
- National Annex for EN 1994-2.

Guidance on the common text is provided in the introduction to the *Designers' Guide to EN 1990. Eurocode: Basis of Structural Design*,[1] and only background information relevant to users of EN 1994-2 is given here.

It is the responsibility of each national standards body to implement each Eurocode part as a national standard. This will comprise, without any alterations, the full text of the Eurocode and its annexes as published by the European Committee for Standardisation, CEN (from its title in French). This will usually be preceded by a National Title Page and a National Foreword, and may be followed by a National Annex.

Each Eurocode recognizes the right of national regulatory authorities to determine values related to safety matters. Values, classes or methods to be chosen or determined at national level are referred to as Nationally Determined Parameters (NDPs). Clauses in which these occur are listed in the *Foreword*.

NDPs are also indicated by notes immediately after relevant clauses. These Notes give recommended values. Many of the values in EN 1994-2 have been in the draft code for over a decade. It is expected that most of the 28 Member States of CEN (listed in the *Foreword*) will specify the recommended values, as their use was assumed in the many calibration studies done during drafting. They are used in this guide, as the National Annex for the UK was not available at the time of writing.

Each National Annex will give or cross-refer to the NDPs to be used in the relevant country. Otherwise the National Annex may contain only the following:[10]

- decisions on the use of informative annexes, and
- references to non-contradictory complementary information to assist the user to apply the Eurocode.

Each national standards body that is a member of CEN is required, as a condition of membership, to withdraw all 'conflicting national standards' by a given date, that is at present March 2010. The Eurocodes will supersede the British bridge code, BS 5400,[11] which should therefore be withdrawn. This will lead to extensive revision of many sets of supplementary design rules, such as those published by the Highways Agency in the UK. Some countries have already adopted Eurocode methods for bridge design; for example, Germany in 2003.[12]

## Additional information specific to EN 1994-2

The information specific to EN 1994-2 emphasises that this standard is to be used with other Eurocodes. The standard includes many cross-references to particular clauses in EN 1990,[13] EN 1991,[14] EN 1992[15] and EN 1993.[16] Similarly, this guide is one of a series on Eurocodes, and is for use with other guides, particularly those for EN 1991,[2] EN 1992-1-1,[6] EN 1993-1-1,[7] EN 1992-2[3] and EN 1993-2.[4]

The *Foreword* refers to a difference between EN 1994-2 and the 'bridge' parts of the other Eurocodes. In Eurocode 4, the 'general' provisions of Part 1-1 are repeated word for word in Part 2, with identical numbering of clauses, paragraphs, equations, etc. Such repetition breaks a rule of CEN, and was permitted, for this code only, to shorten chains of cross-references, mainly to Eurocodes 2 and 3. This determined the numbering and location of the provisions for bridges, and led to a few gaps in the sequences of numbers.

The same policy has been followed in the guides on Eurocode 4. Where material in the *Designers' Guide to EN 1994-1-1*[5] is as relevant to bridges as to buildings, it is repeated here, so this guide is self-contained, in respect of composite bridges, as is EN 1994-2.

A very few 'General' clauses in EN 1994-1-1 are not applicable to bridges. They have been replaced in EN 1994-2 by clearly labelled 'bridge' clauses; for example, *clause 3.2*, '*Reinforcing steel for bridges*'.

The *Foreword* lists the 15 clauses of EN 1994-2 in which national choice is permitted. Five of these relate to values for partial factors, three to shear connection, and seven to provision of 'further guidance'. Elsewhere, there are cross-references to clauses with NDPs in other codes; for example, partial factors for steel and concrete, and values that may depend on climate, such as the free shrinkage of concrete.

Otherwise, the Normative rules in the code must be followed, if the design is to be 'in accordance with the Eurocodes'.

In EN 1994-2, *Sections 1* to *9* are Normative. Only its *Annex C* is 'Informative', because it is based on quite recent research. A National Annex may make it normative in the country concerned, and is itself normative in that country, but not elsewhere. The 'non-contradictory complementary information' referred to above could include, for example, reference to a document based on provisions of BS 5400 on matters not treated in the Eurocodes. Each country can do this, so some aspects of the design of a bridge will continue to depend on where it is to be built.

# CHAPTER I

# General

This chapter is concerned with the general aspects of EN 1994-2, *Eurocode 4: Design of Composite Steel and Concrete Structures, Part 2: General Rules and Rules for Bridges*. The material described in this chapter is covered in *Section 1*, in the following clauses:

## I.I. Scope

### I.I.I. Scope of Eurocode 4

The scope of EN 1994 (all three Parts) is outlined in *clause 1.1.1*. It is to be used with EN 1990, *Eurocode: Basis of Structural Design*, which is the head document of the Eurocode suite, and has an Annex A2, 'Application for bridges'. *Clause 1.1.1(2)* emphasizes that the Eurocodes are concerned with structural behaviour and that other requirements, e.g. thermal and acoustic insulation, are not considered.

*Clause 1.1.1*

*Clause 1.1.1(2)*

The basis for verification of safety and serviceability is the partial factor method. EN 1990 recommends values for load factors and gives various possibilities for combinations of actions. The values and choice of combinations are set by the National Annex for the country in which the structure is to be constructed.

Eurocode 4 is also to be used in conjunction with EN 1991, *Eurocode 1: Actions on Structures*[14] and its National Annex, to determine characteristic or nominal loads. When a composite structure is to be built in a seismic region, account needs to be taken of EN 1998, *Eurocode 8: Design of Structures for Earthquake Resistance*.[17]

*Clause 1.1.1(3)*, as a statement of intention, gives undated references. It supplements the normative rules on dated reference standards, given in *clause 1.2*, where the distinction between dated and undated standards is explained.

*Clause 1.1.1(3)*

The Eurocodes are concerned with design and not execution, but minimum standards of workmanship are required to ensure that the design assumptions are valid. For this reason, *clause 1.1.1(3)* lists the European standards for the execution of steel structures and the execution of concrete structures. The standard for steel structures includes some requirements for composite construction – for example, for the testing of welded stud shear connectors.

### I.I.2. Scope of Part I.I of Eurocode 4

The general rules referred to in *clause 1.1.2(1)* appear also in EN 1994-2, so there is (in general) no need for it to cross-refer to Part 1-1, though it does refer (in *clause 6.6.3.1(4)*)

*Clause 1.1.2(1)*

*Clause 1.1.2(2)*   to Annex B of Part 1-1. The list of the titles of sections in **clause 1.1.2(2)** is identical to that in *clause 1.1.3*, except for those of Sections 8 and 9. In *Sections 1–7* of EN 1994-2, all 'for buildings' clauses of EN 1994-1-1 are omitted, and 'for bridges' clauses are added.

### 1.1.3. Scope of Part 2 of Eurocode 4

*Clause 1.1.3(1)*   **Clause 1.1.3(1)** refers to the partial coverage of design of cable-stayed bridges. This is the only reference to them in EN 1994-2. It was considered here, and in EC2 and EC3, that for this rapidly evolving type of bridge, it was premature to codify much more than the design of their components (e.g. cables, in EN 1993-1-11), although EN 1993-1-11 does contain some requirements for global analysis. Composite construction is attractive for cable-stayed bridges, because the concrete deck is well able to resist longitudinal compression. There is an elegant example in central Johannesburg.[18]

*Clause 1.1.3(2)*   **Clause 1.1.3(2)** lists the titles of the sections of Part 2. Those for *Sections 1–7* are the same as in all the other material-dependent Eurocodes. The contents of *Sections 1* and *2* similarly follow an agreed model.

The provisions of Part 2 cover the design of the following:

- beams in which a steel section acts compositely with concrete
- concrete-encased or concrete-filled composite columns
- composite plates (where the steel member is a flat steel plate, not a profiled section)
- composite box girders
- tapered or non-uniform composite members
- structures that are prestressed by imposed deformations or by tendons.

Joints in composite beams and between beams and steel or composite columns appear in *clause 5.1.2, Joint modelling*, which refers to EN 1993-1-8.[19] There is little detailed coverage, because the main clauses on joints in Part 1-1 are 'for buildings'.

*Section 5, Structural analysis* concerns connected members and frames, both unbraced and braced. The provisions define their imperfections and include the use of second-order global analysis and prestress by imposed deformations.

The scope of Part 2 includes double composite action, and also steel sections that are partially encased. The web of the steel section is encased by reinforced concrete, and shear connection is provided between the concrete and the steel. This is a well-established form of construction in buildings. The primary reason for its choice is improved resistance in fire.

Fully-encased composite beams are not included because:

- no satisfactory model has been found for the ultimate strength in longitudinal shear of a beam without shear connectors
- it is not known to what extent some design rules (e.g. for moment–shear interaction and redistribution of moments) are applicable.

A fully-encased beam with shear connectors can usually be designed as if partly encased or uncased, provided that care is taken to prevent premature spalling of encasement in compression.

Prestressing of composite members by tendons is rarely used, and is not treated in detail. Transverse prestress of a deck slab is covered in EN 1992-2.[3]

The omission of application rules for a type of member or structure should not prevent its use, where appropriate. Some omissions are deliberate, to encourage the use of innovative design, based on specialised literature, the properties of materials, and the fundamentals of equilibrium and compatibility. However, the principles given in the relevant Eurocodes must still be followed. This applies, for example, to:

- members of non-uniform section, or curved in plan
- types of shear connector other than welded headed studs.

EN 1994-2 has a single Informative annex, considered in Chapter 10 of this book.

The three annexes in EN 1994-1-1 were not copied into EN 1994-2 because they are 'Informative' and, except for tests on shear connectors, are for buildings. They are:

- Annex A, Stiffness of joint components in buildings
- Annex B, Standard tests (for shear connectors and for composite slabs)
- Annex C, Shrinkage of concrete for composite structures for buildings.

In ENV 1994-1-1,[20] design rules for many types of shear connector were given. All except those for welded headed studs were omitted, *clause 1.1.3(3)*, mainly in response to requests for a shorter code. The Note to this clause enables national annexes to refer to rules for any type of shear connector. In the UK, this is being done for block connectors with hoops and for channels, and in France for angle connectors, based on the rules in ENV 1994-1-1. Research on older types of connector and the development of new connectors continues.[21–25]

*Clause 1.1.3(3)*

## 1.2. Normative references

References are given only to other European standards, all of which are intended to be used as a package. Formally, the Standards of the International Organization for Standardization (ISO) apply only if given an EN ISO designation. National standards for design and for products do not apply if they conflict with a relevant EN standard.

As Eurocodes may not cross-refer to national standards, replacement of national standards for products by EN or ISO standards is in progress, with a timescale similar to that for the Eurocodes.

During the period of changeover to Eurocodes and EN standards it is possible that an EN referred to, or its national annex, may not be complete. Designers who then seek guidance from national standards should take account of differences between the design philosophies and safety factors in the two sets of documents.

The lists in *clause 1.2* are limited to standards referred to in the text of EN 1994-1-1 or 1994-2. The distinction between dated and undated references should be noted. Any relevant provision of the general reference standards, *clause 1.2.1*, should be assumed to apply.

*Clause 1.2*

*Clause 1.2.1*

EN 1994-2 is based on the concept of the initial erection of structural steel members, which may include prefabricated concrete-encased members. The placing of formwork (which may or may not become part of the finished structure) follows. The addition of reinforcement and *in situ* concrete completes the composite structure. The presentation and content of EN 1994-2 therefore relate more closely to EN 1993 than to EN 1992. This may explain why this list includes execution of steel structures, but not EN 13670, on execution of concrete structures, which is listed in *clause 1.1.1*.

**Table 1.1.** References to EN 1992, *Eurocode 2: Design of Concrete Structures*

| Title of Part | Subjects referred to from EN 1994-2 |
|---|---|
| EN 1992-1-1, *General Rules and Rules for Buildings* | Properties of concrete, reinforcement, and tendons<br>General design of reinforced and prestressed concrete<br>Partial factors $\gamma_M$, including values for fatigue<br>Resistance of reinforced concrete cross-sections to bending and shear<br>Bond, anchorage, cover, and detailing of reinforcement<br>Minimum areas of reinforcement; crack widths in concrete<br>Limiting stresses in concrete, reinforcement and tendons<br>Combination of actions for global analysis for fatigue<br>Fatigue strengths of concrete, reinforcement and tendons<br>Reinforced concrete and composite tension members<br>Transverse reinforcement in composite columns<br>Vertical shear and second-order effects in composite plates<br>Effective areas for load introduction into concrete |
| EN 1992-2, *Rules for Bridges* | Many subjects with references also to EN 1992-1-1 (above)<br>Environmental classes; exposure classes<br>Limitation of crack widths<br>Vertical shear in a concrete flange<br>Exemptions from fatigue assessment for reinforcement and concrete<br>Verification for fatigue; damage equivalent factors |

*Clause 1.2.2*

*Clause 1.2.3*

The '*other reference standards*' in **clause 1.2.2** receive both general references, as in *clause 2.3.2(1)* (to EN 1992-1-1[15]), and specific references to clauses, as in *clause 3.1(1)*, which refers to EN 1992-1-1, 3.1. For composite bridges, further standards, of either type, are listed in **clause 1.2.3**.

For actions, the main reference is in *clause 2.3.1(1)*, to '*the relevant parts of EN 1991*', which include those for unit weights of materials, wind loads, snow loads, thermal actions, and actions during execution. The only references in *clause 1.2* are to EN 1991-2, 'Traffic loads on bridges',[26] and to Annex A2 of EN 1990, which gives combination rules and recommended values for partial factors and combination factors for actions for bridges. EN 1990 is also referred to for modelling of structures for analysis, and general provisions on serviceability limit states and their verification.

### Cross-references from EN 1994-2 to EN 1992 and EN 1993

The parts of EN 1992 and EN 1993 most likely to be referred to in the design of a steel and concrete composite bridge are listed in Tables 1.1 and 1.2, with the relevant aspects of design.

**Table 1.2.** References to EN 1993, *Eurocode 3: Design of Steel Structures*

| Title of Part | Subjects referred to from EN 1994-2 |
|---|---|
| EN 1993-1-1, *General Rules and Rules for Buildings* | Stress–strain properties of steel; $\gamma_M$ for steel<br>General design of unstiffened steelwork<br>Classification of cross-sections<br>Resistance of composite sections to vertical shear<br>Buckling of members and frames; column buckling curves |
| EN 1993-1-5, *Plated Structural Elements* | Design of cross-sections in slenderness Class 3 or 4<br>Effects of shear lag in steel plate elements<br>Design of beams before a concrete flange hardens<br>Design where transverse, longitudinal, or bearing stiffeners are present<br>Transverse distribution of stresses in a wide flange<br>Shear buckling; flange-induced web buckling<br>In-plane transverse forces on webs |
| EN 1993-1-8, *Design of Joints* | Modelling of flexible joints in analysis<br>Design of joints and splices in steel and composite members<br>Design using structural hollow sections<br>Fasteners and welding consumables |
| EN 1993-1-9, *Fatigue Strength of Steel Structures* | Fatigue loading<br>Classification of details into fatigue categories<br>Limiting stress ranges for damage-equivalent stress verification<br>Fatigue verification in welds and connectors |
| EN 1993-1-10, *Material Toughness and Through-thickness Properties* | For selection of steel grade (Charpy test, and Z quality) |
| EN 1993-1-11, *Design of Structures with Tension Components* | Design of bridges with external prestressing or cable support, such as cable-stayed bridges |
| EN 1993-2, *Rules for Bridges* | Global analysis; imperfections<br>Buckling of members and frames<br>Design of beams before a concrete flange hardens<br>Limiting slenderness of web plates<br>Distortion in box girders<br>$\gamma_M$ for fatigue strength; $\gamma_F$ for fatigue loading<br>Damage equivalent factors<br>Limiting stresses in steel; fatigue in structural steel<br>Limits to deformations<br>Vibration |

Many references to EN 1992-2[27] and EN 1993-2[28] lead to references from them to EN 1992-1-1 and EN 1993-1-1, respectively. Unfortunately, the method of drafting of these two bridge parts was not harmonised. For many subjects, some of the clauses needed are 'general' and so are located in Part 1-1, and others are 'for bridges' and will be found in Part 2. There are examples in *clauses 3.2(1)*, *7.2.2(2)* and *7.4.1(1)*.

Other Eurocode parts that may be applicable are:

EN 1993-1-7     *Strength and Stability of Planar Plated Structures Transversely Loaded*
EN 1993-1-12    *Supplementary Rules for High Strength Steel*
EN 1997         *Geotechnical Design, Parts 1 and 2*
EN 1998         *Design of Structures for Earthquake Resistance*
EN 1999         *Design of Aluminium Structures.*

## 1.3. Assumptions

It is assumed in EN 1994-2 that the general assumptions of ENs 1990, 1992, and 1993 will be followed. Commentary on them will be found in the relevant Guides of this series.

Various clauses in EN 1994-2 assume that EN 1090 will be followed in the fabrication and erection of the steelwork. This is important for the design of slender elements, where the methods of analysis and buckling resistance formulae rely on imperfections from fabrication and erection being limited to the levels in EN 1090. EN 1994-2 should therefore not be used for design of bridges that will be fabricated or erected to specifications other than EN 1090, without careful comparison of the respective requirements for tolerances and workmanship. Similarly, the requirements of EN 13670 for execution of concrete structures should be complied with in the construction of reinforced or prestressed concrete elements.

## 1.4. Distinction between principles and application rules

Clauses in the Eurocodes are set out as either Principles or Application Rules. As defined by EN 1990:

- 'Principles comprise general statements for which there is no alternative and requirements and analytical models for which no alternative is permitted unless specifically stated.'
- 'Principles are distinguished by the letter "P" following the paragraph number.'
- 'Application Rules are generally recognised rules which comply with the principles and satisfy their requirements.'

There may be other ways to comply with the Principles, that are at least equivalent to the Application Rules in respect of safety, serviceability, and durability. However, if these are substituted, the design cannot be deemed to be fully in accordance with the Eurocodes.

Eurocodes 2, 3 and 4 are consistent in using the verbal form 'shall' only for a Principle. Application rules generally use 'should' or 'may', but this is not fully consistent.

There are relatively few Principles in Parts 1.1 and 2 of ENs 1992 and 1994. Almost all of those in EN 1993-1-1 and EN 1993-2 were replaced by Application Rules at a late stage of drafting.

It has been recognized that a requirement or analytical model for which 'no alternative is permitted unless specifically stated' can rarely include a numerical value, because most values are influenced by research and/or experience, and may change over the years. (Even the specified elastic modulus for structural steel is an approximate value.) Furthermore, a clause cannot be a Principle if it requires the use of another clause that is an Application Rule; effectively that clause also would become a Principle.

It follows that, ideally, the Principles in all the codes should form a consistent set, referring only to each other, and intelligible if all the Application Rules were deleted. This overriding principle strongly influenced the drafting of EN 1994.

## 1.5. Definitions

### 1.5.1. General

In accordance with the model specified for *Section 1*, reference is made to the definitions given in clauses 1.5 of EN 1990, EN 1992-1-1, and EN 1993-1-1. Many types of analysis are defined in clause 1.5.6 of EN 1990. It should be noted that an analysis based on the deformed geometry of a structure or element under load is termed 'second-order', rather than 'non-linear'. The latter term refers to the treatment of material properties in structural analysis. Thus, according to EN 1990, 'non-linear analysis' includes 'rigid-plastic'. This convention is not followed in EN 1994-2, where the heading 'Non-linear global analysis for bridges' (*clause 5.4.3*) does not include 'rigid-plastic global analysis'. There is no provision for use of the latter in bridges, so relevant rules are found in the 'buildings' clause 5.4.5 of EN 1994-1-1.

*Clause 1.5.1(1)* References from *clause 1.5.1(1)* include clause 1.5.2 of EN 1992-1-1, which defines prestress as an action caused by the stressing of tendons. This is not sufficient for EN 1994-2, because prestress by jacking at supports, which is outside the scope of EN 1992-1-1, is within the scope of EN 1994-2.

The definitions in clauses 1.5.1 to 1.5.9 of EN 1993-1-1 apply where they occur in clauses in EN 1993 to which EN 1994 refers. None of them uses the word 'steel'.

### 1.5.2. Additional terms and definitions

*Clause 1.5.2* Most of the 15 definitions in *clause 1.5.2* include the word 'composite'. The definition of '*shear connection*' does not require the absence of separation or slip at the interface between steel and concrete. Separation is always assumed to be negligible, but explicit allowance may need to be made for effects of slip, for example in *clauses 5.4.3, 6.6.2.3* and *7.2.1*.

The definition of '*composite frame*' is relevant to the use of *Section 5*. Where the behaviour is essentially that of a reinforced or prestressed concrete structure, with only a few composite members, global analysis should be generally in accordance with EN 1992.

These lists of definitions are not exhaustive, because all the codes use terms with precise meanings that can be inferred from their contexts.

Concerning use of words generally, there are significant differences from British codes. These arose from the use of English as the base language for the drafting process, and the resulting need to improve precision of meaning, to facilitate translation into other European languages. In particular:

- 'action' means a load and/or an imposed deformation
- 'action effect' (*clause 5.4*) and 'effect of action' have the same meaning: any deformation or internal force or moment that results from an action.

## 1.6. Symbols

The symbols in the Eurocodes are all based on ISO standard 3898.[29] Each code has its own list, applicable within that code. Some symbols have more than one meaning, the particular meaning being stated in the clause. A few rarely-used symbols are defined only in clauses where they appear (e.g. $A_{c,eff}$ in *7.5.3(1)*).

There are a few important changes from previous practice in the UK. For example, an $x$–$x$ axis is along a member, a $y$–$y$ axis is parallel to the flanges of a steel section (clause 1.7(2) of EN 1993-1-1), and a section modulus is $W$, with subscripts to denote elastic or plastic behaviour.

This convention for member axes is more compatible with most commercially available analysis packages than that used in previous British bridge codes. The $y$–$y$ axis generally represents the major principal axis, as shown in Fig. 1.1(a) and (b). Where this is not a principal axis, the major and minor principal axes are denoted $u$–$u$ and $v$–$v$, as shown in Fig. 1.1(c). It is possible for the major axis of a composite cross-section to be the minor axis of its structural steel component.

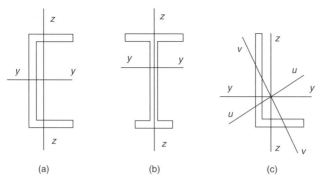

**Fig. 1.1.** Sign convention for axes of members

Wherever possible, definitions in EN 1994-2 have been aligned with those in ENs 1990, 1992 and 1993; but this should not be assumed without checking the list in *clause 1.6*. Some quite minor differences are significant.

The symbol $f_y$ has different meanings in ENs 1992 and 1993. It is retained in EN 1994-2 for the nominal yield strength of structural steel, though the generic subscript for that material is 'a', based on the French word for steel, 'acier'. Subscript 'a' is not used in EN 1993, where the partial factor for steel is not $\gamma_A$, but $\gamma_M$. The symbol $\gamma_M$ is also used in EN 1994-2. The characteristic yield strength of reinforcement is $f_{sk}$, with partial factor $\gamma_S$.

The use of upper-case subscripts for $\gamma$ factors for materials implies that the values given allow for two types of uncertainty: in the properties of the material and in the resistance model used.

*Clause 1.6*

9

# CHAPTER 2

# Basis of design

The material described in this chapter is covered in *Section 2* of EN 1994-2, in the following clauses:

| | |
|---|---|
| • Requirements | *Clause 2.1* |
| • Principles of limit states design | *Clause 2.2* |
| • Basic variables | *Clause 2.3* |
| • Verification by the partial factor method | *Clause 2.4* |

The sequence follows that of EN 1990, Sections 2 to 4 and 6.

## 2.1. Requirements

Design is to be in accordance with the general requirements of EN 1990. The purpose of *Section 2* is to give supplementary provisions for composite structures.

*Clause 2.1(3)* reminds the user again that design is based on actions in accordance with EN 1991, combinations of actions and load factors at the various limit states in accordance with EN 1990 (Annex A2), and the resistances, durability and serviceability provisions of EN 1994 (through extensive references to EC2 and EC3).

*Clause 2.1(3)*

The use of partial safety factors for actions and resistances (the 'partial factor method') is expected but is not a requirement of Eurocodes. The method is presented in Section 6 of EN 1990 as one way of satisfying the basic requirements set out in Section 2 of that standard. This is why use of the partial factor method is given 'deemed to satisfy' status in *clause 2.1(3)*. To establish that a design was in accordance with the Eurocodes, the user of any other method would normally have to demonstrate, to the satisfaction of the regulatory authority and/or the client, that the method satisfied the basic requirements of EN 1990.

The design working life for bridges and components of bridges is also given in EN 1990. This predominantly affects calculations on fatigue. Temporary structures (that will not be dismantled and reused) have an indicative design life of 10 years, while bearings have a life of 10–25 years and a permanent bridge has an indicative design life of 100 years. The design lives of temporary bridges and permanent bridges can be varied in project specifications and the National Annex respectively. For political reasons, the design life for permanent bridges in the UK may be maintained at 120 years.

To achieve the design working life, bridges and bridge components should be designed against corrosion, fatigue and wear and should be regularly inspected and maintained. Where components cannot be designed for the full working life of the bridge, they need to be replaceable. Further detail is given in Chapter 4 of this guide.

## 2.2. Principles of limit states design

The clause provides a reminder that it is important to check strength and stability throughout all stages of construction in addition to the final condition. The strength of bare steel beams during pouring of the deck slab must be checked, as the restraint to the top flange provided by the completed deck slab is absent in this condition.

A beam that is in Class 1 or 2 when completed may be in Class 3 or 4 during construction, if a greater depth of web is in compression. Its stresses must then be built up allowing for the construction history. For cross-sections that are in Class 1 or 2 when completed, final verifications of resistances can be based on accumulation of bending moments and shear forces, rather than stresses, as plastic bending resistances can be used. The serviceability checks would still necessitate consideration of the staged construction.

All resistance formulae for composite members assume that the specified requirements for materials, such as ductility, fracture toughness and through-thickness properties, are met.

## 2.3. Basic variables

*Clause 2.3.1*

**Clause 2.3.1** on actions refers only to EN 1991. Its Part 2, 'Traffic loads on bridges', defines load patterns and leaves clients, or designers, much choice over intensity of loading. Loads during construction are specified in EN 1991-1-6, 'Actions during execution'.[30]

Actions include imposed deformations, such as settlement or jacking of supports, and effects of temperature and shrinkage. Further information is given in comments on *clause 2.3.3.*

*Clause 2.3.2(1)*

**Clause 2.3.2(1)** refers to EN 1992-1-1 for shrinkage and creep of concrete, where detailed and quite complex rules are given for prediction of free shrinkage strain and creep coefficients. These are discussed in comments on *clauses 3.1* and *5.4.2.2*. Effects of creep of concrete are not normally treated as imposed deformations. An exception arises in *clause 5.4.2.2(6)*.

*Clause 2.3.3*

The classification of effects of shrinkage and temperature in *clause 2.3.3* into 'primary' and 'secondary' will be familiar to designers of continuous beams. Secondary effects are to be treated as 'indirect actions', which are 'sets of imposed deformations' (clause 1.5.3.1 of EN 1990), not as action effects. This distinction is relevant in *clause 5.4.2.2(7)*, where indirect actions may be neglected in analyses for some verifications of composite members with all cross-sections in Class 1 or 2. This is because resistances are based on plastic analysis and there is therefore adequate rotation capacity to permit the effects of imposed deformations to be released.

## 2.4. Verification by the partial factor method
### 2.4.1. Design values

*Clause 2.4.1*

**Clause 2.4.1** illustrates the treatment of partial factors. Recommended values are given in Notes, in the hope of eventual convergence between the values for each partial factor that will be specified in the national annexes. This process was adopted because the regulatory bodies in the member states of CEN, rather than CEN itself, are responsible for setting safety levels. The Notes are informative, not normative (i.e. not part of the preceding provision), so that there are no numerical values in the principles, as explained earlier.

*Clause 2.4.1.1(1)*

The Note below *clause 2.4.1.1(1)* recommends $\gamma_P = 1.0$ (where subscript 'P' represents prestress) for controlled imposed deformations. Examples of these include jacking up at supports or jacking down by the removal of packing plates. The latter might be done to increase the reaction at an adjacent end support where there is a risk of uplift occurring.

*Clause 2.4.1.2*

The Notes to *clause 2.4.1.2* link the partial factors for concrete, reinforcing steel and structural steel to those recommended in EN 1992-1-1 and EN 1993. Design would be more difficult if the factors for these materials in composite structures differed from the values in reinforced concrete and steel structures. The reference to EN 1993, as distinct from EN 1993-1-1, is required because some $\gamma_M$ factors differ for bridges and buildings.

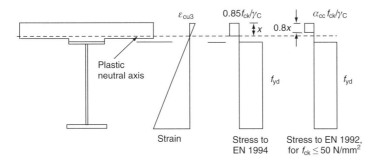

**Fig. 2.1.** Rectangular stress blocks for concrete in compression at ultimate limit states

The remainder of EN 1994-2 normally refers to design strengths, rather than to characteristic or nominal values with partial factors. Characteristic values are 5% lower fractiles for an infinite test series, predicted from experience and a smaller number of tests. Nominal values (e.g. the yield strength of structural steel) are used where distributions of test results cannot be predicted statistically. They are chosen to correspond to characteristic values.

The design strength for concrete is given by:

$$f_{cd} = f_{ck}/\gamma_C \tag{2.1}$$

where $f_{ck}$ is the characteristic cylinder strength. This definition is stated algebraically because it differs from that of EN 1992-2, in which an additional coefficient $\alpha_{cc}$ is applied:

$$f_{cd} = \alpha_{cc} f_{ck}/\gamma_C \tag{D2.1}$$

The coefficient is explained in EN 1992-2 as taking account of long-term effects and of unfavourable effects resulting from the way the load is applied. The value for $\alpha_{cc}$ is to be given in national annexes to EN 1992-2, and 'should lie between 0.80 and 1.00'. The value 1.00 has been used in EN 1994-2, without permitting national choice, for several reasons:

- The plastic stress block for use in resistance of composite sections, defined in *clause 6.2.1.2*, consists of a stress $0.85f_{cd}$ extending to the neutral axis, as shown in Fig. 2.1. The depth of the stress block in EN 1992-2 is only 80% of this distance. The factor 0.85 is not fully equivalent to $\alpha_{cc}$; it allows also for the difference between the stress blocks.
- Predictions using the stress block of EN 1994 have been verified against test results for composite members conducted independently from verifications for concrete bridges.
- The EN 1994 block is easier to apply. The Eurocode 2 rule was not used in Eurocode 4 because resistance formulae become complex where the neutral axis is close to or within the steel flange adjacent to the concrete slab.
- Resistance formulae for composite elements given in EN 1994 are based on calibrations using its stress block, with $\alpha_{cc} = 1.0$.

The definition of $f_{cd}$ in *equation (2.1)* is applicable to verifications of all composite cross-sections, but not where the section is reinforced concrete only; for example, in-plane shear in a concrete flange of a composite beam. For reinforced concrete, EN 1992-2 applies, with $\alpha_{cc}$ in equation (D2.1) as given in the National Annex. It is expected that the rules in the UK's Annex will include:

$\alpha_{cc} = 0.85$ for flexure and axial compression

This is consistent with EN 1994-2, as the coefficient 0.85 appears in the resistance formulae in *clauses 6.2.1.2* and *6.7.3.2*. In these cases, the values $0.85f_{cd}$ in EN 1994-2 and $f_{cd}$ in EN 1992-2 are equal, so the values of symbols $f_{cd}$ are not equal. There is a risk of error when switching between calculations for composite sections and for reinforced concrete elements such as a deck slab both for this reason and because of the different depth of stress block.

**Table 2.1.** Partial factors from EN 1992-2 for materials, for ultimate limit states

| Design situations | $\gamma_C$, for concrete | $\gamma_S$, reinforcing steel | $\gamma_S$, prestressing steel |
|---|---|---|---|
| Persistent and transient | 1.5 | 1.15 | 1.15 |
| Accidental | 1.2 | 1.0 | 1.0 |

Care is needed also with symbols for steels. The design strengths in EN 1994 are $f_{yd}$ for structural steel and $f_{sd}$ for reinforcement, but reinforcement in EN 1992 has $f_{yd}$, not $f_{sd}$.

The recommended partial factors given in EN 1992-2 (referring to EN 1992-1-1) for materials for ultimate limit states other than fatigue are repeated in Table 2.1. For serviceability limit states, the recommended value is generally 1.0, from clause 2.4.2.4(2).

The $\gamma_M$ values for structural steel are denoted $\gamma_{M0}$ to $\gamma_{M7}$ in clause 6.1 of EN 1993-2. Those for ultimate limit states other than fatigue are given in Table 2.2. Further values are given in clauses on fatigue. No distinction is made between persistent, transient, and accidental design situations, though it could be, in a national annex.

For simplicity, $\gamma_M$ for resistances of shear connectors (denoted $\gamma_V$), given in a Note to *clause 6.6.3.1(1)*, was standardised at 1.25, because this is the recommended value for most joints in steelwork. Where calibration led to a different value, a coefficient in the resistance formula was modified to enable 1.25 to be used.

*Clause 2.4.1.3*

*Clause 2.4.1.3* refers to 'product standards hEN' and to 'nominal values'. The 'h' stands for 'harmonised'. This term from the *Construction Products Directive*[31] is explained in the *Designers' Guide to EN 1990*.[1]

Generally, global analysis and resistances of cross-sections may be based on the 'nominal' values of dimensions, which are given on the project drawings or quoted in product standards. Geometrical tolerances as well as structural imperfections (such as welding residual stresses) are accounted for in the methods specified for global analyses and for buckling checks of individual structural elements. These subjects are discussed further in sections 5.2 and 5.3, respectively, of this guide.

*Clause 2.4.1.4*

*Clause 2.4.1.4*, on design resistances to particular action effects, refers to expressions (6.6a) and (6.6c) given in clause 6.3.5 of EN 1990. Resistances in EN 1994-2 often need more than one partial factor, and so use expression (6.6a) which is:

$$R_d = R\{(\eta_i X_{k,i}/\gamma_{M,i}); a_d\} \quad i \geq 1 \tag{D2.2}$$

**Table 2.2.** Partial factors from EN 1993-2 for materials, for ultimate limit states

| Resistance type | Factor | Recommended value |
|---|---|---|
| Resistance of members and cross-sections | | |
| • Resistance of cross-sections to excessive yielding including local buckling | $\gamma_{M0}$ | 1.00 |
| • Resistance of members to instability assessed by member checks | $\gamma_{M1}$ | 1.10 |
| • Resistance to fracture of cross-sections in tension | $\gamma_{M2}$ | 1.25 |
| Resistance of joints | | |
| • Resistance of bolts, rivets, pins and welds | $\gamma_{M2}$ | 1.25 |
| • Resistance of plates in bearing | $\gamma_{M2}$ | 1.25 |
| • Slip resistance: | | |
| – at an ultimate limit state | $\gamma_{M3}$ | 1.25 |
| – at a serviceability limit state | $\gamma_{M3,ser}$ | 1.10 |
| • Bearing resistance of an injection bolt | $\gamma_{M4}$ | 1.10 |
| • Resistance of joints in hollow section lattice girders | $\gamma_{M5}$ | 1.10 |
| • Resistance of pins at serviceability limit state | $\gamma_{M6,ser}$ | 1.00 |
| • Pre-load of high-strength bolts | $\gamma_{M7}$ | 1.10 |

For example, *clause 6.7.3.2(1)* gives the plastic resistance to compression of a cross-section as the sum of terms for the structural steel, concrete and reinforcement:

$$N_{pl,Rd} = A_a f_{yd} + 0.85 A_c f_{cd} + A_s f_{sd} \qquad (6.30)$$

In this case, there is no separate term $a_d$ for the influence of geometrical data on resistance, because uncertainties in areas of cross-sections are allowed for in the $\gamma_M$ factors.

In terms of characteristic strengths, from *clause 2.4.1.2, equation (6.30)* becomes:

$$N_{pl,Rd} = A_a f_y / \gamma_M + 0.85 A_c f_{ck} / \gamma_C + A_s f_{sk} / \gamma_S \qquad (D2.3)$$

where:

- the characteristic material strengths $X_{k,i}$ are $f_y$, $f_{ck}$ and $f_{sk}$;
- the conversion factors, $\eta_i$ in EN 1990, are 1.0 for steel and reinforcement and 0.85 for concrete. These factors enable allowance to be made for the difference between the material property obtained from tests and its *in situ* contribution to the particular resistance considered. In general, it is also permissible to allow for this effect in the values of $\gamma_{M,i}$;
- the partial factors $\gamma_{M,i}$ are written $\gamma_M$, $\gamma_C$ and $\gamma_S$ in EN 1994-2.

Expression (6.6c) of EN 1990 is:

$$R_d = R_k / \gamma_M$$

It applies where characteristic properties and a single partial factor can be used; for example, in expressions for the shear resistance of a headed stud (*clause 6.6.3.1*). It is widely used in EN 1993, where only one material, steel, contributes to a resistance.

## 2.4.2. Combination of actions

*Clause 2.4.2* refers to the combinations of actions given in EN 1990. As in current practice, variable actions are included in a combination only in regions where they contribute to the total action effect considered.

*Clause 2.4.2*

For permanent actions and ultimate limit states, the situation is more complex. Normally the same factor $\gamma_F$ (favourable or unfavourable as appropriate) is applied throughout the structure, irrespective of whether both favourable and unfavourable loading regions exist. Additionally, the characteristic action is a mean (50% fractile) value. Exceptions are covered by clause 6.4.3.1(4)P of EN 1990:

'Where the results of a verification are very sensitive to variations of the magnitude of a permanent action from place to place in the structure, the unfavourable and the favourable parts of this action shall be considered as individual actions.'

A design permanent action is then $\gamma_{Ed,min} G_{k,min}$ in a 'favourable' region, and $\gamma_{Ed,max} G_{k,max}$ in an 'unfavourable' region. Recommendations on the choice of these values and the application of this principle are given in EN 1990, with guidance in the *Designers' Guide to EN 1990*.[1]

## 2.4.3. Verification of static equilibrium (EQU)

The preceding quotation from EN 1990 evidently applies to checks on static equilibrium, *clause 2.4.3(1)*. It draws attention to the role of anchors and bearings in ensuring static equilibrium.

*Clause 2.4.3(1)*

The abbreviation EQU in this clause comes from EN 1990, where four types of ultimate limit state are defined in clause 6.4.1:

- EQU for loss of static equilibrium
- FAT for fatigue failure

- GEO for failure or excessive deformation of the ground
- STR for internal failure or excessive deformation of the structure.

As explained above, the main feature of EQU is that, unlike STR, the partial factor $\gamma_F$ for permanent actions is not uniform over the whole structure. It is higher for destabilizing actions than for those relied on for stability. This guide mainly covers ultimate limit states of types STR and FAT. Use of type GEO arises in design of foundations to EN 1997.[32]

# CHAPTER 3

# Materials

This chapter concerns the properties of materials needed for the design of composite structures. It corresponds to *Section 3*, which has the following clauses:

- Concrete   *Clause 3.1*
- Reinforcing steel for bridges   *Clause 3.2*
- Structural steel for bridges   *Clause 3.3*
- Connecting devices   *Clause 3.4*
- Prestressing steel and devices   *Clause 3.5*
- Tension components in steel   *Clause 3.6*

Rather than repeating information given elsewhere, *Section 3* consists mainly of cross-references to other Eurocodes and EN standards. The following comments relate to provisions of particular significance for composite structures.

## 3.1. Concrete

*Clause 3.1(1)* *Clause 3.1(1)* refers to EN 1992-1-1 for the properties of concrete. For lightweight-aggregate concrete, several properties are dependent on the oven-dry density, relative to $2200 \, \text{kg/m}^3$.

Comprehensive sets of time-dependent properties are given in its clause 3.1 for normal concrete and clause 11.3 for lightweight-aggregate concrete. For composite structures built unpropped, with several stages of construction, simplification may be needed. A simplification for considerations of creep is provided in *clause 5.4.2.2(2)*. Specific properties are now discussed. (For thermal expansion, see Section 3.3 below.)

### Compressive strength

Strength and deformation characteristics are summarized in EN 1992-1-1, Table 3.1 for normal concrete and Table 11.3.1 for lightweight-aggregate concrete.

Strength classes for normal concrete are defined as $Cx/y$, where $x$ and $y$ are respectively the cylinder and cube compressive strengths in $\text{N/mm}^2$ units, determined at age 28 days. All compressive strengths in design rules in Eurocodes are cylinder strengths, so an unsafe error occurs if a specified cube strength is used in calculations. It should be replaced at the outset by the equivalent cylinder strength, using the relationships given by the strength classes.

Most cube strengths in Table 3.1 are rounded to $5 \, \text{N/mm}^2$. The ratios $f_{\text{ck}}/f_{\text{ck,cube}}$ range from 0.78 to 0.83, for grades up to C70/85.

Classes for lightweight concrete are designated $LCx/y$. The relationships between cylinder and cube strengths differ from those of normal concrete; for example, C40/50 and LC40/44. The ratios $f_{\text{ck}}/f_{\text{ck,cube}}$ for the LC grades range from 0.89 to 0.92. Thus, cylinder strengths are about 80% of cube strengths for normal-weight concrete and 90% for lightweight concrete.

Comment on the design compressive strength, $f_{cd} = f_{ck}/\gamma_C$, is given at *clause 2.4.1.2*.

*Tensile strength*

EN 1992 defines concrete tensile strength as the highest stress reached under concentric tensile loading. Values for the mean axial tensile strength of normal-weight concrete at 28 days, $f_{ctm}$, are given in Table 3.1 of EN 1992-1-1. They are based on the following formulae, in $N/mm^2$ units:

$$f_{ctm} = 0.30(f_{ck})^{2/3}, \quad f_{ck} \le C50/60 \tag{D3.1}$$
$$f_{ctm} = 2.12\ln[1 + (f_{cm}/10)], \quad f_{ck} > C50/60 \tag{D3.2}$$

This table also gives the 5% and 95% fractile values for tensile strength. The appropriate fractile value should be used in any limit state verification that relies on either an adverse or beneficial effect of the tensile strength of concrete. Tensile strengths for lightweight concrete are given in Table 11.3.1 of EN 1992-1-1.

Mean tensile stress, $f_{ctm}$, is used in several places in EN 1994-2 where the effects of tension stiffening are considered to be important. These include:

- *clause 5.4.2.3(2)*: rules on allowing for cracking in global analysis
- *clause 5.4.2.8(6)*: calculation of internal forces in concrete tension members in bowstring arches
- *clause 5.5.1(5)*: minimum area of reinforcement required in concrete tension flanges of composite beams
- *clause 7.4.2(1)*: rules on minimum reinforcement to ensure that cracking does not cause yielding of reinforcement in the cracked region
- *clause 7.4.3(3)*: rules on crack width calculation to allow for the increase in stress in reinforcement caused by tension stiffening.

*Elastic deformation*

All properties of concrete are influenced by its composition. The values for the mean short-term modulus of elasticity in Tables 3.1 and 11.3.1 of EN 1992-1-1 are given with a warning that they are 'indicative' and 'should be specifically assessed if the structure is likely to be sensitive to deviations from these general values'.

The values are for concrete with quartzite aggregates. Corrections for other types of aggregate are given in EN 1992-1-1, clause 3.1.3(2). All these are secant values; typically, $0.4f_{cm}/$(strain at $0.4f_{cm}$), and so are slightly lower than the initial tangent modulus, because stress–strain curves for concrete are non-linear from the origin.

Table 3.1 in EN 1992-1-1 gives the analytical relation:

$$E_{cm} = 22[(f_{ck} + 8)/10]^{0.3}$$

with $E_{cm}$ in GPa or $kN/mm^2$ units, and $f_{ck}$ in $N/mm^2$. For $f_{ck} = 30$, this gives $E_{cm} = 32.8$ $kN/mm^2$, whereas the entry in the table is rounded to $33\,kN/mm^2$.

A formula for the increase of $E_{cm}$ with time, in clause 3.1.3(3) of EN 1992-1-1, gives the two-year value as 6% above $E_{cm}$ at 28 days. The influence in a composite structure of so small a change is likely to be negligible compared with the uncertainties in the modelling of creep.

*Clause 3.1(2)*

*Clause 3.1(2)* limits the scope of EN 1994-2 to the strength range C20/25 to C60/75 for normal concrete and from LC20/22 to LC60/66 for lightweight concrete. The upper limits to these ranges are lower than that given in EN 1992-2 (C70/85) because there is limited knowledge and experience of the behaviour of composite members with very strong concrete. This applies, for example, to the load/slip properties of shear connectors, the redistribution of moments in continuous beams and the resistance of columns. The use of rectangular stress blocks for resistance to bending (*clause 6.2.1.2(d)*) relies on the strain capacity of the materials. The relevant property of concrete in compression, $\varepsilon_{cu3}$ in Table 3.1 of EN 1992-1-1, is 0.0035 for classes up to C50/60, but then falls, and is only 0.0026 for class C90/105.

*Shrinkage*

The shrinkage of concrete referred to in ***clause 3.1(3)*** is (presumably) both the drying shrinkage that occurs after setting and the autogenous shrinkage, but not the plastic shrinkage that precedes setting.

Drying shrinkage is associated with movement of water through and out of the concrete and therefore depends on relative humidity and effective section thickness as well as on the concrete mix. It takes several years to be substantially complete. The mean drying shrinkage strain (for unreinforced concrete) is given in clause 3.1.4(6) of EN 1992-1-1 as a function of grade of concrete, ambient relative humidity, effective thickness of the concrete cross-section, and elapsed time since the end of curing. It is stated that actual values have a coefficient of variation of about 30%. This implies a 16% probability that the shrinkage will exceed the prediction by at least 30%.

A slightly better predictor is given in Annex B of EN 1992-1-1, as the type of cement is included as an additional parameter.

Autogenous shrinkage develops during the hydration and hardening of concrete. It is that which occurs in enclosed or sealed concrete, as in a concrete-filled steel tube, where no loss of moisture occurs. This shrinkage strain depends only on the strength of the concrete, and is substantially complete in a few months. It is given in clause 3.1.4(6) of EN 1992-1-1 as a function of concrete grade and the age of the concrete in days. The time coefficient given is $[1 - \exp(-0.2t^{0.5})]$, so this shrinkage should be 90% complete at age 19 weeks. The 90% shrinkage strain for a grade C40/50 concrete is given as $67 \times 10^{-6}$. It has little influence on cracking due to direct loading, and the rules for minimum reinforcement (*clause 7.4.2*) take account of its effects.

The rules in EN 1992-1-1 become less accurate at high concrete strengths, especially if the mix includes silica fume. Data for shrinkage for concrete grades C55/67 and above are given in informative Annex B of EN 1992-2.

Section 11 of EN 1992-2 gives supplementary requirements for lightweight concretes.

The shrinkage of reinforced concrete is lower than the 'free' shrinkage, to an extent that depends on the reinforcement ratio. The difference is easily calculated by elastic theory, if the concrete is in compression. In steel–concrete composite bridges, restraint of reinforced concrete shrinkage by the structural steel leads to locked-in stresses in the composite section. In indeterminate bridges, secondary moments and forces from restraint to the free deflections also occur. Shrinkage, being a permanent action, occurs in every combination of actions. It increases hogging moments at internal supports, often a critical region, and so can influence design.

The specified shrinkage strains will typically be found to be greater than that used in previous UK practice, but the recommended partial load factor, in clause 2.4.2.1 of EN 1992-1-1, is $\gamma_{SH} = 1.0$, lower than the value of 1.2 used in BS 5400.

There is further comment on shrinkage in Chapter 5.

*Creep*

In EN 1994-2, the effects of creep are generally accounted for using an effective modulus of elasticity for the concrete, rather than by explicit calculation of creep deformation. However, it is still necessary to determine the creep coefficient $\phi(t, t_0)$ (denoted $\phi_t$ in EN 1994) from clause 3.1.4 of EN 1992-1-1. Guidance on deriving modular ratios is given in section 5.4.2 of this guide.

## 3.2. Reinforcing steel for bridges

For properties of reinforcement, ***clause 3.2(1)*** refers to clause 3.2 of EN 1992-1-1, which in turn refers to its normative Annex C for bond characteristics. EN 1992 allows the use of bars, de-coiled rods and welded fabric as suitable reinforcement. Its rules are applicable to ribbed and weldable reinforcement only, and therefore cannot be used for plain round bars. The rules are valid for characteristic yield strengths between $400 \, \text{N/mm}^2$ and $600 \, \text{N/mm}^2$. Wire fabrics with nominal bar size 5 mm and above are included. Exceptions to the rules for

**Table 3.1.** Ductility classes for reinforcement

| Class | Characteristic strain at maximum force, $\varepsilon_{uk}$ (%) | Minimum value of $k = (f_t/f_y)_k$ |
|---|---|---|
| A | $\geq 2.5$ | $\geq 1.05$ |
| B | $\geq 5$ | $\geq 1.08$ |
| C | $\geq 7.5$ | $\geq 1.15, <1.35$ |

fatigue of reinforcement may be given in the National Annex, and could refer to the use of wire fabric.

In this section 3.2, symbols $f_{yk}$ and $f_{yd}$ are used for the yield strengths of reinforcement, as in EN 1992, although $f_{sk}$ and $f_{sd}$ are used in EN 1994, to distinguish reinforcement from structural steel.

The grade of reinforcement denotes the specified characteristic yield strength, $f_{yk}$. This is obtained by dividing the characteristic yield load by the nominal cross-sectional area of the bar. Alternatively, for products without a pronounced yield stress, the 0.2% proof stress, $f_{0.2k}$ may be used in place of the yield stress.

*Elastic deformation*

*Clause 3.2(2)*

For simplicity, *clause 3.2(2)* permits the modulus of elasticity of reinforcement to be taken as $210 \, kN/mm^2$, the value given in EN 1993-1-1 for structural steel, rather than $200 \, kN/mm^2$, the value in EN 1992-1-1. This simplification means that it is not necessary to 'transform' reinforcement into structural steel or vice versa when calculating cracked section properties of composite beams.

*Ductility*

*Clause 3.2(3)*

*Clause 3.2(3)* refers to clause 3.2.4 of EN 1992-2; but provisions on ductility in Annex C of EN 1992-1-1 also apply. Reinforcement shall have adequate ductility, defined by the ratio of tensile strength to the yield stress, $(f_t/f_y)_k$, and the strain at maximum force, $\varepsilon_{uk}$. The requirements for the three classes for ductility are given in Table 3.1, from EN 1992-1-1.

Clause 3.2.4(101)P of EN 1992-2 recommends that Class A reinforcement is not used for bridges, although this is subject to variation in the National Annex. The reason is that high strain can occur in reinforcement in a reinforced concrete section in flexure before the concrete crushes. *Clause 5.5.1(5)* prohibits the use of Class A reinforcement in composite beams which are designed as either Class 1 or 2 for a similar reason: namely, that very high strains in reinforcement are possible due to plastification of the whole composite section.

Class 3 and 4 sections are limited to first yield in the structural steel and so the reinforcement strain is limited to a relatively low value. The recommendations of EN 1992 and EN 1994 lead to some ambiguity with respect to ductility requirements for bars in reinforced concrete deck slabs forming part of a composite bridge with Class 3 or 4 beams. Where main longitudinal bars in the deck slab of a composite section are significantly stressed by local loading, it would be advisable to follow the recommendations of EN 1992 and not to use Class A reinforcement.

*Stress–strain curves*

The characteristic stress–strain diagram and the two alternative design diagrams defined in clause 3.2.7 of EN 1992-1-1 are shown in Fig. 3.1. The design diagrams (labelled B in Fig. 3.1) have:

(a) an inclined top branch with a strain limit of $\varepsilon_{ud}$ and a maximum stress of $kf_{yk}/\gamma_S$ at $\varepsilon_{uk}$ (for symbols $k$ and $\varepsilon_{uk}$, see Table 3.1), and
(b) a horizontal top branch without strain limit.

A value for $\varepsilon_{ud}$ may be found in the National Annex to EN 1992-1-1, and is recommended as $0.9\varepsilon_{uk}$.

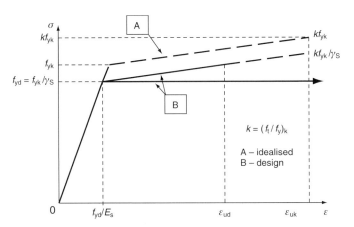

**Fig. 3.1.** Characteristic and design stress–strain diagrams for reinforcement (tension and compression)

From *clause 6.2.1.4*, reinforcement diagram (a) is only relevant when the non-linear method for bending resistance is used. Elastic and plastic bending resistances assume that the reinforcement stress is limited to the design yield strength.

The minimum ductility properties of wire fabric given in Table C.1 of EN 1992-1-1 may not be sufficient to satisfy *clause 5.5.1(6)*, as this requires demonstration of sufficient ductility to avoid fracture when built into a concrete slab. It has been found in tests on continuous composite beams with fabric in tension that the cross-wires initiate cracks in concrete, so that tensile strain becomes concentrated at the locations of the welds in the fabric.[33]

## 3.3. Structural steel for bridges

*Clause 3.3(1)* refers to EN 1993-2, which in turn refers to EN 1993-1-1. This lists in its Table 3.1 steel grades with nominal yield strengths up to 460 N/mm², and allows other steel products to be included in national annexes. The nominal values of material properties have to be adopted as characteristic values in all design calculations.

Two options for selecting material strength are provided. Either the yield strength and ultimate strength should be obtained from the relevant product standard or the simplified values provided in Table 3.1 of EN 1993-1-1 should be used. The National Annex for EC3-1-1 may make this choice. In either case, the strength varies with thickness, and the appropriate thickness must be used when determining the strength.

The elastic constants for steel, given in clause 3.2.6 of EN 1993-1-1, are familiar values. In the notation of EN 1994, they are: $E_a = 210 \,\text{kN/mm}^2$, $G_a = 81 \,\text{kN/mm}^2$, and $\nu_a = 0.3$.

Moduli of elasticity for tension rods and cables of different types are not covered by this clause and are given in EN 1993-1-11.

*Clause 3.3(2)* sets the same upper limit to nominal yield strength as in EN 1993-1-1, namely 460 N/mm², for use in composite bridges. EN 1993-1-12 covers steels up to grade S700. A comprehensive report on high-performance steels appeared in 2005,[34] and there has been extensive research on the use in composite members of structural steels with yield strengths exceeding 355 N/mm².[35–37] It was found that some design rules need modification for use with steel grades higher than S355, to avoid premature crushing of concrete. This applies to:

- plastic resistance moment (*clause 6.2.1.2(2)*), and
- resistance of columns (*clause 6.7.3.6(1)*).

*Ductility*
Many design clauses in EN 1994 rely on the ductile behaviour of structural steel after yield. Ductility is covered by the references in *clause 3.3(1)* to EN 1993.

The ductility characteristics required by clause 3.2.2 of EN 1993-1-1 are for a minimum ratio $f_u/f_y$ of the specified values; a minimum elongation; and a minimum strain at the

*Clause 3.3(1)*

*Clause 3.3(2)*

specified ultimate tensile strength, $f_u$. Recommended values are given, all of which can be modified in the National Annex. The steel grades in Table 3.1 of EN 1993-1-1 all provide the recommended level of ductility. It follows that the drafting of this part of a national annex to EN 1993-1-1 should consider both steel and composite structures.

*Thermal expansion*
For the coefficient of linear thermal expansion of steel, clause 3.2.6 of EN 1993-1-1 gives a value of $12 \times 10^{-6}$ 'per °C' (also written in Eurocodes as /K or $K^{-1}$). This is followed by a Note that for calculating the 'structural effects of unequal temperatures' in composite structures, the coefficient may be taken as $10 \times 10^{-6}$ per °C, which is the value given for normal-weight concrete in clause 3.1.3(5) of EN 1992-1-1. This avoids the need to calculate the internal restraint stresses from uniform temperature change, which would result from different coefficients of thermal expansion for steel and concrete. Movement due to change of uniform temperature (or force due to restraint of movement) should however be calculated using $\alpha = 12 \times 10^{-6}$ per °C for all the structural materials (*clause 5.4.2.5(3)*).

Thermal expansion of reinforcement is not mentioned in EN 1992-1-1, presumably because it is assumed to be the same as that of normal-weight concrete. For reinforcement in composite members the coefficient should be taken as $10 \times 10^{-6}$ per °C. This is not in EN 1994.

Coefficients of thermal expansion for lightweight-aggregate concretes can range from $4 \times 10^{-6}$ to $14 \times 10^{-6}$ per °C. Clause 11.3.2(2) of EN 1992-1-1 states that: 'The differences between the coefficients of thermal expansion of steel and lightweight aggregate concrete need not be considered in design', but 'steel' here means reinforcement, not structural steel. The effects of the difference from $10 \times 10^{-6}$ per °C should be considered in design of composite members for situations where the temperatures of the concrete and the structural steel could differ significantly.

## 3.4. Connecting devices
### 3.4.1. General
Reference is made to EN 1993, *Eurocode 3: Design of Steel Structures, Part 1-8: Design of Joints*[19] for information relating to fasteners, such as bolts, and welding consumables. Provisions for 'other types of mechanical fastener' are given in clause 3.3 of EN 1993-1-3.[38]

*Composite joints*
Composite joints are defined in *clause 1.5.2.8*. In bridges, they are essentially steelwork joints across which a reinforced or prestressed concrete slab is continuous, and cannot be ignored. Composite joints are covered in Section 8 and Annex A of EN 1994-1-1, with extensive reference to EN 1993-1-8. These clauses are written 'for buildings', and so are not copied into EN 1994-2, though many of them are relevant. Commentary on them will be found in Chapters 8 and 10 of the *Designers' Guide to EN 1994-1-1*.[5]

The joints classified as 'rigid' or 'full-strength' occur also in bridge construction. Where bending resistances of beams in Class 1 or 2 are determined by plastic theory, joints in regions of high bending moment must either have sufficient rotation capacity, or be stronger than the weaker of the members joined. The rotation capacity needed in bridges, where elastic global analysis is always used, is lower than in buildings.

Tests, mainly on beam-to-column joints, have found that reinforcing bars of diameter up to 12 mm may fracture. *Clause 5.5.1* gives rules for minimum reinforcement that apply also to joints, but does not exclude small-diameter bars.

### 3.4.2. Headed stud shear connectors
Headed studs are the only type of shear connector for which detailed provisions are given in EN 1994-2, throughout *clause 6.6*. Their use is referred to elsewhere; for example, in *clause 6.7.4.2(4)*. Their performance has been validated for diameters up to 25 mm.[39] Research on

larger studs is in progress. Studs attached to steel top flanges present a hazard during construction, and other types of connector are sometimes used.[23] These must satisfy *clause 6.6.1.1*, which gives the basis of design for shear connection. Research on perforated plate connectors (known initially as 'Perfobond') of S355 and S460 steel in grade C50/60 concrete has found slip capacities from 8–15 mm, which is better than the 6 mm found for 22-mm studs.[25] The use of adhesives on a steel flange is unlikely to be suitable. See also the comment on *clause 1.1.3(3)*.

***Clause 3.4.2*** refers to EN 13918 *Welding – Studs and Ceramic Ferrules for Arc Stud Welding*.[40] This gives minimum dimensions for weld collars. Other methods of attaching studs, such as spinning, may not provide weld collars large enough for the resistances of studs given in *clause 6.6.3.1(1)* to be applicable.

Shear connection between steel and concrete by bond or friction is permitted only in accordance with *clause 6.7.4*, for columns.

*Clause 3.4.2*

## 3.5. Prestressing steel and devices
Properties of materials for prestressing tendons and requirements for anchorage and coupling of tendons are covered in clauses 3.3 and 3.4, respectively, of EN 1992-1-1. Prestressing by tendons is rarely used for steel and concrete composite members and is not discussed further.

## 3.6. Tension components in steel
The scope of EN 1993-1-11 is limited to bridges with adjustable and replaceable steel tension components. It identifies three generic groups: tension rod systems, ropes, and bundles of parallel wires or strands; and provides information on stiffness and other material properties. The analysis of cable-supported bridges, including treatment of load combinations and non-linear effects, is also covered. These are not discussed further here but some discussion can be found in the *Designers' Guide to EN 1993-2*.[4]

# CHAPTER 4

# Durability

This chapter corresponds to *Section 4*, which has the following clauses:

- General *Clause 4.1*
- Corrosion protection at the steel–concrete interface in bridges *Clause 4.2*

## 4.1. General

Almost all aspects of the durability of composite structures are covered by cross-references in *clause 4.1(1)* to ENs 1990, 1992 and 1993. Bridges must be sufficiently durable to remain serviceable throughout their design life. Clause 2.4 of EN 1990 lists ten factors to be taken into account, and gives the following general requirement: *Clause 4.1(1)*

> 'The structure shall be designed such that deterioration over its design working life does not impair the performance of the structure below that intended, having due regard to its environment and the anticipated level of maintenance.'

The specific provisions given in EN 1992 and EN 1993 focus on corrosion protection to reinforcement, tendons and structural steel.

### Reinforced concrete

The main durability provision in EN 1992 is the specification of concrete cover as a defence against corrosion of reinforcement and tendons. The following outline of the procedure is for reinforcement only. In addition to the durability aspect, adequate concrete cover is essential for the transmission of bond forces and for providing sufficient fire resistance (which is of less significance for bridge design). The minimum cover $c_{min}$ to satisfy the durability requirements is defined in clause 4.4.1.2 of EN 1992-1-1 by the following expression:

$$c_{min} = \max\{c_{min,b}; c_{min,dur} + \Delta c_{dur,\gamma} - \Delta c_{dur,st} - \Delta c_{dur,add}; 10\,\text{mm}\} \qquad (D4.1)$$

where: $c_{min,b}$    is the minimum cover due to bond requirements and is defined in Table 4.2 of EN 1992-1-1. For aggregate sizes up to 32 mm it is equal to the bar diameter (or equivalent bar diameter for bundled bars),

$c_{min,dur}$    is the minimum cover required for the environmental conditions,

$\Delta c_{dur,\gamma}$    is an additional safety element which EC2 recommends to be 0 mm,

$\Delta c_{dur,st}$    is a reduction of minimum cover for the use of stainless steel, which, if adopted, should be applied to all design calculations, including bond. The recommended value in EC2 without further specification is 0 mm,

$\Delta c_{dur,add}$    is a reduction of minimum cover for the use of additional protection. This could cover coatings to the concrete surface or reinforcement (such as epoxy coating). EC2 recommends taking a value of 0 mm.

**Table 4.1.** Minimum cover $c_{min,dur}$ for reinforcement. (Source: based on Table 4.4N of EN 1992-1-1[15])

Environmental Requirements for $c_{min}$ (mm)

| Structural Class | Exposure Class (from Table 4.1 of EN 1992-1-1) | | | | | | |
|---|---|---|---|---|---|---|---|
| | X0 | XC1 | XC2/XC3 | XC4 | XD1/XS1 | XD2/XS2 | XD3/XS3 |
| 1 | 10 | 10 | 10 | 15 | 20 | 25 | 30 |
| 2 | 10 | 10 | 15 | 20 | 25 | 30 | 35 |
| 3 | 10 | 10 | 20 | 25 | 30 | 35 | 40 |
| 4 | 10 | 15 | 25 | 30 | 35 | 40 | 45 |
| 5 | 15 | 20 | 30 | 35 | 40 | 45 | 50 |
| 6 | 20 | 25 | 35 | 40 | 45 | 50 | 55 |

The minimum cover for durability requirements, $c_{min,dur}$, depends on the relevant 'exposure class' taken from Table 4.1 of EN 1992-1-1.

There are 18 exposure classes, ranging from X0, 'no risk of corrosion', to XA3, 'highly aggressive chemical environment'. It should be noted that a particular element may have more than one exposure class, e.g. XD3 and XF4. The XF and XA designations affect the minimum required concrete grade (via EN 1992-1-1 Annex E) and the chemical composition of the concrete. The XC and XD designations affect minimum cover and crack width requirements, and XD, XF and XS affect a stress limit for concrete under the characteristic combination, from clause 7.2(102) of EN 1992-2. The exposure classes most likely to be appropriate for composite bridge decks are:

- XC3 for a deck slab protected by waterproofing (recommended in clause 4.2(105) of EN 1992-2)
- XC3 for a deck slab soffit protected from the rain by adjacent girders
- XC4 for other parts of the deck slab exposed to cyclic wetting and drying
- XD3 for parapet edge beams in the splash zone of water contaminated with de-icing salts; and also XF2 or XF4 if exposed to both freeze–thaw and de-icing agents (recommended in clause 4.2(106) of EN 1992-2).

Informative Annex E of EN 1992-1-1 gives 'indicative strength classes' (e.g. C30/37) for each exposure class, for corrosion of reinforcement and for damage to concrete.

The cover $c_{min,dur}$ is given in Table 4.4N of EN 1992-1-1 in terms of the exposure class and the structural class, and the structural class is found from Table 4.3N. These are reproduced here as Tables 4.1 and 4.2, respectively. Table 4.2 gives modifications to the initial structural class, which is recommended (in a Note to clause 4.4.1.2(5) of EN 1992-1-1) to be class 4, assuming a service life of 50 years and concrete of the indicative strength.

Taking exposure class XC4 as an example, the indicative strength class is C30/37. Starting with Structural Class 4, and using Tables 4.1 and 4.2:

- for 100-year life, increase by 2 to Class 6
- for use of C40/50 concrete, reduce by 1 to Class 5
- where the position of the reinforcement is not affected by the construction process, reduce by 1 to Class 4.

'Special quality control' (Table 4.2) is not defined, but clues are given in the Notes to Table 4.3N of EN 1992-1-1. Assuming that it will not be provided, the Class is 4, and Table 4.1 gives $c_{min,dur} = 30$ mm. Using the recommendations that follow equation (D4.1),

$c_{min} = 30$ mm

The cover to be specified on the drawings, $c_{nom}$, shall include a further allowance for deviation ($\Delta c_{dev}$) according to clause 4.4.1.3(1)P of EN 1992-1-1, such that:

$c_{nom} = c_{min} + \Delta c_{dev}$

**Table 4.2.** Recommended structural classification. (Source: based on Table 4.3N of EN 1992-1-1[15])

| | Structural Class | | | | | | |
|---|---|---|---|---|---|---|---|
| | Exposure Class (from Table 4.1 of EN 1992-1-1) | | | | | | |
| Criterion | X0 | XC1 | XC2/XC3 | XC4 | XD1 | XD2/XS1 | XD3/XS2/XS3 |
| Service life of 100 years | Increase class by 2 | Increase class by 2 | Increase class by 2 | Increase class by 2 | Increase class by 2 | Increase class by 2 | Increase class by 2 |
| Strength Class (see notes 1 and 2) | $\geq$C30/37 Reduce class by 1 | $\geq$C30/37 Reduce class by 1 | $\geq$C35/45 Reduce class by 1 | $\geq$C40/50 Reduce class by 1 | $\geq$C40/50 Reduce class by 1 | $\geq$C40/50 Reduce class by 1 | $\geq$C45/55 Reduce class by 1 |
| Member with slab geometry (position of reinforcement not affected by construction process) | Reduce class by 1 | Reduce class by 1 | Reduce class by 1 | Reduce class by 1 | Reduce class by 1 | Reduce class by 1 | Reduce class by 1 |
| Special Quality Control of the concrete ensured | Reduce class by 1 | Reduce class by 1 | Reduce class by 1 | Reduce class by 1 | Reduce class by 1 | Reduce class by 1 | Reduce class by 1 |

Note 1: The strength class and water/cement ratio are considered to be related values. The relationship is subject to a national code. A special composition (type of cement, w/c value, fine fillers) with the intent to produce low permeability may be considered.
Note 2: The limit may be reduced by one strength class if air entrainment of more than 4% is applied.

The value of $\Delta c_{dev}$ for buildings and bridges is defined in the National Annex and is recommended in clause 4.4.1.3(2) of EN 1992-1-1 to be taken as 10 mm. This value may be reduced in situations where accurate measurements of cover achieved can be taken and non-conforming elements rejected. This could apply to precast units.

Almost all the provisions on cover, but not the process to be followed, can be modified in the National Annex to EN 1992-1-1.

*Structural steel*
The rules in Section 4 of EN 1993-1-1 cover the need for access for in-service inspection, maintenance, and possible reconstruction of parts susceptible to corrosion, wear or fatigue. Further provisions relevant to fatigue are given in Section 4 of EN 1993-2, and a list is given of parts that may need to be replaceable. Corrosion allowances for inaccessible surfaces may be given in the National Annex. Further discussion on durability of structural steel is presented in the *Designers' Guide to EN 1993-2*.[4]

Access to shear connectors is not possible, so they must be protected from corrosion. *Clause 4.1(2)* refers to *clause 6.6.5*, which includes relevant detailing rules, for cover and for haunches.

*Clause 4.1(2)*

## 4.2. Corrosion protection at the steel–concrete interface in bridges

The side cover to stud connectors must be at least 50 mm (*clause 6.6.5.4(2)*). *Clause 4.2(1)* requires provision of a minimum of 50 mm of corrosion protection to each edge of a steel flange at an interface with concrete. This does not imply that the connectors must be protected.

*Clause 4.2(1)*

For precast deck slabs, the reference to *Section 8* is to *clause 8.4.2*, which requires greater corrosion protection to a steel flange that supports a precast slab without bedding. Normal UK practice when using 'Omnia' planks has been to extend the corrosion protection a minimum of 25 mm beyond the plank edge and its seating material, with due allowance for placing tolerance. The connectors are not mentioned. They are usually surrounded by *in situ* concrete, whether bedding is used (as is usual) or not. Corrosion protection to the connectors is not normally required. It is possible that a thick coating could reduce their stiffness in shear.

# CHAPTER 5

# Structural analysis

This chapter corresponds to *Section 5* of EN 1994-2, which has the following clauses:

- Structural modelling for analysis                                    *Clause 5.1*
- Structural stability                                                 *Clause 5.2*
- Imperfections                                                        *Clause 5.3*
- Calculation of action effects                                        *Clause 5.4*
- Classification of cross-sections                                     *Clause 5.5*

Structural analysis is performed at three levels: global analysis, member analysis and local analysis. *Section 5* of EN 1994-2 covers the structural idealization of bridges and the methods of global analysis required in different situations to determine deformations and internal forces and moments. It also covers classification of cross-sections of members, for use in determining resistances by methods given in Sections 6 of EN 1993-2 and EN 1994-2. Much reference has to be made to other parts of EC3, especially EN 1993-1-5[41] for the effects of shear lag and plate buckling.

Wherever possible, analyses for serviceability and ultimate limit states use the same methods. It is therefore more convenient to specify them in a single section, rather than to include them in *Sections 6* and *7*.

The division of material between *Section 5* and *Section 6* (Ultimate limit states) is not always obvious. Calculation of vertical shear is clearly 'analysis', but longitudinal shear is in *Section 6*. For composite columns, 'Methods of analysis and member imperfections' is in *clause 6.7.3.4*. This separation of imperfections in frames from those in columns requires care, and receives detailed explanation in the *Designers' Guide to EN 1994-1-1*.[5]

Two flow charts for global analysis, Figs 5.15 and 5.16, are given, with comments, at the end of this chapter. They include relevant provisions from *Section 6*.

## 5.1. Structural modelling for analysis
### 5.1.1. Structural modelling and basic assumptions
The clause of EN 1990 referred to in *clause 5.1.1(1)P* says, in effect, that models shall be appropriate and based on established theory and practice and that the variables shall be relevant.

*Clause 5.1.1(1)P*

The basic requirement is that analysis should realistically model the expected behaviour of the bridge and its constituent elements. For composite bridges, important factors in analysis are the effects on stiffness of shear lag and concrete cracking. For composite members, different rules for shear lag apply for concrete flanges and for the steel parts. The former is dealt with in *clause 5.4.1.2* and the latter in Section 3 of EN 1993-1-5. They are discussed in this Guide under *clause 5.4.1.2*.

The effects of cracking of concrete can be taken into account either by using cracked section properties in accordance with *clause 5.4.2.3* or, for filler-beam decks only, by redistributing the moments determined from an uncracked analysis away from the cracked sections in accordance with *clause 5.4.2.9*. For Class 4 sections, plate buckling effects, which have to be considered in accordance with clause 2.2 of EN 1993-1-5, can also lead to a reduction in stiffness of cross-sections. This is discussed in this Guide under *clause 5.4.1.1*.

Global analysis can be significantly affected by flexibility at connections and by interaction of the bridge structure with the soil, particularly in fully integral bridges. Guidance on modelling joints and ground–structure interaction are given in *clauses 5.1.2* and *5.1.3*, respectively.

Composite members and joints are commonly used in conjunction with others of structural steel. *Clause 5.1.1(2)* makes clear that this is the type of construction envisaged in *Section 5*. Significant differences between Sections 5 of EC3 and EC4 are referred to in this chapter.

*Clause 5.1.1(2)*

### 5.1.2. Joint modelling

In analysis of bridges, it is generally possible to treat joints as either rigid or pinned, as appropriate. *Clause 5.1.2(1)* refers to 'semi-continuous' joints as an exception. They are neither 'rigid' nor 'pinned', and have sufficient flexibility to influence the bending moment transmitted. This could occur, for example, from the flexure of thin end-plates in a bolted end-plate connection.

*Clause 5.1.2(1)*

The three simplified joint models listed in *clause 5.1.2(2)* – simple, continuous and semi-continuous – are those given in EN 1993. Joints in steelwork have their own Eurocode part, EN 1993-1-8.[19] Its design methods are for joints 'subjected to predominantly static loading' (its clause 1.1(1)). Resistance to fatigue is covered in EN 1993-1-9[42] and in *clause 6.8*.

*Clause 5.1.2(2)*

*Clause 5.1.2(3)* prohibits the use of semi-continuous *composite joints* (defined in *clause 1.5.2.8*) in bridges. An example of such a prohibited joint might be a composite main beam joined together through end-plate connections. Semi-continuous non-composite joints should also be avoided where possible, so that fatigue can be assessed using the detail categories in EN 1993-1-9.

*Clause 5.1.2(3)*

Semi-continuous joints may, in some situations, be unavoidable, such as end-plate connections between composite cross-beams and main beam webs in some U-frame bridges, but these would not be composite joints due to the lack of continuity of the slab reinforcement. The flexibility of such a joint would have to be considered in deriving the restraint provided to the compression flange by the U-frame. Design rules are given in EN 1993-1-8 and in EN 1994-1-1.

Another apparent exception to the above rule concerns the slip of bolts. This is discussed under *clause 5.4.1.1(7)*.

### 5.1.3. Ground–structure interaction

*Clause 5.1.3(1)P* refers to 'deformation of supports', so the stiffness of the bearings, piers, abutments and ground have to be taken into account in analysis. This also includes consideration of stiffness in determining effective lengths for buckling or resistance to buckling by analysis. For further guidance on this, see Section 5.2 below.

*Clause 5.1.3(1)P*

The effects of differential settlement must also be included in analysis, although from *clause 5.1.3(3)* they may be neglected in ultimate limit state checks. Similar considerations apply to other indirect actions, such as differential temperature and differential creep. They are discussed in this Guide under *clause 5.4.2.2(6)*.

*Clause 5.1.3(3)*

## 5.2. Structural stability

The following comments refer to both entire bridges and isolated members. They assume that the global analyses will be based on elastic theory. The exception in *clause 5.4.3* is discussed later. All design methods must take account of:

- errors in the initial positions of joints (global geometric imperfections) and in the initial geometry of members (member geometric imperfections)

- the effects of cracking of concrete and of any semi-rigid or nominally pinned joints
- residual stresses in compression members (structural imperfections).

The stage at which each of these is considered or allowed for can be selected by the designer, which leads to some complexity in *clauses 5.2 to 5.4*.

### 5.2.1. Effects of deformed geometry of the structure

In its clause 1.5.6, EN 1990 defines types of analysis. 'First-order' analysis is performed on the initial geometry of the structure. 'Second-order' analysis takes account of the deformations of the structure, which are a function of its loading. Clearly, second-order analysis may always be applied. With appropriate software increasingly available, second-order analysis is now relatively straightforward to perform. The criteria for neglect of second-order effects given in *clauses 5.2.1(2)P* and *5.2.1(3)* need not then be considered. The analysis allowing for second-order effects will usually be iterative but normally the iteration will take place within the software. Methods for second-order analysis are described in text books such as that by Trahair *et al.*[43]

A disadvantage of second-order analysis is that the principle of superposition does not apply and entire load combinations must be applied to the bridge model. In this case, the critical load combinations can still first be estimated using first-order analysis, influence lines (or surfaces) and superposition of load cases.

Second-order effects apply to both in-plane and out-of-plane modes of buckling, including lateral–torsional buckling. The latter behaviour is more complex and requires a finite-element analysis using shell elements to model properly second-order effects and instability. A method of checking beams for out-of-plane instability while modelling only in-plane second-order effects is given in clause 6.3.4 of EN 1993-1-1 and discussed in section 6.4.3 of this guide. Out-of-plane second-order effects can only be neglected in bridge beams where there is sufficient lateral bracing present. In-plane second-order effects in the beams will usually be negligible and lateral–torsional buckling may be checked using one of the simplified methods permitted in *clause 6.4*. Integral bridges, with high axial load in the beams caused by earth pressure, may be an exception.

*Clause 5.2.1(3)* provides a basis for the use of first-order analysis. The check is done for a particular load combination and arrangement. The provisions in this clause are similar to those for elastic analysis in the corresponding clause in EN 1993-2. *Clause 5.2.1(3)* is not just for a sway mode. This is because *clause 5.2.1* is relevant not only to complete frames but also to the design of individual columns (see *clause 6.7.3.4* for composite columns, and comments on it). Such members may be held in position against sway but still be subject to significant second-order effects due to bowing. Second-order effects in local and global modes are illustrated in Fig. 5.1.

In an elastic frame, second-order effects are dependent on the proximity of the design loads to the elastic critical buckling load. This is the basis for *expression (5.1)*, in which $\alpha_{cr}$ is defined as '*the factor . . . to cause elastic instability*'. This may be taken as the load factor at which bifurcation of equilibrium occurs. For a column or frame, it is assumed that there are no member imperfections, and that only vertical loads are present, usually at their maximum design values. These are replaced by a set of loads that produce the same set of member axial forces without any bending. An eigenvalue analysis then gives the factor

*Clause 5.2.1(2)P*
*Clause 5.2.1(3)*

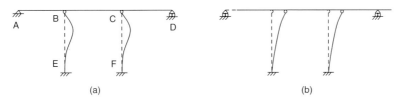

(a)  (b)

**Fig. 5.1.** Examples of local and global instability: (a) local second-order effects; (b) global second-order effects

$\alpha_{cr}$, applied to the whole of the loading, at which the system stiffness vanishes and elastic instability occurs.

To sufficient accuracy, $\alpha_{cr}$ may also be determined by a second-order load–deflection analysis. The non-linear load–deflection response approaches asymptotically to the elastic critical value. This may be useful as some software will perform this analysis but not an elastic critical buckling analysis.

The use of *expression (5.1)* is one way of determining if first-order analysis will suffice. *Clause 5.2.1(3)* also states that second-order effects may be ignored where the increases in internal actions due to the deformations from first-order analysis are less than 10%. Hence, for members braced against lateral buckling:

$$M_I / \Delta M_I \geq 10 \tag{D5.1}$$

where $M_I$ is the moment from first-order analysis, including the effects of initial imperfections, and $\Delta M_I$ is the increase in bending moments calculated from the deflections obtained from first-order analysis (the $P$–$\Delta$ moments). By convention, the symbols $\Delta$ or $\delta$ are used for deformations. They should not be confused with $\Delta$, as used here in $\Delta M_I$.

Application of this criterion, in principle, avoids the need for elastic critical buckling analysis but its use has some problems as discussed below. For the case of a pin-ended strut with sinusoidal bow of magnitude $a_0$, expression (D5.1) is the same as *expression (5.1)*. This can be shown as follows.

The extra deflection from a first-order analysis can easily be shown to be given by:

$$\Delta a = a_0 F_{Ed} / F_{cr} \tag{D5.2}$$

where $F_{Ed}$ is the applied axial load and $F_{cr}$ is the elastic critical buckling load. It follows that the extra moment from the first-order deflection is:

$$\Delta M_I = F_{Ed}(a_0 F_{Ed} / F_{cr}) \tag{D5.3}$$

Putting equation (D5.3) into equation (D5.1) gives *expression (5.1)*:

$$M_I / \Delta M_I = \frac{F_{Ed} a_0}{F_{Ed}(a_0 F_{Ed} / F_{cr})} = \frac{F_{cr}}{F_{Ed}} = \alpha_{cr} \geq 10$$

This direct equivalence is only valid for a pin-ended strut with a sinusoidal bow and hence sinusoidal curvature but it generally remains sufficiently accurate. (Note: It is found for a strut with equal end moments that:

$$M_I / \Delta M_I = \frac{8}{\pi^2} \left( \frac{F_{cr}}{F_{Ed}} \right)$$

For anything other than a pin-ended strut or statically determinate structure, it will not be easy to determine $\Delta M_I$ from the deflections found by first-order analysis. This is because in indeterminate structures, the extra moment cannot be calculated at all sections directly from the local '$P$–$\Delta$' because of the need to maintain compatibility.

In the example shown in Fig. 5.2, it would be conservative to assume that at mid-height, $\Delta M_I = N\Delta$. (This is similar to secondary effects of prestressing in prestressed structures.) A more accurate value could be found from a further first-order analysis that models the first-order deflected shape found by the previous analysis. To avoid the problem that low ratios $M_I / \Delta M_I$ can be obtained near points of contraflexure, the condition $M_I / \Delta M_I \geq 10$ should be applied only at the peak moment positions between each adjacent point of contraflexure. The maximum $P$–$\Delta$ bending moment in the member can again be used as a conservative estimate of $\Delta M_I$.

*Clause 5.2.1(4)P*    *Clause 5.2.1(4)P* is a reminder that the analysis shall account for the reductions in stiffness arising from cracking and creep of concrete and from possible non-linear behaviour of the joints. In general, such effects are dependent on the internal moments and forces, so calculation is iterative. Simplified methods are therefore given in *clauses 5.4.2.2* and *5.4.2.3*, where further comment is given.

Manual intervention may be needed, to adjust stiffness values before repeating an analysis. It is expected however that advanced software will be written for EN 1994 to account

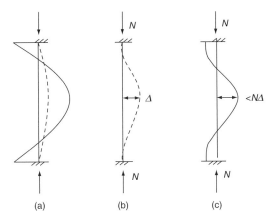

**Fig. 5.2.** Extra bending moments from deflection: (a) first-order moment due to imperfections; (b) first-order deflection; (c) additional moment from deflection

automatically for these effects. The designer may of course make assumptions, although care is needed to ensure these are conservative. For example, assuming that joints have zero rotational stiffness (resulting in simply-supported composite beams) could lead to neglect of the reduction in beam stiffness due to cracking. The overall lateral stiffness would probably be a conservative value, but this is not certain.

*Clause 6.7.3.4(2)* gives an effective flexural stiffness for doubly symmetric columns which may be used to determine $\alpha_{cr}$ (*clause 6.7.3.4(3)*) and which makes allowance for the stiffness of the concrete, including the effects of cracking, and the reinforcement. The use of this stiffness in checking composite columns is discussed in section 6.7.3 of this guide.

For asymmetric composite compression members in general, such as a composite bridge deck beam in an integral bridge, the effective stiffness usually depends on the direction of bowing of the member. This is influenced by the initial camber and by the deflection under the loading considered. The deflection under design ultimate load and after creep usually exceeds the initial camber. The direction of bow is then downwards.

A conservative possibility for determining $\alpha_{cr}$ is to ignore completely the contribution of the concrete to the flexural stiffness, including reinforcement only; this is done in Example 6.6 to determine the elastic critical buckling load under axial force. An even more conservative possibility is to base the flexural stiffness on the steel section alone. If second-order analysis is necessary, this simplification will not usually be satisfactory as the use of cracked properties throughout the structure, irrespective of the sign of the axial force in the concrete, would not satisfy the requirements of *clause 5.4.2.3* regarding cracking. Generally the results of a first-order analysis can be used to determine which areas of the structure are cracked and the section properties for second-order analysis can then be modified as necessary. The stiffness of cracked areas can be based on the above simplification. The procedure can be iterative if the extent of cracked zones is significantly altered by the second-order analysis. An effective modulus of elasticity for compressed concrete is also required to calculate the flexural stiffness of uncracked areas. *Clause 6.7.3.3(4)* provides a formula.

### 5.2.2. Methods of analysis for bridges
Where it is necessary to take second-order effects and imperfections into account, EN 1993-2 clause 5.2.2 provides the following three alternative methods by reference to EN 1993-1-1 clause 5.2.2(3).

• Use of second-order analysis including both 'global' system imperfections and 'local' member imperfections as discussed in section 5.3 below. If this method is followed, no individual checks of member stability are required and members are checked for cross-section resistance only. An alternative method for bare steel members is discussed under *clause 5.3.1(2)*. For each composite member, it is necessary to use an appropriate flexural stiffness covering the effects of cracking and creep as discussed in section 5.2.1 above.

If lateral–torsional buckling is to be covered totally by second-order analysis, appropriate finite-element analysis capable of modelling the behaviour will be required.

- Use of second-order analysis including 'global' system imperfections only. For individual bare steel members, stability checks are then required according to EN 1993-2 clause 6.3. Since the member end forces and moments include second-order effects from global behaviour, the effective length of individual members is then based on the member length, rather than a greater effective length that includes the effects of global sway deformations. Note that when clause 6.3.3 of EN 1993-1-1 is used for member checks of bare steel members, the member moments will be further amplified by the '$k_{ij}$' parameters. Since the second-order analysis will already have amplified these moments, providing sufficient nodes have been included along the member in the analysis model, this is conservative and it would be permissible to set the '$k_{ij}$' parameters equal to unity where they exceed unity. However, the imperfections within the members have not been considered or amplified by the second-order analysis. These are included via the first term in the equations in this clause:

$$\frac{N_{Ed}}{\chi N_{Rk}/\gamma_{M1}}$$

For composite members in compression and bending, buckling resistance curves cannot be used, and the moments from member imperfections in the member length should be added. Second-order effects within the member are accounted for by magnifying the resulting moments from the local imperfections within the length of the member according to *clauses 6.7.3.4(4)* and *6.7.3.4(5)* using an effective length based on the member length, and then checking the resistance of cross-sections. Only the local member imperfections need to be amplified if sufficient nodes have been included along the member in the analysis model, as all other moments will then have been amplified by the second-order global analysis. Further comment and a flow chart are given under *clause 6.7.3.4*.

- Use of first-order analysis without modelled imperfections. For bare steel members, the verification can be made using clause 6.3 of EN 1993-2 with appropriate effective lengths. All second-order effects are then included in the relevant resistance formulae. This latter method will be most familiar to bridge engineers in the UK, as tables of effective lengths for members with varying end conditions of rotational and positional fixity have commonly been used. The use of effective lengths for this method is discussed in the *Designers' Guide to EN 1993-2*.[4]

For composite compression members, this approach is generally not appropriate. The method of *clause 6.7.3* is based on calculation of second-order effects within members, followed by checks on resistance of cross-sections. No buckling resistance curves are provided. Composite beams in bending alone can however be checked for lateral–torsional buckling satisfactorily following this method.

Second-order analysis itself can be done either by direct computer analysis that accounts for the deformed geometry or by amplification of the moments from a first-order analysis (including the effects of imperfections) using clause 5.2.2(5) of EN 1993-2. Where either approach is used, it should only be performed by experienced engineers because the guidance on the use of imperfections in terms of shapes, combinations and directions of application is not comprehensive in EC3 and EC4 and judgement must be exercised.

## 5.3. Imperfections
### 5.3.1. Basis

*Clause 5.3.1(1)P*   *Clause 5.3.1(1)P* lists possible sources of imperfection. Subsequent clauses (and also *clause 5.2*) describe how these should be allowed for. This may be by inclusion in the global analyses or in methods of checking resistance, as explained above.

Imperfections comprise geometric imperfections and residual stresses. The term 'geometric imperfection' is used to describe departures from the intended centreline setting-out dimensions found on drawings, which occur during fabrication and erection. This is inevitable as construction work can only be executed to certain tolerances. Geometric imperfections include lack of verticality, lack of straightness, lack of fit and minor joint eccentricities. The behaviour of members under load is also affected by residual stresses within the members. Residual stresses can lead to yielding of steel occurring locally at lower applied external load than predicted from stress analysis ignoring such effects. The effects of residual stresses can be modelled by additional geometric imperfections. The equivalent geometric imperfections given in EC3 and EC4 cover both geometric imperfections and residual stresses.

*Clause 5.3.1(2)* requires imperfections to be in the most unfavourable direction and form. The most unfavourable geometric imperfection normally has the same shape as the lowest buckling mode. This can sometimes be difficult to find, but it can be assumed that this condition is satisfied by the Eurocode methods for checking resistance that include effects of member imperfections (see comments on *clause 5.2.2*). Clause 5.3.2(11) of EN 1993-1-1 covers the use of a unique global and local system imperfection based on the lowest buckling mode. This can generally only be used for bare steel members as the imperfection parameter $\alpha$ is required and this is not provided for composite members. The method is discussed in the *Designers' Guide to EN 1993-2*.[4]

Clause 5.3.1(2)

## 5.3.2. Imperfections for bridges
Generally, an explicit treatment of geometric imperfections is required for composite frames. In both EN 1993-1-1 and EN 1994-1-1 the values are equivalent rather than measured values (*clause 5.3.2(1)*) because they allow for effects such as residual stresses, in addition to imperfections of shape.

Clause 5.3.2(1)

*Clause 5.3.2(2)* covers bracing design. In composite bridges, the deck slab acts as plan bracing. Compression flanges that require bracing occur in hogging regions of beam-and-slab bridges and in sagging regions of half-through bridges, bowstring arches and similar structures. The bracing of compression flanges in sagging regions differs little from that in all-steel bridges, and is discussed in the *Designers' Guide to EN 1993-2*.[4]

Clause 5.3.2(2)

Steel bottom flanges in hogging regions of composite bridges are usually restrained laterally by continuous or discrete transverse frames. For deep main beams, plan bracing at bottom-flange level may also be used. Where the main beams are rolled I-sections, their webs may be stiff enough to serve as the vertical members of continuous inverted-U frames, which are completed by the shear connection and the deck slab. These systems are discussed under *clause 6.4.2*.

Discrete U-frame bracing can be provided at the location of vertical web stiffeners. These frames need transverse steel members. If these are provided just below the concrete deck, they should be designed as composite. Otherwise, design for shrinkage and temperature effects in the transverse direction becomes difficult. This problem is often avoided by placing the steel cross-member at lower level, so creating an H-frame. Both types of frame provide elastic lateral restraint at bottom-flange level, with a spring stiffness that is easily calculated.

The design transverse forces for these frames, or for plan bracing, arise from lateral imperfections in the compressed flanges. For these imperfections, *clause 5.3.2(2)* refers to EN 1993-2, which in turn refers to clauses 5.3.2 to 5.3.4 of EN 1993-1-1. The design transverse forces, $F_{Ed}$, and a design method are given in clause 6.3.4.2 of EN 1993-2, though it refers specifically only to U-frame restraints. Comments on these clauses are in the relevant Guides in this series.[4,7]

The relevant imperfections for analysis of the bracing system are not necessarily the same as those for the bridge beams themselves.

In hogging regions of continuous beam-and-slab bridges, distortional lateral buckling is usually the critical mode. It should not be assumed that a point of contraflexure is a lateral restraint, for the buckling half-wavelength can exceed the length of flange in compression.[44]

Where the restraint forces are to be transmitted to end supports by a system of plan bracing, this system should be designed to resist the more onerous of the transverse forces $F_{Ed}$ from each restraint within a length equal to the half wavelength of buckling, and the forces generated by an overall flange bow in each flange according to clause 5.3.3 of EN 1993-1-1.

For the latter case, the overall bow is given as $e_0 = \alpha_m L/500$, where $\alpha_m$ is the reduction factor for the number of interconnected beams ($\alpha_m = 0.866$ for two beams), and $L$ is the span. The plan bracing may be designed for an equivalent uniformly-distributed force per beam of $8N_{Ed}(e_0 + \delta_q)/L$, where $\delta_q$ is the deflection of the bracing, and $N_{Ed}$ is the maximum compressive force in the flange.

For very stiff bracing, the total design lateral force for the bracing is:

$$\left(8\sum N_{Ed}/L\right)(\alpha_m L/500) = \sum N_{Ed}\alpha_m/62.5$$

*Clause 5.3.2(2)* should also be used for system imperfections for composite columns, although its scope is given as 'stabilizing transverse frames'. Its reference to clause 5.3 of EN 1993-2 leads to relevant clauses in EN 1993-1-1, as follows.

Initial out-of-plumb of a column is given in clause 5.3.2(3) of EN 1993-1-1 which, although worded for 'frames', is applicable to a single column or row of columns. Where a steel column is very slender and has a moment-resisting joint at one or both ends, clause 5.3.2(6) of EN 1993-1-1 requires its local bow imperfection to be included in the second-order global analysis used to determine the action effects at its ends. 'Very slender' is defined as:

$$\bar{\lambda} > 0.5\sqrt{Af_y/N_{Ed}}$$

It is advised that this rule should be used also for composite columns, in the form $\alpha_{cr} < 4$, with $\alpha_{cr}$ as defined in *clause 5.2.1(3)*. This is obtained by replacing $Af_y$ by $N_{pl}$.

**Clause 5.3.2(3)**   *Clause 5.3.2(3)* covers imperfections in composite columns and compression members (e.g. in trusses), which must be considered explicitly. It refers to material in *clause 6.7.3*, which appears to be limited, by *clause 6.7.3(1)*, to uniform members of doubly symmetrical cross-section. *Clause 6.7.2(9)*, which is of general applicability, also refers to *Table 6.5* of *clause 6.7.3* for member imperfections; but the table only covers typical cross-sections of columns. Imperfections in compressed beams, which occur in integral bridges, appear to be outside the scope of EN 1994.

The imperfections for buckling curve d in Table 5.1 of EN 1993-1-1 could conservatively be used for second-order effects in the plane of bending. For composite bridges with the deck slab on top of the main beams, lateral buckling effects can subsequently be included by a check of the compression flange using the member resistance formulae in clause 6.3 of EN 1993-1-1. Guidance on verifying beams in integral bridges in bending and axial load is discussed in section 6.4 of this guide.

**Clause 5.3.2(4)**   *Clause 5.3.2(4)* covers global and local imperfections in steel compression members, by reference to EN 1993-2. Imperfections for arches are covered in Annex D of EN 1993-2.

## 5.4. Calculation of action effects
### 5.4.1. Methods of global analysis
EN 1990 defines several types of analysis that may be appropriate for ultimate limit states. For global analysis of bridges, EN 1994-2 gives three methods: linear elastic analysis, with or without corrections for cracking of concrete, and non-linear analysis. The latter is discussed in section 5.4.3 below, and is rarely used in practice.

**Clause 5.4.1.1(1)**   *Clause 5.4.1.1(1)* permits the use of elastic global analysis even where plastic (rectangular-stress-block) theory is used for checking resistances of cross-sections. For resistance to flexure, these sections are in Class 1 or 2, and commonly occur in mid-span regions.

There are several reasons[45-47] why the apparent incompatibility between the methods used for analysis and for resistance is accepted. It is essentially consistent with UK practice, but

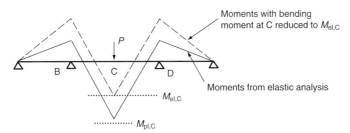

**Fig. 5.3.** Effect of mixing section classes, and an approximate method for checking bending moments at internal supports

care should be taken with mixing section classes within a bridge when elastic analysis is used. An example is a continuous bridge, with a mid-span section designed in bending as Class 2 and the section at an internal support as Class 3. The Class 3 section may become over-stressed by the elastic moments shed from mid-span while the plastic section resistance develops there and stiffness is lost.

There is no such incompatibility for Class 3 or 4 sections, as resistance is based on elastic models.

Mixed-class design has rarely been found to be a problem, as the load cases producing maximum moment at mid-span and at a support rarely coexist, except where adjacent spans are very short compared to the span considered. A relevant design rule is given in *clause 6.2.1.3(2)*.

If redistribution is required to be checked, the conservative method illustrated in Fig. 5.3 may be used. In this example there is a Class 2 section at mid-span of the central span, and the support sections are Class 3. A simplified load case that produces maximum sagging moment is shown. Elastic analysis for the load $P$ gives a bending moment at cross-section C that exceeds the elastic resistance moment, $M_{el,C}$. The excess moment is redistributed from section C, giving the distribution shown by the dashed line. In reality, the moment at C continues to increase, at a reduced rate, after the elastic value $M_{el,C}$ is reached, so the true distribution lies between those shown in Fig. 5.3. The upper distribution therefore provides a safe estimate of the moments at supports B and D, and can be used to check that the elastic resistance moment is not exceeded at these points.

Elastic global analysis is required for serviceability limit states (*clause 5.4.1.1(2)*) to enable yielding of steel to be avoided. Linear elastic analysis is based on linear stress–strain laws, so for composite structures, '*appropriate corrections for . . . cracking of concrete*' are required. These are given in *clause 5.4.2.3*, and apply also for ultimate limit states.

*Clause 5.4.1.1(2)*

*Clause 5.4.1.1(3)* requires elastic analysis for fatigue, to enable realistic ranges of fatigue stress to be predicted.

*Clause 5.4.1.1(3)*

The effects of shear lag, local buckling of steel elements and slip of bolts must also be considered where they significantly influence the global analysis. Shear lag and local buckling effects can reduce member stiffness, while slip in bolt holes causes a localized loss of stiffness. Shear lag is discussed under *clause 5.4.1.2*, and plate buckling and bolt slip are discussed below.

Methods for satisfying the principle of *clause 5.4.1.1(4)P* are given for local buckling in *clauses 5.4.1.1(5)* and *(6)*. These refer to the classification of cross-sections, the established method of allowing for local buckling of steel flanges and webs in compression. It determines the available methods of global analysis and the basis for resistance to bending. The classification system is defined in *clause 5.5*.

*Clause 5.4.1.1(4)P*
*Clause 5.4.1.1(5)*
*Clause 5.4.1.1(6)*

### Plate buckling

In Class 4 sections (those in which local buckling will occur before the attainment of yield), plate buckling can lead to a reduction of stiffness. The in-plane stiffness of perfectly flat plates suddenly reduces when the elastic critical buckling load is reached. In 'real' plates that have imperfections, there is an immediate reduction in stiffness from that expected from the gross

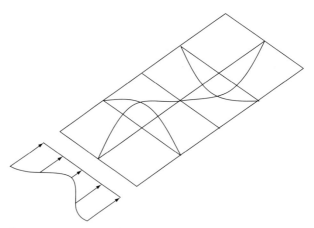

**Fig. 5.4.** Stress distribution across width of slender plate

plate area because of the growth of the bow imperfections under load. This stiffness continues to reduce with increasing load. This arises because non-uniform stress develops across the width of the plate as shown in Fig. 5.4. The non-uniform stress arises because the development of the buckle along the centre of the plate leads to a greater developed length of the plate along its centreline than along its edges. Thus the shortening due to membrane stress, and hence the membrane stress itself, is less along the centreline of the plate.

This loss of stiffness must be considered in the global analysis where significant. It can be represented by an effective area or width of plate, determined from clause 2.2 of EN 1993-1-5. This area or width is greater than that used for resistance, which is given in clause 4.3 of EN 1993-1-5.

The loss of stiffness may be ignored when the ratio of effective area to gross cross-sectional area exceeds a certain value. This ratio may be given in the National Annex. The recommended value, given in a Note to clause 2.2(5) of EN 1993-1-5, is 0.5. This should ensure that plate buckling effects rarely need to be considered in the global analysis. It is only likely to be of relevance for the determination of pre-camber of box girders under self-weight and wet concrete loads. After the deck slab has been cast, buckling of the steel flange plate will be prevented by its connection to the concrete flange via the shear connection.

*Effects of slip at bolt holes and shear connectors*

**Clause 5.4.1.1(7)**     **Clause 5.4.1.1(7)** requires consideration of '*slip in bolt holes and similar deformations of connecting devices*'. This applies to both first- and second-order analyses. There is a similar rule in clause 5.2.1(6) of EN 1993-1-1. No specific guidance is given in EN 1993-2 or EN 1994-2. Generally, bolt slip will have little effect in global analysis. It has often been practice in the UK to design bolts in main beam splices to slip at ultimate limit states (Category B to clause 3.4.1 of EN 1993-1-8). Although slip could alter the moment distribution in the beam, this is justifiable. Splices are usually near to the point of contraflexure, so that slip will not significantly alter the distribution of bending moment. Also, the loading that gives maximum moment at the splice will not be fully coexistent with that for either the maximum hogging moment or maximum sagging moment in adjacent regions.

It is advised that bolt slip should be taken into account for bracing members in the analysis of braced systems. This is because a sudden loss of stiffness arising from bolt slip gives an increase in deflection of the main member and an increased force on the bracing member, which could lead to overall failure. Ideally, therefore, bolts in bracing members should be designed as non-slip at ultimate limit state (Category C to EN 1993-1-8).

The 'similar deformations' quoted above could refer to slip at an interface between steel and concrete, caused by the flexibility of shear connectors. The provisions on shear connection in EN 1994 are intended to ensure that slip is too small to affect the results of elastic global analysis or the resistance of cross-sections. **Clause 5.4.1.1(8)**     global analysis or the resistance of cross-sections. **Clause 5.4.1.1(8)** therefore permits internal moments and forces to be determined assuming full interaction where shear connection is provided in accordance with EN 1994.

Slip of shear connectors can also affect the flexural stiffness of a composite joint. A relevant design method is given in clause A.3 of EN 1994-1-1. It is mainly applicable to semi-continuous joints, and so is not included in EN 1994-2.

An exception to the rules on allowing for cracking of concrete is given in *clause 5.4.1.1(9)*, for the analysis of transient situations during erection stages. This permits uncracked global analysis to be used, for simplicity.

*Clause 5.4.1.1(9)*

### Effective width of flanges for shear lag

Shear lag is defined in *clause 5.4.1.2(1)* with reference to the 'flexibility' of flanges due to in-plane shear. Shear lag in wide flanges causes the longitudinal bending stress adjacent to the web to exceed that expected from analysis with gross cross-sections, while the stress in the flange remote from the web is much lower than expected. This shear lag also leads to an apparent loss of stiffness of a section in bending which can be important in determining realistic distributions of moments in analysis. The determination of the actual distribution of stress is a complex problem.

*Clause 5.4.1.2(1)*

The Eurocodes account for both the loss of stiffness and localized increase in flange stresses by the use of an effective width of flange which is less than the actual available flange width. The effective flange width concept is artificial but, when used with engineering bending theory, leads to uniform stresses across the whole reduced flange width that are equivalent to the peak values adjacent to the webs in the true situation.

The rules that follow provide effective widths for resistance of cross-sections, and simpler values for use in global analyses. The rules use the word 'may' because *clause 5.4.1.2(1)* permits 'rigorous analysis' as an alternative. This is not defined, but should take account of the many relevant influences, such as the cracking of concrete.

### Steel flanges

For 'steel plate elements' *clause 5.4.1.2(2)* refers to EN 1993-1-1. This permits shear lag to be neglected in rolled sections and welded sections 'with similar dimensions', and refers to EN 1993-1-5 for more slender flanges. In these, the stress distribution depends on the stiffening to the flanges and any plasticity occurring for ultimate limit state behaviour. The elastic stress distribution can be modelled using finite-element analysis with appropriate shell elements.

*Clause 5.4.1.2(2)*

The rules in EN 1993-1-5 are not discussed further in this guide but are covered in the *Designers' Guide to EN 1993-2*.[4] Different values of effective width apply for cross-section design for serviceability and ultimate limit states, and the value appropriate to the location of the section along the beam should be used. Simplified effective widths, taken as constant throughout a span, are allowed in the global analysis.

### Concrete flanges

Effective width of concrete flanges is covered in *clauses 5.4.1.2(3)* to *(7)*. The behaviour is complex, being influenced by the loading configuration, and by the extent of cracking and of yielding of the longitudinal reinforcement, both of which help to redistribute the stress across the cross-section. The ability of the transverse reinforcement to distribute the forces is also relevant. The ultimate behaviour in shear of wide flanges is modelled by a truss analogy similar to that for the web of a deep concrete beam.

*Clauses 5.4.1.2(3) to (7)*

The values for effective width given in this clause are simpler than those in BS 5400:Part 5, and similar to those in BS 5950:Part 3.1:1990.[48] The effective width at mid-span and internal supports is given by *equation (5.3)*:

$$b_{\text{eff}} = b_0 + \sum b_{\text{ei}} \qquad (5.3)$$

where $b_0$ is the distance between the outer shear connectors and $b_{\text{ei}}$ is either $b_{\text{e1}}$ or $b_{\text{e2}}$, as shown in Fig. 5.5, or the available width $b_1$ or $b_2$, if lower.

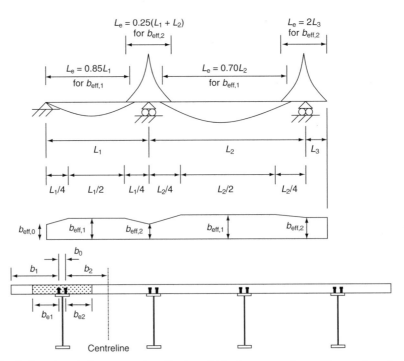

**Fig. 5.5.** Symbols and equivalent spans, for effective width of concrete flange (Source: based on Fig. 5.1 of EN 1994-2)

Each width $b_{ei}$ is limited to $L_e/8$, where $L_e$ is the assumed distance between points of zero bending moment. It depends on the region of the beam considered and on whether the bending moment is hogging or sagging. This is shown in Fig. 5.5, which is based on *Fig. 5.1*.

The values are generally lower than those in EN 1992-1-1 for reinforced concrete T-beams. To adopt those would often increase the number of shear connectors. Without evidence that the greater effective widths are any more accurate, the established values for composite beams have mainly been retained.

In EN 1992-1-1, the sum of the lengths $L_e$ for sagging and hogging regions equals the span of the beam. In reality, points of contraflexure are dependent on the load arrangement. EN 1994, like EN 1993, therefore gives a larger effective width at an internal support. In sagging regions, the assumed distances between points of contraflexure are the same in all three codes.

Although there are significant differences between effective widths for supports and mid-span regions, it is possible to ignore this in elastic global analysis (*clause 5.4.1.2(4)*). This is because shear lag has limited influence on the results. There can however be some small advantage to be gained by modelling in analysis the distribution of effective width along the members given in Fig. 5.5 or *Fig. 5.1*, as this will tend to shed some moment from the hogging regions into the span. It would also be appropriate to model the distribution of effective widths more accurately in cable-stayed structures, but *Fig. 5.1* does not cover these. Example 5.1 below illustrates the calculation of effective width.

Some limitations on span length ratios when using *Fig. 5.1* should be made so that the bending-moment distribution within a span conforms with the assumptions in the figure. It is suggested that the limitations given in EN 1992 and EN 1993 are adopted. These limit the use to cases where adjacent spans do not differ by more than 50% of the shorter span and a cantilever is not longer than half the adjacent span. For other span ratios or moment distributions, the distance between points of zero bending moment, $L_e$, should be calculated from the moment distribution found from an initial analysis.

*Clause 5.4.1.2(8)*   Where it is necessary to determine a more realistic distribution of longitudinal stress across the width of the flange, *clause 5.4.1.2(8)* refers to clause 3.2.2 of EN 1993-1-5. This might be necessary, for example, in checking a deck slab at a transverse diaphragm between main beams at a support, where the deck slab is in tension under global bending and also subjected to a local hogging moment from wheel loads. The use of EN 1993-1-5 can be beneficial here, as often the greatest local effects in a slab occur in the middle of the slab between webs where the global longitudinal stresses are lowest.

*Composite plate flanges*
*Clause 5.4.1.2(8)* recommends the use of its stress distribution for both concrete and steel flanges. Where the flange is a composite plate, shear connection is usually concentrated near the webs, so this stress distribution is applicable. Effective widths of composite plates in bridges are based on *clause 5.4.1.2*, but with a different definition of $b_0$, given in *clause 9.1(3)*.

*Composite trusses*
*Clause 5.4.1.2(9)* applies where a longitudinal composite beam is also a component of a larger structural system, such as a composite truss. For loading applied to it, the beam is continuous over spans equal to the spacing of the nodes of the truss. For the axial force in the beam, the relevant span is that of the truss.

*Clause 5.4.1.2(9)*

### Example 5.1: effective widths of concrete flange for shear lag
A composite bridge has the span layout and cross-section shown in Fig. 5.6. The effective width of top flange for external and internal beams is determined for the mid-span regions BC and DE, and the region CD above an internal support.

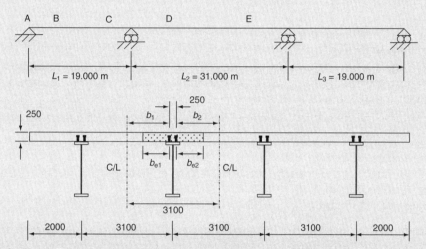

**Fig. 5.6.** Elevation and typical cross-section of bridge for Example 5.1

The effective spans $L_e$, from Fig. 5.5, and the lengths $L_e/8$ are shown in Table 5.1. For an external beam, the available widths on each side of the shear connection are:

$b_1 = 1.875\,\text{m}, b_2 = 1.425\,\text{m}.$

**Table 5.1.** Effective width of concrete flange of composite T-beam

| | External beam | | | Internal beam | | |
|---|---|---|---|---|---|---|
| Region | BC | CD | DE | BC | CD | DE |
| $L_e$ (m) | 16.15 | 12.50 | 21.70 | 16.15 | 12.50 | 21.70 |
| $L_e/8$ (m) | 2.019 | 1.563 | 2.712 | 2.019 | 1.563 | 2.712 |
| $b_{eff}$ (m) | 3.550 | 3.238 | 3.550 | 3.100 | 3.100 | 3.100 |

The effective widths are the lower of these values and $L_e/8$, plus the width of the shear connection, as follows:

> for BC and DE,   $b_{\text{eff}} = 1.875 + 1.425 + 0.25 = \mathbf{3.550\,m}$
>
> for CD,                $b_{\text{eff}} = 1.563 + 1.425 + 0.25 = \mathbf{3.238\,m}$

For an internal beam, the available widths on each side of the shear connection are:

> $b_1 = b_2 = 1.425\,m$

These available widths are both less than $L_e/8$, and so govern. The effective widths are:

> for BC, CD, and DE, $b_{\text{eff}} = 2 \times 1.425 + 0.25 = \mathbf{3.100\,m}$

### 5.4.2. Linear elastic analysis

*Clause 5.4.2.1(1)*

Cracking, creep, shrinkage, sequence of construction, and prestressing, listed in *clause 5.4.2.1(1)*, can all affect the distribution of action affects in continuous beams and frames. This is always important for serviceability limit states, but can in some situations be ignored at ultimate limit states, as discussed under *clause 5.4.2.2(6)*. Cracking of concrete is covered in *clause 5.4.2.3*.

*Creep and shrinkage of concrete*

*Clause 5.4.2.2*

The rules provided in *clause 5.4.2.2* allow creep to be taken into account using a modular ratio $n_L$, that depends on the type of loading, and on the concrete composition and age at loading. This modular ratio is used both for global analysis and for elastic section analysis.

*Clause 5.4.2.2(2)*

It is defined in *clause 5.4.2.2(2)* by:

$$n_L = n_0(1 + \psi_L \phi(t, t_0)) \tag{5.6}$$

where $n_0$ is the modular ratio for short-term loading, $E_a/E_{cm}$. The concrete modulus $E_{cm}$ is obtained from EN 1992 as discussed in section 3.1 of this guide. The creep coefficient $\phi(t, t_0)$ is also obtained from EN 1992.

The creep multiplier $\psi_L$ takes account of the type of loading. Its values are given in *clause 5.4.2.2(2)* as follows:

- for permanent load, $\psi_L = 1.1$
- for the primary and secondary effects of shrinkage (and also the secondary effects of creep, *clause 5.4.2.2(6)*), $\psi_L = 0.55$
- for imposed deformations, $\psi_L = 1.5$.

The reason for the factor $\psi_L$ is illustrated in Fig. 5.7. This shows three schematic curves of the change of compressive stress in concrete with time. The top one, labelled S, is typical of stress caused by the increase of shrinkage with time. Concrete is more susceptible to creep when young, so there is less creep ($\psi_L = 0.55$) than for the more uniform stress caused by permanent loads (line P). The effects of imposed deformations can be significantly reduced by creep when the concrete is young, so the curve is of type ID, with $\psi_L = 1.5$. The value for permanent loading on reinforced concrete is 1.0. It is increased to 1.1 for composite

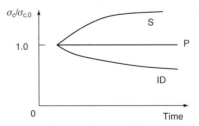

**Fig. 5.7.** Time-dependent compressive stress in concrete, for three types of loading

**Table 5.2.** Values of $\phi_0 = \phi(\infty, t_0)$ and modular ratio $n_L$

|  | $h_0 = 250$ mm | $h_0 = 500$ mm |
|---|---|---|
| $t_0 = 7$ days | 2.48, 23.7 | 2.30, 22.4 |
| $t_0 = 28$ days | 1.90, 19.6 | 1.78, 18.8 |

members because the steel component does not creep. Stress in concrete is reduced by creep less than it would be in a reinforced member, so there is more creep.

These values are based mainly on extensive theoretical work on composite beams of many sizes and proportions.[49]

The factor $\psi_L$ performs a similar function to the ageing coefficient found in Annex KK of EN 1992-2 and in the calculation for loss of prestress in clause 5.10.6 of EN 1992-1-1.

The creep factor $\phi(t, t_0)$ depends on the age of the concrete, $t$, at which the modular ratio is being calculated (usually taken as infinity) and the age of the concrete at first loading, $t_0$. For age $t_0$, *clauses 5.4.2.2(3)* and *(4)* make recommendations for permanent load and shrinkage, respectively. Since most bridges will follow a concrete pour sequence rather than have all the concrete placed in one go, this age at first loading could vary throughout the bridge. *Clause 5.4.2.2(3)* permits an assumed 'mean' value of $t_0$ to be used throughout. This simplification is almost a necessity as it is rare for the designer to have sufficient knowledge of the construction phasing at the design stage to be more accurate than this, but some estimate of the expected timings is still required. *Clause 5.4.2.2(3)*

'First loading' could occur at an age as low as a week, for example, from erection of precast parapets, but the mean age for a multi-span bridge is unlikely to be less than a month.

The creep coefficient depends also on the effective thickness of the concrete element considered, $h_0$. There is no moisture loss through sealed surfaces, so these are assumed to be at mid-thickness of the member. After striking of formwork, a deck slab of thickness, say, 250 mm, has two free surfaces, and an effective thickness of 250 mm. The application of waterproofing to the top surface increases this thickness to 500 mm, which reduces subsequent creep. The designer will not know the age(s) of the deck when waterproofed, and so must make assumptions on the safe side.

Fortunately, the modular ratio is not sensitive to either the age of loading or the effective thickness. As resistances are checked for the structure at an early age, it is on the safe side for the long-term checks to overestimate creep.

As an example, let us suppose that the short-term modular ratio is $n_0 = 6.36$ (as found in a subsequent example), and that a concrete deck slab has a mean thickness of 250 mm, with waterproofing on one surface. The long-term modular ratio is calculated for $t_0 = 7$ days and 28 days, and for $h_0 = 250$ mm and 500 mm. For 'outdoor' conditions with relative humidity 70%, the values of $\phi(\infty, t_0)$ given by Annex B of EN 1992-1-1 with $\psi_L = 1.1$ are as shown in Table 5.2.

The resulting range of values of the modular ratio $n_L$ is from 18.8 to 23.7. A difference of this size has little effect on the results of a global analysis of continuous beams with all spans composite, and far less than the effect of the difference between $n = 6.4$ for imposed load and around 20 for permanent load.

For stresses at cross-sections of slab-on-top decks, the modular ratio has no influence in regions where the slab is in tension. In mid-span regions, compression in concrete is rarely critical, and maximum values occur at a low age, where creep is irrelevant. In steel, bottom-flange tension is the important outcome, and is increased by creep. From Table 5.2, $h_0$ has little effect, and the choice of the low value of 7 days for age at first loading is on the safe side.

Modular ratios are calculated in Example 5.2 below.

*Shrinkage modified by creep*

For shrinkage, the advice in *clause 5.4.2.2(4)* to assume $t_0 = 1$ day rarely leads to a modular ratio higher than that for permanent actions, because of the factor $\psi_L = 0.55$. Both the *Clause 5.4.2.2(4)*

**Table 5.3.** Effects of shrinkage

| $h_0$ (mm) | RH (%) | $10^6 \varepsilon_{sh}$ | $n_L$ |
|---|---|---|---|
| 250 | 70 | 340 | 18.8 |
| 500 | 70 | 304 | 18.0 |
| 250 | 75 | 305 | 19.2 |

long-term shrinkage strain and the creep coefficient are influenced by the assumed effective thickness $h_0$.

For the preceding example, the 1-day rule gives the values in rows 1 and 2 of Table 5.3. It shows that doubling $h_0$ has negligible effect on $n_L$, but reduces shrinkage strain by 10%. Increasing the assumed mean relative humidity (RH) by only 5% has the same effect on shrinkage strain as doubling $h_0$, and negligible effect on $n_L$. The error in an assumed RH may well exceed 5%.

For this example, the 'safe' choices for shrinkage effects are $h_0 = 250$ mm, and an estimate for RH on the low side. As the concession in *clause 5.4.2.2(3)* (the use of a single time $t_0$ for all creep coefficients) refers to 'loads', not to 'actions', it is not clear if shrinkage may be included. It is conservative to do so, because when $t_0$ is assumed to exceed 1 day, the relief of shrinkage effects by creep is reduced. Hence, a single value of $n_L(\infty, t_0)$ may usually be used in analyses for permanent actions, except perhaps in special situations, to which *Clause 5.4.2.2(5)* *clause 5.4.2.2(5)* refers.

### Secondary effects of creep
Where creep deflections cause a change in the support reactions, this leads to the development of secondary moments. This might occur, for example, where there are mixtures of reinforced concrete and steel–composite spans in a continuous structure. The redistribution arises because the 'free' creep deflections are not proportional everywhere to the initial elastic deflections and therefore the 'free' creep deflection would lead to some non-zero deflection at the supports. Other construction sequences could produce a similar effect but this does not affect normal steel–composite bridges to any significant extent. *Clause 5.4.2.2(6)* *Clause 5.4.2.2(6)* is however a prompt that the effects should be considered in the more unusual situations.

Calculation of creep redistribution is more complex than for purely concrete structures, and is explained, with an example, in Ref. 50. The redistribution effects develop slowly with time, so $\psi_L = 0.55$.

### Cross-sections in Class 1 or 2
*Clause 5.4.2.2(6)* is one of several places in EN 1994-2 where, in certain global analyses, various 'indirect actions', that impose displacements and/or rotations, are permitted to be ignored where all cross-sections are either Class 1 or 2. Large plastic strains are possible for beams where cross-sections are Class 1. Class 2 sections exhibit sufficient plastic strain to attain the plastic section capacity but have limited rotation capacity beyond this point. This is however normally considered adequate to relieve the effects of imposed deformations derived from elastic analysis, and EN 1994 therefore permits such relief to be taken. The corresponding clause 5.4.2(2) in EN 1993-2 only permits the effects of imposed deformations to be ignored where all sections are Class 1, so there is an inconsistency at present.

In EN 1994, the effects which can be neglected in analyses for ultimate limit states other than fatigue, provided that all sections are Class 1 or 2, are as follows:

- differential settlement: *clause 5.1.3(3)*
- secondary creep redistribution of moments: *clause 5.4.2.2(6)*
- primary and secondary shrinkage and creep: *clause 5.4.2.2(7)*
- effects of staged construction: *clause 5.4.2.4(2)*
- differential temperature: *clause 5.4.2.5(2)*.

The further condition that there should not be any reduction of resistance due to lateral–torsional buckling is imposed in all of these clauses, and is discussed under *clause 6.4.2(1)*.

*Primary and secondary effects of creep and shrinkage*

**Clause 5.4.2.2(7)** requires 'appropriate' account to be taken of both the primary and secondary effects of creep and shrinkage of the concrete. The recommended partial factor for shrinkage effects at ultimate limit states is $\gamma_{SH} = 1$, from clause 2.4.2.1 of EN 1992-1-1.

*Clause 5.4.2.2(7)*

In a fully-restrained member with the slab above the steel beam, shrinkage effects can be split into a hogging bending moment, an axial tensile force, and a set of self-equilibrated longitudinal stresses, as shown in Example 5.3 below.

Where bearings permit axial shortening, there is no tensile force. In a statically determinate system, the hogging bending moment is released, causing sagging curvature. These, with the locked-in stresses, are the primary effects. They are reduced almost to zero where the concrete slab is cracked through its thickness.

In a statically indeterminate system, such as a continuous beam, the primary shrinkage curvature is incompatible with the levels of the supports. It is counteracted by bending moments caused by changes in the support reactions, which increase at internal supports and reduce at end supports. The moments and the associated shear forces are the *secondary effects* of shrinkage.

*Clause 5.4.2.2(7)* permits both types of effect to be neglected in some checks for ultimate limit states. This is discussed under *clause 5.4.2.2(6)*.

**Clause 5.4.2.2(8)** allows the option of neglecting primary shrinkage curvature in cracked regions.[51] It would be reasonable to base this cracked zone on the same 15% of the span allowed by *clause 5.4.2.3(3)*, where this is applicable. The use of this option reduces the secondary hogging bending at supports. These moments, being a permanent effect, enter into all load combinations, and may influence design of what is often a critical region.

*Clause 5.4.2.2(8)*

The long-term effects of shrinkage are significantly reduced by creep, as illustrated in *clause 5.4.2.2(4)*. Where it is necessary to consider shrinkage effects within the first year or so after casting, a value for the relevant free shrinkage strain can be obtained from clause 3.1.4(6) of EN 1992-1-1.

Primary effects of shrinkage are calculated in Example 5.3 below.

The influence of shrinkage on serviceability verifications is dealt with in Chapter 7.

For creep in columns, **clause 5.4.2.2(9)** refers to *clause 6.7.3.4(2)*, which in turn refers to an effective modulus for concrete given in *clause 6.7.3.3(4)*. If separate analyses are to be made for long-term and short-term effects, *clause 6.7.3.3(4)* can be used assuming ratios of permanent to total load of 1.0 and zero, respectively.

*Clause 5.4.2.2(9)*

Shrinkage effects in columns are unimportant, except in very tall structures.

**Clause 5.4.2.2(10)** excludes the use of the preceding simplified methods for members with both flanges composite and uncracked. The 'uncracked' condition is omitted from *clause 5.4.2.2(2)*, which is probably an oversight. This exclusion is not very restrictive, as new designs of this type are unusual in the UK. It may occur in strengthening schemes where the resistance of the compression flange is increased by making it composite over a short length.

*Clause 5.4.2.2(10)*

*Torsional stiffness of box girders*

For box girders with a composite top flange or with a concrete flange closing the top of an open U-section, the torsional stiffness is usually calculated by reducing the thickness of the gross concrete flange on the basis of the appropriate long- or short-term modular ratio, and maintaining the centroid of the transformed flange in the same position as that of the gross concrete flange. From **clause 5.4.2.2(11)**, the short-term modular ratio should be based on the ratio of shear moduli, $n_{0,G} = G_a/G_{cm}$, where for steel, $G_a = 81.0 \, \text{kN/mm}^2$ from clause 3.2.6 of EN 1993-1-1 and, for concrete:

*Clause 5.4.2.2(11)*

$$G_{cm} = E_{cm}/[2(1 + \nu_c)]$$

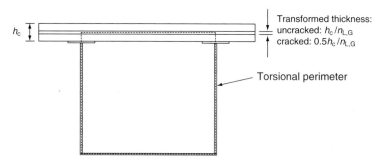

**Fig. 5.8.** Torsional stiffness of composite box girder

Clause 3.1.3(4) of EN 1992-1-1 gives Poisson's ratio ($\nu_c$) as 0.2 or zero, depending on whether the concrete is uncracked or cracked. For this application it is accurate enough to assume $\nu_c = 0.2$ everywhere. The method of *clause 5.4.2.2(2)* should be used for the modular ratio:

$$n_{L,G} = n_{0,G}(1 + \psi_L \phi(t, t_0))$$

The calculation of the torsional second moment of area (in 'steel' units) then follows the usual procedure such that:

$$I_T = \frac{4A_0^2}{\oint \dfrac{ds}{t(s)}}$$

where $A_0$ is the area enclosed by the torsional perimeter running through the centreline of the box walls. This is shown in Fig. 5.8. For closed steel boxes, the location of the centroid of the composite flange can, for simplicity, be located on the basis of first moment of area. The integral $\oint(ds/t(s))$ is the summation of the lengths of each part of the perimeter divided by their respective thicknesses. It is usual to treat the parts of the web projection into the flange as having the thickness of the steel web.

The torsional stiffness is also influenced by flexural cracking, which can cause a significant reduction in the in-plane shear stiffness of the concrete flange. To allow for this in regions where the slab is assumed to be cracked, *clause 5.4.2.3(6)* recommends a 50% reduction in the effective thickness of the flange.

### Effects of cracking of concrete

*Clause 5.4.2.3*

*Clause 5.4.2.3* is applicable to beams, at both serviceability and ultimate limit states. The flow chart of Fig. 5.15 below illustrates the procedure.

In conventional composite beams with the slab above the steel section, cracking of concrete reduces the flexural stiffness in hogging moment regions, but not in sagging regions. The change in relative stiffness needs to be taken into account in elastic global analysis. This is unlike analysis of reinforced concrete beams, where cracking occurs in both hogging and sagging bending, and uncracked cross-sections can be assumed throughout.

A draft of EN 1994-2 permitted allowance for cracking by redistribution of hogging moments from 'uncracked' analysis by up to 10%. Following detailed examination of its effects,[52] this provision was deleted.

*Clause 5.4.2.3(2)*

*Clause 5.4.2.3(2)* provides a general method. This is followed in *clause 5.4.2.3(3)* by a simplified approach of limited application. Both methods refer to the 'uncracked' and 'cracked' flexural stiffnesses $E_a I_1$ and $E_a I_2$, which are defined in *clause 1.5.2*. The flexural rigidity $E_a I_1$ can usually be based on the gross concrete area excluding reinforcement with acceptable accuracy. In the general method, the first step is to determine the expected extent of cracking in beams. The envelope of moments and shears is calculated for characteristic combinations of actions, assuming uncracked sections and including long-term effects. The section is assumed to crack if the extreme-fibre tensile stress in concrete exceeds twice the mean value of the axial tensile strength given by EN 1992-1-1.

The reasons for 'twice' in this assumption are as follows:

- The concrete is likely to be stronger than specified, although this is partly catered for by the use of a mean rather than characteristic tensile strength.
- Test results for tensile strength show a wide scatter when plotted against compressive strength.
- Reaching $f_{ctm}$ at the surface may not cause the slab to crack right through, and even if it does, the effects of tension stiffening are significant at the stage of initial cracking.
- Until after yielding of the reinforcement, the stiffness of a cracked region is greater than $E_a I_2$, because of tension stiffening between the cracks.
- The calculation uses an envelope of moments, for which regions of slab in tension are more extensive than they are for any particular loading.

The global model is then modified to reduce the beam stiffness to the cracked flexural rigidity, $E_a I_2$, over this region, and the structure is reanalysed.

**Clause 5.4.2.3(3)** provides a non-iterative method, but one that is applicable only to some situations. These include conventional continuous composite beams, and beams in braced frames. The cracked regions could differ significantly from the assumed values in a bridge with highly unequal span lengths. Where the conditions are not satisfied, the general method of *clause 5.4.2.3(2)* should be used. *Clause 5.4.2.3(3)*

The influence of cracking on the analysis of braced and unbraced frames is discussed in the *Designers' Guide to EN 1994-1-1.*[5]

For composite columns, **clause 5.4.2.3(4)** makes reference to *clause 6.7.3.4* for the calculation of cracked stiffness. The scope of the latter clause is limited (to double symmetry, etc.) by *clause 6.7.3.1(1)*, where further comment is given. The reduced value of *EI* referred to here is intended for verifications for ultimate limit states, and may be inappropriate for analyses for serviceability. *Clause 5.4.2.3(4)*

For column cross-sections without double symmetry, cracking and tension in columns are referred to in *clause 6.7.2(1)P* and *clause 6.7.2(5)P*, respectively; but there is no guidance on the extent of cracking to be assumed in global analysis.

The assumption in **clause 5.4.2.3(5)**, that effects of cracking in transverse composite members may be neglected, does not extend to decks with only two main beams. Their behaviour is influenced by the length of cantilever cross-beams, if any, and the torsional stiffness of the main beams. The method of *clause 5.4.2.3(2)* is applicable. *Clause 5.4.2.3(5)*

**Clause 5.4.2.3(6)** supplements *clause 5.4.2.2(11)*, where comment on *clause 5.4.2.3(6)* is given. *Clause 5.4.2.3(6)*

For the effects of cracking on the design longitudinal shear for the shear connection at ultimate limit states, **clause 5.4.2.3(7)** refers to *clause 6.6.2.1(2)*. This requires uncracked section properties to be used for uncracked members and for members assumed to be cracked in flexure where the effects of tension stiffening have been ignored in global analysis. *Clause 5.4.2.3(7)*

Where tension stiffening and possible over-strength of the concrete (using upper characteristic values of the tensile strength) have been explicitly considered in the global analysis, then the same assumptions may be made in the determination of longitudinal shear flow. The reason for this is that tension stiffening can lead to a greater force being attracted to the shear connection than would be found from a fully cracked section analysis.

The simplest and most conservative way to consider this effect is to determine the longitudinal shear with an uncracked concrete flange. The same approach is required for fatigue where tension stiffening could again elevate fatigue loads on the studs according to *clauses 6.8.5.4(1)* and *6.8.5.5(2)*.

For longitudinal shear at serviceability limit states, **clause 5.4.2.3(8)** gives, in effect, the same rules as for ultimate limit states, explained above. *Clause 5.4.2.3(8)*

*Stages and sequence of construction*
The need to consider staged construction is discussed in section 2.2 of this guide. The reason for allowing staged construction to be ignored at the ultimate limit state, if the conditions of **clause 5.4.2.4(2)** are met, is discussed under *clause 5.4.2.2(6)*. However, it would not be *Clause 5.4.2.4(2)*

common to do this, as a separate analysis considering the staged construction would then be required for the serviceability limit state.

*Temperature effects*

Clause 5.4.2.5(1)
*Clause 5.4.2.5(1)* refers to EN 1991-1-5[53] for temperature actions. These are uniform temperature change and temperature gradient through a beam, often referred to as differential temperature. Differential temperature produces primary and secondary effects in a similar way to shrinkage. The reason for allowing temperature to be ignored at the ultimate
Clause 5.4.2.5(2)
limit state, if the conditions of *clause 5.4.2.5(2)* are met, is discussed under *clause 5.4.2.2(6)*.

Recommended combination factors for temperature effects are given in Tables A2.1 to A2.4 of Annex A2 of EN 1990. If they are confirmed in the National Annex (as the further comments assume), temperature will be included in all combinations of actions for persistent and transient design situations. In this respect, design to Eurocodes will differ from previous practice in the UK. However, the tables for road bridges and footbridges have a Note which recommends that $\psi_0$ for thermal actions 'may in most cases be reduced to zero for ultimate limit states EQU, STR and GEO'. Only FAT (fatigue) is omitted. It is unlikely that temperature will have much influence on fatigue life. The table for railway bridges refers to EN 1991-1-5. The purpose may be to draw attention to its rules for simultaneity of uniform and temperature difference components, and the need to consider differences of temperature between the deck and the rails.

With $\psi_0 = 0$, temperature effects appear in the ultimate and characteristic combinations only where temperature is the leading variable action. It will usually be evident which members and cross-sections need to be checked for these combinations.

The factors $\psi_1$ and $\psi_2$ are required for the frequent and quasi-permanent combinations used for certain serviceability verifications. The recommended values are $\psi_1 = 0.6$, $\psi_2 = 0.5$. Temperature will rarely be the leading variable action, as the following example shows.

For the effects of differential temperature, EN 1991-1-5 gives two approaches, from which the National Annex can select. The 'Normal Procedure' in Approach 2 is equivalent to the procedure in BS 5400.[11] If this is used, both heating and cooling differential temperature cases tend to produce secondary sagging moments at internal supports where crack widths are checked in continuous beams. These effects of temperature will not normally add to other effects.

*Combinations of actions that involve temperature*

A cross-section is considered where the characteristic temperature action effect is $T_k$, and the action effect from traffic load model 1 (LM1) for road bridges is $Q_k$. The recommended combination factors are given in Table 5.4.

The frequent combinations of variable action effects are:

- with load model 1 leading:   $\psi_1 Q_k + \psi_2 T_k = (0.75 \text{ or } 0.40)Q_k + 0.5 T_k$
- with temperature leading:   $\psi_1 T_k + \psi_2 Q_k = 0.6 T_k$

The second of these governs only where $0.1 T_k > (0.75 \text{ or } 0.4)Q_k$.

Thus, temperature should be taken as the leading variable action only where its action effect is at least 7.5 times (for TS) or 4 times (for UD) that from traffic load model 1.

**Table 5.4.** Recommended combination factors for traffic load and temperature according to EN 1990 Annex A2

| Action effect from: | $\psi_0$ | $\psi_1$ | $\psi_2$ |
|---|---|---|---|
| Tandem system (TS), from LM1 | 0.75 | 0.75 | 0 |
| Uniform loading (UD), from LM1 | 0.40 | 0.40 | 0 |
| Temperature (non-fire) | 0.6 or zero | 0.6 | 0.5 |

The uncertainty about which variable action leads does not arise in quasi-permanent combinations, because the combination factor is always $\psi_2$. Temperature and construction loads are the only variable actions for which $\psi_2 > 0$ is recommended. Both the $\psi$ values and the combination to be used can be changed in the National Annex.

*Prestressing by controlled imposed deformations*

As a principle, *clause 5.4.2.6(1)* requires that possible deviations from the intended amount of imposed deflection be considered, such as might occur due to the tolerance achievable with the specified jacking equipment. The effect of variations in material properties on the action effects developed must also be considered. However, *clause 5.4.2.6(2)* permits these effects to be determined using characteristic or nominal values, '*if the imposed deformations are controlled*'. The nature of the control required is not specified. It should take account of the sensitivity of the structure to any error in the deformation.

    At the ultimate limit state, *clause 2.4.1.1* recommends a load factor of 1.0 for imposed deformations, regardless of whether effects are favourable or unfavourable. It is recommended here that where a structure is particularly sensitive to departures from the intended amount of imposed deformation, tolerances should be determined for the proposed method of applying these deformations and upper and lower bound values considered in the analysis.

*Prestressing by tendons*

Prestressing composite bridges of steel and concrete is uncommon in the UK and is therefore not covered in detail here. *Clause 5.4.2.6(1)* refers to EN 1992 for the treatment of prestress forces in analysis. This is generally sufficient, although EN 1994 itself emphasises, in *clause 5.4.2.6(2)*, the distinction between bonded and unbonded tendons. Essentially, this is that while the force in bonded tendons increases everywhere in proportion to the local increase of strain in the adjacent concrete, the force in unbonded tendons changes in accordance with the overall deformation of the structure; that is, the change of strain in the adjacent concrete averaged over the length of the tendon.

*Tension members in composite bridges*

The purpose of the definitions (a) and (b) in *clause 5.4.2.8(1)* is to distinguish between the two types of structure shown in Fig. 5.9, and to define the terms in italic print.

    In Fig. 5.9(a), the *concrete tension member* AB is shear-connected to the steel structure, represented by member CD, only at its ends ('*concrete*' here means reinforced concrete). No design rules are given for a concrete member where cracking is prevented by prestressing.

    Figure 5.9(b) shows a *composite tension member*, which has normal shear connection. Its concrete flange is the *concrete tension member*. In both cases, there is a tensile force $N$ from the rest of the structure, shared between the concrete and steel components.

    A member spanning between nodes in a sagging region of a composite truss with a deck at bottom-chord level could be of either type. The difference between members of types (a) and (b) is similar to that between unbonded and bonded tendons in prestressed concrete.

    *Clause 5.4.2.8(2)* lists the properties of concrete that should be considered in global analyses. These influence the stiffness of the concrete component, and hence the magnitude

*Clause 5.4.2.6(1)*

*Clause 5.4.2.6(2)*

*Clause 5.4.2.8(1)*

*Clause 5.4.2.8(2)*

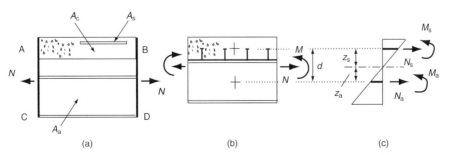

**Fig. 5.9.** Two types of tension member, and forces in the steel and concrete parts: (a) concrete tension member; (b) composite tension member; (c) action effects equivalent to $N$ and $M$

of the force $N$, and the proportions of it resisted by the two components. Force $N$ is assumed to be a significant action effect. There will normally be others, arising from transverse loading on the member.

The distribution of tension between the steel and concrete parts is greatly influenced by tension stiffening in the concrete (which is in turn affected by over-strength of the concrete). It is therefore important that an accurate representation of stiffness is made. This clause allows a rigorous non-linear method to be used. It could be based on Annex L of ENV 1994-2, 'Effects of tension stiffening in composite bridges'.[54] This annex was omitted from EN 1994-2, as being 'text-book material'. Further information on the theory of tension stiffening and its basis in tests is given in Ref. 55, in its references, and below.

The effects of over-strength of concrete in tension can in principle be allowed for by using the upper 5% fractile of tensile strength, $f_{ctk,0.95}$. This is given in Table 3.1 of EN 1992-1-1 as 30% above the mean value, $f_{ctm}$. However, tension is caused by shrinkage, transverse loading, etc., as well as by force $N$, so simplified rules are given in *clauses 5.4.2.8(5)* to *(7)*.

*Clause 5.4.2.8(3)*      *Clause 5.4.2.8(3)* requires effects of shrinkage to be included in 'calculations of the internal forces and moments' in a cracked concrete tension member. This means the axial force and bending moment, which are shown as $N_s$ and $M_s$ in Fig. 5.9(c). The simplification given here overestimates the mean shrinkage strain, and 'should be used' for the secondary effects. This clause is an exception to *clause 5.4.2.2(8)*, which permits shrinkage in cracked regions to be ignored.

*Clause 5.4.2.8(4)*      *Clause 5.4.2.8(4)* refers to simplified methods. The simplest of these, *clause 5.4.2.8(5)*,
*Clause 5.4.2.8(5)*    which requires both 'uncracked' and 'cracked' global analyses, can be quite conservative.
*Clause 5.4.2.8(6)*    *Clause 5.4.2.8(6)* gives a more accurate method for members of type (a) in Fig. 5.9. The longitudinal stiffness of the concrete tension member for use in global analysis is given by *equation (5.6-1)*:

$$(EA_s)_{eff} = E_s A_s / [1 - 0.35/(1 + n_0 \rho_s)] \qquad (5.6-1)$$

where:    $A_s$ is the reinforcement in the tension member,
             $A_c$ is the effective cross-sectional area of the concrete, $\rho_s = A_s/A_c$, and
             $n_0$ is the short-term modular ratio.

This equation is derived from the model of Annex L of ENV 1994-2 for tension stiffening, shown in Fig. 5.10. The figure relates mean tensile strain, $\varepsilon$, to tensile force $N$, in a concrete tension member with properties $A_s$, $A_c$, $\rho_s$ and $n_0$, defined above. Lines 0A and 0B represent uncracked and fully cracked behaviour, respectively.

Cracking first occurs at force $N_{c,cr}$, when the strain is $\varepsilon_{sr1}$. The strain at the crack at once increases to $\varepsilon_{sr2}$, but the mean strain hardly changes. As further cracks occur, the mean strain follows the line CD. If the local variations in the tensile strength of concrete are neglected, this becomes line CE. The effective stiffness within this 'stage of single cracking' is the slope of a line from 0 to some point within CE. After cracking has stabilized, the stiffness is given by a line such as 0F. The strain difference $\beta \Delta \varepsilon_{sr}$ remains constant until

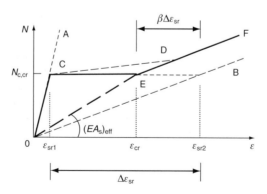

**Fig. 5.10.** Normal force and mean strain for a reinforced concrete tension member

the reinforcement yields. It represents tension stiffening, the term used for the stiffness of the concrete between the cracks.

It has been found that in bridges, the post-cracking stiffness is given with sufficient accuracy by the slope of line 0E, with $\beta \approx 0.35$. This slope, *equation (5.6-1)*, can be derived using Fig. 5.10, as follows.

At a force of $N_{c,cr}$ the following strains are obtained:

fully cracked strain: $\quad \varepsilon_{sr2} = N_{c,cr}/E_s A_s$

uncracked strain: $\quad \varepsilon_{sr1} = N_{c,cr}/(E_s A_s + E_c A_c)$

Introducing $\rho_s = A_s/A_c$ and the short-term modular ratio $n_0$ gives:

$$\varepsilon_{sr1} = N_{c,cr} n_0 \rho_s / [E_s A_s (1 + n_0 \rho_s)]$$

From Fig. 5.10, the strain at point E is:

$$\varepsilon_{cr} = \varepsilon_{sr2} - \beta(\varepsilon_{sr2} - \varepsilon_{sr1}) = \left(\frac{N_{c,cr}}{E_s A_s}\right)\left[1 - \beta\left\{1 - \left(\frac{n_0 \rho_s}{(1 + n_0 \rho_s)}\right)\right\}\right]$$

This can also be expressed in terms of effective stiffness as

$$\varepsilon_{cr} = N_{c,cr}/(E_s A_s)_{eff}$$

Eliminating $\varepsilon_{cr}$ from the last two equations and dividing by $N_{c,cr}$ gives:

$$1/(E_s A_s)_{eff} = 1/(E_s A_s) - \beta[1 - n_0 \rho_s/(1 + n_0 \rho_s)]/(E_s A_s)$$
$$= [1 - 0.35/(1 + n_0 \rho_s)]/(E_s A_s)$$

which is *equation (5.6-1)*.

In Ref. 56, a study was made of the forces predicted in the tension members of a truss using a very similar factor to that in *equation (5.6-1)*. Comparison was made against predictions from a non-linear analysis using the tension field model proposed in Annex L of ENV 1994-2.[54] The two methods generally gave good agreement, with most results being closer to those from a fully cracked analysis than from an uncracked analysis.

The forces given by global analysis using stiffness $(EA_s)_{eff}$ are used for the design of the steel structure, but not the concrete tension member. The tension in the latter is usually highest just before cracking. For an axially loaded member it is, in theory:

$$N_{Ed} = A_c f_{ct,eff}(1 + n_0 \rho_s) \tag{D5.4}$$

with $f_{ct,eff}$ being the tensile strength of the concrete when it cracks and other notation as above. Usually, there is also tensile stress in the member from local loading or shrinkage. This is allowed for by the assumption that $f_{ct,eff} = 0.7f_{ctm}$, given in *clause 5.4.2.8(6)*. Equation (D5.4) is given in this clause with partial factors 1.15 and 1.45 for serviceability and ultimate limit states, respectively. These allow for approximations in the method. Thus, for ultimate limit states:

$$N_{Ed,ult} = 1.45 A_c (0.7 f_{ctm})(1 + n_0 \rho_s) = 1.02 f_{ctm}[A_c + (E_s/E_c)A_s] \tag{D5.5}$$

which is the design tensile force at cracking at stress $f_{ctm}$.

*Clause 5.4.2.8(7)* covers composite members of type (b) in Fig. 5.9. The cross-section properties are found using *equation (5.6-1)* for the stiffness of the cracked concrete flange, and are used in global analyses. As an example, it is assumed that an analysis for an ultimate limit state gives a tensile force $N$ and a sagging moment $M$, as shown in Fig. 5.9(b). These are equivalent to action effects $N_a$ and $M_a$ in the steel component plus $N_s$ and $M_s$ in the concrete component, as shown. This clause requires the normal force $N_s$ to be calculated.

*Clause 5.4.2.8(7)*

Equations for this de-composition of $N$ and $M$ can be derived from elastic section analysis, neglecting slip, as follows.

The crosses in Fig. 5.9(b) indicate the centres of area of the cross-sections of the concrete flange (or the reinforcement, for a cracked flange) and the structural steel section. Let $z_s$,

$z_a$ and $d$ be as shown in Fig. 5.9(c) and $I$, $I_a$ and $I_s$ be the second moments of area of the composite section, the steel component, and the concrete flange, respectively.

For $M = 0, N_{a,N} + N_{s,N} = N$, and $N_{s,N}z_s = N_{a,N}z_a$, whence $N_{s,N} = N(z_a/d)$       (a)

For $N = 0$,    $N_{s,M} = -N_{a,M}$       (b)

Equating curvatures,    $M/I = M_s/I_s = M_a/I_a$       (c)

For equilibrium,    $M = M_s + M_a + N_{a,M}z_a - N_{s,M}z_s$       (d)

From equations (b) to (d), with $z_a + z_s = d$,

$M = M(I_s/I + I_a/I) - N_{s,M}d$, whence $N_{s,M}d = M(I_s + I_a - I)/I$       (e)

For $N$ and $M$ together, from equations (a), (c) and (e):

$$N_s = N(z_a/d) - M(I - I_a - I_s)/Id$$       (D5.6)

$$M_s = MI_s/I$$       (D5.7)

In practice, $I_s \ll I_a$, so $I_s$, and hence $M_s$, can often be taken as zero. The area of reinforcement in the concrete tension member ($A_s$, not $A_{s,eff}$) must be sufficient to resist the greater of force $N_s$ (plus $M_s$, if not negligible) and the force $N_{Ed}$ given by equation (D5.5).

### Filler beam decks for bridges

There are a great number of geometric, material and workmanship-related restrictions which have to be met in order to use the application rules for the design of filler beams. These restrictions are discussed in section 6.3, which deals with the resistances of filler beams, and are necessary because these clauses are based mainly in existing practice in the UK. There is very little relevant research.

*Clause 5.4.2.9(1)*     The same restrictions apply in the use of *clause 5.4.2.9(1)*, which allows the effects of slip at the concrete–steel interface and shear lag to be neglected in global analysis only if these conditions are met. One significant difference from previous practice in the UK is that fully-encased filler beams are not covered by EN 1994. This is because there are no widely accepted design rules for longitudinal shear in fully-encased beams without shear connectors.

*Clause 5.4.2.9(2)*     *Clause 5.4.2.9(2)* covers the transverse distribution of imposed loading. Its option of assuming rigid behaviour in the transverse direction may be applicable to a small single-

*Clause 5.4.2.9(3)*     track railway bridge, but generally, one of the methods of *clause 5.4.2.9(3)* will be used. These assume that there are no transverse steel members within the span. It is therefore essential that continuous transverse reinforcement in both top and bottom faces of the concrete is provided in accordance with the requirements of *clause 6.3*.

*Clause 5.4.2.9(3)* permits global analysis by non-linear methods to *clause 5.4.3*, but normally orthotropic plate or grillage analysis will be used. For the longitudinal flexural stiffness, 'smearing of the steel beams' involves calculating the stiffness of the whole width of the deck, and hence finding a mean stiffness per unit width. It is inferred from *clause*

*Clause 5.4.2.9(4)*     *5.4.2.9(4)* that cracking may be neglected, though *clause 5.4.2.9(7)* provides an alternative for some analyses for serviceability.

The flexural stiffness per unit width in the transverse direction is calculated for the uncracked concrete slab, neglecting reinforcement. The result is a plate with different properties in orthogonal directions, i.e. orthogonally anisotropic or orthotropic for short.

For grillage analysis, uncracked section properties should generally be used (as required by *clause 5.4.2.9(4)*) but it is permissible to account for the loss of stiffness in the transverse direction caused by cracking, by reducing the torsional and flexural stiffnesses of the transverse concrete members by 50%. This can be advantageous, as it reduces the transverse moments, and hence the stresses in the reinforcement.

The longitudinal moments obtained from elastic analysis of an orthotropic slab or grillage may not be redistributed to allow for cracking. This is because cracking can occur in both hogging and sagging regions, and there is insufficient test evidence on which to base design rules. However, *clause 5.4.2.9(5)* permits, for some analyses, up to 15% redistribution of hogging moments for beams in Class 1 at internal supports. This is less liberal than it may appear, because *clause 5.5.3*, which covers classification, does not relax the normal rules for Class 1 webs or flanges to allow for restraint from encasement. The concrete does, however, reduce the depth of web in compression. *Clause 5.4.2.9(5)*

There are no provisions for creep of concrete at ultimate limit states, so *clause 5.4.2.2* applies in the longitudinal direction. In the transverse direction, clause 3.1 of EN 1992-1-1 presumably applies. The modular ratios in the two directions may be found to be different, because of the $\psi_L$ factors in EN 1994.

These comments on creep also apply for deformations, from *clause 5.4.2.9(6)*. Shrinkage can be neglected, because it causes little curvature where there is little difference between the levels of the centroids of the steel and concrete cross-sections. *Clause 5.4.2.9(6)*

*Clause 5.4.2.9(7)* gives a simplified rule for the effects of cracking of concrete on deflections and camber. *Clause 5.4.2.9(8)* permits temperature effects to be ignored, except in certain railway bridges. *Clause 5.4.2.9(7)* *Clause 5.4.2.9(8)*

---

### Example 5.2: modular ratios for long-term loading and for shrinkage

For the bridge of Example 5.1 (Fig. 5.6), modular ratios are calculated for:

- imposed load (short-term loading)
- superimposed dead load (long-term loading)
- effects of shrinkage (long-term).

Modular ratios for long-term loading depend on an assumed effective thickness for the concrete deck slab and a mean 'age at first loading'. The choice of these values is discussed in comments on *clause 5.4.2.2*. Here, it is assumed that superimposed dead load is applied when the concrete has an average age of 7 days, and that the effective thickness of the deck slab is the value before application of waterproofing, which is its actual thickness, 250 mm. The deck concrete is grade C30/37 and the relative humidity is 70%.

*Live load*

From Table 3.1 of EN 1992-1-1, $E_{cm} = 33\,kN/mm^2$

From clause 3.2.6 of EN 1993-1-1, $E_a = 210\,N/mm^2$
for structural steel,

The short-term modular ratio, $n_0 = E_a/E_{cm} = 210/33 = \mathbf{6.36}$

*Superimposed dead load (long term), from Annex B of EN 1992-1-1*

From equation (B.1) of EN 1992-1-1, the creep coefficient $\phi(t, t_0) = \phi_0 \beta_c(t, t_0)$, where $\beta_c(t, t_0)$ is a factor that describes the amount of creep that occurs at time $t$. When $t \to \infty$, $\beta_c = 1$. The total creep is therefore given by:

$$\phi_0 = \phi_{RH}\beta(f_{cm})\beta(t_0) \qquad \text{(B.2) in EN 1992-1-1}$$

where $\phi_{RH}$ is a factor to allow for the effect of relative humidity on the notional creep coefficient. Two expressions are given, depending on the size of $f_{cm}$.

From Table 3.1 of EN 1992-1-1, $f_{cm} = f_{ck} + 8 = 30 + 8 = 38\,N/mm^2$

$$\text{For } f_{cm} > 35\,MPa, \quad \phi_{RH} = \left[1 + \frac{1 - RH/100}{0.1 \cdot \sqrt[3]{h_0}} \cdot \alpha_1\right] \cdot \alpha_2 \qquad \text{(B.3b) in EN 1992-1-1}$$

$RH$ is the relative humidity of the ambient environment in percentage terms; here, 70%.

The factors $\alpha_1$ and $\alpha_2$ allow for the influence of the concrete strength:

$$\alpha_1 = \left[\frac{35}{f_{cm}}\right]^{0.7} = \left[\frac{35}{38}\right]^{0.7} = 0.944$$

$$\alpha_2 = \left[\frac{35}{f_{cm}}\right]^{0.2} = \left[\frac{35}{38}\right]^{0.2} = 0.984 \qquad \text{(B.8c) in EN 1992-1-1}$$

From equation (B.3b) of EN 1992-1-1:

$$\phi_{RH} = \left[1 + \frac{1 - 70/100}{0.1 \times \sqrt[3]{250}} \times 0.944\right] \times 0.984 = 1.43$$

From equation (B.4) of EN 1992-1-1, the factor $\beta(f_{cm})$, that allows for the effect of concrete strength on the notional creep coefficient, is:

$$\beta(f_{cm}) = \frac{16.8}{\sqrt{f_{cm}}} = \frac{16.8}{\sqrt{38}} = 2.73$$

The effect of the age of the concrete at first loading on the notional creep coefficient is given by the factor $\beta(t_0)$ according to equation (B.5) of EN 1992-1-1. For loading at 7 days this gives:

$$\beta(t_0) = \frac{1}{(0.1 + t_0^{0.20})} = \frac{1}{(0.1 + 7^{0.20})} = 0.63$$

This expression is only valid as written for normal or rapid-hardening cements.

The final creep coefficient from equation (B.2) of EN 1992-1-1 is then:

$$\phi(\infty, t_0) = \phi_0 = \phi_{RH}\beta(f_{cm})\beta(t_0) = 1.43 \times 2.73 \times 0.63 = 2.48$$

From *equation (5.6)*, the modular ratio is given by:

$$n_L = n_0(1 + \psi_L\phi(t, t_0)) = 6.36(1 + 1.1 \times 2.48) = \mathbf{23.7}$$

where $\psi_L = 1.1$ for permanent load.

### Effects of shrinkage, from Annex B of EN 1992-1-1

The calculation of the creep factor is as above, but the age at loading is assumed to be one day, from *clause 5.4.2.2*. For the factor $\beta(t_0)$ this gives:

$$\beta(t_0) = \frac{1}{(0.1 + t_0^{0.20})} = \frac{1}{(0.1 + 1^{0.20})} = 0.91$$

The final creep coefficient from equation (B.2) of EN 1992-1-1 is then:

$$\phi(\infty, t_0) = \phi_0 = \phi_{RH}\beta(f_{cm})\beta(t_0) = 1.43 \times 2.73 \times 0.91 = 3.55$$

From *equation (5.6)*, the modular ratio is given by:

$$n_L = n_0(1 + \psi_L\phi(t, t_0)) = 6.36(1 + 0.55 \times 3.55) = \mathbf{18.8}$$

where $\psi_L = 0.55$ for the primary and secondary effects of shrinkage.

### Example 5.3: primary effects of shrinkage

For the bridge in Example 5.1 (Fig. 5.6) the plate thicknesses of an internal beam at mid-span of the main span are as shown in Fig. 5.11. The primary effects of shrinkage at this cross-section are calculated. The deck concrete is grade C30/37 and the relative humidity is 70%.

It is assumed that, for the majority of the shrinkage, the length of continuous concrete deck is such that shear lag effects are negligible. The effective area of the concrete flange is taken as the actual area, for both the shrinkage and its primary effects. The secondary effects arise from changes in the reactions at the supports. For these, the effective widths should be those used for the other permanent actions.

The free shrinkage strain is found first, from clause 3.1.4 of EN 1992-1-1. By interpolation, Table 3.2 of EN 1992-1-1 gives the drying shrinkage as $\varepsilon_{cd,0} = 352 \times 10^{-6}$.

The factor $k_h$ allows for the influence of the shape and size of the concrete cross-section. From Example 5.2, $h_0 = 250$ mm. From Table 3.3 of EN 1992-1-1, $k_h = 0.80$.

The long-term drying shrinkage strain is $0.80 \times 352 \times 10^{-6} = 282 \times 10^{-6}$.

The long-term autogenous shrinkage strain is:

$$\varepsilon_{ca}(\infty) = 2.5(f_{ck} - 10) \times 10^{-6} = 2.5 \times (30 - 10) \times 10^{-6} = 50 \times 10^{-6}$$

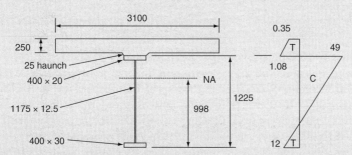

**Fig. 5.11.** Cross-section of beam for Example 5.3, and primary shrinkage stresses with $n_L = 18.8$ (T: tension; C: compression)

From clause 2.4.2.1 of EN 1992-1-1, the recommended partial factor for shrinkage is $\gamma_{SH} = 1.0$, so the design shrinkage strain, for both serviceability and ultimate limit states, is:

$$\varepsilon_{sh} = 1.0 \times (282 + 50) \times 10^{-6} = \mathbf{332 \times 10^{-6}}$$

From Example 5.2, the modular ratio for shrinkage is $n_L = 18.8$.

The tensile force $F_c$ to restore the slab to its length before shrinkage applies to the concrete a tensile stress:

$$332 \times 10^{-6} \times 210 \times 10^3 / 18.8 = 3.71 \text{ N/mm}^2$$

The area of the concrete cross-section is:

$$A_c = 3.1 \times 0.25 + 0.4 \times 0.025 = 0.785 \text{ m}^2$$

therefore

$$F_c = \varepsilon_{sh} A_c E_a / n_L = 332 \times 0.785 \times 210 / 18.8 = 2913 \text{ kN}$$

For $n_L = 18.8$, the location of the neutral axis of the uncracked unreinforced section is as shown in Fig. 5.11. This is 375 mm below the centroid of the concrete area. Relevant properties of this cross-section are:

$$I = 21\,890 \times 10^6 \text{ mm}^4 \text{ and } A = 76\,443 \text{ mm}^2$$

The total external force is zero, so force $F_c$ is balanced by applying a compressive force of 2913 kN and a sagging moment of $2913 \times 0.375 = 1092$ kNm to the composite section.

The long-term primary shrinkage stresses in the cross-section are as follows, with compression positive:

at the top of the slab,

$$\sigma = -3.71 + \left(\frac{2913 \times 10^3}{76\,443} + \frac{1092 \times 502}{21\,890}\right)\frac{1}{18.8} = -0.35 \text{ N/mm}^2$$

at the interface, in concrete,

$$\sigma = -3.71 + \left(\frac{2913 \times 10^3}{76\,443} + \frac{1092 \times 227}{21\,890}\right)\frac{1}{18.8} = -1.08 \text{ N/mm}^2$$

at the interface, in steel,

$$\sigma = +\frac{2913 \times 10^3}{76\,443} + \frac{1092 \times 227}{21\,890} = +49.4\,\text{N/mm}^2$$

at the bottom of the steel beam,

$$\sigma = +\frac{2913 \times 10^3}{76\,443} + \frac{1092 \times 998}{21\,890} = -11.7\,\text{N/mm}^2$$

### 5.4.3. Non-linear global analysis for bridges

*Clause 5.4.3*

The provisions of EN 1992 and EN 1993 on non-linear analysis are clearly relevant, but are not referred to from *clause 5.4.3*. It gives Principles, but no Application Rules. It is stated in EN 1992-2 that clause 5.7(4)P of EN 1992-1-1 applies. It requires stiffnesses to be represented 'in a realistic way' taking account of the 'uncertainties of failure', and concludes 'Only those design formats which are valid within the relevant fields of application shall be used'.

Clause 5.7 of EN 1992-2, 'Non-linear analysis', consists mainly of Notes that give recommendations to national annexes. The majority of the provisions can be varied in the National Annex as agreement could not be obtained at the time of drafting over the use of the safety format proposed. The properties of materials specified in the Notes have been derived so that a single safety factor can be applied to all materials in the verification. Further comment is given under *clause 6.7.2.8*.

Clause 5.4.1 of EN 1993-2 requires the use of an elastic analysis for 'all persistent and transient design situations'. It has a Note that refers to the use of 'plastic global analysis' for accidental design situations, and to the relevant provisions of EN 1993-1-1. These include clause 5.4, which defines three types of non-linear analysis, all of which refer to 'plastic' behaviour. One of them, 'rigid-plastic analysis', should not be considered for composite bridge structures. This is evident from the omission from EN 1994-2 of a clause corresponding to clause 5.4.5 of EN 1994-1-1, 'Rigid plastic global analysis for buildings'.

This method of drafting arises from Notes to clauses 1.5.6.6 and 1.5.6.7 of EN 1990, which make clear that all of the methods of global analysis defined in clauses 1.5.6.6 to 1.5.6.11 (which include 'plastic' methods) are 'non-linear' in Eurocode terminology. 'Non-linear' in these clauses of EN 1990 refers to the deformation properties of the materials, and not to geometrical non-linearity (second-order effects), although these have to be considered when significant, as discussed in section 5.2 above.

Non-linear analysis must satisfy both equilibrium and compatibility of deformations when using non-linear material properties. These broad requirements are given to enable methods more advanced than linear-elastic analysis to be developed and used within the scope of the Eurocodes.

Unlike clause 5.4.1 of EN 1993-2, EN 1994-2 makes no reference to the use of plastic analysis for accidental situations, such as vehicular impact on a bridge pier or impact on a parapet. The National Annex to EN 1993-2 will give guidance. It is recommended that this be followed also for composite design.

Further guidance on non-linear analysis is given in EN 1993-1-5, Annex C, on finite-element modelling of steel plates.

### 5.4.4. Combination of global and local action effects

A typical local action is a wheel load on a highway bridge. It is expected that the National Annex for the UK will require the effects of such loads to be combined with the global effects of coexisting actions for serviceability verifications, but not for checks for ultimate limit states. This is consistent with current practice to BS 5400.[11]

*Clause 5.4.4(1)*

The Note to *clause 5.4.4(1)* refers to Normative Annex E of EN 1993-2. This annex was written for all-steel decks, where local stresses in welds can be significant and where local and global stresses always combine unfavourably. It recommends a combination factor $\psi$ for local and global effects that depends on the span and ranges from 0.7 to 1.0. The application of this rule to reinforced concrete decks that satisfy the serviceability requirements for the combined effects is believed to be over-conservative, because of the beneficial local effects of membrane and arching action. By contrast, if the EN 1993 rules are adopted, global compression in the slab is usually favourable so consideration of 70% of the maximum compressive global stress when checking local effects may actually be unconservative.

## 5.5. Classification of cross-sections

The classification of cross-sections of composite beams is the established method of taking account in design of local buckling of plane steel elements in compression. It determines the available methods of global analysis and the basis for resistance to bending, in the same way as for steel members. Unlike the method in EN 1993-1-1, it does not apply to columns. The Class of a steel element (a flange or a web) depends on its edge support conditions, $b/t$ ratio, distribution of longitudinal stress across its width, yield strength, and in composite sections, the restraint provided against buckling by any attached concrete or concrete encasement.

A flow diagram for the provisions of *clause 5.5* is given in Fig. 5.12. The clause numbers given are from EN 1994-2, unless noted otherwise.

*Clause 5.5*

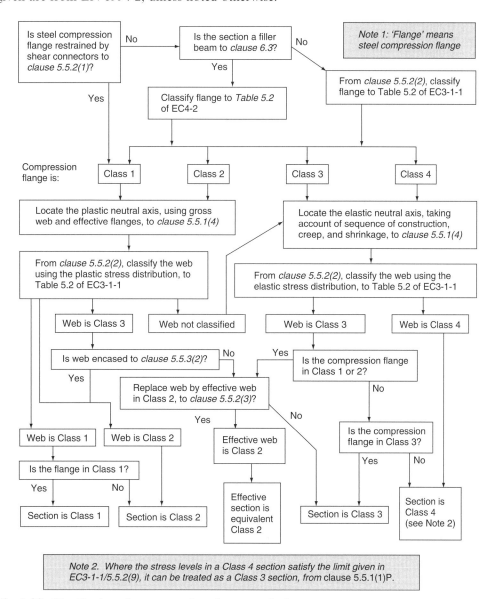

**Fig. 5.12.** Classification of a cross-section of a composite beam

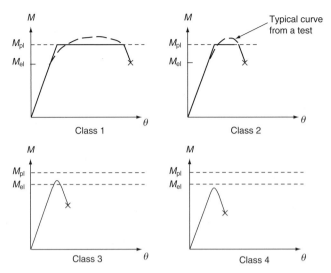

**Fig. 5.13.** Idealized moment–rotation relationships for sections in Classes 1 to 4

*Clause 5.5.1(1)P*

*Clause 5.5.1(2)*

**Clause 5.5.1(1)P** refers to EN 1993-1-1 for definitions of the four Classes and the slendernesses that define the Class boundaries. Classes 1 to 4 correspond respectively to the terms 'plastic', 'compact', 'semi-compact' and 'slender' that were formerly used in BS 5950.[48] The classifications are done separately for steel flanges in compression and steel webs. The Class of the cross-section is the less favourable of the Classes so found, *clause 5.5.1(2)*, with one exception: the 'hole-in-web' option of *clause 5.5.2(3)*.

Idealized moment–rotation curves for members in the four Classes are shown in Fig. 5.13. In reality, curves for sections in Class 1 or 2 depart from linearity as soon as (or even before) the yield moment is reached, and strain-hardening leads to a peak bending moment higher than $M_{pl}$, as shown.

The following notes supplement the definitions given in clause 5.5.2(1) of EN 1993-1-1:

- *Class 1* cross-sections can form a plastic hinge and tolerate a large plastic rotation without loss of resistance. It is a requirement of EN 1993-1-1 for the use of rigid-plastic global analysis that the cross-sections at all plastic hinges are in Class 1. For composite bridges, EN 1994-2 does not permit rigid-plastic analysis. A Note to clause 5.4.1(1) of EN 1993-2 enables its use to be permitted, in a National Annex, for certain accidental design situations for steel bridges.
- *Class 2* cross-sections can develop their plastic moment resistance, $M_{pl,Rd}$, but have limited rotation capacity after reaching it because of local buckling. Regions of sagging bending in composite beams are usually in Class 1 or 2. The resistance $M_{pl,Rd}$ exceeds the resistance at first yield, $M_{el,Rd}$, by between 20% and 40%, compared with about 15% for steel beams. Some restrictions are necessary on the use of $M_{pl,Rd}$ in combination with elastic global analysis, to limit the post-yield shedding of bending moment to adjacent cross-sections in Class 3 or 4. These are given in *clauses 6.2.1.2(2)* and *6.2.1.3(2)*.
- *Class 3* cross-sections become susceptible to local buckling before development of the plastic moment of resistance. In *clause 6.2.1.5(2)* their bending resistance is defined as the '*elastic resistance*', governed by stress limits for all three materials. A limit may be reached when the compressive stress in all restrained steel elements is below yield. Some rotation capacity then remains, but it is impracticable to take advantage of it in design.
- *Class 4* cross-sections are those in which local buckling will occur before the attainment of yield stress in one or more parts of the cross-section. This is assumed in EN 1993 and EN 1994 to be an ultimate limit state. The effective cross-section should be derived in accordance with EN 1993-1-5. Guidance is given in comments on *clause 6.2.1.5(7)*, which defines the procedure, and in the *Designers' Guide to EN 1993-2*.[4]

The Class of a cross-section is determined from the width-to-thickness ratios given in Table 5.2 of EN 1993-1-1 for webs and flanges in compression. The numbers appear different from those in BS 5400:Part 3:2000[11] because the coefficient that takes account of yield strength, $\varepsilon$, is defined as $\sqrt{(235/f_y)}$ in the Eurocodes, and as $\sqrt{(355/f_y)}$ in BS 5400. After allowing for this, the limits for webs at the Class 2/3 boundary agree closely with those in BS 5400, but there are differences for flanges. For outstand flanges, EN 1993 is more liberal at the Class 2/3 boundary, and slightly more severe at the Class 3/4 boundary. For internal flanges of boxes, EN 1993 is considerably more liberal for all Classes.

Reference is sometimes made to a beam in a certain Class. This may imply a certain distribution of bending moment. *Clause 5.5.1(2)* warns that the Class of a composite section depends on the sign of the bending moment (sagging or hogging), as it does for a steel section that is not symmetrical about its neutral axis for bending.

*Clause 5.5.1(3)* permits account to be taken of restraint from concrete in determining the classification of elements, providing that the benefit has been established. Further comment is given at *clause 5.5.2(1)* on spacing of shear connectors.

*Clause 5.5.1(3)*

Since the Class of a web depends on the level of the neutral axis, which is different for elastic and plastic bending, it may not be obvious which stress distribution should be used for a section near the boundary between Classes 2 and 3. *Clause 5.5.1(4)* provides the answer: the plastic distribution. This is because the use of the elastic distribution could place a section in Class 2, for which the bending resistance would be based on the plastic distribution, which in turn could place the section in Class 3.

*Clause 5.5.1(4)*

Elastic stress distributions should be built up by taking the construction sequence into account, together with the effects of creep (generally through the use of different modular ratios for the different load types) and shrinkage.

Where a steel element is longitudinally stiffened, it should be placed in Class 4 unless it can be classified in a higher Class by ignoring the longitudinal stiffeners.

Where both axial load and moment are present, these should be combined when deriving the plastic stress block. Alternatively, the web Class can conservatively be determined on the basis of compressive axial load alone.

*Clause 5.5.1(5)*, on the minimum area of reinforcement for a concrete flange, appears here, rather than in *Section 6*, because it gives a further condition for a cross-section to be placed in Class 1 or 2. The reason is that these sections must maintain their bending resistance, without fracture of the reinforcement, while subjected to higher rotation than those in Class 3 or 4. This is ensured by disallowing the use of bars in ductility Class A (the lowest), and by requiring a minimum cross-sectional area, which depends on the tensile force in the slab just before it cracks.[55] *Clause 5.5.1(6)*, on welded mesh, has the same objective. Clause 3.2.4 of EN 1992-2 does not recommend the use of Class A reinforcement for bridges in any case, but this recommendation can be modified in a National Annex.

*Clause 5.5.1(5)*

*Clause 5.5.1(6)*

During the construction of a composite bridge, it is quite likely that a beam will change its section Class, because the addition of the deck slab both prevents local buckling of the top flange and significantly shifts the neutral axis of the section. Typically, a mid-span section could be in Class 1 or 2 after casting the slab but in Class 3 or 4 prior to this. *Clause 5.5.1(7)* requires strength checks at intermediate stages of construction to be based on the relevant classification at the stage being checked.

*Clause 5.5.1(7)*

The words '*without concrete encasement*' in the title of *clause 5.5.2* are there because this clause is copied from EN 1994-1-1, where it is followed by a clause on beams with web encasement. These are outside the scope of EN 1994-2.

*Clause 5.5.2*

*Clause 5.5.2(1)* is an application of *clause 5.5.1(3)*. The spacing rules to which it refers may be restrictive where full-thickness precast deck slabs are used. *Clause 5.5.2(2)* adds little to *clause 5.5.1*.

*Clause 5.5.2(1)*

*Clause 5.5.2(2)*

### The hole-in-web method

This useful device first appeared in BS 5950-3-1.[48] It is now in clause 6.2.2.4 of EN 1993-1-1, which is referred to from *clause 5.5.2(3)*.

*Clause 5.5.2(3)*

In beams subjected to hogging bending, it often happens that the bottom flange is in Class 1 or 2, and the web is in Class 3. The initial effect of local buckling of the web would be a small reduction in the bending resistance of the section. The assumption that a defined depth of web, the 'hole', is not effective in bending enables the reduced section to be upgraded from Class 3 to Class 2, and removes the sudden change in the bending resistance that would otherwise occur. The method is analogous to the use of effective areas for Class 4 sections, to allow for local buckling.

There is a limitation to its scope that is not evident in the following wording, from EN 1993-1-1:

> The proportion of the web in compression should be replaced by a part of $20\varepsilon t_w$ adjacent to the compression flange, with another part of $20\varepsilon t_w$ adjacent to the plastic neutral axis of the effective cross-section.

It follows that for a design yield strength $f_{yd}$, the compressive force in the web is limited to $40\varepsilon t_w f_{yd}$. For a composite beam in hogging bending, the tensile force in the longitudinal reinforcement in the slab can exceed this value, especially where $f_{yd}$ is reduced to allow for vertical shear. The method is then not applicable, because the second 'element of $20\varepsilon t_w$' is not *adjacent* to the plastic neutral axis, which lies within the top flange. The method, and this limitation, are illustrated in Examples in the *Designers' Guide to EN 1994-1-1*.[5]

It should be noted that if a Class 3 cross-section is treated as an equivalent Class 2 cross-section for section design, it should still be treated as Class 3 when considering the actions to consider in its design. Indirect actions, such as differential settlement, which may be neglected for true Class 2 sections, should not be ignored for effective Class 2 sections. The primary self-equilibrating stresses could reasonably be neglected, but not the secondary effects.

*Clause 5.5.3(2)*

*Clause 5.5.3(2)* and *Table 5.2* give allowable width-to-thickness ratios for the outstands of exposed flanges of filler beams. Those for Class 2 and 3 are greater than those from Table 5.2 of EN 1993-1-1. This is because even though a flange outstand can buckle away from the concrete, rotation of the flange at the junction with the web is prevented (or at least the rotational stiffness is greatly increased) by the presence of the concrete.

---

**Example 5.4: classification of composite beam section in hogging bending**

The classification of the cross-section shown in Fig. 5.14 is determined for hogging bending moments. The effective flange width is 3.1 m. The top layer of reinforcement comprises pairs of 20 mm bars at 150 mm centres. The bottom layer comprises single 20 mm bars at 150 mm centres. All reinforcement has $f_{sk} = 500\,\text{N/mm}^2$ and $\gamma_S = 1.15$. These bars are shown in assumed locations, which would in practice depend on the specified covers and the diameter of the transverse bars.

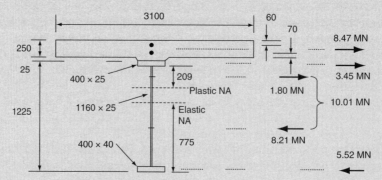

**Fig. 5.14.** Cross-section of beam for Example 5.4

The yield strength of structural steel is thickness-dependent and is $345\,\text{N/mm}^2$ from EN 10025 for steel between 16 mm and 40 mm thick. (If Table 3.1 of EN 1993-1-1 is used, the yield strength can be taken as $355\,\mathrm{N/mm^2}$ for steel up to 40 mm thick. The choice of method can be specified in the National Annex. It is likely that this will require the value from the relevant product standard to be used.)

Hence, $\varepsilon = \sqrt{235/345} = 0.825$.

*Steel bottom flange*
Ignoring the web-to-flange welds, the flange outstand $c = (400 - 25)/2 = 187.5\,\mathrm{mm}$. From Table 5.2 of EN 1993-1-1, the condition for Class 1 is:

$$c/t < 9\varepsilon = 9 \times 0.825 = 7.43$$

For the flange, $c/t = 187.5/40 = 4.7$, so the flange is Class 1.

*Steel web*
To check if the web is in Class 1 or 2, the plastic neutral axis must be determined, using design material strengths.

The total area of reinforcement is:

$$A_\mathrm{s} = 3 \times \pi \times 100 \times 3100/150 = 19\,480\,\mathrm{mm^2}$$

so its tensile force at yield is:

$$19.48 \times 0.5/1.15 = 8.47\,\mathrm{MN}$$

Similarly, the forces in the structural steel elements at yield are found to be as shown in Fig. 5.14. The total longitudinal force is 27.45 MN, so at $M_\mathrm{pl,Rd}$ the compressive force is $27.45/2 = 13.73\,\mathrm{MN}$. The plastic neutral axis is evidently within the web. The depth of web in compression is:

$$1160 \times (13.73 - 5.52)/10.01 = 951\,\mathrm{mm}$$

From Table 5.2 of EN 1993-1-1, for a 'part subject to bending and compression', and ignoring the depth of the web-to-flange welds:

$$\alpha = 951/1160 = 0.82, >0.5$$

The web is in Class 2 if:

$$c/t \leq 456\varepsilon/(13\alpha - 1) = 456 \times 0.825/9.66 = 39.0$$

Its ratio $c/t = 1160/25 = 46.4$, so it is not in Class 2. By inspection, it is in Class 3, but the check at the Class 3/4 boundary is given, as an example. It should be based on the built-up elastic stresses, which may not be available. It is conservative to assume that all stresses are applied to the composite section as this gives the greatest depth of web in compression.

The location of the elastic neutral axis in hogging bending must be found, for the cracked reinforced composite section. There is no need to use a modular ratio for re-inforcement as its modulus may be taken equal to that for structural steel, according to *clause 3.2(2)*. The usual 'first moment of area' calculation finds the neutral axis to be as shown in Fig. 5.14, so the depth of web in compression is $775 - 40 = 735\,\mathrm{mm}$.

Again neglecting the welds, from Table 5.2 of EN 1993-1-1 the stress ratio is

$$\psi = -(1160 - 735)/735 = -0.58$$

and the condition for a Class 3 web is:

$$c/t \leq 42\varepsilon/(0.67 + 0.33\psi) = 42 \times 0.825/(0.67 - 0.19) = 72.4$$

The actual $c/t = 1160/25 = 46.4$, so the composite section is in Class 3 for hogging bending.

## Flow charts for global analysis

The flow charts given in Figs 5.15 and 5.16 are for a bridge with the general layout shown in Fig. 5.1. Figure 5.15, for the superstructure, provides design forces and displacements for the beams and at the four sets of bearings shown. Figure 5.16, for the columns, takes account of system instability shown in Fig. 5.1(b). Instability of members in compression is covered in comments on clause 6.7.3.4.

For simplicity, the scope of these charts is limited by assumptions, as follows:

- Fatigue, vibration, and settlement are excluded.
- Axial force in the superstructure (e.g. from friction at bearings) is negligible.
- The main imposed loading is traffic Load Model 1, from EN 1991-2.
- Only persistent design situations are included.
- The limit states considered are ULS (STR) and SLS (deformation and crack width).
- The superstructure consists of several parallel continuous non-hybrid plate girders without longitudinal stiffeners, composite with a reinforced normal-density-concrete deck slab.
- There are no structural steel transverse members at deck-slab level.
- The only steel cross-sections that may be in Class 4 are the webs near internal supports. The depth of web in compression is influenced by the ratio of non-composite to composite bending moment and the area of reinforcement in the slab. The Class is therefore difficult to predict until some analyses have been done.
- The deck is constructed unpropped, and all structural deck concrete is assumed to be in place before any of the members become composite.
- The formwork is structurally participating precast concrete planks. They are assumed (for simplicity here) to have the same creep and shrinkage properties as the *in situ* concrete of the deck.
- All joints except bearings are assumed to be continuous (*clause 5.1.2*).
- Bearings are 'simple' joints, with or without longitudinal sliding, as shown in Fig. 5.1. Transverse sliding cannot occur.

In the charts, creep and shrinkage effects are considered only as 'long-term' values ($t \rightarrow \infty$). The values of all Nationally Determined Parameters, such as $\gamma$ and $\psi$ factors, are assumed to be those recommended in the Notes in the Eurocodes.

The following data are assumed to be available, based on preliminary analyses and the strengths of the materials to be used, $f_y$, $f_{sk}$ and $f_{ck}$ (converted from an assumed $f_{cu}$):

- dimensions of the flanges and webs of the plate girders
- dimensions of the cross-sections of the concrete deck and the two supporting systems, BE and CF in Fig. 5.1(a)
- details and weight of the superimposed dead load (finishes, parapets, etc.)
- estimated areas of longitudinal slab reinforcement above internal supports.

Assumptions relevant to out-of-plane system instability are as follows. The deck transmits most of the lateral wind loading to supports A and D, with negligible restraint from the two sets of internal supports. The lateral deflections of nodes B and C influence the design of the columns, but stiffnesses are such that wind-induced system instability is not possible.

The following abbreviations are used:

- 'EC2' means EN 1992-1-1 and/or EN 1992-2; similarly for 'EC3'.
- A clause in EN 1994-2 is referred to as, for example, '5.4.2.2'.
- Symbols $g_{k1}$ and $g_{k2}$ are used for characteristic dead loads on the steelwork, and on composite members, respectively. Superimposed dead load is $g_{k3}$. Shrinkage is $g_{sh}$.
- Characteristic imposed loads are denoted $q_k$ (traffic), $w_k$ (wind) and $t_k$ (temperature).

There is not space to list on Fig. 5.15 the combinations of actions required. The notation in the lists that follow is that each symbol, such as $g_{k2}$, represents the sets of action effects ($M_{Ed}$, $V_{Ed}$, deformations, etc.) resulting from the application of the arrangement of the action $g_{k2}$ that is most adverse for the action effect considered.

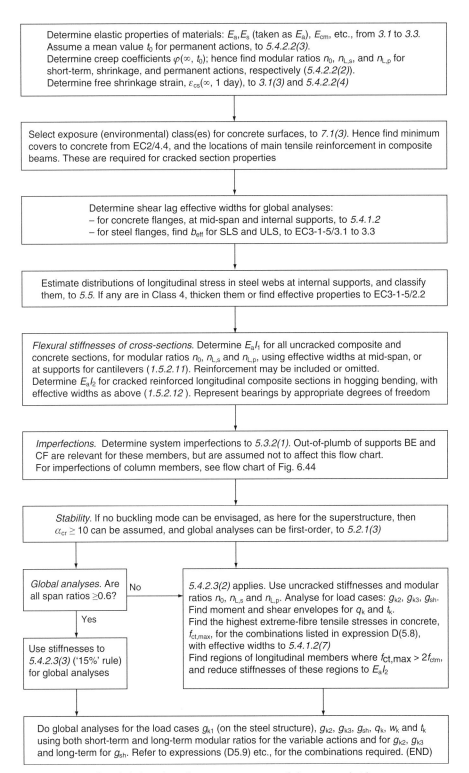

**Fig. 5.15.** Flow chart for global analysis for superstructure of three-span bridge

For the variable actions $q_k$ and $w_k$, different arrangements govern at different cross-sections, so envelopes are required. This may apply also for $t_k$, as several sets of temperature actions are specified.

For finding the 'cracked' regions of longitudinal members, it is assumed that the short-term values are critical, because creep may reduce tensile stress in concrete more than shrinkage increases it. From *clause 5.4.2.3(2)*, the following characteristic combinations are required for finding 'cracked' regions:

- with traffic leading:     $g_{k2} + g_{k3} + q_k + \psi_{0,w}w_k$
- with wind leading:     $g_{k2} + g_{k3} + \psi_{0,q}q_k + w_k$
- with temperature leading:     $g_{k2} + g_{k3} + \psi_{0,q}q_k + \psi_{0,w}w_k + t_k$     (D5.8)

In practice, of course, it will usually be evident which combination governs. Then, only regions in tension corresponding to that combination need be determined.

For finding the most adverse action effects for the limit state ULS (STR), all combinations include the design permanent action effects:

$$\gamma_G(g_{k1} + g_{k2} + g_{k3}) + g_{sh}$$

using the more adverse of the long-term or short-term values. To these are added, in turn, the following combinations of variable action effects:

- with traffic leading:     $1.35q_k + 1.5\psi_{0,w}w_k$
- with wind leading:     $1.35\psi_{0,q}q_k + 1.5w_k$
- with temperature leading:     $1.35\psi_{0,q}q_k + 1.5(\psi_{0,w}w_k + t_k)$     (D5.9)

For serviceability limit states, deformation is checked for frequent combinations. The combination for crack width is for national choice, and 'frequent' is assumed here. These combinations all include the permanent action effects as follows, again using the more adverse of short-term and long-term values:

$$g_{k1} + g_{k2} + g_{k3} + g_{sh}$$

To these are added, in turn, the following combinations of variable action effects:

- with traffic leading:     $\psi_{1,q}q_k + \psi_{2,t}t_k$     because $\psi_{2,w} = 0$
- with wind leading:     $\psi_{1,w}w_k + \psi_{2,t}t_k$     because $\psi_{2,q} = 0$
- with temperature leading:     $\psi_{1,t}t_k$     (D5.10)

As before, it will usually be evident, for each action effect and location, which combination governs.

### Flow chart for supporting systems at internal supports
At each of points B and C in Fig. 5.1, it is assumed that the plate girders are supported on at least two bearings, mounted on a cross-head that is supported by a composite frame or by two or more composite columns, fixed at points E and F. Each bearing acts as a spherical pin. Design action effects and displacements (six per bearing) are known, for each limit state, from analyses of the superstructure.

Preliminary cross-sections for all the members have been chosen. Composite columns are assumed to be within the scope of *clause 6.7.3* (doubly symmetrical, uniform, etc.). The flow chart of Fig. 5.16 is for a single composite column, and is applicable to composite columns generally. For ultimate limit states, only long-term behaviour is considered, as this usually governs.

### Notes on Fig. 5.16
(1) For the elastic critical buckling force $N_{cr}$, the effective length for an unbraced column, as in Fig. 5.1(b), is at least $2L$, where $L$ is the actual length. If the foundation cannot be assumed to be 'rigid', its rotational stiffness should be included in an elastic critical analysis, as the effective length then exceeds $2L$.

In many cases, $\bar{\lambda}$ will be much less than 2, and $\alpha_{cr}$ will far exceed 10. These checks can then be done approximately, by simple hand calculation. Other methods of checking if second-order global analysis is required are discussed under *clause 5.2.1*.

Here, it is assumed that for the transverse direction, $\alpha_{cr} > 10$. No assumption is made for the plane shown in Fig. 5.1. The flow chart of Fig. 5.16, which is for a single column, includes second-order system effects in this plane.

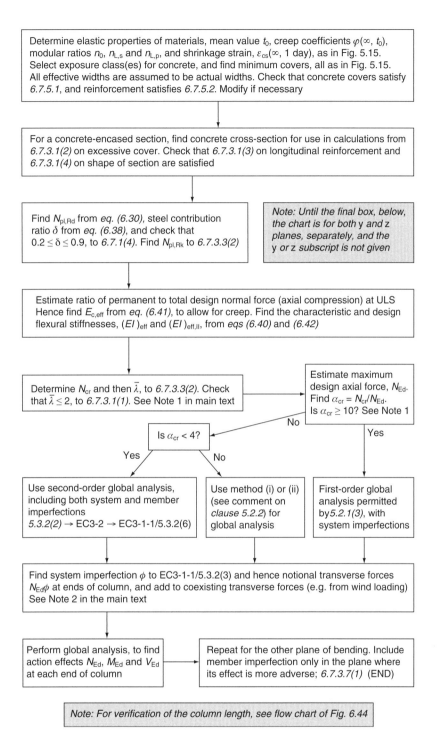

**Fig. 5.16.** Flow chart for global analysis of a composite column

(2) Out-of-plumb of columns, a system imperfection, should be allowed for as follows. Figure 5.17(a) shows a nominally vertical column of length $L$, with design action effects $M$, $N$ and $V$ from a preliminary global analysis. The top-end moment $M$ could represent an off-centre bearing. The design out-of-plumb angle for the column, $\phi$, is found from clause 5.3.2(3) of EN 1993-1-1. Notional horizontal forces $N\phi$ are applied, as shown in Fig. 5.17(b).

Second-order global analysis for the whole structure, including base flexibility, if any, then gives the deformations of the ends of the column and the action effects $N_{Ed}$, etc.,

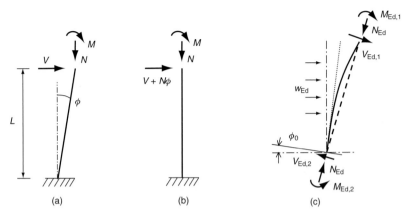

**Fig. 5.17.** System imperfection and global analysis for a column

needed for verification of the column length. In Fig. 5.17(c), $\phi_0$ is the rotation of the column base, and $w_{Ed}$ represents the transverse loading, which may be negligible. For the determination of the bending moments within a column length and its verification, reference should be made to the flow chart of Fig. 6.36 of Ref. 5.

# CHAPTER 6

# Ultimate limit states

This chapter corresponds to *Section 6* of EN 1994-2, which has the following clauses:

*Clauses 6.1* to *6.7* define resistances of cross-sections to static loading, for comparison with action effects determined by the methods of *Section 5*. The ultimate limit state considered is STR, defined in clause 6.4.1(1) of EN 1990 as:

> Internal failure or excessive deformation of the structure or structural members... where the strength of constructional materials of the structure governs.

The self-contained *clause 6.8*, Fatigue, covers steel, concrete, and reinforcement by cross-reference to Eurocodes 2 and 3. Requirements are given for shear connection.

*Clause 6.9* does not appear in EN 1994-1-1 and has been added in EN 1994-2 to cover concrete and composite tension members such as may be found in tied arch bridges and truss bridges.

## 6.1. Beams

### 6.1.1. Beams in bridges – general

*Clause 6.1.1(1)* serves as a summary of the checks that should be performed on the beams themselves (excluding related elements such as bracing and diaphragms). The checks listed are as follows:

*Clause 6.1.1(1)*

- Resistance of cross-sections to bending and shear – *clauses 6.2* and *6.3*. In the Eurocodes, local buckling in Class 4 members, due to direct stress, is covered under the heading of 'cross-section' resistance, even though this buckling resistance is derived considering a finite length of the beam. In Eurocode 3, shear buckling is similarly covered under the heading of 'cross-section' resistance, but this is separately itemized below. A check of the interaction between shear and bending is required in *clause 6.2.2.4*.
- Resistance to lateral–torsional buckling – *clause 6.4*. For lateral–torsional buckling, the resistance is influenced by the properties of the whole member. The rules of Eurocode 4 assume that the member is of uniform cross-section, apart from variations arising from

cracking of concrete and from detailing. The resistance of non-uniform members is covered in clause 6.3.4 of EN 1993-2.

- Resistance to shear buckling and in-plane forces applied to webs – *clauses 6.2.2* and *6.5* respectively. As discussed above, shear buckling resistance is treated as a property of a cross-section.
- Resistance to longitudinal shear – *clause 6.6*. According to *clause 1.1.3(3)*, provisions for shear connection are given only for welded headed studs. This is misleading, for much of *clause 6.6* is more widely applicable, as discussed under *clause 6.6.1*.
- Resistance to fatigue – *clause 6.8*.

The above checks are not exhaustive. Further checks that may be required include the following:

- Interaction with axial force. Axial force is not included in the checks above as *clause 1.5.2.4* defines a composite beam as '*a composite member subjected mainly to bending*'. Axial force does however occur in the beams of composite integral bridges.[57] This is discussed in section 6.4 of this guide.
- Addition of stresses in webs and flanges generated from plan curvature, although this is identified in *clause 6.2.1.1(5)*. No method of combining (or calculating) these effects is provided in Eurocodes 3 or 4. The *Designers' Guide to EN 1993-2*[4] provides some guidance, as do the comments on clause 6.2.1.1(5).
- Flange-induced buckling of the web – *clause 6.5.2* refers.
- Torsion in box girders, which adds to the shear in the webs and necessitates a further check on the flange – Section 7 of EN 1993-1-5 refers. The need to consider combinations of torsion and bending is mentioned in *clause 6.2.1.3(1)*.
- Distortion of box girders, which causes both in-plane and out-of-plane bending in the box walls – clause 6.2.7 of EN 1993-2 refers and the *Designers' Guide to EN 1993-2* provides some guidance.
- Torsion of bare steel beams during construction, which often arises with the use of cantilever forms to construct the deck edge cantilevers. This usually involves a consideration of both St Venant torsion and warping torsion.
- Design of transverse stiffeners – Section 9 of EN 1993-1-5 refers.

Steel cross-sections may be rolled I- or H-section or doubly-symmetrical or mono-symmetrical plate girders. Other possible types include any of those shown in sheet 1 of Table 5.2 of EN 1993-1-1; this includes box girders. Channel and angle sections should not be used unless the shear connection is designed to provide torsional restraint or there is adequate torsional bracing between beams.

### 6.1.2. Effective width for verification of cross-sections
Effective widths for shear lag are discussed in section 5.4.1.2 of this guide. Unlike in global analysis, the effective width appropriate to the cross-section under consideration must be used in calculation of resistance to bending. Distributions of effective width along a span are given in *Figure 5.1*.

## 6.2. Resistances of cross-sections of beams
This clause is for beams without partial or full encasement in concrete. Filler beams with partial encasement are treated in *clause 6.3*. Full encasement is outside the scope of EN 1994.

No guidance is given in EN 1994, or in EN 1993, on the treatment of large holes in steel webs without recourse to finite-element modelling (following the requirements of EN 1993-1-5), but specialized literature is available.[58,59] Bolt holes in steelwork should be treated in accordance with EN 1993-1-1, particularly clauses 6.2.2 to 6.2.6.

### 6.2.1. Bending resistance

#### 6.2.1.1. General

In *clause 6.2.1.1*, three different approaches are given, based on rigid-plastic theory, non-linear theory, and elastic theory. The 'non-linear theory' is that given in *clause 6.2.1.4*. This is not a reference to non-linear global analysis.

*Clause 6.2.1.1(1)* only permits rigid-plastic theory to be used where cross-sections are in Class 1 or 2 and where prestressing by tendons is not used. This is because no explicit check of yielding of bonded tendons is given and therefore non-linear resistance calculation is more appropriate. Comment on this use of plastic resistance with elastic analysis is given under *clause 5.4.1.1(1)*.

*Clause 6.2.1.1(2)* permits non-linear theory and elastic theory to be used for all cross-sections. If unbonded tendons are used, the tendon forces used in section analysis should however be derived in accordance with *clause 5.4.2.7(2)*.

The assumption that composite cross-sections remain plane is always permitted by *clause 6.2.1.1(3)* where elastic and non-linear theory are used, because the conditions set will be satisfied if the design is in accordance with EN 1994. The implication is that longitudinal slip is negligible.

There is no requirement for slip to be determined. This would be difficult because the stiffness of shear connectors is not known accurately, especially where the slab is cracked. Wherever slip may not be negligible, the design methods of EN 1994-2 are intended to allow for its effects.

For beams with curvature in plan, *clause 6.2.1.1(5)* gives no guidance on how to allow for the torsional moments induced or how to assess their significance. Normal practice is to treat the changing direction of the longitudinal force in a flange (and a web, if significant) as a transverse load applied to that flange, which is then designed as a horizontal beam spanning between transverse restraints. It is common to use elastic section resistance in such circumstances to avoid the complexity of producing a plastic stress block for the combined local and global loading. The shear connection and bracing system should be designed for the additional transverse forces.

Similar calculation should be carried out where curvature is achieved using a series of straight sections, except that the transverse forces will be concentrated at the splices between adjacent lengths. Particular care is needed with detailing the splices. Transverse stiffeners and bracing will usually be needed close to each splice to limit the bending in the flange. In box girders, the torsion from curvature will also tend to produce distortion of the box. This must be considered in the design of both the cross-section of the box and its internal restraints.

Bending in transverse planes can also be induced in flanges by curvature of the flange in a vertical plane, and should be considered. *Clause 6.5* covers the transverse forces on webs that this causes, but not the transverse bending in the flange. The latter is covered in the *Designers' Guide to EN 1993-2*.[4]

#### 6.2.1.2. Plastic resistance moment $M_{pl,Rd}$ of a composite cross-section

'Full interaction' in *clause 6.2.1.2(1)(a)* means that no account need be taken of slip or separation at the steel–concrete interface.

'Full interaction' should not be confused with 'full shear connection'. That concept is used only in the rules for buildings, and is explained in clause 6.1.1(7)P of EN 1994-1-1 as follows:

> A span of a beam...has full shear connection when increase in the number of shear connectors would not increase the design bending resistance of the member.

This link of shear connection to bending resistance differs from the method of EN 1994-2, where shear connection is related to action effects, both static and fatigue. Shear connection to Part 2 is not necessarily 'full' according to the above definition (which should strictly read '...number of shear connectors within a critical length...'). It would be confusing to refer to it as 'partial', so this term is never used in Part 2.

*Clause 6.2.1.1(1)*

*Clause 6.2.1.1(2)*

*Clause 6.2.1.1(3)*

*Clause 6.2.1.1(5)*

*Clause 6.2.1.2(1)(a)*

*Reinforcement in compression*

It is usual to neglect slab reinforcement in compression (*clause 6.2.1.2(1)(c)*). Its effect on the bending resistance of the composite section is negligible unless the slab is unusually small. If it is included, and the concrete cover is little greater than the bar diameter, consideration should be given to possible buckling of the bars.

Guidance on detailing is given in clauses 9.5.3(6) and 9.6.3(1) of EN 1992-1-1 for reinforcement in concrete columns and walls respectively. The former requires that no bar within a compression zone should be further than 150 mm from a 'restrained' bar, but 'restrained' is not defined. This could be interpreted as requiring all compression bars in an outer layer to be within 150 mm of a bar held in place by transverse reinforcement. This would usually require link reinforcement in the flange. This interpretation was used in BS 5400 Part 4[11] for compression bars assumed to contribute to the resistance of the section. If the compression flange is classed as a wall, clause 9.6.3 of EN 1992-1-1 requires only that the longitudinal bars are placed inside horizontal (i.e. transverse) reinforcement unless the reinforcement in compression exceeds 2% of the gross concrete area. In the latter case, transverse reinforcement must be provided in accordance with the column rules.

*Stress/strain properties for concrete*

The design compressive strength of concrete, $f_{cd}$, is defined in clause 3.1.6(1)P of EN 1992-1-1 as:

$$f_{cd} = \alpha_{cc} f_{ck}/\gamma_C$$

where:

'$\alpha_{cc}$ is the coefficient taking account of long term effects on the compressive strength and of unfavourable effects resulting from the way the load is applied.

'Note: The value of $\alpha_{cc}$ for use in a country should lie between 0.8 and 1.0 and may be found in its National Annex. The recommended value is 1.'

The reference in *clause 3.1(1)* to EN 1992-1-1 for properties of concrete begins '*unless otherwise given by Eurocode 4*'. Resistances of composite members given in EN 1994-2 are based on extensive calibration studies (e.g. Refs 60, 61). The numerical coefficients given in resistance formulae are consistent with the value $\alpha_{cc} = 1.0$ and the use of either elastic theory or the stress block defined in *clause 6.2.1.2*. Therefore, there is no reference in EN 1994-2 to a coefficient $\alpha_{cc}$ or to a choice to be made in a National Annex. The symbol $f_{cd}$ always means $f_{ck}/\gamma_C$, and for beams and most columns is used with the coefficient 0.85, as in *equation (6.30)* in *clause 6.7.3.2(1)*. An exception, in that clause, is that the 0.85 is replaced by 1.0 for concrete-filled column sections, based on calibration.

The approximation made to the shape of the stress–strain curve is also relevant. Those given in clause 3.1 of EN 1992-1-1 are mainly curved or bilinear, but in clause 3.1.7(3) there is a simpler rectangular stress distribution, similar to the stress block given in the British Standard for the structural use of concrete, BS 8110.[62] Its shape, for concrete strength classes up to C50/60, and the corresponding strain distribution are shown in Fig. 6.1 below.

This stress block is inconvenient for use with composite cross-sections, because the region near the neutral axis assumed to be unstressed is often occupied by a steel flange, and algebraic expressions for resistance to bending become complex.

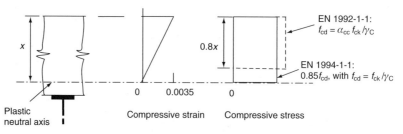

**Fig. 6.1.** Stress blocks for concrete at ultimate limit states

In composite sections, the contribution from the steel section to the bending resistance reduces the significance of that from the concrete. It is thus possible[63] for EN 1994 to allow the use of a rectangular stress block extending to the neutral axis, as shown in Fig. 6.1.

For a member of unit width, the moment about the neutral axis of the EN 1992 stress block ranges from $0.38 f_{ck} x^2 / \gamma_C$ to $0.48 f_{ck} x^2 / \gamma_C$, depending on the value chosen for $\alpha_{cc}$. The value for beams in EN 1994-2 is $0.425 f_{ck} x^2 / \gamma_C$. Calibration studies have shown that this overestimates the bending resistance of cross-sections of columns, so a correction factor $\alpha_M$ is given in *clause 6.7.3.6(1)*. See also the comments on *clause 6.7.3.6*.

### Small concrete flanges

Where the concrete slab is in compression, the method of *clause 6.2.1.2* is based on the assumption that the whole effective areas of steel and concrete can reach their design strengths before the concrete begins to crush. This may not be so if the concrete flange is small compared with the steel section. This lowers the plastic neutral axis, and so increases the maximum compressive strain at the top of the slab, for a given tensile strain in the steel bottom flange.

A detailed study of the problem has been reported.[64] Laboratory tests on beams show that strain hardening of steel usually occurs before crushing of concrete. The effect of this, and the low probability that the strength of both the steel and the concrete will be only at the design level, led to the conclusion that premature crushing can be neglected unless the grade of the structural steel is higher than S355. **Clause 6.2.1.2(2)** specifies a reduction in $M_{pl,Rd}$ where the steel grade is S420 or S460 and the depth of the plastic neutral axis is high.

*Clause 6.2.1.2(2)*

For composite columns, the risk of premature crushing led to a reduction in the factor $\alpha_M$, given in *clause 6.7.3.6(1)*, for S420 and S460 steels.

### Ductility of reinforcement

Reinforcement with insufficient ductility to satisfy *clause 5.5.1(5)*, and welded mesh, should not be included within the effective section of beams in Class 1 or 2 (**clause 6.2.1.2(3)**). This is because laboratory tests on hogging moment regions have shown[33] that some reinforcing bars, and most welded meshes, fracture before the moment–rotation curve for a typical double-cantilever specimen reaches a plateau. The problem with welded mesh is explained in comments on *clause 3.2(3)*.

*Clause 6.2.1.2(3)*

### 6.2.1.3. Additional rules for beams in bridges

*Clause 6.2.1.3(1)* is a reminder that composite beams need to be checked for possible combinations of internal actions that are not specifically covered in EN 1994. The combinations given are biaxial bending, bending and torsion and local and global effects, with a reference to clause 6.2.1(5) of EN 1993-1-1.

*Clause 6.2.1.3(1)*

Significant bending about a vertical axis is rare in composite bridges so biaxial bending is rarely a concern. Despite the reference to EN 1993-1-1, there is little of direct relevance for biaxial bending in composite beams therein. For Class 1 and 2 cross-sections, the interaction of EN 1993-1-1 expression (6.2) could be used for resistance of cross-sections. Rather than computing the resultant plastic stress block for axial load and biaxial bending, a linear interaction is provided:

$$\frac{N_{Ed}}{N_{Rd}} + \frac{M_{y,Ed}}{M_{y,Rd}} + \frac{M_{z,Ed}}{M_{z,Rd}} \leq 1.0$$

where $N_{Rd}$, $M_{y,Rd}$ and $M_{z,Rd}$ are the design resistances for each effect acting individually, with reductions for shear where the shear force is sufficiently large. In theory, it is still necessary to derive the resultant plastic stress block to check whether the cross-section is either Class 1 or 2. This complexity can be avoided by performing the classification under axial compression only. The same expression can be applied to Class 3 and 4 cross-sections or the stresses can be summed using elastic section analysis. Care is needed where the sign of the stress in the slab is different for each constituent action.

In hogging zones of integral bridges, where there is usually a moderate coexistent axial load induced by temperature or soil pressure, it is common to do calculations on the basis of the fully cracked section. The non-linear method of *clause 6.2.1.4* could also be used but this is likely to require the use of computer software. Buckling needs to be checked separately – see section 6.4.

Significant torsion is unlikely to be encountered in most composite I-girder bridges due to the low St Venant torsional stiffness of the steel beams. There are some exceptions including:

- torsion in curved beams as discussed in comments on *clause 6.2.1.1(5)*
- torsion in skew decks at end trimmers
- torsion of bare steel beams where formwork for deck cantilevers is clamped to the outer girders.

EN 1993-1-1 clause 6.2.7(7) permits St Venant torsion to be ignored at ultimate limit states provided that all the torsion is carried by resistance to warping. This is usually the most efficient model and avoids a further interaction with shear stress from vertical shear in the web. If the torque is resisted by opposing bending in the flanges, they can be designed for this bending combined with their axial force. If the length between restraints should be long, then the warping bending stresses would become large and the section would try to resist the torsion predominantly through St Venant shear flow. In that case it might be better to derive the separate contributions from St Venant and warping torsion. Further guidance on shear, torsion and bending is provided in the *Designers' Guide to EN 1993-2*.[4]

Pure torsion in box beams is treated simply by a modification to the shear stress in the webs and flanges, and the design is checked using clause 7.1 of EN 1993-1-5. Pure torsion is however rare and most boxes will also suffer some distortion. This leads to both in-plane warping and out-of-plane bending of the box walls as discussed in Ref. 4.

The reference in *clause 6.2.1.3(1)* to combined local and global effects relates to the steel beam only, because this combination in a concrete deck is a matter for Eurocode 2, unless the deck is a composite plate, when *clause 9.3* applies. Such combinations include bending, shear and transverse load (from wheel loads) according to clause 6.2.8(6) of EN 1993-1-1 and other combinations of local and global load. The Von Mises equivalent stress criterion of EN 1993-1-1 expression (6.1) should be used in the absence of test-based interaction equations for resistances.

*Clause 6.2.1.3(2)*  *Clause 6.2.1.3(2)* relates to the use of plastic resistances in bending, which implies shedding of bending moments, typically from mid-span regions to adjacent supports. Non-linear global analysis allows for this, but linear-elastic analysis does not. The reasons for permitting linear analysis, and for the limitations given in the present clause, are explained in comments on *clause 5.4.1.1(1)*. A method for making use of the limited ductility of support regions has been proposed.[65]

---

**Example 6.1: plastic resistance moment in sagging bending**

For the bridge in Example 5.1 (Fig. 5.6), the resistance moment for an internal beam at mid-span with the cross-section in Fig. 5.11 is determined. The deck concrete is Grade C30/37 and the structural steel is S355 J2 G3. The cross-section is shown in Fig. 6.2 with relevant dimensions, stress blocks and longitudinal forces. The notation is as in *Fig. 6.2* and the concrete stress block as in Fig. 6.1.

Using the partial factors recommended in EN 1992-2 and EN 1993-2, the design strengths are:

$$f_{yd} = 345/1.0 = 345\,\text{N/mm}^2, \ f_{cd} = 30/1.5 = 20\,\text{N/mm}^2$$

The steel yield stress has been taken here as $345\,\text{N/mm}^2$ throughout. This is given in EN 10025 for thicknesses between 16 mm and 40 mm. For the web, $355\,\text{N/mm}^2$ could have been used.

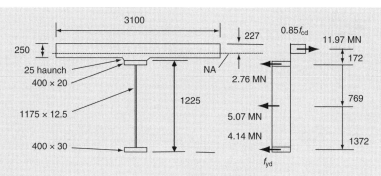

**Fig. 6.2.** Plastic resistance of cross-section to sagging bending, for Example 6.1

Ignoring the haunch and any slab reinforcement, the available compressive force in the concrete is:

$$N_{c,f} = 3.1 \times 0.25 \times 0.85 \times 20 = 13.18 \text{ MN}$$

The available forces in the steel beam are:

in the top flange,  $N_{a,top} = 0.4 \times 0.02 \times 345 = 2.76 \text{ MN}$

in the web,  $N_{a,web} = 1.175 \times 0.0125 \times 345 = 5.07 \text{ MN}$

in the bottom flange,  $N_{a,bot} = 0.4 \times 0.03 \times 345 = 4.14 \text{ MN}$

The total is 11.97 MN. As this is less than 13.18 MN, the neutral axis lies in the concrete slab, at a depth:

$$z_{na} = 250(11.97/13.18) = 227 \text{ mm}$$

The distances below force $N_c$ of the lines of action of the three forces $N_a$ are shown in Fig. 6.2. Hence:

$$\boldsymbol{M_{pl,Rd}} = 2.76 \times 0.172 + 5.07 \times 0.769 + 4.14 \times 1.372 = \boldsymbol{10.05 \text{ MNm}}$$

The cross-section at the adjacent support is in Class 3, so potentially *clause 6.2.1.3(2)* applies. Since the ratio of adjacent spans is 0.61, greater than the limit of 0.6, there is no need to restrict the bending resistance at mid-span to $0.90M_{pl,Rd}$.

## Example 6.2: resistance to hogging bending at an internal support

For the bridge shown in Fig. 5.6, and materials as in Example 6.1, the resistance to hogging bending of the cross-section shown in Fig. 5.14 is studied. It was found in Example 5.4 that the flanges are in Class 1 and the web is in Class 3.

It appears from *clause 5.5.2(3)* that an effective section in Class 2 could be used, to clause 6.2.2.4 of EN 1993-1-1. However, the wording of that clause implies, and its Fig. 6.3 shows, that the plastic neutral axis of the effective section should lie within the web. It is concluded in the *Designers' Guide to EN 1994-1-1*[5] that the hole-in-web approximation should only be used when this is so. As the area of longitudinal reinforcement in the present cross-section is quite high, this condition is checked first.

From clause 6.2.2.4 of EN 1993-1-1, the effective area of web in compression is $40t_w^2\varepsilon$. Using rectangular stress blocks, the condition is:

$$A_s f_{sd} + A_{a,top} f_{yd} < 40t_w^2\varepsilon f_{yd} + A_{a,bot} f_{yd}$$

Hence:

$$A_s < (40t_w^2\varepsilon + A_{a,bot} - A_{a,top})f_{yd}/f_{sd} \tag{D6.1}$$

From Example 5.4:

$$A_s = 19\,480\,\text{mm}^2, \quad \text{and} \quad \varepsilon = \sqrt{235/345} = 0.825$$

From Fig. 5.14:

$$A_{a,bot} - A_{a,top} = 400 \times 15 = 6000\,\text{mm}^2, \; t_w = 25\,\text{mm}$$

For the reinforcement:

$$f_{sd} = 500/1.15 = 435\,\text{N/mm}^2$$

From expression (D6.1):

$$A_s < (40 \times 25^2 \times 0.825 + 6000) \times 345/435 = 21\,120\,\text{mm}^2$$

Thus, expression (D6.1) is satisfied, so $M_{pl,Rd}$ will be found by the hole-in-web method. The longitudinal forces in the reinforcement and the two steel flanges are found as in Example 6.1, and are shown in Fig. 6.3.

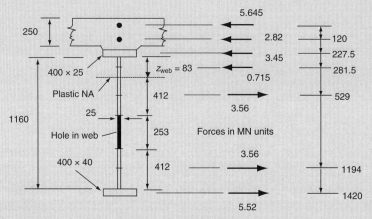

**Fig. 6.3.** Plastic resistance of cross-section to hogging bending, for Example 6.2

The depth of each of the two compressive stress blocks in the web is:

$$20t_w\varepsilon = 20 \times 25 \times 0.825 = 412\,\text{mm}$$

The force in each of them is $20t_w^2\varepsilon f_{yd} = 0.412 \times 0.025 \times 345 = 3.56\,\text{MN}$

The location of the plastic neutral axis is found from longitudinal equilibrium. The tensile force in the web is:

$$T_w = 3.56 \times 2 + 5.52 - 5.645 - 2.82 - 3.45 = 0.715\,\text{MN} = 715\,\text{kN}$$

This force requires a depth of web:

$$z_w = 715/(25 \times 0.345) = 83\,\text{mm}$$

This leads to the depth of the 'hole' in the web, 253 mm, and the distances of the various forces below the level of the top reinforcement, shown in Fig. 6.3. Taking moments about this level gives the bending resistance, which is:

$$M_{pl,Rd} = \textbf{12.64\,MNm}$$

### 6.2.1.4. Non-linear resistance to bending

There are two approaches, described in *clause 6.2.1.4*. With both, the calculations should be done at the critical sections for the design bending moments. The first approach, given in

*Clause 6.2.1.4(1) to (5)*

*clause 6.2.1.4(1)* to *(5)*, enables the resistance of a section to be determined iteratively from the stress–strain relationships of the materials.

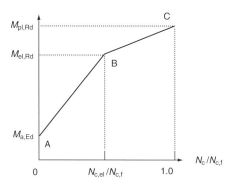

**Fig. 6.4.** Non-linear resistance to bending for Class 1 and 2 cross-sections

A curvature (strain gradient) and neutral-axis position are assumed, the stresses determined from the strains, and the neutral axis moved until the stresses correspond to the external longitudinal force, if any. The assumed strain distributions should allow for the shrinkage strain of the concrete and any strain and/or difference of curvature between steel and concrete caused by temperature. The bending resistance is calculated from this stress distribution. If it exceeds the external moment $M_{Ed}$, the calculation is terminated. If not, the assumed curvature is increased and the process repeated until a value $M_{Rd}$ is found that exceeds $M_{Ed}$. If one of the ultimate strains given in EN 1992-1-1 for concrete and reinforcement is reached first, the cross-section has insufficient resistance. For Class 3 cross-sections or Class 4 effective cross-sections, the compressive strain in the structural steel must not exceed that at first yield.

Clearly, in practice this procedure requires the use of software. For sections in Class 1 or 2, a simplified approach is given in ***clause 6.2.1.4(6)***. This is based on three points on the curve relating longitudinal force in the slab, $N_c$, to design bending moment $M_{Ed}$ that are easily determined. With reference to Fig. 6.4, which is based on *Fig. 6.6*, these points are:

*Clause 6.2.1.4(6)*

- A, where the composite member resists no moment, so $N_c = 0$
- B, which is defined by the results of an elastic analysis of the section, and
- C, based on plastic analysis of the section.

Accurate calculation shows BC to be a convex-upwards curve, so the straight line BC is a conservative approximation. *Clause 6.2.1.4(6)* thus enables hand calculation to be used.

The elastic analysis gives the resistance $M_{el,Rd}$, which is calculated according to *equation (6.4)*. The moment acting on the composite section will generally comprise both short-term and permanent actions and in calculating the stresses from these, appropriate modular ratios should be used in accordance with *clause 5.4.2.2(2)*.

***Clause 6.2.1.4(7)*** makes reference to EN 1993-1-1 for the stress–strain relationship to be used for prestressing steel. The prestrain (which is the initial tendon strain after all losses, calculated in accordance with EN 1992-1-1 clause 5.10.8) must be taken into account in the section design. For bonded tendons, this can be done by displacing the origin of the stress–strain curve along the strain axis by an amount equal to the design prestrain and assuming that the strain change in the tendon is the same as that in the surrounding concrete. For unbonded tendons, the prestress should be treated as a constant force equal to the applied force after all losses. The general method of section analysis for composite columns in *clause 6.7.2* would then be more appropriate.

*Clause 6.2.1.4(7)*

### 6.2.1.5. Elastic resistance to bending
*Clause 6.2.1.4(6)* includes, almost incidentally, a definition of $M_{el,Rd}$ that may seem strange. It is a peculiarity of composite structures that when unpropped construction is used, the elastic resistance to bending depends on the proportion of the total load that is applied before the member becomes composite. Let $M_{a,Ed}$ and $M_{c,Ed}$ be the design bending

moments for the steel and composite sections, respectively, for a section in Class 3. Their total is typically less than the elastic resistance to bending, so to find $M_{el,Rd}$, one or both

*Clause 6.2.1.5(2)*

of them must be increased until one or more of the limiting stresses in ***clause 6.2.1.5(2)*** is reached. To enable a unique result to be obtained, *clause 6.2.1.4(6)* says that $M_{c,Ed}$ is to be increased, and $M_{a,Ed}$ left unchanged. This is because $M_{a,Ed}$ is mainly from permanent actions, which are less uncertain than the variable actions whose effects comprise most of $M_{c,Ed}$.

Unpropped construction normally proceeds by stages, which may have to be considered individually in bridge design. While the sequence of erection of the beams is often known in the design stage, the concrete pour sequence is rarely known. Typically, either a range of possible pour sequences is considered or it is assumed that the whole of the wet concrete is placed simultaneously on the bare steelwork, and the resulting design is rechecked when the pour sequence is known.

The weight of formwork is, in reality, applied to the steel structure and removed from the composite structure. This process leaves self-equilibrated residual stresses in composite cross-sections. Whether or not this is considered in the final situation is a matter for judgement, depending on the significance of the weight of the formwork.

*Clause 6.2.1.5(5)*

One permanent action that influences $M_{el,Rd}$ is shrinkage of concrete. ***Clause 6.2.1.5(5)*** enables the primary stresses to be neglected in cracked concrete, but the implication is that they should be included where the slab is in compression. This provision should not be confused with *clause 5.4.2.2(8)*, although it is consistent with it. The self-equilibrating stresses from the primary effects of shrinkage do not cause any moment but they can give rise to stress. In checking the beam section, if these stresses are adverse, they should be added to those from $M_{a,Ed}$ and $M_{c,Ed}$ when verifying stresses against the limits in *clause 6.2.1.5(2)*. If it is necessary to determine the actual elastic resistance moment, $M_{el,Rd}$, the shrinkage stresses should be added to the stresses from $M_{a,Ed}$ and $kM_{c,Ed}$ when determining $k$ and hence $M_{el,Rd}$. If this addition increases $M_{el,Rd}$, it could be omitted, but this is not a requirement, because shrinkage is classified as a permanent action.

*Clause 6.2.1.5(6)*

***Clause 6.2.1.5(6)*** is a reminder that lateral–torsional buckling should also be checked, which applies equally to the other methods of cross-section design. The calculation of $M_{el,Rd}$ is relevant for Class 3 cross-sections if the method of *clause 6.4.2* is used, but the above problem with shrinkage does not occur as the slab will be in tension in the critical region.

Additional guidance is required for Class 4 cross-sections since the effectiveness of the Class 4 elements (usually only the web for composite I-beams) depends on the stress distributions within them. The loss of effectiveness for local buckling is dealt with by the use of effective widths according to EN 1993-1-5. For staged construction, there is the additional problem that the stress distribution changes during construction and therefore the size and location of the effective part of the element also change at each stage.

*Clause 6.2.1.5(7)*

To avoid the complexity of summing stresses from different effective cross-sections, ***clause 6.2.1.5(7)*** provides a simplified pragmatic rule. This requires that the stress distribution at any stage is built up using gross-section properties. The reference to 'gross' sections is not intended to mean that shear lag can be neglected; it refers only to the neglect of plate buckling. The stress distribution so derived is used to determine an effective web which is then used to determine section properties and stresses at all stages up to the one considered.

The Note to clause 4.4(3) of EN 1993-1-5 provides almost identical guidance, but clarifies that an effective flange should be used together with the gross web to determine the initial stress distribution. 'Effective' in this sense includes the effects of both shear lag and plate buckling. Plate buckling for flanges is likely to be relevant only for box girders. Example 6.3 illustrates the method.

*Clause 6.2.1.5(7)* refers to some clauses in EN 1993-1-5 that permit mid-plane stresses in steel plates to be used in verifications. For compression parts in Class 3, EN 1993-2 follows clause 6.2.1(9) of EN 1993-1-1. This says:

Compressive stresses should be limited to the yield strength at the extreme fibres.

It is followed by the Note:

> The extreme fibres may be assumed at the midplane of the flanges for ULS checks. For fatigue see EN 1993-1-9.

This concession can be assumed to apply also to composite beams.

An assumption in the effective section method is that there is sufficient post-buckling strength to achieve the necessary redistribution of stress to allow all components to be stressed to their individual resistances. This approach is therefore not permitted (and is not appropriate) in a number of situations where there may not be sufficient post-buckling strength or where the geometry of the member is outside prescribed limits. These exceptions are given in EN 1993-1-5, clause 2.3(1).

Where prestressing is used, *clause 6.2.1.5(8)* limits the stress in tendons to the elastic range and makes reference to clause 5.10.8 of EN 1992-1-1 for guidance on initial prestrain. The latter covers both bonded and unbonded prestress.

*Clause 6.2.1.5(9)* provides an alternative method of treating Class 4 cross-sections using Section 10 of EN 1993-1-5. This method can be used where the conditions of EN 1993-1-5 clause 2.3(1) are not met. Section 10 requires that all stresses are calculated on gross sections and buckling checks are then carried out on the component plates of the cross-section. There is usually economic disadvantage in using this method because the beneficial load shedding of stress around the cross-section implicit in the effective section method does not occur. Additionally, the benefit of using test-based interactions between shear and bending is lost.

If the whole member is prone to overall buckling instability, such as flexural or lateral–torsional buckling, these effects must either be calculated by second-order analysis and the additional stresses included when checking panels or by using a limiting stress $\sigma_{\text{limit}}$ in member buckling checks. For flexural buckling, $\sigma_{\text{limit}}$ can be calculated based on the lowest compressive value of axial stress $\sigma_{x,\text{Ed}}$ acting on its own, required to cause buckling failure in the weakest sub-panel or an entire panel, according to the verification formula in Section 10 of EN 1993-1-5. This value of $\sigma_{\text{limit}}$ is then used to replace $f_y$ in the member buckling check. It is conservative, particularly when the critical panel used to determine $\sigma_{\text{limit}}$ is not at the extreme compression fibre of the section where the greatest stress increase during buckling occurs. For lateral–torsional buckling, $\sigma_{\text{limit}}$ can be determined as the bending stress at the extreme compression fibre needed to cause buckling in the weakest panel. This would however again be very conservative where $\sigma_{\text{limit}}$ was determined from buckling of a web panel which was not at the extreme fibre, as the direct stress in a web panel would not increase much during lateral–torsional buckling.

A detailed discussion of the use of Section 10 of EN 1993-1-5 is given in the *Designers' Guide to EN 1993-2*.[4]

*Clause 6.2.1.5(8)*

*Clause 6.2.1.5(9)*

---

**Example 6.3: elastic bending resistance of a Class 4 cross-section**
For the bridge in Example 5.1 (Fig. 5.6), the mid-span section of the internal beam in Fig. 5.11 continues to the splice adjacent to each pier. The top and bottom layers of reinforcement comprise 16 mm bars at 150 mm centres. There are 20 mm transverse bars, with top and bottom covers of 40 mm and 45 mm respectively, so the locations of the 16 mm bars are as shown in Fig. 6.5. All reinforcement has $f_{sk} = 500\,\text{N/mm}^2$ and $\gamma_S = 1.15$. The steel yield stress is taken as 345 N/mm² throughout.

The cross-section is checked for the ultimate limit state hogging moments adjacent to the splice, which are as follows:

steel beam only: $M_{a,\text{Ed}} = 150\,\text{kNm}$

cracked composite beam: $M_{c,\text{Ed}} = 2600\,\text{kNm}$ (including secondary effects of shrinkage)

By inspection, the cross-section is not in Class 1 or 2 so its classification is checked at the Class 3/4 boundary using elastic stresses.

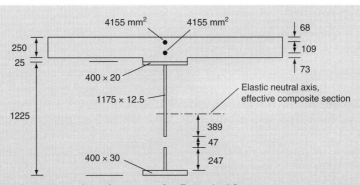

**Fig. 6.5.** Effective section and reinforcement for Example 6.3

*Steel bottom flange*
Ignoring the web-to-flange welds, the flange outstand $c = (400 - 12.5)/2 = 193.8\,\text{mm}$. From Table 5.2 of EN 1993-1-1, the condition for Class 1 is:

$$c/t < 9\varepsilon = 9 \times 0.825 = 7.43$$

For the flange, $c/t = 193.8/30 = 6.46$, so the flange is Class 1.

*Steel web*
The area of each layer of reinforcement is $A_s = \pi \times 64 \times 3100/150 = 4155\,\text{mm}^2$. It would be conservative to assume that all stresses are applied to the composite section as this gives the greatest depth of web in compression. The stresses below are however based on the built-up elastic stresses. The elastic modulus for the reinforcement is taken as equal to *Clause 3.2(2)* that for structural steel, from *clause 3.2(2)*.

The elastic section moduli for the gross cross-section are given in rows 1 and 3 of Table 6.1. The extreme-fibre stresses for the steel section are:

$$\sigma_{a,\text{top}} = 150/12.87 + 2600/25.85 = 112.2\,\text{N/mm}^2 \text{ tension}$$

$$\sigma_{a,\text{bot}} = 150/15.96 + 2600/18.91 = 146.9\,\text{N/mm}^2 \text{ compression}$$

**Table 6.1.** Section moduli for hogging bending of the cross-section of Fig. 6.5, in $10^6\,\text{mm}^3$ units, and height of neutral axis above bottom of section

|  | Section modulus | | | Height of |
|  | Top layer of bars | Top of steel section | Bottom of steel section | neutral axis (mm) |
|---|---|---|---|---|
| Gross steel section | — | 12.87 | 15.96 | 547 |
| Effective steel section | — | 12.90 | 15.77 | 551 |
| Gross composite section | 18.47 | 25.85 | 18.91 | 707 |
| Effective composite section | 18.47 | 25.94 | 18.63 | 713 |

Primary shrinkage stresses are neglected because the deck slab is assumed to be cracked. Using the stresses at the extreme fibres of the web, from Table 5.2 of EN 1993-1-1, the stress ratio is:

$$\psi = -108/140.6 = -0.768$$

and the condition for a Class 3 web is:

$$c/t \le 42\varepsilon/(0.67 + 0.33\psi) = 42 \times 0.825/(0.67 - 0.253) = 83.1$$

Neglecting the widths of the fillet welds, the actual $c/t = 1175/12.5 = 94$, so the composite section is in Class 4 for hogging bending. An effective section must therefore be derived for the web in accordance with *clause 6.2.1.5(7)* using the built-up stresses calculated on the gross cross-section above.

From Table 4.1 of EN 1993-1-5:

$$k_\sigma = 7.81 - 6.29\psi + 9.78\psi^2 = 18.4 \quad \text{for} \quad \psi = -0.768.$$

From clause 4.4(2) of EN 1993-1-5:

$$\bar{\lambda}_p = \frac{\bar{b}/t}{28.4\varepsilon\sqrt{k_\sigma}} = \frac{1175/12.5}{28.4 \times 0.825 \times \sqrt{18.4}} = 0.935 > 0.673$$

so the reduction factor is:

$$\rho = \frac{\bar{\lambda}_p - 0.055(3 + \psi)}{\bar{\lambda}_p^2} = \frac{0.935 - 0.055(3 - 0.768)}{0.935^2} = 0.929$$

$$b_{eff} = \rho\bar{b}/(1 - \psi) = 617\,\text{mm}, \quad b_{e1} = 0.4 \times 617 = 247\,\text{mm}, \quad b_{e2} = 0.6 \times 617 = 370\,\text{mm}$$

Including the 'hole', the depth of web in compression is $b_{eff}/\rho$, which is 664 mm, so the width of the hole is $664 - 617 = 47$ mm. The stress ratio for the web now differs from that for the gross section, but the effect of this on the properties of the net section can be neglected. It is clear from clause 4.4(3) of EN 1993-1-5 that $\psi$ (and hence $\rho$ and $b_{eff}$) need not be recalculated. The level of the elastic neutral axis for this net section is found to be as shown in Table 6.1; consequently, the depth $b_{e2}$ is in fact 389 mm, not 370 mm. The new section moduli are given in rows 2 and 4 of Table 6.1.

The effective section is as shown in Fig. 6.5. The final stresses are as follows:

$$\sigma_{a,top} = 150/12.90 + 2600/25.94 = 111.8\,\text{N/mm}^2 \text{ tension} < 345\,\text{N/mm}^2$$

$$\sigma_{a,bot} = 150/15.77 + 2600/18.63 = 149.1\,\text{N/mm}^2 \text{ compression} < 345\,\text{N/mm}^2$$

$$\sigma_{s,top} = 2600/18.47 = 140.8\,\text{N/mm}^2 < 500/1.15 = 435\,\text{N/mm}^2$$

The stress change caused by the small reduction in web area is negligible in this case.

### Elastic resistance to bending

From *clause 6.2.1.4(6)*, $M_{el,Rd}$ is found by scaling up $M_{c,Ed}$ by a factor $k$ until a stress limit is reached. By inspection of the final stresses, the bottom flange will probably govern. In fact, it does, and:

$$150/15.77 + (2600/18.63)k = 345$$

whence $k = 2.40$, and the elastic resistance moment is:

$$M_{el,Rd} = 150 + 2.40 \times 2600 = \mathbf{6390\,kNm} \text{ (provided that } M_{a,Ed} = 150\,\text{kNm)}$$

## 6.2.2. Resistance to vertical shear

*Clause 6.2.2* is for beams without web encasement. The whole of the vertical shear is usually assumed to be resisted by the steel section, as in previous codes for composite beams. This enables the design rules of EN 1993-1-1 and EN 1993-1-5 to be used. The assumption can be conservative where the slab is in compression. Even where it is in tension and cracked in flexure, consideration of equilibrium shows that the slab must make some contribution to shear resistance, except where the reinforcement has yielded. For solid slabs, the effect is significant where the depth of the steel beam is only twice that of the slab,[66] but diminishes as this ratio increases.

In composite plate girders with vertical stiffeners, the concrete slab can contribute to the anchorage of a tension field in the web,[67] but the shear connectors must then be designed for vertical forces (*clause 6.2.2.3(2)*). The tension field model used in EN 1993-1-5 is discussed in the *Designers' Guide to EN 1993-2*.[4] Since the additional tension field supported by the flanges must be anchored at both upper and lower surfaces of the web, the weaker flange

*Clause 6.2.2*

*Clause 6.2.2.3(2)*

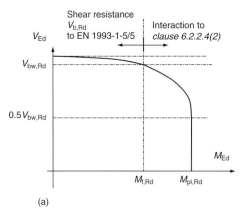
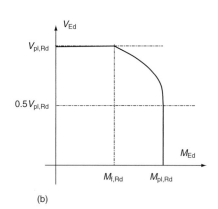

**Fig. 6.6.** Shear–moment interaction for Class 1 and 2 cross-sections (a) with shear buckling and (b) without shear buckling

will govern the contribution of the flanges, $V_{bf,Rd}$, to shear resistance. Comment given later on *clause 6.2.2.5(1)* is relevant here.

*Bending and vertical shear – beams in Class 1 or 2*
Shear stress does not significantly reduce bending resistance unless the shear is quite high. For this reason, the interaction may be neglected until the shear force exceeds half the
**Clause 6.2.2.4(1)** shear resistance (***clause 6.2.2.4(1)***).
**Clause 6.2.2.4(2)** Both EN 1993-1-1 and EN 1994-2 use a parabolic interaction curve. ***Clause 6.2.2.4(2)*** covers the case of Class 1 or 2 cross-sections where the reduction factor for the design yield strength of the web is $(1 - \rho)$, where:

$$\rho = [(2V_{Ed}/V_{Rd}) - 1]^2 \tag{6.5}$$

and $V_{Rd}$ is the resistance in shear (which is either the plastic shear resistance or the shear buckling resistance if lower). The interactions for Class 1 and 2 cross-sections with and without shear buckling are shown in Fig. 6.6.

For a web where the shear buckling resistance is less than the plastic shear resistance and $M_{Ed} < M_{f,Rd}$, the flanges may make a contribution $V_{bf,Rd}$ to the shear resistance according to EN 1993-1-5 clause 5.4(1). For moments exceeding $M_{f,Rd}$ (the plastic bending resistance ignoring the web), this contribution is zero as at least one flange is fully utilized for bending. $V_{Rd}$ is then equal to $V_{bw,Rd}$. For moments less than $M_{f,Rd}$, $V_{Rd}$ is equal to $V_{bw,Rd} + V_{bf,Rd}$.

This definition of $V_{Rd}$ leads to some inconsistency in *clause 6.2.2.4(2)* as the resistance in bending produced therein can never be less than $M_{f,Rd}$. Where there is shear buckling therefore, it is best to consider that the interaction with bending and shear according to *clause 6.2.2.4(2)* is valid for moments in excess of $M_{f,Rd}$ only. For lower moments, the interaction with shear is covered entirely by the shear check to EN 1993-1-5 clause 5.4(1).

Where a Class 3 cross-section is treated as an equivalent Class 2 section and the design yield strength of the web is reduced to allow for vertical shear, the effect on a section in hogging bending is to increase the depth of web in compression. If the change is small, the hole-in-web model can still be used. For a higher shear force, the new plastic neutral axis may be within the top flange, and the hole-in-web method is inapplicable. The section should then be treated as a Class 3 section.

*Bending and vertical shear – beams in Class 3 or 4*
**Clause 6.2.2.4(3)** If the cross-section is either Class 3 or Class 4, then ***clause 6.2.2.4(3)*** applies and the interaction should be checked using EN 1993-1-5 clause 7.1. This clause is similar to that for Class 1 and 2 sections but an interaction equation is provided. This allows the designer to neglect the interaction between shear and bending moment when the design shear force is less than 50% of the shear buckling resistance based on the web contribution alone. Where the design

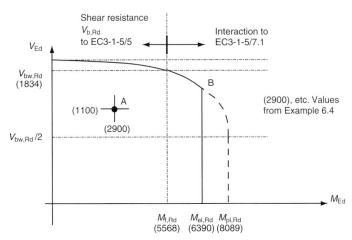

**Fig. 6.7.** Shear–moment interaction for Class 3 and 4 cross-sections to clause 7.1 of EN 1993-1-5

shear force exceeds this value and $M_{Ed} \geq M_{f,Rd}$, the condition to be satisfied is:

$$\bar{\eta}_1 + \left[1 - \frac{M_{f,Rd}}{M_{pl,Rd}}\right](2\bar{\eta}_3 - 1)^2 \leq 1.0 \qquad \text{(7.1) in EN 1993-1-5}$$

where $\bar{\eta}_3$ is the ratio $V_{Ed}/V_{bw,Rd}$ and $\bar{\eta}_1$ is a usage factor for bending, $M_{Ed}/M_{pl,Rd}$, based on the plastic moment resistance of the section. $M_{f,Rd}$ is the design plastic bending resistance based on a section comprising the flanges only. The definition of $M_{f,Rd}$ is discussed under *clause 6.2.2.5(2)* below.

For Class 4 sections, the calculation of $M_{f,Rd}$ and $M_{pl,Rd}$ must consider effective widths for flanges, allowing for plate buckling. $M_{pl,Rd}$ is however calculated using the gross web, regardless of any reduction that might be required for local buckling under direct stress. If axial force is present, EN 1993-1-5 clause 7.1(4) requires appropriate reduction to be made to $M_{f,Rd}$ and $M_{pl,Rd}$. Discussion of axial force is given before Example 6.4.

The interaction for Class 3 and 4 beams is illustrated in Fig. 6.7. The full contribution to the shear resistance from the web, $V_{bw,Rd}$, is obtained at a moment of $M_{f,Rd}$. For smaller moments, the coexisting shear can increase further due to the flange shear contribution, $V_{bf,Rd}$, from clause 5.4 of EN 1993-1-5, provided that the web contribution is less than the plastic resistance. The applied bending moment must additionally not exceed the elastic bending resistance; that is, the accumulated stress must not exceed one of the limits in *clause 6.2.1.5(2)*. This truncates the interaction diagram in Fig. 6.7 at a moment of $M_{el,Rd}$. The moment must also not exceed that for lateral–torsional buckling.

The value of $M_{Ed}$ for use in the interaction with Class 3 and 4 cross-sections is not clearly defined. *Clause 6.2.2.4(3)* states only that EN 1993-1-5 clause 7.1 is applicable '*using the calculated stresses of the composite section*'. These stresses are dependent on the sequence of construction and can include self-equilibrating stresses such as those from shrinkage which contribute no net moment. There was no problem with interpretation in earlier drafts as $\eta_1$, the accumulated stress divided by the appropriate stress limit, was used in the interaction rather than $\bar{\eta}_1$.

For compatibility with the use of $M_{pl,Rd}$ in the interaction expression (based on the cross-section at the time considered) it is recommended here that $M_{Ed}$ is taken as the greatest value of $(\Sigma\sigma_i)W$, where $\Sigma\sigma_i$ is the total accumulated stress at an extreme fibre and $W$ is the elastic modulus of the effective section at the same fibre at the time considered. This bending moment, when applied to the cross-section at the time considered, produces stresses at the extreme fibres which are at least as great as those accumulated.

The reason for the use of plastic bending properties in the interaction for Class 3 and Class 4 beams needs some explanation. Test results on symmetric bare steel beams with Class 3 and Class 4 webs[68] and also computer simulations on composite bridge beams with unequal flanges[69] showed very weak interaction with shear. The former physical tests showed virtually no interaction at all and the latter typically showed some minor interaction only after 80% of the shear resistance had been reached. The use of a plastic resistance moment in the interaction helps to force this observed behaviour as seen in Fig. 6.7.

No distinction is made for beams with longitudinally stiffened webs, which can have less post-buckling strength when overall web panel buckling is critical. There are limited test results for such beams and the approach leads to an interaction with shear only at very high percentages of the web shear resistance. A safe option is to replace $\bar{\eta}_1$ by $\eta_1$ in the interaction expression. For composite beams with longitudinally stiffened webs, $\eta_1$ can be interpreted as the usage factor based on accumulated stress and the stress limits in *clause 6.2.1.5(2)*.

Various theories for post-critical behaviour in shear of webs in Class 3 or 4 under combined bending and vertical shear have been compared with 22 test results from composite beams.[69] It was found that the method of EN 1993-1-5 gives good predictions for web panels of width/depth ratio exceeding 1.5, and is conservative for shorter panels.

Checks of bare steel flanges of box girders are covered in the *Designers' Guide to EN 1993-2*.[4] For open steel boxes, clause 7.1(5) of EN 1993-1-5 clearly does not apply to the reinforced concrete top flange. For composite flanges, this clause should be applied to the steel part of the composite flange, but the effective area of the steel part may be taken as the gross area (reduced for shear lag if applicable) for all loads applied after the concrete flange has been cast, provided that the shear connectors are spaced in accordance with *Table 9.1*. Shear buckling need not be considered in the calculation of $\bar{\eta}_3$. Since most continuous box-girder bridges will be in Class 3 or 4 at supports, the restriction to elastic bending resistance forced by clause 7.1(5) of EN 1993-1-5 should not be unduly conservative. The use of elastic analysis also facilitates addition of any distortional warping and transverse distortional bending stresses developed.

*Bending and vertical shear – all Classes*

Clause 6.2.2.4(4)

*Clause 6.2.2.4(4)* confirms that when the depth of web in compression is increased to allow for shear, the resulting change in the plastic neutral axis should be ignored when classifying the web. The reduction of steel strength to represent the effect on bending resistance of shear is only a model to match test results. To add the sophistication of reclassifying the cross-section would be an unjustified complexity. The scatter of data for section classification further makes reclassification unjustified. The issue of reclassification does not arise when using EN 1993-1-5 clause 7.1 as the interaction with shear is given by an interaction expression. The movement of the neutral axis is never determined.

Clause 6.2.2.5(1)

*Clause 6.2.2.5(1)* refers to the contribution of flanges to the resistance of the web to buckling in shear. It permits the contribution of the flange in EN 1993-1-5 clause 5.4(1) to be based on the bare steel flange even if it has the larger plastic moment resistance. It implies that where this is done, the weaker flange is being assisted by the concrete slab in anchoring the tension field. From *clause 6.2.2.3(2)*, the shear connection should then be designed for the relevant vertical force. This additional check can be avoided by neglecting the concrete contribution in calculating $V_{\text{bf,Rd}}$.

Clause 6.2.2.5(2)

The plastic bending resistance of the flanges, $M_{\text{f,Rd}}$, is defined in *clause 6.2.2.5(2)* for composite sections as the design plastic resistance of the effective section excluding the steel web. This implies a plastic neutral axis within the stronger flange (usually the composite one). Clause 7.1(3) of EN 1993-1-5 allows $M_{\text{f,Rd}}$ to be taken as the product of the strength of the weaker flange and 'the distance between the centroids of the flanges'. This gives a slightly lower result for a composite beam than application of the rule in EN 1994-2. The definition in EN 1994-2 is in fact also used in EN 1993-1-5, clauses 5.4(2) and 7.1(1).

It is stated in clause 7.1(1) of EN 1993-1-5 that the interaction expression for bending and shear is valid only where $\bar{\eta}_1 \geq M_{\text{f,Rd}}/M_{\text{pl,Rd}}$. From the definition of $\bar{\eta}_1$, this condition is $M_{\text{Ed}} \geq M_{\text{f,Rd}}$. Where it is not satisfied (as in Example 6.5), the bending moment $M_{\text{Ed}}$ can be resisted entirely by the flanges of the section. The web is not involved, so there is no interaction between bending and shear unless the shear resistance is to be enhanced by the flange contribution in EN 1993-1-5, clause 5.4. In such cases, the check on interaction between bending and shear is effectively carried out using that clause as illustrated in Figs 6.6 and 6.7. No such condition is stated for $\eta_1$, so it should not be applied when $\bar{\eta}_1$ is replaced by $\eta_1$ when required by clause 7.1(5) of EN 1993-1-5.

*Effect of compressive axial force*
*Clause 6.2.2.5(1)* makes clear that 'axial force' means a force $N_{Ed}$ acting on the composite cross-section, or an axial force $N_{a,Ed}$ applied to the steel element before the member becomes composite. It is not the axial force in the steel element that contributes to the bending resistance of a composite beam.

For Class 1 or 2 cross-sections, the resistance to bending, shear and axial force should be determined by first reducing the design yield strength of the web in accordance with *clause 6.2.2.4(2)* and then checking the resulting cross-section under bending and axial force.

For Class 3 or 4 cross-sections, clause 7.1(4) of EN 1993-1-5 is also relevant. This effectively requires the plastic bending resistance $M_{pl,Rd}$ in the interaction expression of EN 1993-1-5 clause 7.1(1) to be reduced to $M_{pl,N,Rd}$ (using the notation of *clause 6.7.3.6*) where axial force is present. The resistance $M_{f,Rd}$ should be reduced by the factor in clause 5.4(2) of EN 1993-1-5, which is as follows:

$$\left[1 - \frac{N_{Ed}}{(A_{f1} + A_{f2})f_{yf}/\gamma_{M0}}\right] \qquad \text{(5.9) in EN 1993-1-5}$$

This is written for bare steel beams and $A_{f1}$ and $A_{f2}$ are the areas of the steel flanges. These are assumed here to be resisting the whole of the force $N_{Ed}$, presumably because in this tension-field model, the web is fully used already.

For composite beams in hogging zones, equation (5.9) above could be replaced by:

$$\left[1 - \frac{N_{Ed}}{(A_{f1} + A_{f2})f_{yf}/\gamma_{M0} + A_s f_{sd}}\right] \qquad \text{(D6.2)}$$

where $A_s$ is the area of the longitudinal reinforcement in the top slab.

For sagging bending, the shear force is unlikely to be high enough to reduce the resistance to axial force and bending. On the assumption that the axial force is applied only to the composite section, the value of $M_{Ed}$ to use in the interaction expression can be derived from the accumulated stresses as suggested above for checking combined bending and shear, but the uniform stress component from the axial force should not be considered in calculating $\Sigma\sigma_i$. If the axial force, determined as acting at the elastic centroid of the composite section, acts at another level in the model used for the resistance, the moment arising from this change in its line of action should be included in $M_{Ed}$. This is illustrated in Example 6.5.

Clause 7.1(4) and (5) of EN 1993-1-5 requires that where axial force is present such that the whole web is in compression, $M_{f,Rd}$ should be taken as zero in the interaction expression, and $\bar{\eta}_1$ should be replaced by $\eta_1$ (which is defined in EN 1993-1-5 clause 4.6). This leads to the interaction diagram shown in Fig. 6.8. The limit $\bar{\eta}_1 \geq M_{f,Rd}/M_{pl,Rd}$ for validity of expression

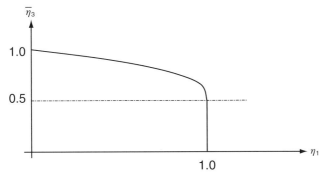

**Fig. 6.8.** Shear–moment interaction for Class 3 and 4 cross-sections with webs fully in compression

(7.1) given in EN 1993-1-5 clause 7.1(1) is not applicable in this case. The expression is applicable where $\eta_1 \geq 0$.

The application of this requirement is unclear for beams built in stages. These could have axial load applied separately to the bare steel section and to the composite section. A safe interpretation, given the relatively small amount of testing on asymmetric sections, would be to take $M_{f,Rd}$ as zero wherever the whole web is in compression under the built-up stresses. For composite bridges, $\eta_1$ can be interpreted as the usage factor based on accumulated stress and the stress limits in *clause 6.2.1.5(2)*. However, this is likely to be conservative at high shear, given the weak interaction between bending and shear found in the tests on composite beams discussed above.

### Vertical shear in a concrete flange

Clause 6.2.2.5(3)  *Clause 6.2.2.5(3)* gives the resistance to vertical shear in a concrete flange of a composite beam (represented here by a design shear strength, $v_{Rd,c}$) by reference to clause 6.2.2 of EN 1992-2. That clause is intended mainly to enable higher shear strengths to be used in the presence of in-plane prestress. A Note in EN 1992-2 recommends values for its three nationally determined parameters (NDPs). Where the flange is in tension, as in a continuous composite beam, the reduced strengths obtained can be over-conservative. In EN 1994-2, the Note recommends different NDPs, based on recent research.[70] With these values, and for effective slab depths $d$ of at least 200 mm and $\gamma_C = 1.5$, the rules are:

$$v_{Rd,c} = 0.10\left(1 + \sqrt{\frac{200}{d}}\right)(100\rho f_{ck})^{1/3} + 0.12\sigma_{cp} \qquad (a)$$

and

$$v_{Rd,c} \geq 0.035\left(1 + \sqrt{\frac{200}{d}}\right)^{3/2} f_{ck}^{1/2} + 0.12\sigma_{cp} \qquad (b)$$

where: $\rho = A_s/bd \leq 0.02$

$$\sigma_{cp} = N_{Ed}/A_c < 0.2f_{cd} \text{ (compression positive)} \qquad (c)$$

and $N_{Ed}$ is the in-plane axial force (negative if tensile) in the slab of breadth $b$ and with tensile reinforcement $A_s$, and $f_{ck}$ is in N/mm$^2$ units.

It can be inferred from Fig. 6.3 in EN 1992-2 that $A_s$ is the reinforcement in tension under the loading 'which produces the shear force considered' (a wording that is used in clause 5.3.3.2 of BS 5400-4). Thus, for shear from a wheel load, only one layer of reinforcement (top or bottom, as appropriate) is relevant, even though both layers may be resisting global tension.

It thus appears from equation (a) that the shear strength depends on the tensile force in the slab. This awkward interaction is usually avoided, because EN 1994-2 gives a further research-based recommendation, that where $\sigma_{cp}$ is tensile, it should not be taken as greater than 1.85 N/mm$^2$. The effect of this is now illustrated, with $d = 200$ mm.

Let the reinforcement ratios be $\rho_1 = 0.010$ for the 'tensile reinforcement', $\rho_2 = 0.005$ for the other layer, with $f_{ck} = 40$ N/mm$^2$, and $\sigma_{cp} = -1.85$ N/mm$^2$. From equation (a) above:

$$v_{Rd,c} = 0.1 \times 2(1.0 \times 40)^{1/3} - 0.12 \times 1.85 = 0.68 - 0.22 = 0.46 \text{ N/mm}^2$$

and equation (b) does not govern. From equation (c) with values of $\sigma_{cp}$, $N_{Ed}$ and $f_s$ all negative:

$$\sigma_{cp} = N_{Ed}/A_c = \Sigma(f_s A_s)/A_c = f_s(0.01 + 0.005)bd/bh = 0.015f_s d/h$$

where the summation is for both layers of reinforcement, because $\sigma_{cp}$ is the mean tensile stress in the slab if uncracked and unreinforced.

For $h = 250$ mm, the stress $\sigma_{cp}$ then reaches $-1.85$ N/mm$^2$ when the mean tensile stress in the reinforcement is 154 N/mm$^2$, which is a low value in practice. At higher values, $v_{Rd,c}$ is independent of the tensile force in the slab, though the resulting shear strength is usually lower than that from BS 5400-4.

In the transverse direction, $N_{Ed}$ is zero unless there is composite action in both directions, so for checking punching shear, two different shear strengths may be relevant.

**Example 6.4: resistance of a Class 4 section to hogging bending and vertical shear**

The cross-section in Example 6.3 (Fig. 6.5) is checked for resistance to a vertical shear force of 1100 kN, combined with bending moments $M_{a,Ed} = 150$ kNm and

$$M_{c,Ed} = 2600 \text{ kNm}$$

From clause 6.2.6(6) of EN 1993-1-1, resistance to shear buckling should be checked if:

$$h_w/t_w > 72\varepsilon/\eta$$

where $\eta$ is a factor for which a Note to clause 5.1.2 of EN 1993-1-5 recommends the value 1.2. For S355 steel and a 12.5 mm thick web plate, $\varepsilon = 0.81$, so:

$$h_w\eta/t_w\varepsilon = 1175 \times 1.2/(12.5 \times 0.81) = 139 > 72$$

The resistance of this unstiffened web to shear buckling is found using clauses 5.2 and 5.3 of EN 1993-1-5. The transverse stiffeners provided at the cross-bracings are conservatively ignored, as is the contribution from the flanges. For stiffeners at supports only, the slenderness is obtained from EN 1993-1-5 equation (5.5):

$$\overline{\lambda}_w = \frac{h_w}{86.4t\varepsilon} = \frac{1175}{86.4 \times 12.5 \times 0.81} = 1.343$$

Away from an end support, the column 'rigid end post' in Table 5.1 of EN 1993-1-5 applies, so:

$$\chi_w = \frac{1.37}{0.7 + \overline{\lambda}_w} = \frac{1.37}{0.7 + 1.343} = 0.67$$

From EN 1993-1-5 equation (5.2):

$$V_{bw,Rd} = \frac{\chi_w f_{yw} h_w t}{\sqrt{3}\gamma_{M1}} = \frac{0.67 \times 355 \times 1175 \times 12.5}{\sqrt{3} \times 1.1} = \mathbf{1834 \text{ kN}}$$

The shear ratio $\overline{\eta}_3 = 1100/1834 = 0.60$. This exceeds 0.5 so interaction with the hogging bending moment must be considered using EN 1993-1-5, clause 7.1. The resistances $M_{f,Rd}$ and $M_{pl,Rd}$ are first determined for the composite section. *Clause 6.2.2.5(2)* requires $M_{f,Rd}$ to be calculated for the composite section neglecting the web. $M_{pl,Rd}$ is calculated using the gross web, regardless of the reduction for local buckling under direct stress. From section analysis, using $f_{yd} = 345$ N/mm$^2$ throughout:

$$M_{f,Rd} = \mathbf{5568 \text{ kNm}}$$

$$M_{pl,Rd} = \mathbf{8089 \text{ kNm}}$$

The applied bending moment $M_{Ed}$ is taken as the greatest value of $(\Sigma\sigma_i)W$, as explained earlier. Using stresses from Example 6.3 and section moduli from Table 6.1, the values of $M_{Ed}$ for the extreme fibres of the steel beam are as follows:

top flange: $M_{Ed} = 111.8 \times 25.94 = \mathbf{2900 \text{ kNm}}$, which governs
bottom flange: $M_{Ed} = 149.1 \times 18.63 = 2778$ kNm

The bending ratio $\overline{\eta}_1 = 2900/8089 = 0.359$.

This is less than the ratio $M_{f,Rd}/M_{pl,Rd}$, which is 0.69, so there is no interaction between bending and shear.

To illustrate the use of interaction expression (7.1) of EN 1993-1-5, let us assume that $M_{Ed}$ is increased, such that $\overline{\eta}_1 = 0.75$, with $\overline{\eta}_3 = 0.60$ as before. Then:

$$\overline{\eta}_1 + \left[1 - \frac{M_{f,Rd}}{M_{pl,Rd}}\right](2\overline{\eta}_3 - 1)^2 = 0.75 + \left[1 - \frac{5568}{8089}\right](2 \times 0.60 - 1)^2 = 0.762 \tag{D6.3}$$

The original action effects are shown as point A in Fig. 6.7. This lies below point B, showing that in this case, the vertical shear does not reduce the resistance to bending.

The check of $\eta_1$ also required by the reference in clause 7.1(1) of EN 1993-1-5 to its clause 4.6 is covered in Example 6.3. The ratio $\eta_1$ is the greatest usage based on accumulated stress, which is $149.5/345 = 0.43$ at the bottom flange. If the moment–shear interaction above is checked conservatively using $\eta_1$, equation (D6.3) becomes:

$$\frac{M_{Ed}}{M_{el,Rd}} + \left[1 - \frac{5568}{8089}\right](2 \times 0.60 - 1)^2 \le 1, \quad \text{or} \quad M_{Ed} \le 0.988 M_{el,Rd}$$

thus giving a slight reduction to the bending resistance. This reduction will always occur when $\bar{\eta}_3 > 0.5$ is used in this interaction expression as can be seen from Fig. 6.8.

### Example 6.5: addition of axial compression to a Class 4 cross-section

The effect of adding an axial compression $N_{Ed} = 4.8\,\text{MN}$ to the composite cross-section studied in Examples 6.3 and 6.4 is now calculated, using the method explained earlier. It is assumed that in the global analysis, the beam was located at the level of the long-term elastic neutral axis of the uncracked unreinforced section at mid-span, with $n_L = 23.7$. This is 951 mm (denoted $z_{elu}$) above the bottom of the 1500 mm deep section. Where the neutral axis of the cross-section being verified is at some lower level, $z$, for example, with $N_{Ed}$ acting at that level, the coexisting hogging bending moment should be reduced by $N_{Ed}(z_{elu} - z)$, to allow for the change in the level of $N_{Ed}$.

The composite section, shown in Fig. 6.5, is also subjected, as before, to hogging bending moments $M_{a,Ed} = 150\,\text{kNm}$ and $M_{c,Ed} = 2600\,\text{kNm}$, and to vertical shear $V_{Ed} = 1100\,\text{kN}$. The concrete slab is assumed to be fully cracked.

It was found in Example 6.4 that for the vertical shear, $\bar{\eta}_3 = 0.60$, so the interaction factor $(2\bar{\eta}_3 - 1)^2$ is only 0.04. The first check is therefore on the elastic resistance of the net section to $N_{Ed}$ plus $M_{Ed}$.

If $N_{Ed}$ is assumed to act at the centroid of the net elastic Class 4 section, allowing for the hole, its line of action, and hence $M_{Ed}$, change at each iteration. It will be found that the whole of the effective web is in compression, so that the interaction with shear should be based on $\eta_1$ (accumulated stresses), not on $\bar{\eta}_1$ (action effects and resistances). This enables stresses from $N_{Ed}$ and $M_{Ed}$ to be added, and a non-iterative method to be used, based on separate effective cross-sections for axial force and for bending. This method can always be used as a conservative approach.

*Stresses from axial compression*
For the gross cracked cross-section, $A = 43\,000\,\text{mm}^2$, so:

$$\sigma_a = 4800/43.0 = 112\,\text{N/mm}^2 \text{ compression}$$

From Table 4.1 in EN 1993-1-5, $\quad \psi = 1$ and $k_\sigma = 4.0$

From Example 6.3, for the web, $\quad \bar{b}/t = c/t = 94$

Assuming $f_y = 345\,\text{N/mm}^2$, as in Example 6.1, then $\varepsilon = 0.825$.
From EN 1993-1-5 clause 4.4(2) and Table 4.1:

$$\bar{\lambda}_p = \frac{\bar{b}/t}{28.4\varepsilon\sqrt{k_\sigma}} = \frac{94}{28.4 \times 0.825 \times \sqrt{4.0}} = 2.01$$

$$\rho = \frac{\bar{\lambda}_p - 0.055(3 + \psi)}{\bar{\lambda}_p^2} = \frac{2.01 - 0.055(3 + 1)}{2.01^2} = 0.444$$

$$b_{eff} = \rho\bar{b} = 0.444 \times 1175 = 522\,\text{mm}, \quad \text{so} \quad b_{e1} = b_{e2} = 261\,\text{mm}$$

The depth of the hole in the web is $1175 - 522 = 653\,\text{mm}$.

The net cross-section for axial compression is shown in Fig. 6.9(a). Its net area is:

$$A_{\text{eff,N}} = 43\,000 - 653 \times 12.5 = 34\,840\,\text{mm}^2$$

The compressive stress from $N_{\text{Ed}}$ is $\sigma_{\text{a,N}} = 4800/34.84 = 138\,\text{N/mm}^2$.
The elastic neutral axis of the net section is 729 mm above the bottom, so the change in neutral axis is $\Delta z = 951 - 729 = 222\,\text{mm}^2$, and $N_{\text{Ed}}\,\Delta z = 1066\,\text{kNm}$.

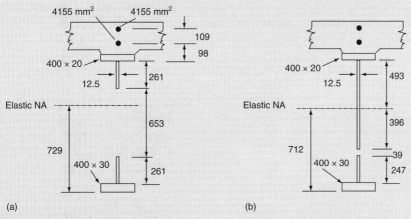

**Fig. 6.9.** Net cross-sections for (a) axial compression and (b) hogging bending

*Stresses from bending moment*
In Example 6.4, $M_{\text{c,Ed}} = 2600\,\text{kNm}$, hogging. The line of action of $N_{\text{Ed}}$ has been moved downwards, so $N_{\text{Ed}}\,\Delta z$ is sagging, and now $M_{\text{c,Ed}} = 2600 - 1066 = 1534\,\text{kNm}$, with $M_{\text{a,Ed}} = 150\,\text{kNm}$, as before.

Using section moduli for the gross cross-section from Example 6.3, the stresses at the edge of the web are:

$$\sigma_{\text{a,top}} = 68.4\,\text{N/mm}^2 \text{ tension}, \quad \sigma_{\text{a,bot}} = 86.5\,\text{N/mm}^2 \text{ compression}$$

Hence,

$$\psi = -68.4/86.5 = -0.790$$

Proceeding as in Example 6.3, the results are as follows:

$$k_\sigma = 18.9, \quad \bar{\lambda}_{\text{p}} = 0.923, \quad \rho = 0.941, \quad b_{\text{eff}} = 618\,\text{mm}, \quad b_{\text{e1}} = 247\,\text{mm}, \quad b_{\text{e2}} = 371\,\text{mm}$$

The hole in the web is 39 mm deep. The effective cross-section is shown in Fig. 6.9(b).
The extreme-fibre stresses from $M_{\text{a,Ed}}$, $M_{\text{c,Ed}}$ and $N_{\text{Ed}}$ respectively are:

$$\sigma_{\text{a,top}} = -(11.6 + 59.1) + 138 = 67\,\text{N/mm}^2$$

$$\sigma_{\text{a,bot}} = +(9.5 + 82.4) + 138 = 230\,\text{N/mm}^2$$

It follows that there is some compression in the deck slab, which has been neglected, for simplicity. The reinforcement is assumed here to carry all the compressive force in the slab.

*Interaction with vertical shear*
The whole of the web is in compression, so from clause 7.1(5) of EN 1993-1-5, $M_{\text{f,Rd}} = 0$ and $\eta_1$, not $\bar{\eta}_1$, is used. For the steel bottom flange, which governs,

$$\eta_1 = 230/345 = 0.67$$

From equation (7.1) of EN 1993-1-5, with $\bar{\eta}_3 = 0.60$ and $M_{\text{f,Rd}} = 0$,

$$\eta_1 + (2\bar{\eta}_3 - 1)^2 = 0.67 + 0.04 = 0.71$$

This is less than 1.0, so the cross-section is verified.

*Method when the web is partly in tension*

This example is now repeated with the axial compression reduced to $N_{Ed} = 2.5\,MN$ and all other data as before, to illustrate the method where $\bar{\eta}_1$ is used and $M_{f,Rd}$ is not zero.

From clause 7.1(4) of EN 1993-1-5, $M_{pl,Rd}$ is reduced to allow for $N_{Ed}$, as follows. For the gross cross-section $M_{pl,Rd} = 8089\,kNm$, and the plastic neutral axis is 876 mm above the bottom. Force $N_{Ed}$ is assumed to act at its level. The depth of web needed to resist it is $h_{w,N} = 2500/(12.5 \times 0.345) = 580\,mm$. This depth is centred on the neutral axis as shown in Fig. 6.10 and remains wholly within the web. Its contribution to $M_{pl,Rd}$ was:

$$(f_{yd}th_{w,N}^2)/4 = 345 \times 12.5 \times 0.58^2/4 = 363\,kNm$$

As its depth is centred on the plastic neutral axis for bending alone,

$$M_{pl,N,Rd} = 8089 - 363 = \mathbf{7726\,kNm}$$

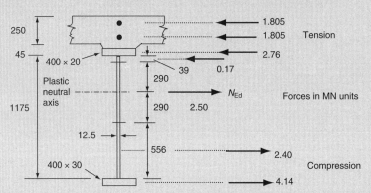

**Fig. 6.10.** Plastic resistance of Class 4 section to hogging bending and axial compression

From Example 6.4, $M_{f,Rd} = 5568\,kNm$. From equation (D6.2) and using forces from Fig. 6.10, the reduction factor that allows for $N_{Ed}$ is:

$$\left[1 - \frac{N_{Ed}}{(A_{f1} + A_{f2})f_{yf}/\gamma_{M0} + A_s f_{sd}}\right] = 1 - \frac{2.50}{2.76 + 4.14 + 2 \times 1.805} = 0.762$$

Hence,

$$M_{f,N,Rd} = 0.762 \times 5568 = \mathbf{4243\,kNm}$$

The bending moment $M_{Ed}$ is found from accumulated stresses, using the Class 4 cross-section for bending. Its elastic properties should strictly be determined with a value for $M_{Ed}$ such that the line of action of $N_{Ed}$ is at the neutral axis of the effective cross-section. This requires iteration. Finally, the line of action of $N_{Ed}$ should be moved to the neutral axis of the plastic section used for the calculation of $M_{pl,Rd}$. This requires a further correction to $M_{Ed}$.

The simpler and sufficiently accurate method used here is to find the Class 4 section properties ignoring any moment from the axial force, to use these to scale up $M_{a,Ed}$, and then to add the correction from $N_{Ed}$. The change in the line of action of $N_{Ed}$ is:

$951 - 876 = 75\,mm$, so $M_{c,Ed} = 2600 - 2500 \times 0.075 = \mathbf{2413\,kNm}$

Calculation similar to that in the section 'Stresses from bending moment', above, finds the depth of the hole in the web to be 322 mm. The top flange is found to govern, and

$$M_{Ed} = M_{a,Ed}(W_{c,top}/W_{a,top}) + M_{c,Ed} = 150 \times 26.6/13.0 + 2413 = \mathbf{2720\,kNm}$$

This bending moment is less than $M_{f,N,Rd}$, so it can be resisted entirely by the flanges, and there is no need to consider interaction with shear in accordance with clause 7.1(1) of EN 1993-1-5.

*Stability of the span in the vertical plane*
Buckling of the whole span in the vertical plane is possible. Its elastic critical axial force is now estimated, treating it as pin-ended, and assuming sagging bending. The modular ratio $n_L = 18.8$ is used, intermediate between the values for short- and long-term loading. The presence of a stiffer cross-section near the supports is ignored.

The result is $N_{cr} = 47\,\text{MN}$. The ratio $\alpha_{cr} = N_{cr}/N_{Ed} = 8.1$ (<10), so from *clause 5.2.1(3)*, second-order effects should be included in $M_{Ed}$. There appears to be a sufficient margin for these, but this has not been checked.

## 6.3. Filler beam decks

### 6.3.1. Scope

The encasement of steel bridge beams in concrete provides several advantages for design:

- It enables a Class 3 web to be upgraded to Class 2, and the slenderness limit for a Class 2 compression flange to be increased by 40% (*clause 5.5.3*).
- It prevents lateral–torsional buckling.
- It prevents shear buckling (*clause 6.3.4(1)*).
- It greatly increases the resistance of the bridge deck to vehicular impact or terrorist attack.

These design advantages may not however lead to the most economic solution. The use of longitudinal filler beams in new construction is not common at present.

There are a great number of geometric, material and workmanship-related restrictions given in *clauses 6.3.1(1) to (4)* which have to be met in order to use the application rules for the design of filler beams. These are necessary because the rules derive mainly from existing practice in the UK and from clause 8 of BS 5400:Part 5.[11] No explicit check of the shear connection between steel beams and concrete (provided by friction and bond only) is required.

*Clause 6.3.1(1)* excludes fully-encased filler beams from the scope of *clause 6.3*. This is because there are no widely-accepted design rules for longitudinal shear in fully-encased beams without shear connectors.

*Clause 6.3.1(2)* requires the beams to be of uniform cross-section and to have a web depth and flange width within the ranges found for rolled H- or I-sections. This is due to the lack of existing examples of filler beams with cross-sections other than these. There is no requirement for the beams to be H- or I-sections, but hollow sections would be outside the scope of *clause 6.3*.

*Clause 6.3.1(3)* permits spans to be either simply supported or continuous with square or skew supports. This clarification is based on existing practice, and takes account of the many other restrictions.

*Clause 6.3.1(4)* contains the majority of the restrictions which relate mainly to ensuring the adequacy of the bond between steel beam and concrete, as follows.

Clause 6.3.1(1)

Clause 6.3.1(2)

Clause 6.3.1(3)

Clause 6.3.1(4)

- Steel beams should not be curved in plan. This is because the torsion produced would lead to additional bond stresses between the structural steel and concrete, for which no application rules are available.
- The deck skew should not exceed 30°. This limits the magnitude of torsional moments, which can become large with high skew.
- The nominal depth, $h$, of the beam should lie between 210 mm and 1100 mm. This is because anything less than 210 mm should be treated as reinforced concrete, and there could in future be rolled sections deeper than 1100 mm.
- A maximum spacing of the steel beams is set: the lesser of $h/3 + 600\,\text{mm}$ and 750 mm. This reflects existing practice and limits the longitudinal shear flow (and bond stresses) between the concrete and the steel beam.
- The minimum concrete cover to the top of the steel beams is restricted to 70 mm. A larger value may however be necessary to provide adequate cover to the reinforcement. The

maximum cover is limited to the lesser of 150 mm and $h/3$, based on existing practice and to limit the longitudinal shear stress developed.

A further restriction is given such that the plastic neutral axis for sagging bending remains below the level of the bottom of the top flange, since cracking of the concrete in the vicinity of the top flange could reduce the bond stress developed. This rule could only govern where the steel beams were unusually small. The side cover to the top flange should be at least 80 mm.

- The clear distance between top flanges should not be less than 150 mm so that the concrete can be adequately compacted. This is essential to ensure that the required bond to the steel is obtained.
- Bottom transverse reinforcement should be provided (through holes in the beam webs) such that transverse moments developed can be carried. A minimum bar size and maximum spacing are specified. Minimum reinforcement, here and elsewhere, should also satisfy the requirements of EN 1992.
- Normal-density concrete should be used. This is because there is little experience of filler-beam construction with concrete other than normal-density, where the bond characteristics could be affected.
- The flange should be de-scaled. This again is to ensure good bond between the concrete and the steel beam.
- For road and railway bridges the holes in steel webs should be drilled. This is discussed under *clause 6.3.2(2)*.

### 6.3.2. General

*Clause 6.3.2(1)*

*Clause 6.3.2(1)* refers to other clauses for the cross-section checks, which should be conducted at ultimate and serviceability limit states. These references do not require a check of torsion as discussed below.

*Clause 6.3.2(2)*

*Clause 6.3.2(2)* requires beams with bolted connections or welding to be checked against fatigue. The implication is that filler beams without these need not be checked for fatigue, even though they will contain stress-raising holes through which the transverse reinforcement passes. For road and railway bridges, where fatigue loading is significant, *clause 6.3.1(4)* requires that all holes in webs are drilled (rather than punched), which improves the fatigue category of the detail.

*Clause 6.3.2(3)*

*Clause 6.3.2(3)* is a reminder to refer to the relaxations for cross-section Class in *clause 5.5.3*.

*Clause 6.3.2(4)*

Mechanical shear connection need not be provided for filler beams (*clause 6.3.2(4)*). This reliance on bond improves the relative economy of filler-beam construction but leads to many of the restrictions noted above under *clause 6.3.1*.

### 6.3.3. Bending moments

*Clause 6.3.3(1)*

The resistance of cross-sections to bending, *clause 6.3.3(1)*, is determined in the same way as for uncased sections of the same Class, with Class determined in accordance with *clause 5.5.3*. The relaxations in *clause 5.5.3* should generally ensure that beams can be designed plastically and thus imposed deformations generally need not be considered at ultimate limit states (the comments made under *clause 5.4.2.2(6)* refer).

Lateral–torsional buckling is not mentioned in *clause 6.3.3(1)* because a filler-beam deck is inherently stable against lateral–torsional buckling in its completed state due to its large transverse stiffness. The steel beams are likely to be susceptible during construction and the title of *clause 6.3.5* provides a warning.

For the influence of vertical shear on resistance to bending, reference is made to the rules for uncased beams. The shear resistance of filler-beam decks is high, so interaction is unlikely, but it should be checked for continuous spans.

*Clause 6.3.3(2)*

In the transverse direction, a filler-beam deck behaves as a reinforced concrete slab. *Clause 6.3.3(2)* therefore makes reference to EN 1992-2 for the bending resistance in the transverse direction. A Note to clause 9.1(103) of EN 1992-2 makes minimum reinforcement a nationally determined parameter.

No requirement is given for a check on torsion, which will be produced to some degree in both longitudinal and transverse directions of the global analysis models allowed by *clause 5.4.2.9(3)*. Neglect of torsion is justified by the limits imposed on geometry in *clause 6.3.1(4)*, particularly the limit on skew angle, and by current UK practice.

### 6.3.4. Vertical shear
The simplest calculation of shear resistance involves basing the resistance on that of the steel beam alone. *Clause 6.3.4(1)* indicates that this resistance can be calculated using the plastic shear resistance and so ignoring shear buckling. The clause does permit a contribution from the concrete to be taken. *Clauses 6.3.4(2)* and *6.3.4(3)*, respectively, cover a method of determining the shear force that may be carried on the reinforced concrete section and the determination of the resistance of this concrete section. *Clause 6.3.4(3)* applies also to shear resistance in the transverse direction.

*Clause 6.3.4(1)*

*Clause 6.3.4(2)*
*Clause 6.3.4(3)*

### 6.3.5. Resistance and stability of steel beams during execution
*Clause 6.3.5(1)* refers to EN 1993-1-1 and EN 1993-2 for the check of the bare steel beams. This covers both cross-section resistance and lateral–torsional buckling. The latter is an important consideration prior to hardening of the concrete.

*Clause 6.3.5(1)*

# 6.4. Lateral–torsional buckling of composite beams
## 6.4.1. General
It is assumed in this section that in completed bridges, the steel top flanges of all composite beams will be stabilized laterally by connection to a concrete or composite slab (*clause 6.4.1(1)*). The rules on maximum spacing of connectors in *clause 6.6.5.5(1)* and *(2)* relate to the classification of the top flange, and thus only to local buckling. For lateral–torsional buckling, the relevant rule, given in *clause 6.6.5.5(3)*, is less restrictive.

*Clause 6.4.1(1)*

Any steel top flange in compression that is not so stabilized should be checked for lateral buckling (*clause 6.4.1(2)*) using clause 6.3.2 of EN 1993-1-1 to determine the reduction factor for buckling. For completed bridges, this applies to the bottom flange adjacent to intermediate supports in continuous construction. In a composite beam, the concrete slab provides lateral restraint to the steel member, and also restrains its rotation about a longitudinal axis. Lateral buckling is always associated with distortion (change of shape) of the cross-section (Fig. 6.11(b)). This is not true 'lateral–torsional' buckling and is often referred to as 'distortional lateral' buckling. This form of buckling is covered by *clauses 6.4.2* and *6.4.3*. The general method of *clause 6.4.2*, based on the use of a computed value of the elastic critical moment $M_{cr}$, is applicable, but no detailed guidance on the calculation of $M_{cr}$ is given in either EN 1993-1-1 or EN 1994-2.

*Clause 6.4.1(2)*

For completed bridges, the bottom flange may be in compression over most of a span when that span is relatively short and lightly loaded and adjacent spans are fully loaded. Bottom flanges in compression should always be restrained laterally at supports. It should not be assumed that a point of contraflexure is equivalent to a lateral restraint.

Design methods for composite beams must take account of the bending of the web, Fig. 6.11(b). They differ in detail from the method of clause 6.3.2 of EN 1993-1-1, but the same imperfection factors and buckling curves are used, in the absence of any better-established alternatives.

The reference in *clause 6.4.1(3)* to EN 1993-1-1 provides a general method for use where the method in *clause 6.4.2* is inapplicable (e.g. for a Class 4 beam). *Clause 6.4.3* makes a similar reference but adds a reference to a further method available in clause 6.3.4.2 of EN 1993-2. During unpropped construction, prior to the presence of a hardened deck slab, the buckling verification can be more complicated and often involves overall buckling

*Clause 6.4.1(3)*

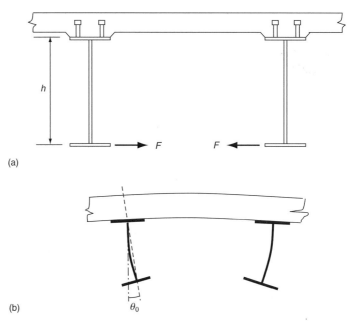

(a)

(b) $\theta_0$

**Fig. 6.11.** (a) U-frame action and (b) distortional lateral buckling

of a braced pair of beams. This situation is discussed further at the end of section 6.4.3.2 of this guide.

### 6.4.2. Beams in bridges with uniform cross-sections in Class 1, 2 and 3

This general method of design is written with distortional buckling of bottom flanges in mind. It would not apply, for example, to a mid-span cross-section of a beam with the slab at bottom-flange level (Fig. 6.12). The reference to 'uniform cross-section' in the title of the clause is not intended to exclude minor changes such as reinforcement details and effects of cracking of concrete. The method cannot be used for Class 4 cross-sections, which is a significant limitation for larger bridges, in which case the methods of *clause 6.4.3* should be used. The latter methods are more general.

The method is based closely on clause 6.3.2 of EN 1993-1-1. There is correspondence in the definitions of the reduction factor $\chi_{LT}$, *clause 6.4.2(1)*, and the relative slenderness, $\bar{\lambda}_{LT}$, *clause 6.4.2(4)*. The reduction factor is applied to the design resistance moment $M_{Rd}$, which is defined in *clauses 6.4.2(2)* and *(3)*. Expressions for $M_{Rd}$ are given by references to *clause 6.2*. It should be noted that these include the design yield strength $f_{yd}$ which should, in this case, be calculated using $\gamma_{M1}$ rather than $\gamma_{M0}$ because this is a check of instability. If the beam is found not to be susceptible to lateral–torsional buckling (i.e. $\chi_{LT} = 1.0$), it would be reasonable to replace $\gamma_{M1}$ with $\gamma_{M0}$.

The determination of $M_{Rd}$ for a Class 3 section differs from that of $M_{el,Rd}$ in *clause 6.2.1.4(6)* only in that the limiting stress $f_{cd}$ for concrete in compression need not be considered. It is necessary to take account of the method of construction.

The buckling resistance moment $M_{b,Rd}$ given by *equation (6.6)* must exceed the highest applied moment $M_{Ed}$ within the unbraced length of compression flange considered.

*Clause 6.4.2(1)*

*Clause 6.4.2(2)*
*Clause 6.4.2(3)*

**Fig. 6.12.** Example of a composite beam with the slab in tension at mid-span

*Lateral buckling for a Class 3 cross-section with unpropped construction*
The influence of method of construction on verification of a Class 3 composite section for lateral buckling is as follows. From *equation (6.4)*,

$$M_{Rd} = M_{el,Rd} = M_{a,Ed} + kM_{c,Ed} \qquad\qquad (a)$$

where subscript c is used for the action effect on the composite member.
From *equation (6.6)*, the verification is:

$$M_{Ed} = M_{a,Ed} + M_{c,Ed} \leq \chi_{LT}M_{el,Rd} \qquad\qquad (b)$$

which is:

$$\chi_{LT} \geq (M_{a,Ed} + M_{c,Ed})/M_{el,Rd} = M_{Ed}/M_{el,Rd} \qquad\qquad (c)$$

The total hogging bending moment $M_{Ed}$ may be almost independent of the method of construction. However, the stress limit that determines $M_{el,Rd}$ may be different for propped and unpropped construction. If it is bottom-flange compression in both cases, then $M_{el,Rd}$ is lower for unpropped construction, and the limit on $\chi_{LT}$ from equation (c) is more severe.

*Elastic critical buckling moment*
***Clause 6.4.2(4)*** requires the determination of the elastic critical buckling moment, taking account of the relevant restraints, so their stiffnesses have to be calculated. The lateral restraint from the slab can usually be assumed to be rigid. Where the structure is such that a pair of steel beams and a concrete flange attached to them can be modelled as an inverted-U frame (***clause 6.4.2(5)*** and *Fig. 6.10*), continuous along the span, the rotational restraining stiffness at top-flange level, $k_s$, can be found from ***clause 6.4.2(6)***. In the definition of stiffness $k_s$, flexibility arises from two sources:

*Clause 6.4.2(4)*

*Clause 6.4.2(5)*
*Clause 6.4.2(6)*

- bending of the slab, which may not be negligible: $1/k_1$ from *equation (6.9)*
- bending of the steel web, which predominates: $1/k_2$ from *equation (6.10)*.

A third source of flexibility is potentially the shear connection but it has been found[71] that this can be neglected providing the requirements of *clause 6.4.2(5)* are met.

There is a similar 'discrete U-frame' concept, which appears to be relevant to composite beams where the steel sections have vertical web stiffeners. The shear connectors closest to those stiffeners would then have to transmit almost the whole of the bending moment *Fh* (Fig. 6.11(a)), where *F* is now a force on a discrete U-frame. The flexibility of the shear connection may then not be negligible, nor is it certain that the shear connection and the adjacent slab would be sufficiently strong.[72] Where stiffeners are present, the resistance of the connection above each stiffener to repeated transverse bending should be established, as there is a risk of local shear failure within the slab. There is at present no simple method of verification. This is the reason for the condition that the web should be unstiffened in *clause 6.4.2(5)(b)*. The restriction need not apply if bracings (flexible or rigid) are attached to the stiffeners, but in this case the model referred to in *clause 6.4.3.2* would be used.

***Clause 6.4.2(7)*** allows the St Venant torsional stiffness to be included in the calculation. This is often neglected in lateral–torsional buckling models based on buckling of the bottom chord, such as that provided in EN 1993-2 clause 6.3.4.2.

*Clause 6.4.2(7)*

No formula is provided for the elastic critical buckling moment for the U-frame model described above. $M_{cr}$ could be determined from a finite-element model of the beam with a lateral and torsional restraint as set out above. Alternatively, textbook solutions could be used. One such method was given in Annex B of ENV 1994-1-1[20] and is now in the *Designers' Guide to EN 1994-1-1*.[5]

## 6.4.3. General methods for buckling of members and frames
### 6.4.3.1. General method
Reference is made to EN 1993-2 clause 6.3.4 where the method of *clause 6.4.2* for beams or the non-linear method of *clause 6.7* for columns does not apply.

EN 1993-1-1 clause 6.3.4 gives a general method of evaluating the combined effect of axial load and mono-axial bending applied in the plane of the structure, without use of an interaction expression. The method is valid for asymmetric and non-uniform members and also for entire plane frames. In principle, this method is more realistic since the structure or member does, in reality, buckle in a single mode with a single 'system slenderness'. Interaction formulae assume separate modes under each individual action with different slendernesses that have to subsequently be combined to give an overall verification. The disadvantage is that software capable of both elastic critical buckling analysis and second-order analysis is required. Additionally, shell elements will be needed to determine elastic critical modes resulting from flexural loading.

An alternative method is to use second-order analysis with imperfections to cover both in-plane and out-of-plane buckling effects as discussed in sections 5.2 and 5.3 of this guide, but this has the same difficulties as above.

The basic verification is performed by determining a single slenderness for out-of-plane buckling, which can include combined lateral and lateral–torsional buckling. This slenderness is a slenderness for the whole system and applies to all members included within it. It takes the usual Eurocode form as follows:

$$\bar{\lambda}_{op} = \sqrt{\frac{\alpha_{ult,k}}{\alpha_{cr,op}}}$$

(6.64) in EN 1993-1-1

where: $\alpha_{ult,k}$ is the minimum load factor applied to the design loads required to reach the characteristic resistance of the most critical cross-section ignoring out-of-plane buckling but including moments from second-order effects and imperfections in-plane, and

$\alpha_{cr,op}$ is the minimum load factor applied to the design loads required to give elastic critical buckling in an out-of-plane mode, ignoring in-plane buckling.

The first stage of calculation requires an analysis to be performed to determine $\alpha_{ult,k}$. In-plane second-order effects and imperfections must be included in the analysis because they are not otherwise included in the resistance formula used in this method. If the structure is not prone to significant second-order effects as discussed in section 5.2 of this guide, then first-order analysis may be used. The flexural stiffness to be used is important in deter-

*Clause 6.4.3.1(1)* mining second-order effects and this is recognized by the text of ***clause 6.4.3.1(1)***. It will be conservative to use the cracked stiffness $E_a I_2$ throughout if the bridge is modelled with beam elements. If a finite-element shell model is used, the reinforcement can be modelled and the concrete neglected so as to avoid an overestimation of stiffness in cracked zones. Out-of-plane second-order effects may need to be suppressed.

Each cross-section is verified using the interaction expression in clause 6.2 of EN 1993-1-1, but using characteristic resistances. Effective cross-sections should be used for Class 4 sections. The loads are all increased by a factor $\alpha_{ult,k}$ until the characteristic resistance is reached. The simple and conservative verification given in clause 6.2.1(7) of EN 1993-1-1 becomes:

$$\frac{N_{Ed}}{N_{Rk}} + \frac{M_{y,Ed}}{M_{y,Rk}} \leq 1.0$$

(D6.4)

where $N_{Rk}$ and $M_{y,Rk}$ include allowance for any reduction necessary due to shear and torsion, if separate checks of cross-section resistance are to be avoided in addition to the buckling check being considered here. $N_{Ed}$ and $M_{y,Ed}$ are the axial forces and moments at a cross-section resulting from the design loads. If first-order analysis is allowable, the load factor is determined from:

$$\alpha_{ult,k}\left(\frac{N_{Ed}}{N_{Rk}} + \frac{M_{y,Ed}}{M_{y,Rk}}\right) = 1.0$$

(D6.5)

which is given in a Note to clause 6.3.4(4) of EN 1993-1-1.

If second-order analysis is necessary, $\alpha_{ult,k}$ is found by increasing the imposed loads progressively until one cross-section reaches failure according to expression (D6.4). This is necessary as the system is no longer linear and results from one analysis cannot simply be factored up when the imposed load is increased.

The second stage is to determine the lowest load factor $\alpha_{cr,op}$ to reach elastic critical buckling in an out-of-plane mode but ignoring in-plane buckling modes. This will typically require a finite-element model with shell elements to predict adequately the lateral–torsional buckling behaviour. The reinforcement can be modelled and the concrete neglected so as to avoid an overestimation of stiffness in cracked zones. If the load factor can only be determined separately for axial loads $\alpha_{cr,N}$ and bending moments $\alpha_{cr,M}$, as might be the case if standard textbook solutions are used, the overall load factor could be determined from a simple interaction equation such as:

$$\frac{1}{\alpha_{cr,op}} = \frac{1}{\alpha_{cr,N}} + \frac{1}{\alpha_{cr,M}}$$

Next, an overall slenderness is calculated for the entire system according to equation (6.64) of EN 1993-1-1. This slenderness refers only to out-of-plane effects as discussed above because in-plane effects are separately included in the determination of action effects. A reduction factor $\chi_{op}$ for this slenderness is then determined. This reduction factor depends in principle on whether the mode of buckling is predominantly flexural or lateral–torsional as the reduction curves can sometimes differ. The simplest solution is to take the lower of the reduction factors for out-of-plane flexural buckling, $\chi$, and lateral–torsional buckling, $\chi_{LT}$, from clauses 6.3.1 and 6.3.2, respectively, of EN 1993-2. For bridges, the recommended reduction factors are the same but the National Annex could alter this. This reduction factor is then applied to the cross-section check performed in stage 1, but this time using design values of the material properties. If the cross-section is verified using the simple inter-action expression (D6.4), then the verification taking lateral and lateral–torsional buckling into account becomes:

$$\frac{N_{Ed}}{N_{Rk}/\gamma_{M1}} + \frac{M_{y,Ed}}{M_{y,Rk}/\gamma_{M1}} \leq \chi_{op} \qquad (D6.6)$$

It follows from equation (D6.5) and expression (D6.6) that the verification is:

$$\frac{\chi_{op}\alpha_{ult,k}}{\gamma_{M1}} \geq 1.0 \qquad (D6.7)$$

Alternatively, separate reduction factors $\chi$ for axial load and $\chi_{LT}$ for bending moment can be determined for each effect separately using the same slenderness. If the cross-section is verified using the simple interaction expression (D6.4), then the verification taking lateral and lateral–torsional buckling into account becomes:

$$\frac{N_{Ed}}{\chi N_{Rk}/\gamma_{M1}} + \frac{M_{y,Ed}}{\chi_{LT} M_{y,Rk}/\gamma_{M1}} \leq 1.0 \qquad (D6.8)$$

It should be noted that this procedure can be conservative where the element governing the cross-section check is not itself significantly affected by the out-of-plane deformations. The method is illustrated in a qualitative example for a steel-only member in the *Designers' Guide to EN 1993-2*.[4]

### 6.4.3.2. Simplified method
A simplified method is permitted for compression flanges of composite beams and chords of composite trusses by reference to EN 1993-2 clause 6.3.4.2. Its clause D2.4 provides the stiffness of U-frames in trusses (and plate girders by analogy). The method is based on representing lateral–torsional buckling by lateral buckling of the compression flange. All subsequent discussion refers to beam flanges but is equally applicable to chords of trusses. The method is primarily intended for U-frame-type bridges but can be used for other types of flexible bracing. It also applies to lengths between rigid restraints of a beam compression flange, as is found in hogging zones in steel and concrete composite construction. The use of the method for half-through bridges is discussed in the *Designers' Guide to EN 1993-2*.

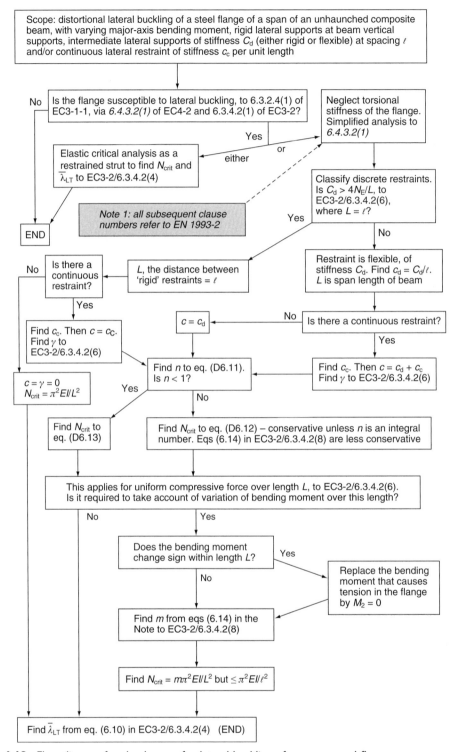

**Fig. 6.13.** Flow diagram for slenderness for lateral buckling of a compressed flange

The method effectively ignores the torsional stiffness of the beam. This may become signifi-cant for rolled steel sections but is generally not significant for deeper fabricated girders.

A flow diagram for determining the slenderness $\bar{\lambda}_{LT}$ for a length of beam of uniform depth between rigid lateral supports is given in Fig. 6.13.

EN 1993-2 clause 6.3.4.2 allows the slenderness for lateral buckling to be determined from an eigenvalue analysis of the compression chord. The flange (with an attached portion of web

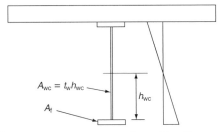

**Fig. 6.14.** Definitions for effective compression zone for a Class 3 cross-section

in the compression zone) is modelled as a strut with area $A_{\text{eff}}$, supported by springs in the lateral direction. These represent restraint from bracings (including discrete U-frames) and from any continuous U-frame action which might be provided by the connection to the deck slab. Buckling in the vertical direction is assumed to be prevented by the web in this model but checks on flange-induced buckling according to Section 8 of EN 1993-1-5 should be made to confirm this assumption. Bracings can be flexible, as is the case of bracing by discrete U-frames, or can be rigid, as is likely to be the case for cross-bracing. Other types of bracing, such as horizontal members at mid-height between beams together with plan bracing or a deck slab, may be rigid or flexible depending on their stiffness as discussed below.

Elastic critical buckling analysis may be performed to calculate the critical buckling load, $N_{\text{crit}}$. The slenderness is then given by EN 1993-2 equation (6.10):

$$\overline{\lambda}_{\text{LT}} = \sqrt{\frac{A_{\text{eff}} f_{\text{y}}}{N_{\text{crit}}}}$$

where $A_{\text{eff}} = A_{\text{f}} + A_{\text{wc}}/3$, as shown in Fig. 6.14. This approximate definition of $A_{\text{eff}}$ (greater than the flange area) is necessary to ensure that the critical stress produced for the strut is the same as that required to produce buckling in the beam under bending moment. For Class 4 cross-sections, $A_{\text{eff}}$ is determined making allowance for the reduction in area due to plate buckling.

If smeared springs are used to model the stiffness of discrete restraints such as discrete U-frames, the buckling load should not be taken as larger than that corresponding to the Euler load of a strut between discrete bracings. If computer analysis is used, there would be no particular reason to use smeared springs for discrete restraints. This approximation is generally only made when a mathematical approach is used based on the beam-on-elastic-foundation analogy, which was used to derive the equations in EN 1993-2.

*Spring stiffnesses for discrete U-frames and other restraints*
Spring stiffnesses for discrete U-frames may be calculated using Table D.3 from Annex D of EN 1993-2, where values of stiffness, $C_{\text{d}}$, can be calculated. (It is noted that the notation $C$ rather than $C_{\text{d}}$ is used in Table D.3.) A typical case covering a pair of plate girders with stiffeners and cross-girders is shown in Fig. 6.15 for which the stiffness (under the unit applied forces shown) is:

$$C_{\text{d}} = \frac{EI_{\text{v}}}{\dfrac{h_{\text{v}}^3}{3} + \dfrac{h^2 b_{\text{q}} I_{\text{v}}}{2I_{\text{q}}}} \tag{D6.9}$$

Section properties for stiffeners should be derived using an attached width of web plate in accordance with Fig. 9.1 of EN 1993-1-5 (stiffener width plus $30\varepsilon t_{\text{w}}$). If the cross-member is composite, its second moment of area should be based on cracked section properties.

Equation (D6.9) also covers steel and concrete composite bridges without stiffeners and cross-girders where the cross-member stiffness is the short-term cracked stiffness of the deck slab and reinforcement, and the vertical-member stiffness is based on the unstiffened web. For continuous U-frames, consideration of this stiffness will have little effect in

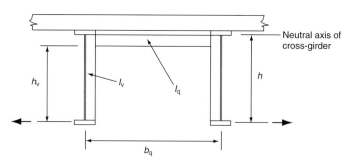

**Fig. 6.15.** Definitions of properties needed to calculate $C_d$

raising the buckling resistance, unless the length between rigid restraints is large, and will necessitate an additional check of the web for the U-frame moments induced. For multiple girders, the restraint to internal girders may be derived by replacing $2I_q$ by $3I_q$ in the expression for $C_d$. Equation (D6.9) is then similar to *equation (6.8)*. That differs only by the inclusion of Poisson's ratio in the stiffness of the web plate and by the assumption that the point of rotation of the compression flange is at the underside of the deck slab, rather than some way within it.

The stiffness of other restraints, such as a channel section placed between members at mid-height, can be derived from a plane frame model of the bracing system. For braced pairs of beams or multiple beams with a common system, it will generally be necessary to consider unit forces applied to the compression flanges such that the displacement of the flange is maximized. For a paired U-frame, the maximum displacement occurs with forces in opposite directions as in Fig. 6.15 but this will not always be the case. For paired beams braced by a mid-height channel, forces in the same direction will probably give greater flange displacement.

A computer model is useful where, for example, the flange section changes or there is a reversal of axial stress in the length of the flange being considered. In other simpler cases the formulae provided in clause 6.3.4.2 of EN 1993-2 are applicable.

*Elastic critical buckling load*
The formula for $N_{crit}$ is derived from eigenvalue analysis with continuous springs. From elastic theory (as set out, for example, in Refs 73 and 74), the critical load for buckling of such a strut is:

$$N_{crit} = n^2 \frac{\pi^2 EI}{L^2} + \frac{cL^2}{n^2\pi^2} \tag{D6.10}$$

where: $I$ is the transverse second moment of area of the effective flange and web,
$L$ is the length between 'rigid' braces,
$c$ is the stiffness of the restraints smeared per unit length, and
$n$ is the number of half waves in the buckled shape.

By differentiation, this is a minimum when:

$$n^4 = \frac{cL^4}{\pi^4 EI} \tag{D6.11}$$

which gives:

$$N_{crit} = 2\sqrt{cEI} \tag{D6.12}$$

Equation (6.12) of EN 1993-2 is:

$$N_{crit} = mN_E$$

where:

$$N_E = \frac{\pi^2 EI}{L^2}, \quad m = (2/\pi^2)\sqrt{\gamma} \geq 1.0, \quad \gamma = \frac{cL^4}{EI} \quad \text{and} \quad c = C_d/l$$

where $C_d$ is equal to the restraint stiffness and $l$ is the distance between restraints. When these terms are substituted into equation (6.12) of EN 1993-2, equation (D6.12) is produced.

When $\gamma = \pi^4 = 97$, then $c = \pi^4 EI/L^4$, and this model gives the results:

$$N_{crit} = 2\pi^2 EI/L^2, \quad n = 1.0$$

It is not valid for lower values of $c$ because then $n < 1$, which implies a buckling half-wavelength that exceeds the length $L$ between rigid restraints, and a value of $N_{crit}$ lower than that corresponding to a length $L$. In this case, the buckling load should be taken as:

$$N_{crit} = \frac{\pi^2 EI}{L^2} + \frac{cL^2}{\pi^2} \tag{D6.13}$$

Equation (D6.10) assumes that the end restraints that define the length $L$ are 'rigid'. The definition of 'rigid' is discussed below. If intermediate bracings are not rigid, their stiffness can be taken to contribute to 'c' but the length $L$ is then defined by the length between rigid bracings. Bracings at supports for typical composite bridges will usually be rigid due to the need for them to provide torsional restraint to the beams.

*Short lengths of beam between rigid bracings*
Equation (D6.12) shows that the critical buckling load from equation (6.12) of EN 1993-2 is independent of the length between rigid restraints. Equation (D6.13) is the basis for the first of equations (6.14) in EN 1993-2 for short lengths between rigid braces. The half wave length of buckling is restricted to the length between braces, and any flexible restraints included in this length increase the buckling load from that for a pin-ended strut of length $L$. The formulae provided also allow the effects of varying end moments and shears to be taken into account, but they are not valid (and are actually unsafe) where the bending moment reverses within length $L$. They are as follows:

$$m_1 = 1 + 0.44(1 + \mu)\Phi^{1.5} + (3 + 2\Phi)\gamma/(350 - 50\mu) \text{ or}$$

$$m_2 = 1 + 0.44(1 + \mu)\Phi^{1.5} + (0.195 + (0.05 + \mu/100)\Phi)\gamma^{0.5} \text{ if less than above}$$

with:

$$\mu = V_2/V_1 \text{ and } \Phi = 2(1 - M_2/M_1)/(1 + \mu) \text{ for } M_2 < M_1 \text{ and } V_2 < V_1$$

The subscripts in the symbols $m_1$ and $m_2$ correspond to the number of buckling half-waves considered, $n$. Figure 6.16 enables the equation that gives the lower result to be found, by

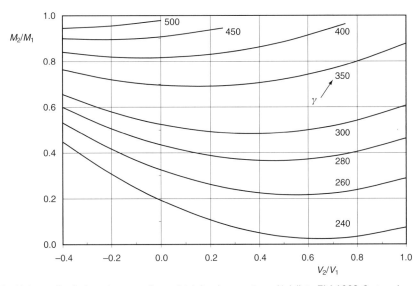

**Fig. 6.16.** Values of $\gamma$ (other than zero) at which both equations (6.14) in EN 1993-2 give the same value for $m$. Below each curve, $m_1$ governs

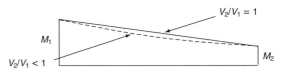

**Fig. 6.17.** Effect of shear ratio on the shape of the moment diagram

giving values of $\gamma$ at which $m_1 = m_2$. If the actual value of $\gamma$ for a buckling length with ratios $V_2/V_1$ and $M_2/M_1$ is lower than that shown in the figure, the equation for $m_1$ governs; if not, $m_2$ governs.

*Uniformly compressed flange*
The beneficial influence of lateral restraint, represented by $\gamma$, is evident for the most adverse case, a uniformly-compressed flange, for which $\mu = 1$, $\Phi = 0$. Then,

$$m_1 = 1.00 + \gamma/100, \quad m_2 = 1.00 + 0.195\gamma^{0.5}$$

These ratios $m$ are equal when $\gamma^{0.5} = 19.5$, or $\gamma = 380$, as shown by the point (1.0, 1.0) in Fig. 6.16. The change from $n = 2$ to $n = 3$ can be found from equation (D6.10) which, in terms of $\gamma$, is:

$$N_{\text{crit}}/N_E = n^2 + \gamma/(n^2\pi^4)$$

This gives $N_{\text{crit}}$ for $n = 3$ equal to that for $n = 2$ when $\gamma = 3500$ and $N_{\text{crit}}/N_E = 13$. The equations for $m_1$ and $m_2$ are more complex than equation (D6.10) because their scope includes non-uniform moment. Within the range of $\gamma$ from 380 to 3000, the value $m_2$ for uniform moment can be up to 10% higher than from equation (D6.10). This 'error' is small and is in part compensated for by the neglect of the torsional stiffness of the beam in this method. At $\gamma = 3500$ it gives $N_{\text{crit}}/N_E = 12.5$, which is more conservative. It then follows closely the results from equation (D6.10) as $\gamma$ increases (and $n$ also increases from 3 to 4). For $\gamma$ up to 20 000, the values of $m_2$ differ from the predictions of (D6.10) by only $\pm 3.6\%$.

The shear ratio, $\mu$, in the equations for $m_1$ and $m_2$, helps to describe the shape of the bending moment diagram between points of restraint. It is linear if $\mu = 1.0$. If $\mu < 1.0$, the moments fall quicker than assumed from a linear distribution as shown in Fig. 6.17 and consequently the flange is less susceptible to buckling.

*Change of sign of axial force within a length between rigid restraints*
The lack of validity for moment reversal of equations (6.14) in EN 1993-2 is a problem for a typical composite beam with cross-bracing adjacent to the internal supports. Where the most distant brace from the pier is still in a hogging zone, the moment in the beam will reverse in the span section between braces as shown in Fig. 6.18. In this region, $m$ should not be assumed to be 1.0 as this could lead to over-design of the beam or unnecessary provision

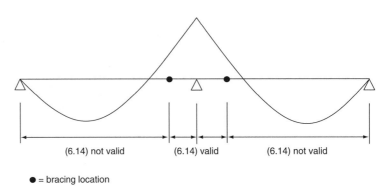

● = bracing location

**Fig. 6.18.** Range of validity of equations (6.14) of EN 1993-2

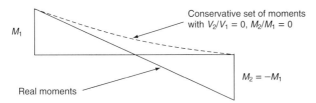

**Fig. 6.19.** Typical calculation of m where bending moment reverses

of additional braces away from the pier, to ensure that the section between innermost braces is entirely sagging and the bottom flange is in tension. A Note to clause 6.3.4.2(7) of EN 1993-2 provides the option of assuming $M_2 = 0$. If benefit from the restraining stiffness of the deck slab is ignored (i.e. $c = 0$), and $V_2$ is conservatively taken equal to $V_1$ then this leads to $m = 1.88$.

Where the top flange is braced continuously by a deck, it may be possible to 'vary' $\mu$ to produce a less conservative moment diagram. For the case in Fig. 6.19, the use of $V_2/V_1 = 0$, $M_2/M_1 = 0$ achieves the same moment gradient at end 1 as the real set of moments, and a distribution that lies everywhere else above the real moments and so is still conservative. Equations (6.14) of EN 1993-2 then give the value $m = 2.24$, again ignoring any U-frame restraint. Providing the top flange is continuously braced, the correct $m$ would be greater.

It is possible to include continuous U-frame action from an unstiffened web between rigid braces in the calculation of the spring stiffness $c$. The benefit is usually small for short lengths between braces, and the web plate, slab and shear connection must be checked for the forces implied by such action. Fig. 6.20 shows a graph of $m$ against $M_2/M_1$ with $c = 0$, for varying $V_2/V_1$.

It is possible to combine equations (6.10) and (6.12) of EN 1993-2 to produce a single formula for slenderness, taking $A_f = bt_f$ for the flange area, as follows:

$$\bar{\lambda}_{LT} = \sqrt{\frac{A_{\mathrm{eff}} f_y}{N_{\mathrm{crit}}}} = \sqrt{\frac{(A_f + A_{\mathrm{wc}}/3) f_y L^2}{m\pi^2 EI}} = L\sqrt{\frac{(1 + A_{\mathrm{wc}}/3A_f)(f_y/Em)}{\dfrac{\pi^2}{12}\dfrac{b^3 t_f}{bt_f}}}$$

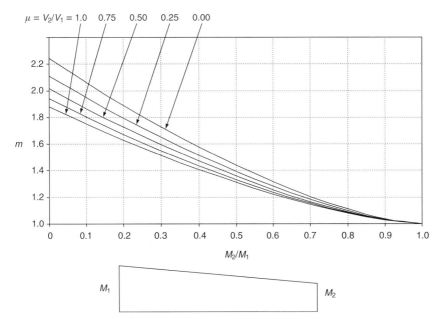

**Fig. 6.20.** Values of m ( $= N_{\mathrm{crit}}/N_E$) between rigid restraints with $\gamma = 0$

so

$$\overline{\lambda}_{LT} = 1.103 \frac{L}{b}\sqrt{\frac{f_y}{Em}}\sqrt{1+\frac{A_{wc}}{3A_f}} \qquad (D6.14)$$

It is still necessary to evaluate $N_{crit}$ when checking the strength of the bracings.

The formulae in clause 6.3.4.2(7) of EN 1993-2 do not apply directly to haunched girders as they assume that the flange force is distributed in the same way as the bending moment. The general method of using an eigenvalue analysis based on the forces in the compression chord is still applicable. Alternatively, the formulae provided could be applied using the least value of the spring stiffness $c$ within the length considered. The flange force ratio $F_2/F_1$ is used instead of the moment ratio $M_2/M_1$, with $V_2/V_1$ taken as 1.0, when applying equation (6.14) of EN 1993-2.

EN 1993-2 clause 6.3.4.2(7) allows the buckling verification to be performed at a distance of $0.25L_k = 0.25L/\sqrt{m}$ (i.e. 25% of the effective length) from the end with the larger moment. (The symbols $L_k$ and $l_k$ are both used for effective length in 6.3.4.2.) This appears to double-count the benefit from moment shape derived in equations (6.14) of EN 1993-2; but it does not do so. The check at $0.25L_k$ reflects the fact that the peak stress from transverse buckling of the flange occurs some distance away from the rigid restraint to the flange, whereas the peak stress from overall bending of the beam occurs at the restraint. (In this model, the beam flange is assumed to be pin-ended at the rigid transverse restraints.) Since these two peak stresses do not coexist they are not fully additive, and the buckling verification can be performed at a 'design' section somewhere between these two locations. The cross-section resistance must still be verified at the point of maximum moment.

There are clearly problems with applying clause 6.3.4.2(7) of EN 1993-2 where the moment reverses as the section $0.25L/\sqrt{m}$ from an end may be a point of contraflexure. In this situation, it is recommended here that the design section be taken as 25% of the distance from the position of maximum moment to the position of zero moment. In addition, if benefit is taken of verification at the $0.25L_k$ cross-section, the calculated slenderness above must be modified so that it refers to this design section. The critical moment value will be less here and the slenderness is therefore increased. This can be done by defining a new slenderness at the $0.25L_k$ section such that

$$\overline{\lambda}_{0.25Lk} = \overline{\lambda}_{LT}\sqrt{\frac{M_1}{M_{0.25Lk}}}$$

where $M_{0.25Lk}$ is the moment at the $0.25L_k$ section. This procedure is illustrated in Example 6.6 below. It should be noted that the k in $M_{0.25Lk}$ does not imply a characteristic value; this is a design value.

### Stiffness of braces
The formulae in EN 1993-2 discussed above are only valid where the end restraints that define the length $L$ are 'rigid'. It is possible to equate $N_{crit} = 2\sqrt{cEI}$ to $\pi^2EI/L^2$ to find a limiting stiffness that gives an effective length equal to the distance between rigid restraints, $L$, but this slightly underestimates the required stiffness. This is because the formulae assume that the restraints are continuously smeared when they are in fact discrete. The former analysis gives a required value for $C_d$ of $\pi^4EI/4L^3$, whereas the 'correct' stiffness is $4\pi^2EI/L^3$, which is 62% higher.

### Interaction with compressive axial load
The interaction with axial load is covered in *clause 6.4*, in *clause 6.4.3.1* only, via the general method given in EN 1993-2. Axial load has several effects including:

- magnification of the main bending moment about the horizontal axis of the beam (the second-order effect)

- increase of stress in the compression flange leading to an increased tendency for lateral buckling.

Most bridge cross-sections are either Class 3 or 4 at supports so the stresses from axial load can simply be assumed to be applied to the cracked composite section, and the elastic section resistance can be used. At mid-span, beams are usually Class 1 or 2 and the calculation of a modified plastic moment resistance in the presence of axial load is relatively simple. The plastic neutral axis is so chosen that the total compressive force exceeds the total tensile force by an amount equal to the axial load.

Care must however be taken to ensure that the bending resistance is obtained about an axis at the height of the applied axial force assumed in the global analysis. This is important for non-symmetric beams as the elastic and plastic neutral axes for bending alone do not coincide, whereas they do for a symmetric section. Most of *clause 6.7* is for doubly-symmetric sections only, but the general method of clause 6.7.2 may be applied to beams provided that compressive stresses do not exceed their relevant limiting values where Class 3 and 4 cross-sections are involved.

Alternatively, the cross-section can be designed using a conservative interaction expression such as that in clause 6.2.1(7) of EN 1993-1-1:

$$\frac{N_{Ed}}{N_{Rd}} + \frac{M_{y,Ed}}{M_{y,Rd}} \leq 1.0$$

where $N_{Rd}$ and $M_{y,Rd}$ are the design resistances for axial force and moment acting individually but with reductions for shear where the shear force is sufficiently large. A similar interaction expression can be used for the buckling verification with the terms in the denominator replaced by the relevant buckling resistances:

$$\frac{N_{Ed}}{N_{b,Rd}} + \frac{M_{Ed}}{M_{b,Rd}} \leq 1.0 \qquad (D6.15)$$

The value for $M_{Ed}$ should include additional moments from in-plane second-order effects (including from in-plane imperfections). Such second-order effects will normally be negligible. The buckling resistance $N_{b,Rd}$ should be calculated on the basis of the axial stress required for lateral buckling of the compression flange. This method is illustrated in Example 6.6 below.

### Beams without plan bracing or decking during construction

During construction it is common to stabilize girders in pairs by connecting them with 'torsional' bracing. Such bracing reduces or prevents torsion of individual beams but does not restrict lateral deflection. Vertical 'torsional' cross-bracing as shown in Fig. 6.21 has been considered in the UK for many years to act as a rigid support to the compression flange, thus restricting the effective length to the distance between braces. Opinion is now somewhat divided on whether such bracing can be considered fully effective and BS

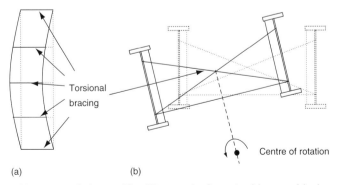

**Fig. 6.21.** Torsional bracing and shape of buckling mode, for paired beams: (a) plan on braced pair of beams showing buckling mode shape; (b) cross-section through braced pair of beams showing buckling mode shape

5400:Part 3:2000[11] introduced a clause to cover this situation which predicts that such bracing is not fully effective.

This situation arises because equilibrium of the braced pair under torsion requires opposing vertical forces to be generated in the two girders. Consequently one girder moves up, one moves down and some twist of the girder pair is generated, albeit much less than for an unbraced pair. If the beam span-to-depth ratio is large, the deflections and hence twists can be significant. The *Designers' Guide to EN 1993-2*[4] suggests a method based on BS 5400 Part 3, but in some cases it may lead to the conclusion that plan bracing is necessary. A better estimate of slenderness can be made using a finite-element analysis.

A finite-element model of a non-composite beam, using shell elements for the paired main beams and beam elements to represent the bracings, can be set up relatively quickly with modern commercially available software. Elastic critical buckling analysis can then be performed and a value of $M_{cr}$ determined directly for use in slenderness calculation to clause 6.3.2 of EN 1993-2. This approach usually demonstrates that the cross-bracing is not fully effective in limiting the effective length of the flange to the distance between bracings, but that it is more effective than is predicted by BS 5400. For simply-supported paired girders, a typical lowest buckling mode under dead load is shown in Fig. 6.21.

## Example 6.6: bending and shear in a continuous composite beam

The locations of the bracings and splices for the bridge used in earlier examples are shown in Fig. 6.22. The two internal beams are Class 3 at each internal support as found in Example 5.4. The cross-sections of the central span of these beams, also shown, are as in Examples 5.4 and 6.1 to 6.4. The neutral axes shown in the cross-section at the piers are for hogging bending of the cracked composite section.

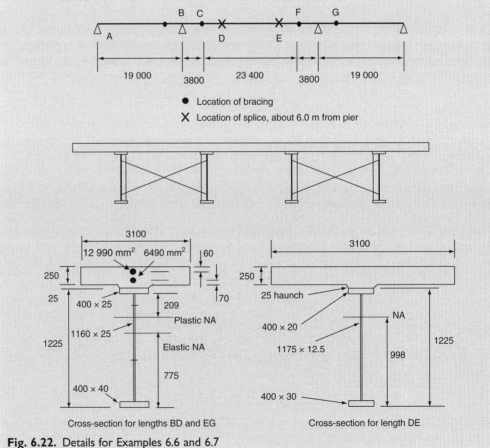

**Fig. 6.22.** Details for Examples 6.6 and 6.7

The design ultimate hogging moments at internal support B are 2213 kNm on the steel section plus 4814 kNm on the composite section, so $M_{\mathrm{Ed}} = 7027$ kNm. The coexisting hogging moment at the braced point C in the central span is 4222 kNm. The vertical shear at point C is 70% of that at the pier B. The hogging bending moment at the splice, where the beam cross-section changes, is 3000 kNm.

Lateral–torsional buckling adjacent to the pier and in the main span beyond the brace is checked and the effect of a coexisting axial compression of 1000 kN applied to the composite section is considered. This could arise in a semi-integral bridge with screen walls at its ends.

*Elastic resistance to bending at an internal support*
The elastic section moduli for the cross-section at point B are given in Table 6.2. These are based on the extreme fibres but it would have been permissible to base them on the centroids of the flanges in accordance with EN 1993-1-1 clause 6.2.1(9). To find $M_{\mathrm{el,Rd}}$, the factor $k$ (*clause 6.2.1.4(6)*) is found for the top and bottom surfaces of the steel beam, as follows. The result will be used in checks on buckling, so $f_{\mathrm{yd}}$ is found using $\gamma_{\mathrm{M1}}$ ($= 1.1$). Primary shrinkage stresses are neglected because the deck slab is assumed to be cracked.

**Table 6.2.** Section moduli at an internal support, in $10^6$ mm$^3$ units

| | Top layer of bars | Top of steel section | Bottom of steel section |
|---|---|---|---|
| Gross steel section | — | 18.28 | 22.20 |
| Cracked composite section | 34.05 | 50.31 | 29.25 |

For the top flange,

$$2213/18.28 + kM_{\mathrm{c,Ed}}/50.31 = 345/1.1 \text{ so } kM_{\mathrm{c,Ed}} = 9688 \text{ kNm}$$

For the bottom flange,

$$2213/22.20 + kM_{\mathrm{c,Ed}}/29.25 = 345/1.1 \text{ so } kM_{\mathrm{c,Ed}} = 6258 \text{ kNm}$$

The elastic resistance is governed by the bottom flange, so that:

$$M_{\mathrm{el,Rd}} = 2213 + 6258 = \mathbf{8471 \text{ kNm}}$$

The maximum compressive stress in the bottom flange is:

$$\sigma_{\mathrm{a,bot}} = 2213/22.2 + 4814/29.25 = 264 \text{ N/mm}^2$$

*Resistance of length BC (Fig. 6.22) to distortional lateral buckling*
Strictly, the stiffness of the bracing should first be checked (or should later be designed) so that the buckling length is confined to the length between braces. This is done in Example 6.7. The bending-moment distribution is shown in Fig. 6.23.

Where no vertical web stiffeners are required, the deck slab provides a small continuous U-frame stiffness. This could be included using Table D.3 of EN 1993-2, case 1a, to calculate a stiffness, $c$. This contribution has been ignored to avoid the complexities of designing the deck slab and shear connection for the forces implied, and because any need to stiffen the web has not yet been considered. Therefore from clause 6.3.4.2(6) of EN 1993-2, $\gamma = cL^4/EI = 0$.

The compression zone of the beam is designed as a pin-ended strut with continuous vertical restraint, and lateral restraint at points 3.80 m apart (Fig. 6.22). Its cross-sectional areas are:

- flange: $A_{\mathrm{f}} = 400 \times 40 = 16\,000$ mm$^2$

- web compression zone: $A_{wc} = 735 \times 25 = 18\,375\,\text{mm}^2$. (Conservatively based on the height of the neutral axis for the composite section. It could be based on the actual depth for the accumulated stress profile, which is 633 mm.)

The second moment of area of the compressed area is calculated for the bottom flange, as the contribution from the web is negligible:

$$I = 40 \times 400^3/12 = 213.3 \times 10^6\,\text{mm}^4$$

The applied bending moments at each end of the equivalent strut are:

$$M_{Ed,1} = 7027\,\text{kNm}; \quad M_{Ed,2} = 4222\,\text{kNm}$$

From EN 1993-2 clause 6.3.4.2(7):

$$M_2/M_1 = 4222/7027 = 0.60 \text{ and } \mu = V_2/V_1 = 0.70$$

$$\Phi = 2(1 - M_2/M_1)/(1 + \mu) = 2(1 - 0.60)/(1 + 0.70) = 0.46$$

When $\gamma = 0$, the first two of equations (6.14) in clause 6.3.4.2(8) of EN 1993-2 both give:

$$m = 1 + 0.44(1 + \mu)\Phi^{1.5} = 1 + 0.44(1 + 0.70)0.46^{1.5} = 1.23$$

If the deck slab is considered to provide U-frame restraint, the value of $m$ for this length of flange is found to be still only 1.26, so there is no real benefit to lateral stability in considering U-frame action over such a short length of beam.

From equation (D6.14):

$$\overline{\lambda}_{LT} = 1.1\frac{L}{b}\sqrt{\frac{f_y}{Em}}\sqrt{1 + \frac{A_{wc}}{3A_f}} = 1.1 \times \frac{3800}{400}\sqrt{\frac{345}{210 \times 10^3 \times 1.23}} \times \sqrt{1 + \frac{18375}{3 \times 16000}} = 0.45$$

This exceeds 0.2 so from clause 6.3.2.2(4) of EN 1993-1-1 this length of flange is prone to lateral–torsional buckling.

The ratio $h/b = 1225/400 = 3.1$ exceeds 2.0, so from Table 6.4 in clause 6.3.2.2 of EN 1993-1-1 the relevant buckling curve is curve d. Hence, $\alpha_{LT} = 0.76$ from Table 6.3.

From equation (6.56) in EN 1993-1-1, clause 6.3.2.2:

$$\Phi_{LT} = 0.5[1 + \alpha_{LT}(\overline{\lambda}_{LT} - 0.2) + \overline{\lambda}_{LT}^2] = 0.5[1 + 0.76(0.45 - 0.2) + 0.45^2] = 0.696$$

$$\chi_{LT} = \frac{1}{\Phi_{LT} + \sqrt{\Phi_{LT}^2 - \overline{\lambda}_{LT}^2}} = \frac{1}{0.696 + \sqrt{0.696^2 - 0.45^2}} = 0.81$$

Applying this reduction factor gives:

$$M_{b,Rd} = \chi_{LT}M_{el,Rd} = 0.81 \times 8471 = \textbf{6862 kNm}$$

At the internal support, $M_{Ed} = 7027\,\text{kNm}$ (2% higher). However, clause 6.3.4.2(7) of EN 1993-2 provides the option of making this check at a distance of $0.25L/\sqrt{m}$ from the support. This distance is:

$$0.25 \times 3800/\sqrt{1.23} = 857\,\text{mm}$$

Using linear interpolation, Fig. 6.23, this gives $M_{Ed} = \textbf{6394 kNm}$. The modified slenderness is:

$$\overline{\lambda}_{0.25Lk} = \overline{\lambda}_{LT}\sqrt{\frac{M_1}{M_{0.25Lk}}} = 0.45\sqrt{\frac{7027}{6394}} = 0.47$$

This reduces $\chi_{LT}$ from 0.81 to 0.80, so the new resistance is:

$$M_{b,Rd} = \chi_{LT}M_{el,Rd} = 0.80 \times 8471 = \textbf{6777 kNm}$$

This exceeds $M_{Ed}$ (6394 kNm), so this check on lateral buckling is satisfied.

The further condition that the elastic resistance (8471 kNm) is not exceeded at the point of peak moment (7027 kNm) is satisfied. This cross-section should also be checked for combined bending and shear, but in this case the shear is less than 50% of the shear resistance and thus no interaction occurs.

*Resistance with a coexisting axial compression of 1000 kN*
An axial force of 1000 kN is applied at the height of the elastic centroidal axis of the cracked cross-section at the internal support. Susceptibility to in-plane second-order effects is first checked. The second moment of area of the cracked composite section at mid-span, $1.326 \times 10^{10}\,\text{mm}^4$, is conservatively used to determine the elastic critical flexural buckling load for major-axis buckling.

$$N_{\text{cr}} = \frac{\pi^2 EI}{L^2} = \frac{\pi^2 \times 210 \times 1.326 \times 10^{10}}{31\,000^2} = 28\,600\,\text{kN}$$

From *clause 5.2.1(3)*:

$$\alpha_{\text{cr}} = \frac{28\,600}{1000} = 29 > 10$$

so in-plane second-order effects may be neglected.

At the internal support, the area of the cracked composite section is $74\,480\,\text{mm}^2$, so the axial compressive stress is $1000 \times 10^3/74\,480 = 13.4\,\text{N/mm}^2$. This changes the total stresses at the extreme fibres of the steel beam to $204\,\text{N/mm}^2$ tension and $278\,\text{N/mm}^2$ compression. This stress distribution is found to leave the cross-section at the pier still in Class 3. The section at the brace is also in Class 3.

The conservative linear interaction between axial and bending resistances of expression (D6.15) will be used:

$$\frac{N_{\text{Ed}}}{N_{\text{b,Rd}}} + \frac{M_{\text{Ed}}}{M_{\text{b,Rd}}} \leq 1.00$$

so $N_{\text{b,Rd}}$ must be found, based on buckling of the web and bottom flange under uniform compression. Since the combined stress distribution leads to a Class 3 cross-section throughout the buckling length, the gross section will be used in this analysis, even for the calculation of the compression resistance, below.

If the section became Class 4, effective properties should be used. These could be derived either separately for moment and axial force or as a unique effective section under the combined stress field. In either case, the moment of the axial force produced by the shift of the neutral axis should be considered.

For axial force alone, the required areas of the cross-sections are:

$$A_{\text{f}} = 400 \times 40 = 16\,000\,\text{mm}^2, \ A_{\text{wc}} = 1160 \times 25 = 29\,000\,\text{mm}^2$$

Neglecting U-frame restraint as before, equations (6.14) in clause 6.3.4.2(7) of EN 1993-2 with $M_1 = M_2$ and $\gamma = 0$ give $m = 1.00$.
From equation (D6.14):

$$\overline{\lambda}_{\text{LT}} = 1.1\frac{L}{b}\sqrt{\frac{f_y}{Em}}\sqrt{1+\frac{A_{\text{wc}}}{3A_{\text{f}}}} = 1.1 \times \frac{3800}{400}\sqrt{\frac{345}{210\times10^3\times1.00}} \times \sqrt{1+\frac{29\,000}{3\times16\,000}} = 0.54$$

From curve d on Fig. 6.4 of EN 1993-1-1, $\chi = 0.74$. The axial buckling resistance of the cracked composite cross-section, based on buckling of the bottom flange, is:

$$N_{\text{b,Rd}} = \chi A f_{\text{yd}} = 0.74 \times 74\,480 \times 345/1.1 = \textbf{17\,285\,kN}$$

It should be noted that $N_{\text{b,Rd}}$ does not represent a real resistance to axial load alone as the cross-section would then be in Class 4 and a reduction to the web area to allow for local buckling in accordance with EN 1993-1-5 would be required. It is however valid to use the gross cross-section in the interaction here as the cross-section is Class 3 under the actual combination of axial force and bending moment. The use of a gross cross-section also avoids the need to consider any additional moment produced by the shift in centroidal axis that occurs when an effective web area is used.

From expression (D6.15),

$$1000/17\,285 + 6394/6777 = 1.00$$

which is just satisfactory, with these conservative assumptions. A check of cross-section resistance is also required at the end of the member, but this is satisfied by the check of combined stresses above.

*Buckling resistance of the mid-span region of the central span*
An approximate check is carried out for the 23.4 m length between the two braced points (C and F in Fig. 6.22), at first using the cross-section at the pier throughout to derive the reduction factor. This is slightly unconservative as the cross-section reduces at the splice. An axial force is not considered in this part of the example.

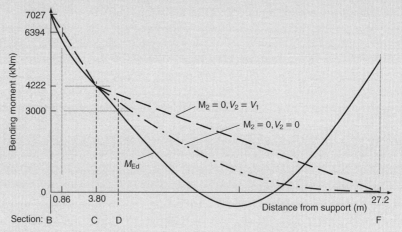

**Fig. 6.23.** Bending action effects and resistances for an internal span

It is assumed that maximum imposed load acts on the two side spans and that only a short length near mid-span is in sagging bending, as sketched in Fig. 6.23. Since the bending moment reverses, equations (6.14) in EN 1993-2 are not directly applicable. If the suggestion of clause 6.3.4.2(7) of EN 1993-2 is followed, and $M_2$ is taken as zero at the other brace (cross-section F), the bending-moment distribution depends on the value assumed for $V_2$, the vertical shear at $F$. Two possibilities are shown in Fig. 6.23.

Their use does not follow directly from the discussion associated with Fig. 6.18, where the moment was assumed to reverse only once in the length between rigid restraints. In Fig. 6.23, the two fictitious sets of moments do not always lie above the real set and are therefore not obviously conservative. However, the interaction of the hogging moment at one end of the beam with the buckling behaviour at the other end is weak when the moment reverses twice in this way.

BS 5400:Part 3[11] included a parameter '$\eta$' which was used to consider the effect of moment shape on buckling resistance. For no reversal, $m$ is in principle equivalent to $1/\eta^2$, although there is not complete numerical equivalence. Figure 6.24 gives comparative values of $m' = 1/\eta^2$. This shows that for the worst real moment distribution, where the moment just remains entirely hogging, the value of $m'$ is greater (less conservative) than for the two possibilities in Fig. 6.23. This shows that the less conservative of these possibilities ($V_2 = 0$) can be used. It gives $m = 2.24$ from equations (6.14).

From equation (D6.14) with $A_{wc} = 25 \times 735 = 18\,375\,\text{mm}^2$:

$$\bar{\lambda}_{LT} = 1.1 \frac{L}{b} \sqrt{\frac{f_y}{Em}} \sqrt{1 + \frac{A_{wc}}{3A_f}}$$

$$= 1.1 \times \frac{23\,400}{400} \sqrt{\frac{345}{210 \times 10^3 \times 2.24}} \times \sqrt{1 + \frac{18\,375}{3 \times 16\,000}} = 2.05 > 0.2$$

Using curve d in Fig. 6.4 of EN 1993-1-1, $\chi_{LT} = 0.17$.

If the slab reinforcement at cross-section C is the same as at the support,

$M_{el,Rd} = 8471\,\text{kNm}$, and $M_{b,Rd} = 0.17 \times 8471 = \mathbf{1440\,kNm}$

This is far too low, so according to this method another brace would be required further from the pier to reduce the buckling length. U-frame action is now considered.

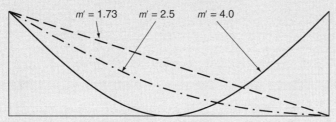

**Fig. 6.24.** Variation of $m'$ with different bending-moment distributions, derived from BS 5400:Part 3[11]

*Use of continuous U-frame action – simplified method of EN 1993-2, clause 6.3.4.2*
The method of *clause 6.4.2* is inapplicable because the cross-section is not uniform along length CF, and a region near the splice is in Class 4 for hogging bending. The method of clause 6.3.4.2 of EN 1993-2 is therefore used. Its spring stiffness $c$ is the lateral force per unit length at bottom-flange level, for unit displacement of the flange. It is related to the corresponding stiffness $k_s$ in *clause 6.4.2* by:

$$k_s = ch_s^2 \tag{D6.16}$$

where $h_s$ is the distance between the centres of the steel flanges (*Fig. 6.10*).

For most of the length CF the web is 12.5 mm thick so the cross-section for length DE (Fig. 6.22) is used for this check, with $h_s = 1200\,\text{mm}$. For the bottom flange,

$$I_{afz} = 30 \times 400^3/12 = 160 \times 10^6\,\text{mm}^4 \tag{D6.17}$$

In comparison with this thin web, the slab component of the U-frame is very stiff, so its flexibility is neglected here, as is the torsional stiffness of the bottom flange. In general, the flexibility of the slab should be included. From *equations (6.8)* and *(6.10)* with $k_1 \gg k_2$, so that $k_s \approx k_2$, and using equation (D6.16),

$$c = k_s/h_s^2 = E_a \left(\frac{t_w}{h_s}\right)^3 /[4(1 - \nu_a^2)] = 210 \times 10^6 (12.5/1200)^3/(4 \times 0.91) = 65.2\,\text{kN/m}^2$$

As an alternative, equation (D6.9) could be used for the calculation of $c$. As discussed in the main text, there are some minor differences in the definition of the height terms, '$h$'. Those in equation (D6.9) seem more appropriate where the slab flexibility becomes important.

From EN 1993-2 clause 6.3.4.2 and result (D6.17),

$$\gamma = cL^4/EI = 65.2 \times 23.4^4/(210 \times 160) = 582$$

The less conservative assumption, $V_2 = 0$, is used with $M_2 = 0$. This gives $\mu = 0$, $\Phi = 2$. From Fig. 6.16, the second of equations (6.14) in clause 6.3.4.2 of EN 1993-2 governs.

With $\mu = 0$ it gives:

$$m = 1 + 0.44\Phi^{1.5} + (0.195 + 0.05\Phi)\gamma^{0.5} = 1 + 1.245 + 7.117 = 9.36$$

U-frame action (the final term) is now a significant contributor to $m$. (For uniform moment and the same $\gamma$, $m = 5.70$.)

The cross-section reduces at the splice position, approximately 6 m from the pier, so the minimum cross-section is conservatively considered throughout. In equation (D6.14) for $\bar{\lambda}_{LT}$, the areas in compression are:

- flange: $A_f = 400 \times 30 = 12\,000\,\text{mm}^2$
- web compression zone: $A_{wc} = (683 - 47) \times 12.5 = 7950\,\text{mm}^2$. (Conservatively based on the height of the neutral axis for the composite section shown in Fig. 6.5, which is 683 mm above the bottom flange.)

Hence from equation (D6.14):

$$\bar{\lambda}_{LT} = 1.1 \frac{L}{b} \sqrt{\frac{f_y}{Em}} \sqrt{1 + \frac{A_{wc}}{3A_f}}$$

$$= 1.1 \times \frac{23\,400}{400} \sqrt{\frac{345}{210 \times 10^3 \times 9.36}} \times \sqrt{1 + \frac{7950}{3 \times 12\,000}} = 0.942$$

Curve d of Fig. 6.4 in EN 1993-1-1 gives $\chi_{LT} = 0.49$. With $M_{el,Rd}$ from Example 6.3, the buckling resistance $\chi_{LT} M_{el,Rd}$ is:

$$M_{b,Rd} = 0.49 \times 6390 = \mathbf{3131\,kNm}$$

which is less than 4222 kNm (the moment at the brace). By inspection, a check at the $0.25L_k$ design section will also not pass.

These checks are however conservative as they assume the minimum cross-section throughout. If reference is made back to the expressions for slenderness given in equations (6.10) of EN 1993-2 and *(6.7)*, it is seen that:

$$\bar{\lambda}_{LT} = \sqrt{\frac{A_{eff}f_y}{N_{crit}}} = \sqrt{\frac{M_{Rk}}{M_{crit}}}$$

so that $M_{crit}$ measured at the brace is effectively

$$M_{crit} = \frac{M_{Rk}}{\bar{\lambda}_{LT}^2} = \frac{6390 \times 1.1}{0.942^2} = 7921\,\text{kNm}$$

For the length of the beam with the larger cross-section, $M_{Rk}$ is larger than assumed above. The buckling moment $M_{crit}$ is however mainly influenced by the long length of smaller cross-section so that it will be similar to that found above, even if the short lengths of stiffer end section are considered in the calculation.

*Use of continuous U-frame action – general method of EN 1993-1-1, clause 6.3.4*
A revised slenderness can be determined using the method of EN 1993-1-1 clause 6.3.4. From equation (D6.5) with $N_{Ed} = 0$, within the span between braces, the minimum value of

$$\alpha_{ult,k} = \frac{M_{y,Rk}}{M_{y,Ed}}$$

is

$$\frac{8471 \times 1.1}{4222} = 2.21$$

at the brace location, where:

$$M_{y,Rd} = 8471\,\text{kNm}$$

(For the weaker section at the splice location, $M_{y,Rk}/M_{y,Ed} = 6390 \times 1.1/3000 = 2.34$).

The minimum load factor to cause lateral–torsional buckling is:

$$\alpha_{\mathrm{cr,op}} = \frac{M_{\mathrm{crit}}}{M_{\mathrm{y,Ed}}} = \frac{7921}{4222} = 1.88$$

The system slenderness of the span between the braces, from equation (6.64) of EN 1993-1-1, is:

$$\bar{\lambda}_{\mathrm{op}} = \sqrt{\frac{\alpha_{\mathrm{ult,k}}}{\alpha_{\mathrm{cr,op}}}} = \sqrt{\frac{2.21}{1.88}} = 1.08$$

and hence the reduction factor, from curve d of Fig. 6.4 in EN 1993-1-1, is $\chi_{\mathrm{op}} = 0.43$. The verification is then performed according to equation (D6.7):

$$\frac{\chi_{\mathrm{op}}\alpha_{\mathrm{ult,k}}}{\gamma_{\mathrm{M1}}} = \frac{0.43 \times 2.21}{1.1} = 0.86 < 1.0$$

so the beam is still inadequate. This verification is equivalent to $M_{\mathrm{b,Rd}} = 0.43 \times 8471 = 3643\,\mathrm{kNm}$ at the brace, which is still less than the applied moment of $4222\,\mathrm{kNm}$.

It would be possible to improve this verification further by determining a more accurate value of $M_{\mathrm{crit}}$ from a finite-element model. However, inclusion of U-frame action has the disadvantage that the web and shear connection would have to be designed for the resulting effects. A better alternative could be the addition of another brace adjacent to the splice location.

## Example 6.7: stiffness and required resistance of cross-bracing

The bracing of the continuous bridge beam in Example 6.6 comprises cross-bracing made from $150 \times 150 \times 18$ angle and attached to $100 \times 20$ stiffeners on a 25 mm thick web. The bracings are checked for rigidity and the force in them arising from bracing the flanges is determined. The effects of the 1000 kN axial compressive force are included.

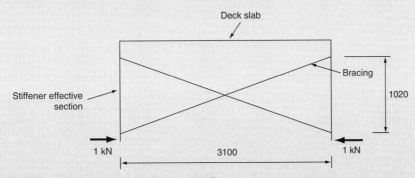

**Fig. 6.25.** Cross-bracing for Examples 6.6 and 6.7

The stiffness of the brace was first calculated from the plane-frame model shown in Fig. 6.25. From Fig. 9.1 of EN 1993-1-5, the effective section of each stiffener includes a width of web:

$$30\varepsilon t_{\mathrm{w}} + t_{\mathrm{st}} = 30 \times 0.81 \times 25 + 20 = 628\,\mathrm{mm}$$

Hence,

$$A_{\mathrm{st}} = 628 \times 25 + 100 \times 20 = 17\,700\,\mathrm{mm}^2$$

This leads to $I_{\mathrm{st}} = 9.41 \times 10^6\,\mathrm{mm}^4$.

The deck slab spans 3.1 m. From *clause 5.4.1.2* its effective span is $3.1 \times 0.7 = 2.17\,\mathrm{m}$, and its effective width for stiffness is $0.25 \times 2.17 = 0.542\,\mathrm{m}$. Its stiffness is conservatively based on the cracked section, with the concrete modulus taken as $E_{cm}/2$ to represent the fact that some of the loading is short term and some is long term. Greater accuracy is not warranted here as the concrete stiffness has little influence on the overall stiffness of the cracked section.

From elastic analysis for the forces shown in Fig. 6.25, the stiffness is:

$$C_d = 80\,\text{kN/mm}$$

From clause 6.3.4.2(6) of EN 1993-2, the condition for a lateral support to a compressed member to be 'rigid' is:

$$C_d \geq 4\pi^2 EI/L_b^3$$

where, for length BC in Fig. 6.23,

$$L_b = 3.80\,\text{m}$$

and

$$I = 213.3 \times 10^6\,\text{mm}^4$$

Hence,

$$C_d \geq 4\pi^2 \times 210 \times 213.3/(3.8^3 \times 1000) = 32.2\,\text{kN/mm}$$

The support is 'rigid'.

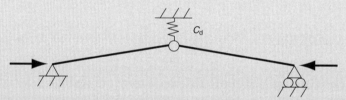

**Fig. 6.26.** Elastic stiffness of bracing to a pin-ended strut

The formula in EN 1993-2 here assumes that supports are present every 3.8 m such that the buckling length is restricted to 3.8 m each side of this brace and that the force in the flange is constant each side of the brace. The limiting spring stiffness for $C_d$ is analogous to that required for equilibrium of a strut with a pin joint in it at the spring position, such that buckling of the lengths each side of the pin joint occurs before buckling of the whole strut into the brace – see Fig. 6.26. A small displacement of the strut at the pin joint produces a kink in the strut and a lateral force on the brace, which must be stiff enough to resist this force at the given displacement. For a given displacement, the kink angle and thus the force on the spring is increased by reducing the length of the strut each side of the spring. This kink force is also increased because the critical buckling load for the lengths each side of the spring is increased by the reduction in length. Here, the flange force is not the same each side of the brace and the length of unbraced flange is greater than 3.8 m on one side of the brace. The kink force is therefore overestimated and the calculated value for $C_d$ is conservative. This confirms the use in Example 6.6 of $L$ as the length between braces.

The design lateral force for the bracing is now found, using clause 6.3.4.2(5) of EN 1993-2. From Example 6.6, $\bar{\lambda}_{LT} = 0.45$, and the effective area of the compressed flange is:

$$A_{eff} = 16\,000 + 18\,375/3 = 22\,120\,\text{mm}^2$$

From equations in EN 1993-2, clause 6.3.4.2,

$$\ell_k = \pi(EI/N_{crit})^{1/2} = \pi[EI\bar{\lambda}_{LT}^2/(A_{eff}f_y)]^{1/2} = \pi \times 0.45\left(\frac{210 \times 213.3 \times 1000}{22\,120 \times 345}\right)^{1/2} = 3.43\,\text{m}$$

The distance between braced points is $\ell = 3.8\,\text{m}$, so $\ell_k < 1.2\,\ell$.

(Since the brace has been found to be 'rigid', and from Example 6.6, $m > 1$ so that $N_{\text{crit}} > \pi^2 EI/\ell^2$, $\ell_k$ is obviously less than $\ell$, and this check was unnecessary.)

From clause 6.3.4.2(5), the lateral force applied by each bottom flange to the brace is:

$$F_{\text{Ed}} = N_{\text{Ed}}/100$$

From Example 6.6, the greatest compressive stress in the bottom flange at the pier is $278\,\text{N/mm}^2$.

Hence:

$$F_{\text{Ed}} = \frac{N_{\text{Ed}}}{100} = 278 \times 22\,120/(100 \times 1000) = 61.5\,\text{kN}$$

The axial force in the bracing is then approximately:

$$\frac{61.5}{\cos(\tan^{-1}1020/3100)} = 64.7\,\text{kN}$$

There will also be some bending moment in the bracing members due to joint eccentricities.

## 6.5. Transverse forces on webs

The local resistance of an unstiffened and unencased web to forces (typically, vertical forces) applied through a steel flange can be assumed to be the same in a composite member as in a steel member, so *clause 6.5* consists mainly of references to EN 1993-1-5. High transverse loads are relatively uncommon in bridge design other than during launching operations or from special vehicles or heavy construction loads, such as from a crane outrigger. Theoretically, wheel loads should be checked but are unlikely ever to be significant. *Clause 6.5*

The patch loading rules given in EN 1993-1-5 Section 6 make allowance for failure by either plastic failure of the web, with associated plastic bending deformation of the flange, or by buckling of the web. More detail on the derivation and use of the rules is given in the *Designers' Guide to EN 1993-2.*[4] The rules for patch loading can only be used if the geometric conditions in EN 1993-1-5 clause 2.3 are met; otherwise EN 1993-1-5 Section 10 should be used. Clause 6.1(1) of EN 1993-1-5 also requires that the compression flange is 'adequately restrained' laterally. It is not clear what this means in practice, but the restraint requirement should be satisfied where the flange is continuously braced by, for example, a deck slab or where there are sufficient restraints to prevent lateral–torsional buckling.

*Clause 6.5.1(1)* states that the rules in EN 1993-1-5 Section 6 are applicable to the non-composite flange of a composite beam. If load is applied to the composite flange, the rules could still be used by ignoring the contribution of the reinforced concrete to the plastic bending resistance of the flange. No testing is available to validate inclusion of any contribution. A spread of load could be taken through the concrete flange to increase the stiff loaded length on the steel flange. There is limited guidance in EN 1992 on what angle of spread to assume; clause 8.10.3 of EN 1992-1-1 recommends a dispersion angle of $\tan^{-1}2/3$, i.e. 34°, for concentrated prestressing forces. It would be reasonable to use 45° here, which would be consistent with previous bridge design practice in the UK. *Clause 6.5.1(1)*

*Clause 6.5.1(2)* makes reference to EN 1993-1-5 clause 7.2 for the interaction of transverse force with axial force and bending. This gives: *Clause 6.5.1(2)*

$$\eta_2 + 0.8\eta_1 \leq 1.4$$

where:

$$\eta_2 = \frac{\sigma_{z,\text{Ed}}}{f_{\text{yw}}/\gamma_{\text{M1}}} = \frac{F_{\text{Ed}}}{f_{\text{yw}}L_{\text{eff}}t_w/\gamma_{\text{M1}}} = \frac{F_{\text{Ed}}}{F_{\text{Rd}}}$$

is the usage factor for transverse load acting alone, and

$$\eta_1 = \frac{\sigma_{x,Ed}}{f_y/\gamma_{M0}} = \frac{N_{Ed}}{f_y A_{eff}/\gamma_{M0}} + \frac{M_{Ed} + N_{Ed}e_N}{f_y W_{eff}/\gamma_{M0}}$$

is the usage factor for direct stress alone, calculated elastically. The calculation of $\eta_1$ should take account of the construction sequence as discussed in section 6.2.1.5 of this guide. It can be seen that this interaction expression does not allow for a plastic distribution of stress for bending and axial force. Even if the cross-section is Class 1 or 2, this will not lead to any discontinuity with the plastic bending resistance at low transverse load as only 80% of the elastic bending stress is considered and the limiting value of the interaction is 1.4. The ratio between the plastic and elastic resistances to bending for typical composite beams is less than 1.4.

*Clause 6.5.2*  *Clause 6.5.2* covers flange-induced buckling of webs by reference to EN 1993-1-5 Section 8. If the flange is sufficiently large and the web is very slender, it is possible for the whole flange to buckle in the plane of the web by inducing buckling in the web itself. If the compression flange is continuously curved in elevation, whether because of the soffit profile or because the whole beam is cambered, the continuous change in direction of the flange force causes a radial force in the plane of the web. This force increases the likelihood of flange-induced buckling into the web. Discussion on the use of Section 8 of EN 1993-1-5 is provided in the *Designers' Guide to EN 1993-2*.[4]

## 6.6. Shear connection
### 6.6.1. General
#### 6.6.1.1. Basis of design

*Clause 6.6.1.1(1)*  *Clause 6.6* is applicable to shear connection in composite beams. *Clause 6.6.1.1(1)* refers also to '*other types of composite member*'. Shear connection in composite columns is addressed in *clause 6.7.4*, but reference is made to *clause 6.6.3.1* for the design resistance of headed stud connectors.

*Clause 6.6.1.1(2)P*  Although the uncertain effects of bond are excluded by *clause 6.6.1.1(2)P*, friction is not excluded. Its essential difference from bond is that there must be compressive force across the relevant surfaces. This usually arises from wedging action. Provisions for shear connection by friction are given in *clause 6.7.4.2(4)* for columns.

*Clause 6.6.1.1(3)P*  '*Inelastic redistribution of shear*' (*clause 6.6.1.1(3)P*) is most relevant to building design in the provisions of EN 1994-1-1 for partial shear connection. Inelastic redistribution of shear is allowed in a number of places for bridges including:

- *clause 6.6.1.2* (which allows redistribution over lengths such that the design resistance is not exceeded by more than 10%)
- *clause 6.6.2.2* (which permits assumptions about the distribution of the longitudinal shear force within an inelastic length of a member)
- *clauses 6.6.2.3(3)* and *6.6.2.4(3)* for the distribution of shear in studs from concentrated loads.

*Clause 6.6.1.1(4)P*  *Clause 6.6.1.1(4)P* uses the term '*ductile*' for connectors that have deformation capacity
*Clause 6.6.1.1(5)*  sufficient to assume ideal plastic behaviour of the shear connection. *Clause 6.6.1.1(5)* quantifies this as a characteristic slip capacity of 6 mm.[75]
*Clause 6.6.1.1(6)P*  The need for compatibility of load/slip properties, *clause 6.6.1.1(6)P*, is one reason why neither bond nor adhesives can be used to supplement the shear resistance of studs. The combined use of studs and block-and-hoop connectors has been discouraged for the same reason, though there is little doubt that effectively rigid projections into the concrete slab, such as bolt heads and ends of flange plates, contribute to shear connection. This Principle is particularly important in bridges, where the fatigue loading on individual connectors may otherwise be underestimated. This applies also where bridges are to be strengthened by retro-fitting additional shear connectors.

'*Separation*', in **clause 6.6.1.1(7)P**, means separation sufficient for the curvatures of the *Clause 6.6.1.1(7)P* two elements to be different at a cross-section, or for there to be a risk of local corrosion. None of the design methods in EN 1994-2 takes account of differences of curvature, which can arise from a very small separation. Even where most of the load is applied by or above the slab, as is usual, tests on beams with unheaded studs show separation, especially after inelastic behaviour begins. This arises from local variations in the flexural stiffnesses of the concrete and steel elements, and from the tendency of the slab to ride up on the weld collars. The standard heads of stud connectors have been found to be large enough to control separation, and the rule in **clause 6.6.1.1(8)** is intended to ensure that other types *Clause 6.6.1.1(8)* of connector, with anchoring devices if necessary, can do so.

Resistance to uplift is much influenced by the reinforcement near the bottom of the slab, so if the resistance of an anchor is to be checked by testing, reinforcement in accordance with *clause 6.6.6* should be provided in the test specimens. Anchors are inevitably subjected also to shear.

**Clause 6.6.1.1(9)** refers to '*direct tension*'. Load from a maintenance cradle hanging from *Clause 6.6.1.1(9)* the steel member is an example of how tension may arise. It can also be caused by the differential deflections of adjacent beams under certain patterns of imposed load, although the resulting tensions are usually small. Greater tension can be produced near bracings as identified by *clause 6.6.1.1(13)*. Where tension is present in studs, its design magnitude should be determined and checked in accordance with *clause 6.6.3.2*.

**Clause 6.6.1.1(10)P** is a principle that has led to many application rules. The shear forces *Clause* are inevitably '*concentrated*'. One research study[76] found that 70% of the shear on a stud was *6.6.1.1(10)P* resisted by its weld collar, and that the local (triaxial) stress in the concrete was several times its cube strength. Transverse reinforcement performs a dual role. It acts as horizontal shear reinforcement for the concrete flanges, and controls and limits splitting. Its detailing is particularly critical where connectors are close to a free surface of the slab or where they are aligned so as to cause splitting in the direction of the slab thickness. To account for the latter, **clause 6.6.1.1(11)** should also include a reference to *clause 6.6.4* for design of *Clause 6.6.1.1(11)* the transverse reinforcement.

Larger concentrated forces occur where precast slabs are used, and connectors are placed in groups in holes in the slabs. This influences the detailing of the reinforcement near these holes, and is referred to in *Section 8*.

**Clause 6.6.1.1(12)** is intended to permit the use of other types of connector. ENV 1994-1-1[20] *Clause 6.6.1.1(12)* included provisions for many types of connector other than studs: block connectors, anchors, hoops, angles, and friction-grip bolts. They have all been omitted because of their limited use and to shorten the code.

*Clause 6.6.1.1(12)* gives scope, for example, to develop ways to improve current detailing practice at the ends of beams in fully integral bridges, where forces need to be transferred abruptly from the composite beams into reinforced concrete piers and abutments. In British practice, the use of 'bars with hoops' is often favoured in these regions, and design rules are given in BS 5400-5.[11] The word 'block' rather than 'bar' is used in this Guide to avoid confusion with reinforcing bars. It is shown in Example 6.8 that the shear resistance of a connector of this type can be determined in accordance with EN 1992 and EN 1993. The height of the block should not exceed four times its thickness if the connector is assumed to be rigid as in Example 6.8.

**Clause 6.6.1.1(13)** identifies a problem that occurs adjacent to cross-frames or diaphragms *Clause 6.6.1.1(13)* between beams. For multi-beam decks, beams are often braced in pairs such that the bracing is not continuous transversely across the deck. The presence of bracing locally significantly stiffens the bridge transversely. Moments and shears in the deck slab are attracted out of the concrete slab and into the bracing as shown in Fig. 6.27 via the transverse stiffeners. This effect is not modelled in a conventional grillage analysis unless the increased stiffness in the location of bracings is included using a shear flexible member with inertia and shear area chosen to match the deflections obtained from a plane frame analysis of the bracing system. Three-dimensional space-frame or finite-element representations of the bridge can be used to model these local effects more directly.

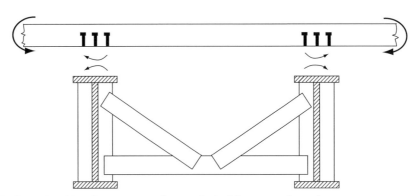

**Fig. 6.27.** Example of bending moments from a deck slab attracted into bracings

The transfer of moment causes tension in the shear connectors on one side of the flange and induces compression between concrete and flange on the other. Welds at tops of stiffeners must also be designed for this moment, which often leads to throat sizes greater than a 'nominal' 6 mm.

In composite box girders, similar effects arise over the tops of the boxes, particularly at the locations of ring frames, bracings or diaphragms.

*6.6.1.2. Ultimate limit states other than fatigue*

*Clause 6.6.1.2*

In detailing the size and spacing of shear connectors, *clause 6.6.1.2* permits the design longitudinal shear flow to be averaged over lengths such that the peak shear flow within each length does not exceed the design longitudinal shear resistance per unit length by more than 10%, and the total design longitudinal shear does not exceed the total design longitudinal shear within this length. This is consistent with previous practice in the UK and sometimes avoids the need to alter locally the number or spacings of shear connectors adjacent to supports. *Clause 6.6.1.2* has little relevance to the inelastic lengths in Class 1 and 2 members covered by *clause 6.6.2.2(2)* since the longitudinal shear is already averaged over the inelastic zone in this method.

> **Example 6.8: shear resistance of a block connector with a hoop**
> Blocks of S235 steel, 250 mm long and 40 mm square, are welded to a steel flange as shown in Fig. 6.28, at a longitudinal spacing of 300 mm. The resistance to longitudinal shear, $P_{Rd}$, in a C30/37 concrete is determined. From *clause 6.6.1.1(8)* the resistance to uplift should be at least $0.1P_{Rd}$. This is provided by the 16 mm reinforcing bars shown. None of the modes of failure involve interaction between concrete and steel, so their own $\gamma_M$ factors are used, rather than 1.25, though the National Annex could decide otherwise. The concrete is checked to EN 1992, so its definition of $f_{cd}$ is used, namely $f_{cd} = \alpha_{cc}f_{ck}/\gamma_C$. Assuming that the National Annex gives $\alpha_{cc} = 1.0$ for this situation, the design strengths of the materials are:
>
> $$f_{yd} \geq 225\,\text{N/mm}^2, \quad f_{sd} = 500/1.15 = 435\,\text{N/mm}^2, \quad f_{cd} = 1 \times 30/1.5 = 20\,\text{N/mm}^2$$
>
> The blocks here are so stiff that the longitudinal shear force can be assumed to be resisted by a uniform stress, $\sigma_{block}$ say, at the face of each block. Lateral restraint enables this stress to exceed $f_{cd}$ to an extent given in clause 6.7 of EN 1992-1-1, 'Partially loaded areas':
>
> $$\sigma_{block} = F_{Rdu}/A_{c0} = f_{cd}\sqrt{A_{c1}/A_{c0}} \leq 3.0f_{cd} \qquad \text{(6.63) in EN 1992-1-1}$$
>
> where $A_{c0}$ is the loaded area and $A_{c1}$ is the 'design distribution area' of similar shape to $A_{c0}$, shown in Fig. 6.29 of EN 1992-1-1.

Clause 6.7 requires the line of action of the force to pass through the centres of both areas, but in this application it can be assumed that the force from area $b_2 d_2/2$ is resisted by the face of the block, of area $b_1 d_1/2$, because the blocks are designed also to resist uplift. The dimensions of area $A_{c1}$ are fixed by clause 6.7 of EN 1992-1-1 as follows:

$$b_2 \leq b_1 + h \quad \text{and} \quad b_2 \leq 3b_1; \qquad d_2 \leq d_1 + h \quad \text{and} \quad d_2 \leq 3d_1$$

Here, from Fig. 6.28,

$$h = 300 - 40 = 260\,\text{mm}, b_1 = 2 \times 40 = 80\,\text{mm}, d_1 = 250\,\text{mm}$$

where $b_2 = 240\,\text{mm}$, $d_2 = 510\,\text{mm}$.

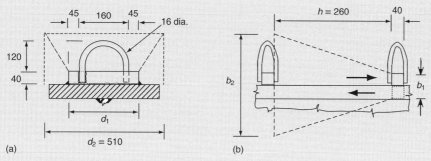

**Fig. 6.28.** Block shear connector with hoop, for Example 6.8

From equation (6.63),

$$\sqrt{A_{c1}/A_{c0}} = \sqrt{(510 \times 240/2)/(250 \times 40)} = 2.47\,(<3.0)$$

and

$$F_{\text{Rdu}} = P_{\text{Rd}} = 0.250 \times 40 \times 2.47 \times 20 = \mathbf{494\,kN}$$

The tensile stress in two 16 mm bars from an uplift force of 49.4 kN is 123 N/mm². The required anchorage length for a hooped bar is given in clause 8.4.4(2) of EN 1992-1-1. It is proportional to the tensile stress in the bar and depends on its lateral containment, which in this application is good. For $\sigma_{\text{sd}} = 123\,\text{N/mm}^2$ the anchorage length is 115 mm, so 120 mm (Fig. 6.28(a)) is sufficient.

The welds between the block and the steel flange are designed for the resulting shear, tension, and bending moment in accordance with EN 1993-1-8. A separate check of fatigue would be required using EN 1993-1-9 to determine the detail category and stress range. The comments on *clause 6.8.6.2(2)* refer. The welds between the bar and the block are designed for the uplift force.

The resistance given by this method is significantly less than that from design to BS 5400-5, where the method is based mainly on tests.[77] The above method based on clause 6.7 of EN 1992-1-1 would strictly require vertical reinforcement to control splitting from the vertical load dispersal. However, as both push tests and practice have shown this reinforcement to be unnecessary even when using the higher resistances to BS 5400-5, vertical reinforcement need not be provided here.

The resistance of a block connector is much higher than that of a shear stud, so where they are used in haunches, the detailing of reinforcement in the haunch needs attention.

EN 1992-1-1 appears to give no guidance on the serviceability stress limit in a region where its clause 6.7 is applied. For shear connectors generally, *clause 7.2.2(6)* refers to *clause 6.8.1(3)*, where the recommended limit is $0.75 P_{\text{Rd}}$. This agrees closely with the corresponding ratio given in BS 5400-5.[11]

### 6.6.2. Longitudinal shear force in beams for bridges

*6.6.2.1. Beams in which elastic or non-linear theory is used for resistances of cross-sections*

*Clause 6.6.2.1(1)* requires that the design longitudinal shear force per unit length (the 'shear flow') at an interface between steel and concrete is determined from the rate of change of force in the concrete or the steel. The second part of the clause states, as a consequence of this, that where elastic bending resistance is used, the shear flow can be determined from the transverse shear at the cross-section considered. To do this, it is implicit that the beam is of uniform cross-section such that the usual expression for longitudinal shear flow,

$$v_{L,Ed} = \frac{V_{c,Ed} A \bar{z}}{I}$$

can be used, where:

> $A$ is the effective transformed area on the side of the plane concerned that does not include the centroid of the section, sometimes named the 'excluded area';
> $\bar{z}$ is the distance in the plane of bending from the member neutral axis to the centroid of area $A$;
> $I$ is the second moment of area of the effective cross-section of the member.

The relevant shear $V_{c,Ed}$ is that acting on the composite section. Where the cross-section varies along its length, the shear flow is no longer directly proportional to the shear on the beam and the following expression should be used:

$$v_{L,Ed} = \frac{d}{dx}\left(\frac{M_{c,Ed} A \bar{z}}{I}\right) = \frac{V_{c,Ed} A \bar{z}}{I} + M_{c,Ed}\frac{d}{dx}\left(\frac{A \bar{z}}{I}\right) \qquad (D6.18)$$

Equation (D6.18) does not directly cover step changes in the steel cross-section as often occur at splices. In such situations, it would be reasonable to assume that the step change occurs uniformly over a length of twice the effective depth of the cross-section when applying equation (D6.18). Where there is a sudden change from bare steel to a composite section, design for the concentrated longitudinal shear force from development of composite action should follow *clause 6.6.2.4*.

The calculated elastic longitudinal shear flow is strongly dependent on whether or not the concrete slab is considered to be cracked. In reality, the slab will be stiffer than predicted by a fully cracked analysis due to tension stiffening. *Clause 6.6.2.1(2)* clarifies that the slab should
therefore be considered to be fully uncracked unless tension stiffening and over-strength of concrete are considered in both global analysis and section design as discussed under *clause 5.4.2.3(7)*.

*Clause 6.6.2.1(3)* requires account to be taken of longitudinal slip where concentrated longitudinal forces are applied, and refers to *clauses 6.6.2.3 and 6.6.2.4*. In other cases, *clause 6.6.2.1(3)* allows slip to be neglected for consistency with *clause 5.4.1.1(8)*.

*Composite box girders*

For box girders with a composite flange, a shear flow across the shear connection can occur due to shear from circulatory torsion, torsional warping and distortional warping. These
effects are discussed in the *Designers' Guide to EN 1993-2*.[4] *Clause 6.6.2.1(4)* requires them to be included 'if appropriate'. This influences the design longitudinal shear stress (*clause 6.6.6.1(5)*), and hence the area of transverse reinforcement, to *clause 6.6.6.2*.

Shear lag and connector slip lead to a non-uniform distribution of force in the shear connectors across the width of the flange. This is discussed in section 9.4 of this Guide.

*6.6.2.2. Beams in bridges with cross-sections in Class 1 or 2*

Where the bending resistance exceeds the elastic resistance and material behaviour is non-linear, shear flows can similarly no longer be calculated from linear-elastic section analysis. To do so using equation (D6.18) would underestimate the shear flow where elastic limits are exceeded as the lever arm of the cross-section implicit in the calculation would be
overestimated and thus the element forces would be underestimated. *Clause 6.6.2.2(1)*

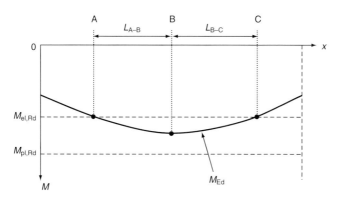

**Fig. 6.29.** Definition of inelastic lengths for Class 1 and 2 cross-sections with the slab in compression

therefore requires that account be taken of inelastic behaviour of the member and its component parts in calculation of longitudinal shear. This differs from previous UK practice but is more soundly based in theory.

*Clause 6.6.2.2(2)* gives specific guidance on how to comply with the above requirements where the concrete slab is in compression. For the length of beam where the bending moment exceeds $M_{el,Rd}$, the longitudinal shear relationship should be determined from the change in slab force. The relevant length is that between the points A and C in Fig. 6.29. The longitudinal shear force in the length A–B is determined as the difference between slab forces $N_{c,el}$ at point A and $N_{c,d}$ at point B. Appropriate shear connection to carry this force is provided within this length. Similar calculation is performed for the length B–C.

*Clause 6.6.2.2(2)*

The spacing of the shear connectors within these lengths is left to the designer. Normally for lengths A–B and B–C, and in the absence of heavy point loads, changes of cross-section, etc., uniform spacing can be used. In a doubtful case, for example within A–B, the slab force $N_c$ at some point within A–B should be determined from the bending moment and appropriate numbers of connectors provided between A and D, say D, and between D and B.

The actual relationship between slab force, $N_c$, and moment, $M_{Ed}$, is shown in Fig. 6.30, together with the approximate expression in *Fig. 6.6* of *clause 6.2.1.4(6)* and the further simplification of *Fig. 6.11*. It can be seen that both the approximations are safe for the design of shear connection, because for a given bending moment, the predicted slab force exceeds the real slab force.

For inelastic lengths where the slab is in tension, *clause 6.6.2.2(3)* requires the calculation of longitudinal shear force to consider the effects of tension stiffening and possible over-strength of the concrete. Failure to do so could underestimate the force attracted to the shear connection, resulting in excessive slip. As an alternative, *clause 6.6.2.2(4)* permits the shear flow to be determined using elastic cross-section analysis based on the uncracked cross-section. Elastic analysis can be justified in this instance because the conservative

*Clause 6.6.2.2(3)*

*Clause 6.6.2.2(4)*

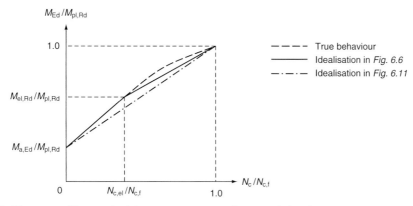

**Fig. 6.30.** Variation of longitudinal force in a concrete flange with bending moment

assumption of fully uncracked concrete offsets the slightly unconservative neglect of inelasticity.

### 6.6.2.3. Local effects of concentrated longitudinal shear force due to introduction of longitudinal forces

Where concentrated longitudinal forces are applied to a composite section, the stress state can easily be determined some distance away from the point of application from considerations of equilibrium and from the usual assumption that plane sections remain plane. Plane sections do not, however, remain plane in the vicinity of the force, and accurate determination of the length over which longitudinal shear transfers between concrete slab and steel flange together with the magnitude of the peak longitudinal shear flow requires complex analysis. This clause is based on parametric finite-element analyses[78] and existing practice.

*Clause 6.6.2.3*

*Clause 6.6.2.3(2)*

*Clause 6.6.2.3* provides simple rules for the determination of the design shear flow between steel and concrete where there is a concentrated longitudinal force, $F_{Ed}$, applied to the concrete slab. *Clause 6.6.2.3(2)* distinguishes between forces applied within the length of the member and those applied at ends of the members. In the former case, the length over which the force is distributed, $L_v$, is equal to the effective width for global analysis, $b_{eff}$, plus $e_d$, which is the loaded length plus twice the lateral distance from the point of application of the force to the web centreline: $L_v = b_{eff} + e_d$.

For forces applied at an end of a concrete flange, the distribution length is half of the above. The reference to effective width for global analysis means that the simple provisions of *clause 5.4.1.2(4)* can be used, rather than the effective width appropriate to the cross-section where the force is applied.

The force cannot, in general, be transferred uniformly by the shear connection over the above lengths and *Fig. 6.12(a)* and *(b)* shows the distribution to be used, leading to *equations (6.12)* and *(6.13)*. Where stud shear connectors are used, these are sufficiently ductile to permit a uniform distribution of shear flow over the above lengths at the ultimate limit

*Clause 6.6.2.3(3)*

state. This leads to *equations (6.14)* and *(6.15)* in *clause 6.6.2.3(3)*. For serviceability or fatigue limit states, the distributions of *equations (6.12)* and *(6.13)* should always be used.

The shear force $V_{L,Ed}$ transferred to the shear connection is not $F_{Ed}$, as can be seen from Fig. 6.31 for the case of a force applied to the end of the concrete slab. Force $V_{L,Ed}$ is the difference between $F_{Ed}$ and the force $N_c$ in the concrete slab where dispersal of $F_{Ed}$ into the cross-section is complete.

*Clause 6.6.2.3(4)*

*Clause 6.6.2.3(4)* allows the dispersal of the force $F_{Ed} - V_{L,Ed}$ (which for load applied to the concrete as shown in Fig. 6.31 is equal to $N_c$) into either the concrete or steel element to be based on an angle of spread of $2\beta$ where $\beta$ is $\tan^{-1} 2/3$. This is the same spread angle used in EN 1992-1-1 clause 8.10.3 for dispersal of prestressing force into concrete. It is slightly less than the dispersal allowed by clause 3.2.3 of EN 1993-1-5 for the spread through steel elements.

### 6.6.2.4. Local effects of concentrated longitudinal shear forces at sudden change of cross-sections

*Clause 6.6.2.4*

*Clause 6.6.2.4* provides simple rules for the determination of the design shear flow between steel and concrete at ends of slabs where:

*Clause 6.6.2.4(1)*

- the primary effects of shrinkage or differential temperature are developed (*clause 6.6.2.4(1)*)

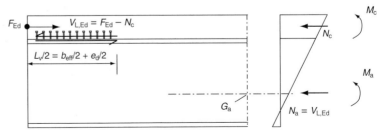

**Fig. 6.31.** Determination of $V_{L,Ed}$ for a concentrated force applied at an end of the slab

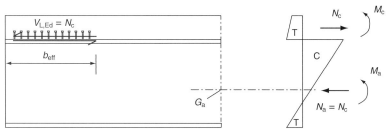

**Fig. 6.32.** Determination of $V_{L,Ed}$ for primary shrinkage at an end of a beam

- there is an abrupt change of cross-section (*clause 6.6.2.4(2)*), such as that shown in Fig. 6.33.     *Clause 6.6.2.4(2)*

The shear $V_{L,Ed}$ transferred across the concrete and steel interface due to shrinkage or temperature may be assumed to be distributed over a length equal to $b_{eff}$, as discussed in section 6.6.2.3 above. Generally, *clause 6.6.2.4(3)* requires the distribution of this force to     *Clause 6.6.2.4(3)* be triangular as shown in *Fig. 6.12(c)*, which leads to *equation (6.16)*. Where stud shear connectors are used, these are again sufficiently ductile to permit a uniform distribution of shear flow over the length $b_{eff}$. This leads to a design shear flow of $V_{L,Ed}/b_{eff}$.

A calculation of primary shrinkage stresses is given in Example 5.3 (Fig. 5.11). The force $N_c$ is found from these. It equals the shear force $V_{L,Ed}$, which is transferred as shown in Fig. 6.32.

The determination of $V_{L,Ed}$ caused by bending at a sudden change in cross-section is shown in Fig. 6.33 for the case of propped construction, in which the total moment at cross-section B–B is:

$$M_{Ed,B} = M_a + M_c + N_c z$$

For unpropped construction, the stress would not vary linearly across the composite section as shown in Fig. 6.33, but the calculation of longitudinal shear from the force in the slab would follow the same procedure.

The length over which the force is distributed and the shape of distribution may be taken according to *clause 6.6.2.4(5)* to be the same as that given in *clause 6.6.2.4(3)*.     *Clause 6.6.2.4(5)*

## 6.6.3. Headed stud connectors in solid slabs and concrete encasement
*Resistance to longitudinal shear*

In BS 5400 Part 5[11] and in earlier UK codes, the characteristic shear resistances of studs are given in a table, applicable only when the stud material has particular properties. There was no theoretical model for the shear resistance.

The Eurocodes must be applicable to a wider range of products, so design equations are essential. Those given in *clause 6.6.3.1(1)* are based on the model that a stud with shank dia-     *Clause 6.6.3.1(1)* meter $d$ and ultimate strength $f_u$, set in concrete with characteristic strength $f_{ck}$ and mean secant modulus $E_{cm}$, fails either in the steel alone or in the concrete alone. The concrete failure is found in tests to be influenced by both the stiffness and the strength of the concrete.

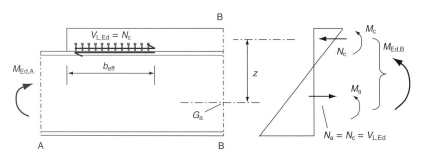

**Fig. 6.33.** Determination of $V_{L,Ed}$ caused by bending moment at a sudden change of cross-section

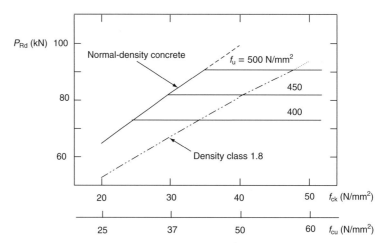

**Fig. 6.34.** Design shear resistances of 19 mm studs with $h/d \geq 4$ in solid slabs

This led to *equations (6.18)* to *(6.21)*, in which the numerical constants and partial safety factor $\gamma_V$ have been deduced from analyses of test data. In situations where the resistances from *equations (6.18)* and *(6.19)* are similar, tests show that interaction occurs between the two assumed modes of failure. An equation based on analyses of test data, but not on a defined model[79]

$$P_{Rd} = k(\pi d^2/4)f_u(E_{cm}/E_a)^{0.4}(f_{ck}/f_u)^{0.35} \qquad (D6.19)$$

gives a curve with a shape that approximates better both to test data and to values tabulated in BS 5400.

In the statistical analyses done for EN 1994-1-1[80,81] both of these methods were studied. Equation (D6.19) gave results with slightly less scatter, but the equations of *clause 6.6.3.1(1)* were preferred because of their clear basis and experience of their use in some countries. Here, and elsewhere in *Section 6*, coefficients from such analyses were modified slightly, to enable a single partial factor, denoted $\gamma_V$ (V for shear), 1.25, to be recommended for all types of shear connection. This value has been used in draft Eurocodes for over 20 years.

It was concluded from this study[81] that the coefficient in *equation (6.19)* should be 0.26. This result was based on push tests, where the mean number of studs per specimen was only six, and where lateral restraint from the narrow test slabs was usually less stiff than in the concrete flange of a composite beam. Strength of studs in many beams is also increased by the presence of hogging transverse bending of the slab. For these reasons the coefficient was increased from 0.26 to 0.29, a value that is supported by a subsequent calibration study[60] based on beams with partial shear connection.

Design resistances of 19 mm stud connectors in solid slabs, given by *clause 6.6.3.1*, are shown in Fig. 6.34. It is assumed that the penalty for short studs, *equation (6.20)*, does not apply. For any given values of $f_u$ and $f_{ck}$, the figure shows which failure mode governs. It can be used for this purpose for studs of other diameters, provided that $h/d \geq 4$. The reference to the slabs as 'solid' means that they are not composite slabs cast on profiled steel sheeting. It does not normally exclude haunched slabs.

The 'overall nominal height' of a stud, used in *equations (6.20)* and *(6.21)*, is about 5 mm greater than the 'length after welding', a term which is also in use.

*Weld collars*

*Clause 6.6.3.1(2)*

*Clause 6.6.3.1(2)* on weld collars refers to EN 13918,[40] which gives 'guide values' for the height and diameter of collars, with the note that these may vary in through-deck stud welding. It is known that for studs with normal weld collars, a high proportion of the shear is transmitted through the collar.[76] It should not be assumed that the shear resistances of *clause 6.6.3.1* are applicable to studs without collars, as noted by *clause 6.6.3.1(4)* (e.g.

where friction welding by high-speed spinning is used). A normal collar should be fused to the shank of the stud. Typical collars in the test specimens from which the design formulae were deduced had a diameter not less than $1.25d$ and a minimum height not less than $0.15d$, where $d$ is the diameter of the shank.

### Splitting of the slab

*Clause 6.6.3.1(3)* refers to '*splitting forces*' in the direction of the slab thickness. These occur where the axis of a stud lies in a plane parallel to that of the concrete slab; for example, if studs are welded to the web of a steel T-section that projects into a concrete flange. These are referred to as 'lying studs' in published research[82] on the local reinforcement needed to prevent or control splitting. Comment on the informative *Annex C* on this subject is given in Chapter 10. A similar problem occurs in composite L-beams with studs close to a free edge of the slab. This is addressed in *clause 6.6.5.3(2)*.

*Clause 6.6.3.1(3)*

### Tension in studs

Pressure under the head of a stud connector and friction on the shank normally causes the stud weld to be subjected to vertical tension before shear failure is reached. This is why *clause 6.6.1.1(8)* requires shear connectors to have a resistance to tension that is at least 10% of the shear resistance. *Clause 6.6.3.2(2)* therefore permits tensile forces that are less than this to be neglected. (The symbol $F_{\text{ten}}$ in this clause means $F_{\text{Ed,ten}}$.)

*Clause 6.6.3.2(2)*

   Resistance of studs to higher tensile forces has been found to depend on so many variables, especially the layout of local reinforcement, that no simple design rules could be given. Relevant evidence from about 60 tests on 19 mm and 22 mm studs is presented in Ref. 74, which gives a best-fit interaction curve. In design terms, this becomes

$$(F_{\text{ten}}/0.85P_{\text{Rd}})^{5/3} + (P_{\text{Ed}}/P_{\text{Rd}})^{5/3} \leq 1 \qquad \text{(D6.20)}$$

Where the vertical tensile force $F_{\text{ten}} = 0.1P_{\text{Rd}}$, this gives $P_{\text{Ed}} \leq 0.93P_{\text{Rd}}$, which is plausible. Expression (D6.20) should be used with caution, because some studs in these tests had ratios $h/d$ as high as 9; but on the conservative side, the concrete blocks were unreinforced.

## 6.6.4. Headed studs that cause splitting in the direction of the slab thickness

There is a risk of splitting of the concrete where the shank of a stud (a 'lying stud') is parallel and close to a free surface of the slab, as shown, for example, in Fig. 6.35. Where the conditions of *clause 6.6.4(1)* to *(3)* are met, the stud resistances of *clause 6.6.3.1* may still be used. The geometric requirements are shown in Fig. 6.35, in which $d$ is the diameter of the stud. A further restriction is that the stud must not also carry shear in a direction transverse to the slab thickness. The example shown in Fig. 6.35 would not comply in this respect unless the steel section were designed to be loaded on its bottom flange. *Clause 6.6.4(3)* requires that the stirrups shown should be designed for a tensile force equal to $0.3P_{\text{Rd}}$ per stud connector. This is analogous with the design of bursting reinforcement at prestressing anchorages. The true tensile force depends on the slab thickness and spacing of the studs and the proposed value is conservative for a single row of studs. No recommendation is given here, or in *Annex C*, on the design of stirrups where there are several rows of studs.

*Clause 6.6.4(1) to (3)*

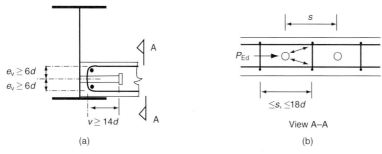

(a)                                        (b)

**Fig. 6.35.** Examples of details susceptible to longitudinal splitting

Some details which do not comply with *clause 6.6.4* can be designed using the rules in the informative *Annex C*, if its use is permitted by the National Annex. In Fig. 6.35, the effects of local loading on the slab and of U-frame action will also cause moment at the shear connection which could cause stud tensions in excess of those allowed by *clause 6.6.3.2*. This detail is therefore best avoided.

Planes of type a–a such as section A–A in Fig. 6.35 should be provided with longitudinal shear reinforcement in accordance with *clause 6.6.6*.

### 6.6.5. Detailing of the shear connection and influence of execution

It is rarely possible to prove the general validity of application rules for detailing, because they apply to so great a variety of situations. They are based partly on previous practice. An adverse experience causes the relevant rule to be made more restrictive. In research, existing rules are often violated when test specimens are designed, in the hope that extensive good experience may enable existing rules to be relaxed.

Rules are often expressed in the form of limiting dimensions, even though most behaviour (excluding corrosion) is more influenced by ratios of dimensions than by a single value. Minimum dimensions that would be appropriate for an unusually large structural member could exceed those given in the code. Similarly, code maxima may be too large for use in a small member. Designers are unwise to follow detailing rules blindly, because no set of rules can be comprehensive.

*Resistance to separation*

*Clause 6.6.5.1(1)*    The object of **clause 6.6.5.1(1)** on resistance to separation is to ensure that failure surfaces in the concrete cannot pass above the connectors and below the reinforcement, intersecting neither. Tests have found that these surfaces may not be plane; the problem is three-dimensional. A longitudinal section through a possible failure surface ABC is shown in Fig. 6.36. The studs are at the maximum spacing allowed by *clause 6.6.5.5(3)*.

*Clause 6.6.5.1* defines only the highest level for the bottom reinforcement. Ideally, its longitudinal location relative to the studs should also be defined, because the objective is to prevent failure surfaces where the angle $\alpha$ (Fig. 6.36) is small. It is impracticable to link detailing rules for reinforcement with those for connectors, or to specify a minimum for angle $\alpha$. In Fig. 6.36, it is less than 8°, which is much too low.

The angle $\alpha$ obviously depends on the level of the bottom bars, the height of the studs, and the spacing of both the bars and the studs. Studs in a bridge deck usually have a length after welding (LAW) that exceeds the 95 mm shown. Assuming LAW = 120 mm, maximum spacings of both bars and studs of 450 mm, and a bottom cover of 50 mm gives $\alpha \geq 17°$, approximately, which is suggested here as a minimum. Studs may need to be longer than 125 mm where permanent formwork is used, as this raises the level of the bottom reinforcement.

Other work reached a similar conclusion in 2004.[83] Referring to failure surfaces as shown in Fig. 6.36, it was recommended that angle $\alpha$ should be at least 15°. In this paper the line AB (Fig. 6.36) is tangential to the top of the bar at B, rather than the bottom, slightly reducing its slope.

*Concreting*

*Clause 6.6.5.2(1)P*    **Clause 6.6.5.2(1)P** requires shear connectors to be detailed so that the concrete can be adequately compacted around the base of the connector. This necessitates the avoidance

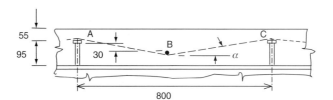

**Fig. 6.36.** Level of bottom transverse reinforcement (dimensions in mm)

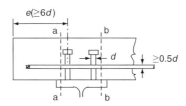

**Fig. 6.37.** Longitudinal shear reinforcement in an L-beam

of excessively close spacings of connectors and the use of connector geometries that might prevent adequate flow of the concrete around the connector. The former could be a consideration at the ends of fully integral bridges where a very high shear flow has to be transferred into the steel beam over a relatively short length. Since the resistances of connectors other than studs are not covered by EN 1994-2, properties of other types of connector could be referred to from a National Annex. The design of a block-and-hoop connector is illustrated in Example 6.8. A novel type of connection could be investigated as part of the testing requirements of *clause 6.6.1.1(12)*.

### Loading of shear connection during execution
*Clause 6.6.5.2(3)* particularly concerns the staged casting of concrete flanges for typical unpropped composite bridges. Partly matured concrete around shear connectors in a recently cast length of beam could possibly be damaged by the effects of concreting nearby. The recommended lower limit on concrete strength, $20\,\text{N/mm}^2$, in effect sets a minimum time interval between successive stages of casting. The rule begins '*Wherever possible*' because there appears to be no evidence of damage from effects of early thermal or shrinkage strains, which also apply longitudinal shear to young concrete.

*Clause 6.6.5.2(3)*

In propped construction, it would be unusual to remove the props until the concrete had achieved a compressive strength of at least $20\,\text{N/mm}^2$, in order to avoid overstressing the beam as a whole. Where the props are removed prior to the concrete attaining the specified strength, verifications at removal of props should be based on an appropriately reduced compressive strength.

### Local reinforcement in the slab
Where shear connectors are close to a longitudinal edge of a concrete flange, use of U-bars is almost the only way of providing the full anchorage required by *clause 6.6.5.3(1)*. The splitting referred to in *clause 6.6.5.3(2)* is a common mode of failure in push-test specimens with narrow slabs (e.g. 300 mm, which has long been the standard width in British codes). It was also found, in full-scale tests, to be the normal failure mode for composite L-beams constructed with precast slabs.[84] Detailing rules are given in *clause 6.6.5.3(2)* for slabs where the edge distance $e$ in Fig. 6.37 is less than 300 mm. The required area of bottom transverse reinforcement, $A_b$ per unit length of beam, should be found using *clause 6.6.6*. In the unhaunched slab shown in Fig. 6.37, failure surface b–b will be critical (unless the slab is very thick) because the shear on surface a–a is low in an L-beam with an asymmetrical concrete flange.

*Clause 6.6.5.3(1)*
*Clause 6.6.5.3(2)*

To ensure that the reinforcement is fully anchored to the left of the line a–a, it is recommended that U-bars be used. These can be in a horizontal plane or, where top reinforcement is needed, in a vertical plane.

### Reinforcement at the end of a cantilever
At the end of a composite cantilever, the force on the concrete from the connectors acts towards the nearest edge of the slab. The effects of shrinkage and temperature can add further stresses[74] that tend to cause splitting in region B in Fig. 6.38, so reinforcement in this region needs careful detailing. *Clause 6.6.5.3(3)P* can be satisfied by providing 'herringbone' bottom reinforcement (ABC in Fig. 6.38) sufficient to anchor the force from the connectors into the slab, and ensuring that the longitudinal bars provided to resist that force are anchored beyond their intersection with ABC.

*Clause 6.6.5.3(3)P*

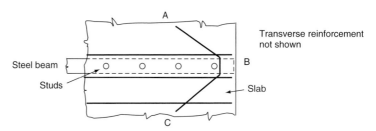

**Fig. 6.38.** Reinforcement at the end of a cantilever

*Haunches*

Haunches are sometimes provided in composite bridges to cater for drainage cross-falls so that the thickness of the slab or deck surfacing need not be varied. The detailing rules of *Clause 6.6.5.4* *clause 6.6.5.4* are based on limited test evidence, but are long-established.[85] In regions of high longitudinal shear, deep haunches should be used with caution because there may be little warning of failure.

*Maximum spacing of connectors*

Situations where the stability of a concrete slab is ensured by its connection to a steel beam are unlikely to occur because a concrete slab that is adequate to resist local bridge loading is unlikely to suffer instability from membrane forces. The converse situation, stabilization of the steel flange, is of interest only where the steel compression flange is not already in Class 1 or 2. Where the steel beam is a plate girder, its proportions will often be chosen such that it is in Class 3 for the bare steel condition during construction. This maximises the lateral buckling resistance for a flange of given cross-sectional area.

*Clause 6.6.5.5(2)* *Clause 6.6.5.5(2)* is not restrictive in practice. As an example, a plate girder is considered, in steel with $f_y = 355\,\text{N/mm}^2$, where the top flange has $t_f = 20\,\text{mm}$, an overall breadth of 350 mm, and an outstand $c$ of 165 mm. The ratio $\varepsilon$ is 0.81 and the slenderness is:

$$c/t_f\varepsilon = 165/(20 \times 0.81) = 10.2$$

so from Table 5.2 of EN 1993-1-1, the flange is in Class 3. From *clause 6.6.5.5(2)*, it can be assumed to be in Class 1 if shear connectors are provided within 146 mm of each free edge, at longitudinal spacing not exceeding 356 mm, for a solid slab.

The ratio 22 in this clause is based on the assumption that the steel flange cannot buckle towards the slab. Where there are transverse ribs (e.g. due to the use of profiled sheeting), the assumption may not be correct, so the ratio is reduced to 15. The maximum spacing in this example is then 243 mm.

Further requirements for composite plates in box girders are given in *clause 9.4(7)*. These also cover limitations on longitudinal and transverse spacings of connectors to ensure Class 3 behaviour. The rule on transverse spacing in *Table 9.1* should be applied also to a wide compression flange of a plate girder.

*Clause 6.6.5.5(3)* The maximum longitudinal spacing in bridges, given in *clause 6.6.5.5(3)*, $4h_c$ but $\leq 800\,\text{mm}$, is more liberal than the equivalent rule of BS 5400 Part 5.[11] It is based mainly on behaviour observed in tests, and on practice with precast slabs in some countries.

*Clause 6.6.5.5(4)* *Clause 6.6.5.5(4)* allows the spacing rules for individual connectors to be relaxed if connectors are placed in groups. This may facilitate the use of precast deck units with discrete pockets for the shear connection (*clause 8.4.3(3)* refers) but many of the deemed-to-satisfy rules elsewhere in EN 1994-2 then no longer apply. The designer should then explicitly consider the relevant effects, which will make it difficult in practice to depart from the application rules. The effects listed are as follows.

- Non-uniform flow of longitudinal shear. If the spacing of the groups of connectors is large compared to the distance between points of zero and maximum moment in the beam, then the normal assumption of plane sections remaining plane will not apply and the calculation of bending resistance to *clause 6.2* will not be valid.

- Greater risk of slip and vertical separation of concrete and steel. The latter carries a corrosion risk for the steel flange which would be hard to quantify without testing.
- Buckling of the steel flange. This can be considered by applying clause 4.4(2) of EN 1993-1-5. The elastic critical buckling stress, $\sigma_{cr}$, can be determined for the discrete supports offered by the particular connection provided, either by finite-element analysis or from standard texts such as Ref. 86. If the latter method is employed, account needs to be taken of the beneficial restraint provided by the concrete against buckling. In the absence of this restraint, the flange would try to buckle in half wavelengths between the studs, alternating towards and away from the concrete. Buckling into the concrete is, in reality, prevented and therefore no rotation of the flange can occur along the line of the studs. Discrete supports which clamp the plate at the stud locations may therefore usually be assumed in determining the critical stress.
- Local resistance of the slab to the concentrated force from the connectors. Groups of studs apply a force analogous to that from an anchorage of a prestressing cable. The region of transverse tension does not coincide with the location of the group. Both the quantity and the location of the transverse reinforcement required may differ from that given by *clause 6.6.6*.

### Dimensions of the steel flange
The rules of *clause 6.6.5.6* are intended to prevent local overstress of a steel flange near a shear connector and to avoid problems with stud welding. Application rules for minimum flange thickness are given in *clause 6.6.5.7(3)* and *(5)*. The minimum edge distance for connectors in *clause 6.6.5.6(2)* is consistent with the requirements of BS 5400:Part 5.[11] The limit is also necessary to avoid a reduction in the fatigue detail category for the flange at the stud location, which from EN 1993-1-9 Table 8.4, is 80 for a compliant stud.

*Clause 6.6.5.6*

*Clause 6.6.5.6(2)*

### Headed stud connectors
*Clause 6.6.5.7(1)* and *(2)* is concerned with resistance to uplift. Rules for resistance of studs, minimum cover and projection of studs above bottom reinforcement usually lead to the use of studs of height greater than $3d$.

*Clause 6.6.5.7(1)*
*Clause 6.6.5.7(2)*

The limit 1.5 for the ratio $d/t_f$ in *clause 6.6.5.7(3)* could, in principle, influence the design of shear connection for closed-top box girders in bridges, effectively requiring the thickness of the top flange to be a minimum of 13 mm where 19 mm diameter studs are used. Studs of this size are preferred by many UK fabricators as they can be welded manually. It is unlikely that a composite box would have a flange this thin as it would then require considerable longitudinal stiffening to support the plate prior to setting of the concrete. *Clause 6.6.5.7(3)* would also apply to plate girders adjacent to cross-braces or transverse diaphragms, but practical sizes of flanges for main beams will satisfy this criterion. It could be a consideration for cross-girders.

*Clause 6.6.5.7(3)*

In *clause 6.6.5.7(4)*, the minimum lateral spacing of studs in 'solid slabs' has been reduced to $2.5d$, compared with the $4d$ of BS 5950-3-1. This facilitates the use of precast slabs supported on the edges of the steel flanges, with projecting U-bars that loop over pairs of studs. Closely spaced pairs of studs must be well confined laterally. The words 'solid slabs' should therefore be understood here to exclude haunches.

*Clause 6.6.5.7(4)*

## 6.6.6. Longitudinal shear in concrete slabs
The subject of *clause 6.6.6* is the avoidance of local failure of a concrete flange near the shear connection, by the provision of appropriate reinforcement. These bars enhance the resistance of a thin concrete slab to in-plane shear in the same way that stirrups strengthen a concrete web in vertical shear. Transverse reinforcement is also needed to control and limit the longitudinal splitting of the slab that can be caused by local forces from individual connectors. In this respect, the detailing problem is more acute than in the flanges of concrete T-beams, where the shear from the web is applied more uniformly.

*Clause 6.6.6*

The principal change from earlier codes is that the equations for the required area of transverse reinforcement have been replaced by cross-reference to EN 1992-1-1. Its provisions are based on a truss analogy, as before, but a more general version of it, in which the angle between members of the truss can be chosen by the designer. It is an application of strut-and-tie modelling, which is widely used in EN 1992.

There is, however, a significant difference between the application of EN 1992 and EN 1994. In the latter, the transverse reinforcement may be placed according to the distribution of vertical shear force envelope, or according to the stud forces for sections where the elastic resistance moment is exceeded. In the former, the transverse reinforcement should be placed according to the location of the web compression struts as they intersect the flanges and their subsequent continuation into the flanges.

*Clause 6.6.6.1(2)P*      The definitions of shear surfaces in *clause 6.6.6.1(2)P* and the basic design method are as before. The method of presentation reflects the need to separate the 'general' provisions, *clauses 6.6.6.1 to 3*, from those restricted to 'buildings', in EN 1994-1-1 clause 6.6.6.4.

*Clause 6.6.6.1(4)*      *Clause 6.6.6.1(4)* requires the design longitudinal shear to be '*consistent with*' that used for the design of the shear connectors. This means that the distribution along the beam of resistance to in-plane shear in the slab should be not less than that assumed for the design of the shear connection. For example, uniform resistance to longitudinal shear flow ($v_L$) should be provided where the connectors are uniformly spaced, even if the vertical shear over the length is not constant. It does not mean, for example, that if, for reasons concerning detailing, $v_{L,Rd} = 1.3 v_{L,Ed}$ for the connectors, the transverse reinforcement must provide the same degree of over-strength.

The reference to '*variation of longitudinal shear across the width of the concrete flange*' means that transverse reinforcement could be reduced away from the beam centre-lines, where the longitudinal shear reduces, if flexural requirements permit.

*Clause 6.6.6.1(5)*      In applying *clause 6.6.6.1(5)*, it is sufficiently accurate to assume that longitudinal bending stress in the concrete flange is constant across its effective width, and zero outside it. The clause is relevant, for example, to finding the shear on plane a–a in the haunched beam shown in *Fig. 6.15*, which, for a symmetrical flange, is less than half the shear resisted by the connectors.

### Resistance of a concrete flange to longitudinal shear

*Clause 6.6.6.2(1)*      *Clause 6.6.6.2(1)* refers to clause 6.2.4 of EN 1992-1-1, which is written for a design longitudinal shear stress $v_{Ed}$ acting on a cross-section of thickness $h_f$. This must be distinguished from the design longitudinal shear flow $v_{L,Ed}$ used in EN 1994 which is equal to $v_{Ed}h_f$. The clause requires the area of transverse reinforcement $A_{sf}$ at spacing $s_f$ to satisfy

$$A_{sf} f_{yd} / s_f > v_{Ed} h_f / \cot \theta_f \qquad \text{(6.21) in EN 1992-1-1}$$

and the longitudinal shear stress to satisfy

$$v_{Ed} < \nu f_{cd} \sin \theta_f \cos \theta_f \qquad \text{(6.22) in EN 1992-1-1}$$

where $\nu = 0.6(1 - f_{ck}/250)$, with $f_{ck}$ in N/mm$^2$ units. (The Greek letter $\nu$ (nu) used here in EN 1992-1-1 should not be confused with the Roman letter $v$ (vee), which is used for shear stress.)

The angle $\theta_f$ between the diagonal strut and the axis of the beam is chosen (within limits) by the designer. It should be noted that the recommended limits depend on whether the flange is in tension or compression, and can be varied by a National Annex.

EN 1992-1-1 does not specify the distribution of the required transverse reinforcement between the upper and lower layers in the slab. It was a requirement of early drafts of EN 1992-2 that the transverse reinforcement provided should have the same centre of resistance as the longitudinal force in the slab. This was removed, presumably because it has been common practice to consider the shear resistance to be the sum of the resistances from the two layers. *Clause 6.6.6.2(3)* refers to *Fig. 6.15* which clarifies that the reinforcement to be considered on plane a–a for composite beams is the total of the two layers, $A_b + A_t$. It should be noted that application of Annex MM of EN 1992-2 would necessitate provision of transverse reinforcement with the same centre of resistance as the longitudinal force in the slab.

The use of the method is illustrated in Example 6.9.

The reference in *clause 6.6.6.2(1)* is to the whole of clause 6.2.4 of EN 1992-1-1. This includes clause 6.2.4(5) which requires a check of the interaction with transverse bending in the concrete slab on planes of type a–a. This requires the amount of transverse reinforcement to be the greater of that required for longitudinal shear alone and half that required for longitudinal shear plus that required for transverse bending.

This rule is illustrated in Fig. 6.39(b), in which $A_{req'd}$ is the total reinforcement required, and subscripts s and b refer to the reinforcement required for shear and bending, respectively. The rule is more onerous than that in BS 5400 Part 5, where no interaction is needed to be considered on planes of type a–a. This was because a transverse bending moment produces no net axial force in the slab. Reinforcement in tension is then associated with concrete that has a resistance to shear enhanced by the presence of transverse compression. Test evidence supported this model.

Consideration of this interaction according to EN 1992-1-1, rather than simple addition of bending and shear requirements, is rational as the truss angle in the upper and lower layers of the slab can be varied to account for the relative demands imposed on them of shear and either direct tension or compression. Annex MM of EN 1992-2 reinforces this, although its use suggests that the '50% of longitudinal shear' rule is optimistic. The interaction on surfaces around the studs differs slightly as discussed below under the heading '*Shear planes and surfaces*'.

Clause 6.2.4(105) of EN 1992-2 adds an additional interaction condition for the concrete struts, which was largely due to the strength of belief in its Project Team that the neglect of this check was unsafe. It was less to do with any inherent difference between the behaviour of buildings and bridges. Considerations of equilibrium suggest that EN 1992-2 is correct. The reference in EN 1994-2 to EN 1992-1-1 rather than to EN 1992-2 is therefore significant as it excludes the check. No check of the effect of moment on the concrete struts was required by BS 5400 Part 5.

Clause 6.2.4(105) of EN 1992-2 refers to the compression from transverse bending. It is however equally logical to consider the slab longitudinal compression in the check of the concrete struts, although this was not intended. Once again, the use of Annex MM of EN 1992-2 would require this to be considered. It is rare in practice for a concrete flange to be subjected to a severe combination of longitudinal compression and in-plane shear. It could occur near an internal support of a continuous half-through bridge. It is shown in Example 6.11 that the reduction in resistance to bending would usually be negligible, if this additional interaction were to be considered.

Neither EN 1992 nor EN 1994 deals with the case of longitudinal shear and coexistent transverse tension in the slab. This can occur in the transverse beams of ladder decks near the intersection with the main beams in hogging zones where the main beam reinforcement is in global tension. In such cases, there is clearly a net tension in the slab and the reinforcement requirements for this tension should be fully combined with that for longitudinal shear on planes a–a.

### Shear planes and surfaces

*Clause 6.6.6.1(3)* refers to shear '*surfaces*' because some of them are not plane. Those of types b–b, c–c and d–d in *Fig. 6.15* are different from the type a–a surface because they resist almost the whole longitudinal shear, not (typically) about half of it. The relevant reinforcement intersects them twice, as shown by the factors 2 in the table in *Fig. 6.15*.

For a surface of type c–c in a beam with the steel section near one edge of the concrete flange, it is clearly wrong to assume that half the shear crosses half of the surface c–c. However, in this situation the shear on the adjacent plane of type a–a will govern, so the method is not unsafe.

*Clause 6.6.6.2(2)* refers to EN 1992-1-1 clause 6.2.4(4) for resistance to longitudinal shear for surfaces passing around the shear studs. This does not include a check of the interaction with transverse bending in the slab. This does not mean that such a check may be ignored.

*Clause 6.6.6.2(2)*

Interaction of longitudinal shear and bending should be considered for the reinforcement crossing shear surfaces around the connectors. Slab bottom reinforcement is particularly important since most of the shear transferred by stud connectors is transferred over the bottom part of the stud. The bottom reinforcement crossing surfaces passing around the studs must control the localized splitting stresses generated by the high stud pressures. For surfaces of type b–b and c–c in *Fig. 6.15*, it is clear that the reinforcement crossing the surface must provide both the resistance to longitudinal shear and any transverse sagging moment present. The reinforcement requirements for coexisting shear and sagging moment should therefore be fully added.

For coexisting shear and hogging moment, there is transverse compression at the base of the connectors. BS 5400 Part 5 permitted a corresponding reduction in the bottom reinforcement. This could be the basis of a '*more accurate calculation*' permitted by *clause 6.6.6.2(2)*.

For surfaces of type d–d in *Fig. 6.15*, the haunch reinforcement crossed by the studs will not be considered in the sagging bending resistance and therefore it need only be designed for longitudinal shear. These recommendations are consistent with those in BS 5400 Part 5.

*Minimum transverse reinforcement*

*Clause 6.6.6.3*

*Clause 6.6.6.3* on this subject is discussed under *clause 6.6.5.1* on resistance to separation.

### Example 6.9: transverse reinforcement for longitudinal shear

Figure 6.39(a) shows a plan of an area ABCD of a concrete flange of thickness $h_f$, assumed to be in longitudinal compression, with shear stress $v_{Ed}$ and transverse reinforcement $A_{sf}$ at spacing $s_f$. The shear force per transverse bar is:

$$F_v = v_{Ed} h_f s_f$$

acting on side AB of the rectangle shown. It is transferred to side CD by a concrete strut AC at angle $\theta_f$ to AB, and with edges that pass through the mid-points of AB, etc., as shown, so that the width of the strut is $s_f \sin \theta_f$.

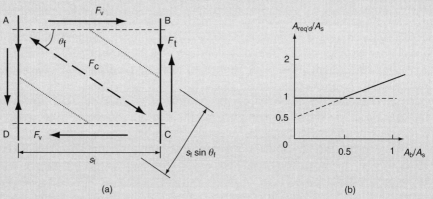

(a)

(b)

**Fig. 6.39.** In-plane shear in a concrete flange: (a) truss analogy; and (b) interaction of longitudinal shear with bending

For equilibrium at A, the force in the strut is:

$$F_c = F_v \sec \theta_f \tag{D6.21}$$

For equilibrium at C, the force in the transverse bar BC is:

$$F_t = F_c \sin \theta_f = F_v \tan \theta_f \tag{D6.22}$$

For minimum area of transverse reinforcement, $\theta_f$ should be chosen to be as small as possible. For a flange in compression, the limits to $\theta_f$ given in clause 6.2.4(4) of EN 1992-1-1 are:

$$45° \geq \theta_f \geq 26.5° \tag{D6.23}$$

so the initial choice for $\theta_f$ is 26.5°. Then, from equation (D6.22),

$$F_t = 0.5F_v \qquad\qquad (D6.24)$$

From equation (6.22) in EN 1992-1-1, above,

$$v_{Ed} < 0.40\nu f_{cd}$$

If this inequality is satisfied, then the value chosen for $\theta_f$ is satisfactory. However, let us assume that the concrete strut is overstressed, because $v_{Ed} = 0.48\nu f_{cd}$.
To satisfy equation (6.22), $\sin\theta_f \cos\theta_f \geq 0.48$, whence $\theta_f \geq 37°$.
The designer increases $\theta_f$ to 40°, which satisfies expression (D6.23).
From equation (D6.22), $F_t = F_v \tan 40° = 0.84F_v$.
From equation (D6.24), the change in $\theta_f$, made to limit the compressive stress in the concrete strut AC, increases the required area of transverse reinforcement by 68%.

The lengths of the sides of the triangle ABC in Fig. 6.39(a) are proportional to the forces $F_v$, $F_t$ and $F_c$. For given $F_v$ and $s_f$, increasing $\theta_f$ increases $F_c$, but for $\theta_f < 45°$ (the maximum value recommended), the increase in the width $s_t \sin\theta_f$ is greater, so the stress in the concrete is reduced.

## Example 6.10: longitudinal shear checks
The bridge shown in Fig. 6.22 is checked for longitudinal shear, (i) adjacent to an internal support, (ii) at mid-span of the main span and (iii) at an end support. Creep of concrete reduces longitudinal shear, so for elastic theory, the short-term modular ratio is used.

### (i) Adjacent to an internal support
The $19 \times 150$ mm stud connectors are assumed to be 145 mm high after welding. Their arrangement and the transverse reinforcement are shown in Fig. 6.40 and the dimensions of the cross-section in Fig. 6.22. The shear studs are checked first. Although the concrete is assumed to be cracked at the support in both global analysis and cross-section design, the slab is considered to be uncracked for longitudinal shear design in accordance with *clause 6.6.2.1(2)*. The longitudinal shear is determined from the vertical shear using elastic analysis in accordance with *clause 6.6.2.1(1)* since the bending resistance was based on elastic analysis.

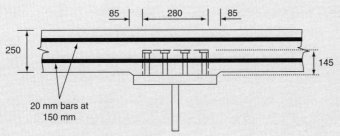

**Fig. 6.40.** Shear studs and transverse reinforcement adjacent to an internal support

From Example 5.2, the modular ratio $n_0$ is 6.36. From Example 5.4, the area of longitudinal reinforcement is $A_s = 19\,480\,\text{mm}^2$, which is 2.5% of the effective cross-section of the concrete flange. Relevant elastic properties of the cross-section are given in Table 6.3 for the uncracked unreinforced section (subscript U) and the uncracked reinforced section (subscript UR). The effect on these values of including the reinforcement is not negligible when the long-term modular ratio is used. However, the significant reduction in longitudinal shear caused by cracking is being ignored, so it is accurate enough to use the unreinforced section when calculating longitudinal shear.

The height $z$ to the neutral axis is measured from the bottom of the cross-section. The property $A\bar{z}/I$, for the whole of the effective concrete flange, is appropriate for checking the shear resistance of the studs, and slightly conservative for the shear surface of type b–b shown in Fig. 6.40.

**Table 6.3.** Elastic properties of cross-section at internal support

| Modular ratio | $z_U$ (mm) | $I_U$ (m²mm²) | $(A\bar{z}/I)_U$ (m⁻¹) | $z_{UR}$ (mm) | $I_{UR}$ (m²mm²) | $(A\bar{z}/I)_{UR}$ (m⁻¹) |
|---|---|---|---|---|---|---|
| 6.36 | 1120 | 38 530 | 0.8098 | 1146 | 39 890 | 0.8380 |
| 23.63 | 862 | 26 390 | 0.6438 | 959 | 31 200 | 0.7284 |

The calculation using $n_0$ is:

$$\frac{A\bar{z}}{I} = \frac{\left(\frac{3100}{6.36} \times 250\right) \times (1375 - 1120) + \left(\frac{400}{6.36} \times 25\right) \times (1238 - 1120)}{38\,530 \times 10^3} = 0.810\,\text{m}^{-1}$$

The design vertical shear forces on the composite section are: long-term, $V_{Ed} = 827\,\text{kN}$; short-term, $V_{Ed} = 1076\,\text{kN}$; total, 1903 kN.

From equation (D6.18),

$$v_{L,Ed} = 1903 \times 0.810 = \mathbf{1541\,kN/m}$$

Groups of four 19 mm diameter studs with $f_u = 500\,\text{N/mm}^2$ are provided at 150 mm centres. Their resistance is governed by *equation (6.19)*:

$$P_{Rd} = \frac{0.29\alpha d^2\sqrt{f_{ck}E_{cm}}}{\gamma_V} = \frac{0.29 \times 19^2\sqrt{30 \times 33 \times 10^3}}{1.25 \times 1000} = 83.3\,\text{kN/stud}$$

Thus $v_{L,Rd} = 83.3 \times 4/0.15 = \mathbf{2222\,kN/m}$ which exceeds the 1541 kN/m applied.

Longitudinal shear in the concrete is checked next. The surface around the studs is critical for the reinforcement check as it has the same reinforcement as the plane through the deck (i.e. two 20 mm diameter bars) but almost twice the longitudinal shear. It is assumed here that there is no significant sagging bending over the top of the main beams adjacent to the internal supports. From equation (6.21) in clause 6.2.4(4) of EN 1992-1-1, assuming a 45° truss angle:

$$A_{sf}f_{yd}/s_f > v_{Ed}h_f/\cot\theta_f \quad \text{where} \quad v_{Ed}h_f = 1541\,\text{kN/m}$$

$$A_{sf} \geq 1541 \times 150/(\cot 45° \times 500/1.15) = 532\,\text{mm}^2 < 628\,\text{mm}^2 \text{ from two 20 mm bars}$$

The planes through the deck slab are critical for the concrete stress check since the length of each concrete shear plane is 250 mm compared to 570 mm for the surface around the studs, which carries twice the shear. The shear stress is:

$$v_{Ed} = 1541/(2 \times 250) = 3.08\,\text{N/mm}^2$$

From equations (6.6N) in clause 6.2.2(6) and (6.22) in clause 6.2.4(4) of EN 1992-1-1:

$$v_{Ed} < \nu f_{cd}\sin\theta_f\cos\theta_f = 0.6(1 - 30/250) \times (30/1.5) \times 0.5 = 5.28\,\text{N/mm}^2$$

so the shear stress is satisfactory.

It should be noted that there is another surface around the studs which intersects the top of the haunch with length of 582 mm. It would be possible for such a plane to be more critical.

### (ii) Mid-span of the main span
The maximum spacing of groups of studs as shown in Fig. 6.41 is now found. The transverse reinforcement is as before and the cross-sectional dimensions of the beam are shown in Fig. 6.22. In the real bridge, the moment at mid-span was less than the elastic resistance

to bending and therefore a similar calculation to that in (i) could have been performed. For the purpose of this example, the sagging bending moment at mid-span is considered to be increased to 8.0 MNm, comprising 2.0 MNm on the bare steel section, 2.0 MNm on the 'long-term' composite section and 4.0 MNm live load on the 'short-term' composite section.

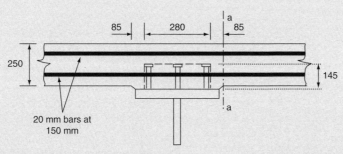

**Fig. 6.41.** Shear studs and transverse reinforcement at mid-span and adjacent to an end support

The distance between the point of maximum moment and the point where the elastic resistance to bending is just exceeded is assumed here to be 4.5 m. The longitudinal shear force between these points is determined by rearranging *equation (6.3)* and substituting $M_{Ed}$ for $M_{Rd}$ so that:

$$V_{L,Ed} = N_c - N_{c,el} = \frac{(N_{c,f} - N_{c,el})(M_{Ed} - M_{el,Rd})}{(M_{pl,Rd} - M_{el,Rd})}$$

It is not obvious which modular ratio gives the more adverse result for this region, so calculations are done using both $n_0$ and $n_L$ for the long-term loading. The elastic resistance to bending is governed by the tensile stress in the bottom flange. From *clause 6.2.1.4(6)*, $M_{el,Rd}$ is found by scaling down $M_{c,Ed}$ by a factor $k$ until a stress limit is reached. The relevant section moduli in $m^2mm$ units are 15.96 for the steel section, and 23.39 short term and 21.55 long term for the composite section. Hence,

$$2000/15.96 + (4000/23.39 + 2000/21.55)k = 345 - 11.7$$

where 11.7 N/mm$^2$ is the stress due to the primary effects of shrinkage from Example 5.3. (The secondary effects of shrinkage have been ignored here as they are relieving.)

This gives $k = 0.788$, and the elastic resistance moment is:

$$M_{el,Rd} = 2000 + 0.788 \times (4000 + 2000) = 6728 \text{ kNm}$$

From Example 6.1, $M_{pl,Rd} = 10\,050$ kNm.

The compressive force $N_{c,el}$ in the composite slab at $M_{el,Rd}$ is now required. The primary shrinkage stress, although tensile, is included for consistency with the calculation of $M_{el,Rd}$. Its value at mid-depth of the 250 mm flange, from Example 5.3, is 0.68 N/mm$^2$. The effect of the stresses in the haunch is negligible here. Using the section moduli for mid-depth of the flange, given in Table 6.4, the mean stress is:

$$\sigma_{c,mean} = 0.788 \times (4000/969.1) + (2000/1143) - 0.68 = 3.95 \text{ N/mm}^2$$

**Table 6.4.** Section moduli at mid-span for uncracked unreinforced section

| Modular ratio | $z_U$ (mm) | $I_U$ (m$^2$mm$^2$) | $(A\bar{z}/I)_U$ (m$^{-1}$) | $W_c$, top of slab (m$^2$mm) | $W_c$, mid slab (m$^2$mm) | $W_c$, mid haunch (m$^2$mm) | $W_a$, bottom flange (m$^2$mm) |
|---|---|---|---|---|---|---|---|
| 6.36 | 1192 | 27 880 | 0.8024 | 575.9 | 969.1 | 3890 | 23.39 |
| 23.7 | 951 | 20 500 | 0.6843 | 882.7 | 1143 | 1692 | 21.55 |

Hence,

$$N_{c,el} = 3.1 \times 0.25 \times 3.95 = 3.06\,\text{MN}$$

The force for full interaction, $N_{c,f}$, is based on rectangular stress blocks:

$$N_{c,f} = 3.1 \times 0.25 \times 0.85 \times 30/1.5 = 13.18\,\text{MN}$$

From *equation (6.3)*:

$$V_{L,Ed} = N_c - N_{c,el} = \frac{(N_{c,f} - N_{c,el})(M_{Ed} - M_{el,Rd})}{(M_{pl,Rd} - M_{el,Rd})} = \frac{(13.18 - 3.06)(8.0 - 6.728)}{(10.05 - 6.728)}$$

$$= 3875\,\text{kN}$$

The shear flow is therefore $v_{L,Ed} = 3875/4.5 = \mathbf{861\,kN/m}$

Similar calculations using $n_0 = 6.36$ for all loading give: $M_{el,Rd} = 6858\,\text{kNm}$, $\sigma_{c,mean} = 4.33\,\text{N/mm}^2$, and $N_{c,el} = 3.36\,\text{MN}$, from which $v_{L,Ed} = 781\,\text{kN/m}$, which does not govern.

From (i) above, $P_{Rd} = 83.3\,\text{kN/stud}$, so the required spacing of groups of three is:

$$s_v = 83.3 \times 3/861 = 0.290\,\text{m}$$

Groups at 250 mm spacing could be used, unless a fatigue or serviceability check is found to govern.

Longitudinal shear in the concrete is adequate by inspection, as the shear flow is less than that at the internal support but both the thickness of the slab and the reinforcement are the same.

### (iii) End support

The shear stud arrangement and transverse reinforcement are as shown in Fig. 6.41 and the cross-sectional dimensions are shown in Fig. 6.22. The studs are checked first. The longitudinal shear is determined from the vertical shear using elastic analysis in accordance with *clause 6.6.2.1(1)* since the bending moment is less than the elastic resistance.

From similar calculations to those for the pier section, the longitudinal shear flow, excluding that from shrinkage and temperature, is found to be $v_{L,Ed} = 810\,\text{kN/m}$. The combination factor $\psi_0$ for effects of temperature recommended in Annex A2 of EN 1990 is 0.6, with a Note that it 'may in most cases be reduced to 0 for ultimate limit states EQU, STR, and GEO'. Temperature effects are not considered here.

The primary and secondary effects of shrinkage are both beneficial, and so are not considered. With $P_{Rd} = 83.3\,\text{kN/stud}$, the resistance of groups of three at 250 mm spacing is 1000 kN/m, which is sufficient.

Longitudinal shear in the concrete is adequate by inspection, as the shear flow is less than that at the internal support but both concrete slab thickness and reinforcement are the same.

The studs in all three cases above should also be checked at serviceability according to *clause 6.8.1(3)*. This has not been done here.

### Example 6.11: influence of in-plane shear in a compressed flange on bending resistances of a beam

The mid-span region of an internal beam in the main span of the bridge is studied. Its cross-section is shown in Fig. 6.22. The imposed sagging bending moments are as in Example 6.10(ii): $M_{Ed,a} = 2.0\,\text{MNm}$, $M_{Ed,c} = 2.0\,\text{MNm}$ short term plus 4.0 MNm long term. Shear flow is reduced by creep, so the short-term modular ratio, $n_0 = 6.36$, is used for all loading, and shrinkage effects are ignored. The section is in Class 2, but the full plastic resistance moment, $M_{pl,Rd}$, is unlikely to be needed. Properties found earlier are as follows:

- from Example 6.1, $M_{pl,Rd} = 10\,050\,\text{kNm}$

- from Fig. 6.2, at $M_{\mathrm{pl,Rd}}$, depth of slab in compression $= 227\,\mathrm{mm}$
- from Example 6.10, $M_{\mathrm{el,Rd}} = 6858\,\mathrm{kNm}$.

Elastic properties of the cross-section are given in Table 6.4.

Situations are studied in which a layer of thickness $h_{\mathrm{v}}$ at the bottom of the slab is needed for the diagonal struts of the truss model for in-plane shear. The bending resistance is found using only the remaining thickness, $h_{\mathrm{m}} = 250 - h_{\mathrm{v}}$ (mm units). This is 'the depth of compression considered in the bending assessment' to which clause 6.2.4(105) of EN 1992-2 could be assumed to refer. As discussed in the main text, it was only intended to refer to transverse bending moment. The haunch is included in the elastic properties, and neglected in calculations for $M_{\mathrm{pl,Rd}}$.

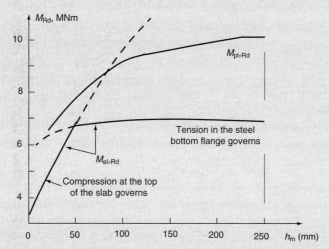

**Fig. 6.42.** Influence of thickness of slab in compression on resistance to bending

The effect on the bending resistances of reducing the flange thickness from 250 mm to $h_{\mathrm{m}}$ is shown in Fig. 6.42. Reduction in $M_{\mathrm{pl,Rd}}$ does not begin until $h_{\mathrm{m}} < 227\,\mathrm{mm}$, and is then gradual, until the plastic neutral axis moves into the web, at $h_{\mathrm{m}} = 122\,\mathrm{mm}$. When $h_{\mathrm{m}} = 100\,\mathrm{mm}$, the reduction is still less than 10%.

The elastic resistance is governed by stress in the bottom flange, and at first increases as $h_{\mathrm{m}}$ is reduced. Compressive stress in concrete does not govern until $h_{\mathrm{m}}$ is less than 50 mm, as shown. For $h_{\mathrm{m}} = 100\,\mathrm{mm}$, $M_{\mathrm{el,Rd}}$ is greater than for 250 mm.

The vertical shear for which $h_{\mathrm{m}} = 100\,\mathrm{mm}$, $h_{\mathrm{v}} = 150\,\mathrm{mm}$ is now found and compared with the shear resistance of the steel web, $V_{\mathrm{bw,Rd}} = 1834\,\mathrm{kN}$ from Example 6.4. The method is explained in comments on *clause 6.6.6.2(1)*. The optimum angle $\theta_{\mathrm{f}}$ for the concrete struts, which is 45°, is used. It is assumed that the transverse reinforcement does not govern. The property $A\bar{z}/I$ should continue to be based on the full slab thickness, not on $h_{\mathrm{m}}$, to provide a margin for over-strength materials, inelastic behaviour, etc.

Equation (6.22) in EN 1992-1-1 is $v_{\mathrm{Ed}} < \nu f_{\mathrm{cd}} \sin\theta_{\mathrm{f}} \cos\theta_{\mathrm{f}}$.
From Example 6.10(i) with $f_{\mathrm{ck}} = 30\,\mathrm{N/mm^2}$, $\theta_{\mathrm{f}} = 45°$; this gives $v_{\mathrm{Ed}} < 5.28\,\mathrm{N/mm^2}$.
From Fig. 6.41, the width of flange excluded by the shear plane a–a is:

$$(3100 - 450)/2 = 1325\,\mathrm{mm}$$

The shear flow on this plane is:

$$v_{\mathrm{L,Ed}} = v_{\mathrm{Ed}} h_{\mathrm{v}} = (1325/3100) V_{\mathrm{Ed}} (A\bar{z}/I) \qquad \text{(D6.25)}$$

From equation (D6.25) with $h_{\mathrm{v}} = 150\,\mathrm{mm}$ and $A\bar{z}/I$ from Table 6.4,

$$\mathbf{V_{Ed}} < 5.28 \times 150 \times (3100/1325)/0.8024 = \mathbf{2309\,kN}$$

This limit is 26% above the shear resistance of the steel web. Evidently, interaction between in-plane shear and bending resistance is negligible for this cross-section.

## 6.7. Composite columns and composite compression members

### 6.7.1. General

*Scope*

A composite column is defined in *clause 1.5.2.5* as '*a composite member subjected mainly to compression or to compression and bending*'. The title of *clause 6.7* includes '*compression members*' to make clear that its scope is not limited to vertical members, but includes, for example, composite members in trusses.

Composite columns are more widely used in buildings than in bridges, so their treatment here is less detailed than in the *Designers' Guide to EN 1994-1-1*.[5] Its Example 6.10 on a concrete-encased I-section column is supplemented here by Example 6.12 on a concrete-filled steel tube.

In this Guide, references to 'columns' include other composite compression members, unless noted otherwise, and 'column' means a length of member between adjacent lateral restraints. The concept of the 'effective length' of a column is not used in *clause 6.7*. Instead, the 'relative slenderness' is defined, in *clause 6.7.3.3(2)*, in terms of $N_{cr}$, '*the elastic critical normal force for the relevant buckling mode*'. This use of $N_{cr}$ is explained in the comments on *clause 6.7.3.3*.

*Clause 6.7.1(1)P* refers to *Fig. 6.17*, in which all the cross-sections shown have double symmetry; but *clause 6.7.1(6)* makes clear that the scope of the general method of *clause 6.7.2* includes members of non-symmetrical section.[87]

*Clause 6.7* is not intended for application to members subjected mainly to transverse loading and also resisting longitudinal compression, such as longitudinal beams in an integral bridge. These are treated in this Guide in the comments on beams.

The bending moment in a compression member depends on the assumed location of the line of action of the axial force, $N$. Where the cross-section has double symmetry, as in most columns, this is taken as the intersection of the axes of symmetry. In other cases the choice, made in the modelling for global analysis, should be retained for the analysis of the cross-sections. A small degree of asymmetry (e.g. due to an embedded pipe) can be allowed for by ignoring in calculations concrete areas elsewhere, such that symmetry is restored.

No shear connectors are shown in the cross-sections in *Fig. 6.17*, because within a column length, the longitudinal shear is normally much lower than in a beam, and sufficient inter-action may be provided by bond or friction. Shear connectors are normally required for load introduction, following *clause 6.7.4*.

Where the design axial compression is less than $N_{pm,Rd}$, shown in *Fig. 6.19* and Fig. 6.47, it is on the safe side to ignore it in verification of cross-sections. Where there is moderate or high transverse shear, shear connectors may be needed throughout the member. Example 6.11 of Ref. 5 is relevant.

The strengths of materials in *clause 6.7.1(2)P* are as for beams, except that class C60/75 and lightweight-aggregate concretes are excluded. For these, additional provisions (e.g. for creep, shrinkage and strain capacity) would be required.[88,89]

*Clause 6.7.1(3)* and *clause 5.1.1(2)* both concern the scope of EN 1994-2, as discussed above.

The steel contribution ratio, *clause 6.7.1(4)*, is the proportion of the squash load of the section that is provided by the structural steel member. If it is outside the limits given, the member should be treated as reinforced concrete or as structural steel, as appropriate.

*Independent action effects*

*Clause 6.7.1(7)* relates to the $N$–$M$ interaction curve for a cross-section of a column shown in *Fig. 6.19* and as a polygon in Fig. 6.47. It applies where the factored axial compression $\gamma_F N_{Ek}$ is less than $N_{pm,Rd}/2$, so that reduction in $N_{Ed}$ reduces $M_{Rd}$. As this could be unsafe where $N_{Ed}$ and $M_{Ed}$ result from independent actions, the factor $\gamma_F$ for $N_{Ek}$ is reduced, as illustrated in Fig. 6.34 of Ref. 5.

The 'bulge' in the interaction curve is often tiny, as shown in Fig. 6.47. A simpler and more conservative rule, that ignores the bulge, was given in ENV 1994-1-1. It is that if $M_{Rd}$ corresponding to $\gamma_F N_{Ek}$ is found to exceed $M_{pl,Rd}$, $M_{Rd}$ should be taken as $M_{pl,Rd}$. It is applicable unless the bending moment $M_{Ed}$ is due solely to the eccentricity of the force $N_{Ed}$.

It is doubtful if the 20% rule of *clause 6.7.1(7)* was intended to be combined with the reduction of $\gamma_F$ from 1.35 to 1.0 for a permanent action with a relieving effect. Where that is done, use of the simpler rule given above is recommended (e.g. in Fig. 6.47, to replace boundary BDC by BC).

### Local buckling

The principle of **clause 6.7.1(8)P** is followed by application rules in **clause 6.7.1(9)**. They ensure that the concrete (reinforced in accordance with *clause 6.7.5*) restrains the steel and prevents it from buckling even when yielded. Columns are, in effect, treated in *clause 6.7* as Class 2 sections. Restraint from the concrete enables the slenderness limits for Class 2 to be increased to the values given in *Table 6.3*. For example, the factor 90 given for a circular hollow section replaces 70 in EN 1993-1-1. Members in Class 3 or 4 are outside the scope of *clause 6.7*.

*Clause 6.7.1(8)P*
*Clause 6.7.1(9)*

### Fatigue

Verification of columns for fatigue will rarely be needed, but fatigue loading could occur in composite members in a truss or in composite columns in integral bridges. Verification, if required, should be to *clause 6.8*.

## 6.7.2. General method of design

The 'general method' of **clause 6.7.2** is provided for members outside the scope of the simplified method of *clause 6.7.3*, and also to enable advanced software-based methods to be used. It is more a set of principles than a design method. Writing software that satisfies them is a task for specialists.

*Clause 6.7.2*

Much of *clause 6.7.3* and the comments on it provide further guidance on design of compression members that are outside its scope.

**Clause 6.7.2(3)P** refers to '*internal forces*'. These are the action effects within the compression member, found from global analysis to *Section 5* that includes global and local imperfections and second-order effects.

*Clause 6.7.2(3)P*

*Clause 6.7.2(3)P* also refers to '*elasto-plastic analysis*'. This is defined in clause 1.5.6.10 of EN 1990 as 'structural analysis that uses stress/strain or moment/curvature relationships consisting of a linear elastic part followed by a plastic part with or without hardening'.

As the three materials in a composite section follow different non-linear relationships, direct analysis of cross-sections is not possible. One has first to assume the dimensions and materials of the member, and then determine the axial force $N$ and bending moment $M$ at a cross-section from assumed values of axial strain and curvature $\phi$, using the relevant material properties. The $M$–$N$–$\phi$ relationship for each section can be found from many such calculations. This becomes more complex where biaxial bending is present.[90]

Integration along the length of the member then leads to a non-linear member stiffness matrix that relates axial force and end moments to the axial change of length and the end rotations.

**Clause 6.7.2(8)** on stress–strain curves was drafted, as a 'General' rule, before clause 5.7 of EN 1992-2 was available and refers only to the Parts 1-1 of Eurocodes 2 and 3. At that time these rules appeared to be incompatible for use for composite structures. Hence, no application rules on non-linear global analysis are given in *clause 5.4.3*, where further comment is given.

*Clause 6.7.2(8)*

In clause 5.7 of EN 1992-2, the intention is that realistic stiffnesses, not design stiffnesses, should be used, on the basis that a small amount of material at the critical section with 'design' properties will not alter the overall response. For bridges, the recommended stress–strain curves are based on the characteristic strengths. This is consistent with Informative

Annex C of EN 1993-1-5, for structural steel. Both Eurocodes 2 and 3 refer to their national annexes for this subject. In the absence of references in EN 1994-2 to these Parts of Eurocodes 2 and 3, guidance should be sought from the National Annex.

Where characteristic properties are used in non-linear global analysis, further checks on cross-sections are required. An attractive proposition therefore is to use design values of material properties throughout, so that the non-linear analysis itself becomes the verification, provided that the resistance found exceeds the factored loading. This approach is permitted by clause 5.7 of EN 1992-2. However, it may not be conservative for serviceability limit states if significant internal forces arise from indirect actions such that greater stiffness attracts greater internal effects. There is a caveat to this effect in clause 5.7 of EN 1992-2.

### 6.7.3. Simplified method of design

*Scope of the simplified method*

*Clause 6.7.3.1*

*Clause 6.7.3.1(1)*

The method has been calibrated by comparison with test results.[91,92] Its scope, *clause 6.7.3.1*, is limited mainly by the range of results available, which leads to the restriction $\bar{\lambda} \leq 2$ in *clause 6.7.3.1(1)*. For most columns, the method requires explicit account to be taken of imperfections and second-order effects. The use of strut curves is limited in *clause 6.7.3.5(2)* to axially-loaded members.

The restriction on unconnected steel sections in *paragraph (1)* is to prevent loss of stiffness due to slip, that would invalidate the formulae for $EI$ of the column cross-section. The limits

*Clause 6.7.3.1(2)*

to concrete cover in *clause 6.7.3.1(2)* arise from concern over strain softening of concrete invalidating the interaction diagram (*Fig. 6.19*), and from the limited test data for columns with thicker covers. These provisions normally ensure that for each axis of bending, the flexural stiffness of the steel section makes a significant contribution to the total stiffness. Greater cover can be used by ignoring in calculation the concrete that exceeds the stated limits.

*Clause 6.7.3.1(3)*

The limit of 6% in *clause 6.7.3.1(3)* on the reinforcement used in calculation is more liberal than the 4% (except at laps) recommended in EN 1992-1-1. This limit and that on maximum slenderness are unlikely to be restrictive in practice.

*Clause 6.7.3.1(4)*

*Clause 6.7.3.1(4)* is intended to prevent the use of sections susceptible to lateral–torsional buckling.

*Resistance of cross-sections*

Reference to the partial safety factors for the materials is avoided by specifying resistances in terms of design values for strength, rather than characteristic values; for example in *equation*

*Clause 6.7.3.2(1)*

*(6.30)* for plastic resistance to compression in *clause 6.7.3.2(1)*. This resistance, $N_{pl,Rd}$, is the design ultimate axial load for a short column, assuming that the structural steel and reinforcement are yielding and the concrete is crushing.

For concrete-encased sections, the crushing stress is taken as 85% of the design cylinder strength, as explained in the comments on *clause 3.1*. For concrete-filled sections, the concrete component develops a higher strength because of the confinement from the steel section, and the 15% reduction is not made; see also the comments on *clause 6.7.3.2(6)*.

*Resistance to combined compression and bending*

The bending resistance of a column cross-section, $M_{pl,Rd}$, is calculated as for a composite

*Clause 6.7.3.2(2)*

beam in Class 1 or 2, *clause 6.7.3.2(2)*. Points on the interaction curve shown in *Figs 6.18* and *6.19* represent limiting combinations of compressive axial load $N$ and moment $M$ which correspond to the plastic resistance of the cross-section.

The resistance is found using rectangular stress blocks. For simplicity, that for the concrete extends to the neutral axis, as shown in Fig. 6.43 for resistance to bending (point B in *Fig. 6.19* and Fig. 6.47). As explained in the comments on *clause 3.1(1)*, this simplification is unconservative in comparison with stress/strain curves for concrete and the rules of EN 1992-1-1. To compensate for this, the plastic resistance moment for the cross-section is reduced by a factor $\alpha_M$ in *clause 6.7.3.6(1)*.

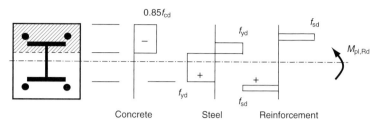

**Fig. 6.43.** Stress distributions for resistance in bending

As axial compression increases, the neutral axis moves; for example, towards the lower edge of the section shown in Fig. 6.43, and then outside the section. The interaction curve is therefore determined by moving the neutral axis in increments across the section, and finding pairs of values of $M$ and $N$ from the corresponding stress blocks. This requires a computer program, unless the simplification given in *clause 6.7.3.2(5)* is used. Simplified expressions for the coordinates of points B, C and D on the interaction curve are given in Appendix C of Ref. 5. Further comment is given in Examples 6.10 and C.1 in that Guide and in Example 6.12 here.

*Influence of transverse shear*
***Clauses 6.7.3.2(3)*** and ***(4)***, on the influence of transverse shear on the interaction curve, are generally the same as *clause 6.2.2.4* on moment–shear interaction in beams. One assumes first that the shear $V_{\mathrm{Ed}}$ acts on the structural steel section alone. If it is less than $0.5V_{\mathrm{pl,a,Rd}}$, it has no effect on the curve. If it is greater, there is an option of sharing it between the steel and reinforced concrete sections, which may reduce that acting on the steel to below $0.5V_{\mathrm{pl,a,Rd}}$. If it does not, then a reduced design yield strength is used for the shear area, as for the web of a beam. In a column the shear area depends on the plane of bending considered, and may consist of the flanges of the steel section. It is assumed that shear buckling does not occur.

*Clause 6.7.3.2(3)*
*Clause 6.7.3.2(4)*

Shear high enough for $V_{\mathrm{c,Rd}}$ to be relied on in design is unlikely to occur in a composite column, so the code does not go into detail here. The reference in *clause 6.7.3.2(3)* to the use of EN 1992 does not include EN 1992-2, where clause 6.2 was not drafted with columns in mind. Equation (6.2.b) in EN 1992-1-1, which gives a minimum shear strength for concrete regardless of reinforcement content, is not valid for unreinforced concrete as it assumes that minimum reinforcement will be provided according to EN 1992 requirements. It can be inferred that for a concrete-filled tube with no longitudinal reinforcement (permitted by *clause 6.7.5.2(1)*), the shear resistance $V_{\mathrm{c,Rd}}$ according to EN 1992 should be taken as zero.

*Simplified interaction curve*
***Clause 6.7.3.2(5)*** explains the use of the polygonal diagram BDCA in *Fig. 6.19* as an approximation to the interaction curve, suitable for hand calculation. The method applies to any cross-section with biaxial symmetry, not just to encased I-sections.

*Clause 6.7.3.2(5)*

First, the location of the neutral axis for pure bending is found, by equating the longitudinal forces from the stress blocks on either side of it. Let this be at distance $h_{\mathrm{n}}$ from the centroid of the uncracked section, as shown in *Fig. 6.19(B)*. It is shown in Appendix C of Ref. 5 that the neutral axis for point C on the interaction diagram is at distance $h_{\mathrm{n}}$ on the other side of the centroid, and the neutral axis for point D passes through the centroid. The values of $M$ and $N$ at each point are easily found from the stress blocks shown in *Fig. 6.19*. For concrete-filled steel tubes the factor 0.85 may be omitted.

*Concrete-filled tubes of circular or rectangular cross-section*
***Clause 6.7.3.2(6)*** is based on the lateral expansion that occurs in concrete under axial compression. This causes circumferential tension in the steel tube and triaxial compression in the concrete. This increases the crushing strength of the concrete[91] to an extent that

*Clause 6.7.3.2(6)*

outweighs the reduction in the effective yield strength of the steel in vertical compression. The coefficients $\eta_a$ and $\eta_c$ given in this clause allow for these effects.

This containment effect is not present to the same extent in concrete-filled rectangular tubes because less circumferential tension can be developed. In all tubes the effects of containment reduce as bending moments are applied, because the mean compressive strain in the concrete and the associated lateral expansion are reduced. With increasing slenderness, bowing of the member under load increases the bending moment, and therefore the effectiveness of containment is further reduced. For these reasons, $\eta_a$ and $\eta_c$ are dependent on the eccentricity of loading and on the slenderness of the member.

*Properties of the column or compression member*
For composite compression members in a frame, some properties of each member are needed before or during global analysis of the frame:

<table>
<tr><td>Clause 6.7.3.3(1)</td><td>•</td><td>the steel contribution ratio, clause 6.7.3.3(1)</td></tr>
<tr><td>Clause 6.7.3.3(2)</td><td>•</td><td>the relative slenderness $\bar{\lambda}$, clause 6.7.3.3(2)</td></tr>
<tr><td>Clause 6.7.3.3(3)</td><td>•</td><td>the effective flexural stiffnesses, clauses 6.7.3.3(3) and 6.7.3.4(2), and</td></tr>
<tr><td>Clause 6.7.3.3(4)</td><td>•</td><td>the creep coefficient and effective modulus for concrete, clause 6.7.3.3(4).</td></tr>
</table>

The steel contribution ratio is explained in the comments on *clause 6.7.1(4)*.

The relative slenderness $\bar{\lambda}$ is needed to check that the member is within the scope of the simplified method, *clause 6.7.3.1(1)*. Often it will be evident that $\bar{\lambda} < 2$. The calculation can then be omitted, as $\bar{\lambda}$ is not needed again unless the member resists axial load only.

The unfactored quantities $E$, $I$ and $L$ are used in the calculation of $N_{cr}$, so $\bar{\lambda}$ is calculated using in *equation (6.39)* the characteristic (unfactored) value of the squash load, $N_{pl,Rk}$, and the characteristic flexural stiffness $(EI)_{eff}$ from *clause 6.7.3.3(3)*. This is the only use of this stiffness in *Section 6*. The upper limit on $\bar{\lambda}$ is somewhat arbitrary and does not justify great precision in $N_{cr}$.

Creep of concrete increases the lateral deformation of the member. This is allowed for by replacing the elastic modulus $E_{cm}$ (in *equation (6.40)*) by a reduced value $E_{c,eff}$ from *equation (6.41)*. This depends on the creep coefficient $\phi_t$, which is a function of the age at which concrete is stressed and the duration of the load. The effective modulus depends also on the proportion of the design axial load that is permanent. The design of the member is rarely sensitive to the influence of the creep coefficient on $E_{c,eff}$, so conservative assumptions can be made about uncertainties. Normally, a single value of effective modulus can be used for all compression members in a structure. Further discussion is given under *clause 5.4.2.2*.

The correction factor $K_e$ is to allow for loss of stiffness caused by possible cracking of concrete.

The condition for ignoring second-order effects within the member is explained in comments on *clause 5.2.1(3)*. Where the ratio $\alpha_{cr}$ ($= N_{cr}/N_{Ed}$) is used, the critical load $N_{cr}$ is the axial force in the member in the lowest buckling mode of the structure that involves the member. In the rare cases where both ends of a column are detailed so as to behave as pin-ended (as in Example 6.12), $N_{cr} = \pi^2(EI)_{eff,II}/L^2$. The flexural stiffness $(EI)_{eff,II}$ is obtained from *clause 6.7.3.4(2)*.

In continuous construction, the critical buckling mode involves adjacent members, which must be included in the elastic critical analysis.

*Analyses for verification of a compression member*
For the compression members of a frame or truss that are within the scope of *clause 6.7.3*, a flow chart for calculation routes is given in Fig. 6.44.

The relationship between the analysis of a frame and the stability of individual members is discussed both in the comments on *clause 5.2.2* and below. If bending is biaxial, the procedure in *clause 6.7.3.4* is followed for each axis in turn.

Clause 6.7.3.4(1)     **Clause 6.7.3.4(1)** requires the use of second-order linear-elastic global analysis except where the option of *clause 6.7.3.4(5)* applies, or route (c) in Fig. 6.44 is chosen and $\alpha_{cr} > 10$ in accordance with *clause 6.7.3.4(3)*. The simplified method of *clause 6.7.3.5(2)*

Flow chart for global analysis (g.a.) and verification of a compression member in a composite frame, with reference to global and member imperfections (g.imp and m.imp). This is for a member of doubly symmetrical and uniform cross-section (*6.7.3.1(1)*) and for a particular loading. See Notes 1 and 2.

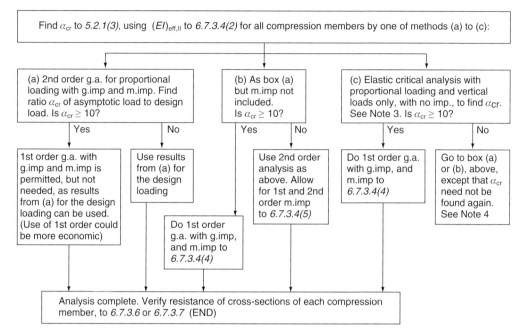

Note 1. 'Loading' means a particular combination of actions, load case and load arrangement. In boxes (a) to (c) the lowest $\alpha_{cr}$ for various loadings is found. The chosen loadings should include that for maximum side-sway, and those that are expected to cause the greatest axial compression in each potentially critical compression member.
Note 2. Analysis (a) includes both $P$–$\Delta$ effects from global imperfections and $P$–$\delta$ effects from member imperfections.
Note 3. For choice of loadings, see Note 1 and the comments on *clause 5.2.1(3)* and *(4)*.
Note 4. No need to return to (a) or (b) where $\alpha_{cr} < 10$ only in a local member mode (pin-ended conditions). Then, do first-order g.a. with amplification to *6.7.3.4(5)* and verify cross-sections.

**Fig. 6.44.** Flow chart for analysis and verification for a compression member

is rarely applicable in practice because some first-order bending moment (other than from imperfections) will usually be present; for example, due to friction at bearings.

 *Clause 6.7.3.4(2)* gives the design flexural stiffnesses for compression members, for use in all analyses for ultimate limit states. The factor $K_{e,II}$ allows for cracking, as is required by the reference in *clause 5.4.2.3(4)* to *clause 6.7.3.4*. The factor $K_0$ is from research-based calibration studies. Long-term effects are allowed for, as before, by replacing $E_{cm}$ in *equation (6.42)* by $E_{c,eff}$ from *equation (6.41)*.

 In *clause 6.7.3.4(3)*, '*the elastic critical load*' refers to the frame at its lowest buckling mode involving the member concerned; and '*second-order effects*' means those in the member due to both its own imperfections and global imperfections. When deciding whether second-order effects of member imperfections can be neglected, the effects of global imperfections can be neglected in an elastic critical analysis (route (c) in Fig. 6.44). A second-order analysis for the asymptotic load, route (a), will give the same value for $\alpha_{cr}$ whether global imperfections are included or not. They are shown in Fig. 6.44 as included because the same analysis can then give the design bending moments for the member concerned.

 *Clause 6.7.3.4(4)* gives the equivalent member imperfection, for use in a global analysis, as an initial bow. It is proportional to the length $L$ of the member between lateral restraints and is defined by $e_0$, the lateral departure at mid-height of its axis of symmetry from the line joining the centres of symmetry at its ends. The value accounts principally for truly geometric imperfections and for the effects of residual stresses. It is independent of the distribution of bending moment along the member. The curved shape is usually assumed to be sinusoidal, but a circular arc is acceptable. The curve is assumed initially to lie in the plane normal to the axes of the bending moments.

*Clause 6.7.3.4(2)*

*Clause 6.7.3.4(3)*

*Clause 6.7.3.4(4)*

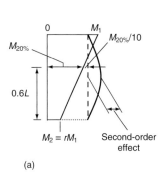
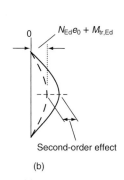
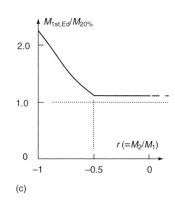

(a)          (b)          (c)

**Fig. 6.45.** Bending moments in a column: (a) end moments from global analysis; (b) initial imperfections and transverse loading; and (c) equivalent first-order bending moment

Clause 6.7.3.4(5)

Where member imperfections are not included in the global analysis and $\alpha_{cr} < 10$, *clause 6.7.3.4(5)* enables these imperfections to be allowed for. It is based on the critical load $N_{cr,eff}$ for the isolated pin-ended member even where the critical buckling mode for the frame involves sway, such that the effective length of the member exceeds its system length. This is consistent with clause 5.2.2(7)(b) of EN 1993-1-1, which is referred to from *clause 5.2.2(1)* via clause 5.2.2 of EN 1993-2. (This route also leads to clause 5.2.2(3) of EN 1993-1-1, which sets out these options in detail and is consistent with Fig. 6.44.)

The reason for this definition for $N_{cr,eff}$ is that where necessary (e.g. where $\alpha_{cr} < 10$), the effects of global imperfections and side-sway have been accounted for in the second-order global analysis. This can be seen by using as an example a 'flagpole'-type column, with both out-of-plumb and initial bow.

### Determination of design bending moment for a compression member

It is now assumed that for a particular member, with or without lateral load within its length, an analysis in which member imperfections were not included has provided a design axial force $N_{Ed}$ and design end moments for one of the principal planes of bending. These are denoted $M_1$ and $M_2$, with $|M_1| \geq |M_2|$, as shown in Fig. 6.45(a). Biaxial bending is considered later. The axial force is normally almost constant along the length of the member. Where it varies, its maximum value can conservatively be assumed to be present throughout its length.

The factor $k$ in *clause 6.7.3.4(5)* is proportional to $\beta$. For the end moments, from *Table 6.4*, $\beta$ lies between 0.44 and 1.1, but for the member imperfection it is always 1.0. These two values are denoted $\beta_1$ and $\beta_2$. The calculation of $\beta_1$ is now explained, assuming that the critical bending moment occurs either at the end where $M_{Ed} = M_1$ (where no member imperfection or resulting second-order effect is assumed) or within the central 20% of the length of the member.

Except where there is lateral loading, the maximum first-order bending moment within this central length is:

$$M_{20\%} = M_1(0.6 + 0.4r)$$

shown in Fig. 6.45(a). This is represented by an 'equivalent' first-order design value, given by *Table 6.4* as:

$$M_{1st,Ed} = M_1(0.66 + 0.44r)$$

with a lower limit of $0.44M_1$. The ratio $M_{1st,Ed}/M_{20\%}$ is shown in Fig. 6.45(c). It is generally 1.1, but increases sharply where $r < -0.5$, which is where the lower limit of $0.44M_1$ is reached. This range of $r$ represents significant double-curvature bending. The increase provides protection against snap-through to single-curvature buckling.

The moment $M_{1st,Ed}$ is increased by the factor

$$\frac{1}{1 - N_{Ed}/N_{cr,eff}}$$

to allow for second-order effects. This factor is an approximation, as shown in Fig. 2.9 of Ref. 93, which is allowed for by the use of the ratio 1.1 shown in Fig. 6.45(c).

Basing $N_{cr,eff}$ on pin-ended conditions can be conservative where the column is braced with end rotational restraints that produce an effective length less than the column height.

Where there is lateral loading within the column length, the bending-moment distribution should be treated as the sum of two distributions, one corresponding to each of the two parts of *Table 6.4*. In the first half of the table, $M_{Ed}$ is then the sum of contributions from member imperfection and lateral load. These are not necessarily in the same direction, because the member imperfection $e_0$ can be in any lateral direction and must be chosen to give the most adverse overall result for the column.

*Equation (6.43)* states that $k$ must be greater than or equal to unity, and this is correct for a single distribution of bending moment. However, for a combination of two distributions, it could be conservative to adjust both values of $k$ in this way when the two sets of moments are treated separately.

At mid-length the component due to end moments depends on their ratio, $r$, and therefore could be small. The appropriate first component is:

$$\frac{\beta_1 M_1}{1 - N_{Ed}/N_{cr,eff}}$$

without the condition that it should exceed $M_1$.

The imperfection $e_0$ causes a first-order bending moment $N_{Ed}e_0$ at mid-length. The resulting contribution to $M_{Ed,max}$ is:

$$\frac{\beta_2 N_{Ed}e_0}{1 - N_{Ed}/N_{cr,eff}}, \quad \text{with } \beta_2 = 1$$

This, plus the contribution from any mid-length moment from lateral loading, is added to the first component. The condition $k \geq 1$ applies to the sum of the two components, and is intended to ensure that the design moment is at least equal to the greatest first-order moment.

In biaxial bending, the initial member imperfection may be neglected in the less critical plane (*clause 6.7.3.7(1)*).

The definitions of $M_{Ed}$ in *clause 6.7.3.4(5)* and *Table 6.4* may appear contradictory. In the text before *equation (6.43)*, $M_{Ed}$ is referred to as a first-order moment. This is because it does not include second-order effects arising within the member. However, *Table 6.4* makes clear that $M_{Ed}$ is to be determined by either first-order or second-order global analysis, as shown in Fig. 6.44.

The simplified method of **clause 6.7.3.5** is rarely applicable, as explained in the comment on *clause 6.7.3.4(1)*, so no comment on it is given.

*Clause 6.7.3.5*

### Verification of cross-sections

For uniaxial bending, the final step is to check that the cross-section can resist $M_{max,Ed}$ with compression $N_{Ed}$. The interaction diagram gives a resistance $\mu_d M_{pl,Rd}$ with axial load $N_{Ed}$, as shown in *Fig. 6.18*. This is unconservative, being based on rectangular stress-blocks, as explained in the comment on *clause 3.1(1)*, so in **clause 6.7.3.6(1)** it is reduced, by the use of a factor $\alpha_M$ that depends on the grade of structural steel. This factor allows for the increase in the compressive strain in the cross-section at yield of the steel (which is adverse for the concrete), when the yield strength of the steel is increased.

*Clause 6.7.3.6(1)*

Where values of $M_{max,Ed}$ have been found for both axes, **clause 6.7.3.7** on biaxial bending applies, in which they are written as $M_{y,Ed}$ and $M_{z,Ed}$. If one is much greater than the other, the relevant check for uniaxial bending, *equation (6.46)*, will govern. Otherwise, the linear interaction given by *equation (6.47)* applies.

*Clause 6.7.3.7*

If the member fails this biaxial condition by a small margin, it may be helpful to recalculate the less critical bending moment omitting the member imperfection, as permitted by *clause 6.7.3.7(1)*.

### 6.7.4. Shear connection and load introduction
*Load introduction*

The provisions for the resistance of cross-sections of columns assume that no significant slip
*Clause 6.7.4.1(1)P* occurs at the interface between the concrete and structural steel components. *Clauses*
*Clause 6.7.4.1(2)P* *6.7.4.1(1)P* and *(2)P* give the principles for limiting slip to an insignificant level in the
critical regions: those where axial load and/or bending moments are applied to the member.

For any assumed '*clearly defined load path*' it is possible to estimate stresses, including
shear at the interface. Shear connection is unlikely to be needed outside regions of load
introduction unless the shear strength $\tau_{Rd}$ from *Table 6.6* is very low, or the member is
also acting as a beam, or has a high degree of double-curvature bending. *Clause*
*Clause 6.7.4.1(3)* *6.7.4.1(3)* refers to the special case of an axially loaded column.

Where axial load is applied through a joint attached only to the steel component, the force
to be transferred to the concrete can be estimated from the relative axial loads in the two
materials given by the resistance model. Accurate calculation is rarely practicable where
the cross-section concerned does not govern the design of the column. In this partly-
plastic situation, the more adverse of the elastic and fully-plastic models give a safe result
*Clause 6.7.4.2(1)* (*clause 6.7.4.2(1)*, last line). In practice, it may be simpler to provide shear connection
based on a conservative (high) estimate of the force to be transferred.

Where axial force is applied by a plate bearing on both materials or on concrete only, the
proportion of the force resisted by the concrete gradually decreases, due to creep and
shrinkage. It could be inferred from *clause 6.7.4.2(1)* that shear connection should be
provided for a high proportion of the force applied. However, models based on elastic
theory are over-conservative in this inherently stable situation, where large strains are
acceptable. The application rules that follow are based mainly on tests.

Few shear connectors reach their design shear strength until the slip is at least 1 mm; but
this is not significant slip for a resistance model based on plastic behaviour and rectangular
stress blocks. However, a long load path implies greater slip, so the assumed path should not
*Clause 6.7.4.2(2)* extend beyond the introduction length given in *clause 6.7.4.2(2)*.

In a concrete-filled tube, shrinkage effects are low, for only the autogenous shrinkage
strain occurs, with a long-term value below $10^{-4}$, from clause 3.1.4(6) of EN 1992-1-1.
Radial shrinkage is outweighed by the lateral expansion of concrete in compression, for
its inelastic Poisson's ratio increases at high compressive stress, and eventually exceeds
0.5. Friction then provides significant shear connection.

Concrete-filled tubular columns with bearings at both ends have found application in
bridge design. Where the whole load is applied to the concrete core through an end plate,
*Clause 6.7.4.2(3)* the conditions of *clause 6.7.4.2(3)* can be satisfied, and no shear connection is required.

This complete reliance on friction for shear transfer is supported by test evidence[94,95]
and by inelastic theory. For columns of circular cross-section, no plausible failure mechanism has been found for an end region that does not involve yielding of the steel casing in
hoop tension and vertical compression. For a large non-circular column, it would be
prudent to check behaviour by finite-element analysis. There is further discussion in
Example 6.12.

Friction is also the basis for the enhanced resistance of stud connectors given in
*Clause 6.7.4.2(4)* *clause 6.7.4.2(4)*.

Detailing at points of load introduction or change of cross-section is assisted by the high
*Clause 6.7.4.2(5)* permissible bearing stresses given in *clauses 6.7.4.2(5)* and *(6)*. An example is given in Ref. 5
*Clause 6.7.4.2(6)* in which the local design compressive strength of the concrete, $\sigma_{c,Rd}$ in *equation (6.48)*, is
found to be 260 N/mm².

*Clause 6.7.4.2(7)* *Clause 6.7.4.2(7)* relates to load introduction to reinforcement in a concrete-filled tube.
This and some other concessions made at the ends of a column length are based mainly
on tests on columns of sizes typical of those used in buildings. Some caution should be
exercised in applying them to members with much larger cross-sections. Unless a column
is free to sway, a hinge forms in its central region before it fails. End regions that are slightly
weaker have little effect on the failure load, because at that stage their bending moments are
lower than at mid-length.

The absence from *clause 6.7.4.2(8)* of a reference to EN 1992-2 is deliberate, as its clause 9.5.3 gives a rule that is not required for composite columns.   *Clause 6.7.4.2(8)*

*Figure 6.23* illustrates the requirement of *clause 6.7.4.2(9)* for transverse reinforcement, which must have a resistance to tension equal to the force $N_{c1}$. If longitudinal reinforcement is ignored, this is given by:   *Clause 6.7.4.2(9)*

$$N_{c1} = A_{c2}/(2nA)$$

where $A$ is the transformed area of the cross-section 1-1 of the column in *Fig. 6.23*, given by:

$$A = A_s + (A_{c1} + A_{c2})/n$$

and $A_{c1}$ and $A_{c2}$ are the unshaded and shaded areas of concrete, respectively, in section 1-1. The modular ratio, $n$, should usually be taken as the short-term value.

*Transverse shear*

*Clause 6.7.4.3* gives application rules (used in Example 6.11 in Ref. 5) relevant to the principle of *clause 6.7.4.1(2)*, for columns with the longitudinal shear that arises from transverse shear. The design shear strengths $\tau_{Rd}$ in *Table 6.6* are far lower than the tensile strength of concrete. They rely on friction, not bond, and are related to the extent to which separation at the interface is prevented. For example, in partially-encased I-sections, lateral expansion of the concrete creates pressure on the flanges, but not on the web, for which $\tau_{Rd} = 0$; and the highest shear strengths are for concrete within steel tubes.   *Clause 6.7.4.3*

Where small steel I-sections are present within a column that is mainly concrete, *clause 6.7.4.3(4)* provides a useful increase to $\tau_{Rd}$, for covers $c_z$ up to 115 mm. The enhancement factor is more simply presented as: $\beta_c = 0.2 + c_z/50 \leq 2.5$.   *Clause 6.7.4.3(4)*

Concern about the attachment of concrete to steel in partially-encased I-sections appears again in *clause 6.7.4.3(5)*, because under weak-axis bending, separation tends to develop between the encasement and the web.   *Clause 6.7.4.3(5)*

## 6.7.5. Detailing provisions

If a steel I-section in an environment in class X0 to EN 1992-1-1 has links in contact with its flange (permitted by *clause 6.7.5.2(3)*), the cover to the steel section could be as low as 25 mm. For a wide steel flange, this thin layer of concrete would have little resistance to buckling outwards, so the minimum thickness is increased to 40 mm in *clause 6.7.5.1(2)*. This is a nominal dimension.   *Clause 6.7.5.1(2)*

Minimum longitudinal reinforcement, *clause 6.7.5.2(1)*, is needed to control the width of cracks, which can be caused by shrinkage even in columns with concrete nominally in compression.   *Clause 6.7.5.2(1)*

*Clause 6.7.5.2(2)* does not refer to EN 1992-2 because its clause 9.5 introduces a nationally-determined parameter, which is not needed for composite columns.   *Clause 6.7.5.2(2)*

*Clause 6.7.5.2(4)* refers to exposure class X0 of EN 1992-1-1. This is a 'very dry' environment, with 'no risk of corrosion or attack', so this clause is unlikely to be applicable in bridges.   *Clause 6.7.5.2(4)*

---

### Example 6.12: concrete-filled tube of circular cross-section

This Example is based on columns used for a motorway interchange, as described in Refs 94 and 96. The column shown in Fig. 6.46 is of circular cross-section. It has spherical rocker bearings at each end, of radii 600 mm (internal) and 605 mm (external). Its length between centres of bearings is 11.5 m. Its design will be checked for a design ultimate load $N_{Ed} = 18.0$ MN. The bearing at its lower end is fixed in position. The deformation of the superstructure at ultimate load causes a maximum eccentricity of load of 75 mm.

Concerning $\gamma_M$ for structural steel, clause 5.2.2(7)(a) of EN 1993-1-1 says that 'no individual stability check for the members according to 6.3 is necessary' when second-order analysis is used with member imperfections; and clause 6.1(1) of EN 1993-1-1 then says that $\gamma_{M1}$ is used for 'instability assessed by member checks'. This appears to permit $\gamma_{M0}$ to be used when second-order analysis and cross-section checks are used, as here, so $\gamma_{M0} = 1.0$ is used.

The properties of the materials, in the usual notation, are as follows.

Structural steel: S355; $f_y = f_{yd} = 355\,\text{N/mm}^2$, based on the use of Table 3.1 of EN 1993-1-1. (The UK's National Annex is likely to require the appropriate value to be taken from EN 10025.) From EN 1993, $E_a = 210\,\text{kN/mm}^2$.

Concrete: C40/50; $f_{ck} = 40\,\text{N/mm}^2$; $f_{cd} = 40/1.5 = 26.7\,\text{N/mm}^2$.
The coarse aggregate is limestone, so from clause 3.1.3(2) of EN 1992-1-1,
$E_{cm} = 0.9 \times 35 = 31.5\,\text{kN/mm}^2$; $n_0 = 210/31.5 = 6.67$.

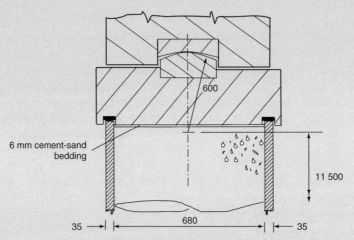

**Fig. 6.46.** Cross-section at each end of concrete-filled tube of Example 6.12

*Geometrical properties of the cross-section*
In the notation of *Fig. 6.17(e)*, $d = 750\,\text{mm}$, $t = 35\,\text{mm}$, giving $d/t = 21.4$.
The limit, from *Table 6.3*, is $d/t \le 90(235/355) = 59.6$.

From *clause 6.7.5.2(1)*, '*normally no longitudinal reinforcement is necessary*' (unless resistance to fire is required), so $A_s = 0$ is assumed.

For the concrete:   area $A_c = \pi \times 340^2 = 363\,200\,\text{mm}^2$
$\qquad\qquad\qquad\qquad\quad I_c = \pi \times 340^4/4 = 10\,500 \times 10^6\,\text{mm}^4$
For the steel tube:   area $A_a = \pi \times 375^2 - 363\,200 = 78\,620\,\text{mm}^2$
$\qquad\qquad\qquad\qquad\quad I_a = \pi \times 375^4/4 - 10\,500 \times 10^6 = 5036 \times 10^6\,\text{mm}^4$

*Design action effects, ultimate limit state*
For the most critical load arrangement, global analysis gives these values:

$$N_{Ed} = \textbf{18.0\,MN}, \text{ of which } N_{G,Ed} = 13.0\,\text{MN} \tag{D6.26}$$

$$M_{Ed,top} = 18 \times 0.075 = \textbf{1.35\,MNm} \tag{D6.27}$$

As the column has circular symmetry and its imperfection is assumed to lie in the plane of bending, there is no need to consider biaxial bending. For a rocker bearing, the effective length should be taken to the points of contact, and is:

$$L = 11.5 + 2 \times 0.6 = \textbf{12.7\,m}$$

Depending on the relationship between the rotation and the displacement of the superstructure at the point of support, it can be shown that the points of contact within the two bearings can be such that the ratio of end moments has any value between $+1$ and $-1$. The worst case for the column, assumed here, is:

$$M_{\text{Ed,top}} = M_{\text{Ed,bot}}$$

(i.e., $r = 1$ in *Table 6.4*). Double-curvature bending ($r = -1$) causes higher transverse shear force in the column, but it is too low to influence the design.

### Creep coefficient
From *clause 6.7.3.3(4)*,

$$E_{\text{c}} = E_{\text{cm}}/[1 + (N_{\text{G,Ed}}/N_{\text{Ed}})\phi_{\text{t}}] \tag{6.41}$$

The creep coefficient $\phi_{\text{t}}$ is $\phi(t, t_0)$ to *clause 5.4.2.2*. The time $t_0$ is taken as 30 days, and $t$ is taken as 'infinity', as creep reduces the stiffness, and hence the stability, of a column.

From clause 3.1.4(5) of EN 1992-1-1, the 'perimeter exposed to drying' is zero, so that the notional size, $h_0 \to \infty$. Assuming 'inside conditions' and the use of normal cement, the graphs in Fig. 3.1 of EN 1992-1-1 give:

$$\phi(\infty, 30) = 1.4 = \phi_{\text{t}}$$

The assumed 'age at first loading' has little influence on the result if it exceeds about 20 days.

From *equation (6.41)*,

$$E_{\text{c,eff}} = 31.5/[1 + 1.4(13/18)] = \textbf{15.7 kN/mm}^2 \tag{D6.28}$$

### Shrinkage
When the upper bearing is placed, the concrete becomes effectively sealed, so its drying shrinkage can be taken as zero. From EN 1992-1-1/3.1.4(6), the autogenous shrinkage is:

$$\varepsilon_{\text{ca}}(\infty) = 2.5(f_{\text{ck}} - 10) \times 10^{-6} = 2.5 \times 30 \times 30 \times 10^{-6} = \textbf{75} \times \textbf{10}^{-6} \tag{D6.29}$$

Ignoring the restraint from the steel tube, this would cause the 11 m length of column to shorten by only 0.8 mm. Its influence on shear connection is discussed later.

### Squash load, elastic critical load, and slenderness
From *clause 6.7.3.2(1)*,

$$
\begin{aligned}
N_{\textbf{pl,Rd}} &= A_{\text{a}}f_{\text{yd}} + A_{\text{c}}f_{\text{cd}} \\
&= 78.62 \times 0.355 + 363.2 \times 0.0267 = 27.9 + 9.70 = \textbf{37.6 MN}
\end{aligned} \tag{D6.30}
$$

From *clause 6.7.3.3(1)*, the steel contribution ratio is:

$$\delta = 27.9/37.6 = 0.74$$

which is within the limits of *clause 6.7.1(4)*.

For $\bar{\lambda}$ to *clause 6.7.3.3(2)*, with $\gamma_{\text{C}} = 1.5$,

$$N_{\textbf{pl,Rk}} = 27.9 + 1.5 \times 9.70 = \textbf{42.46 MN} \tag{D6.31}$$

From *clause 6.7.3.3(3)*,

$$
\begin{aligned}
(EI)_{\text{eff}} &= E_{\text{a}}I_{\text{a}} + K_{\text{e}}E_{\text{c,eff}}I_{\text{c}} \\
&= 210 \times 5036 + 0.6 \times 15.7 \times 10\,500 = 1.156 \times 10^6 \,\text{kN m}^2
\end{aligned} \tag{6.40}
$$

Hence,

$$N_{\text{cr}} = \pi^2(EI)_{\text{eff}}/L^2 = 1.156 \times 10^3 \pi^2/12.7^2 = 70.74 \,\text{MN}$$

From *equation (6.39)*,

$$\bar{\lambda} = (N_{\text{pl,Rk}}/N_{\text{cr}})^{0.5} = (42.46/70.74)^{0.5} = \textbf{0.775}$$

The non-dimensional slenderness does not exceed 2.0, so *clause 6.7.3.1(1)* is satisfied. *Clause 6.7.3.2(6)*, on the effect of containment on the strength of concrete, does not apply, as $\bar{\lambda} > 0.5$.

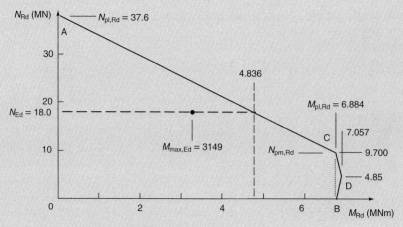

**Fig. 6.47.** Interaction polygon for concrete-filled tube

*Interaction polygon*
The interaction polygon corresponding to *Fig. 6.19* is determined using formulae that are given and explained in Appendix C of Ref. 5. *Clause 6.7.3.2(5)* permits it to be used as an approximation to the $N$–$M$ interaction curve for the cross-section.
The data are: $h = b = d = 750\,\text{mm}$; $r = d/2 - t = 375 - 35 = 340\,\text{mm}$.
From result (D6.30),

$$N_{\text{pl,Rd}} = 27.9 + 9.70 = \mathbf{37.6\,MN}$$

The equation numbers (C.) refer to those given in Ref. 5. From equation (C.29) with $W_{\text{ps}} = 0$,

$$W_{\text{pc}} = \frac{(b - 2t)(h - 2t)^2}{4} - \frac{2}{3}r^3 = 680^3/4 - 2 \times 340^3/3 = 52.4 \times 10^6\,\text{mm}^3$$

From equation (C.30):

$$W_{\text{pa}} = \frac{(bh^2)}{4} - \frac{2}{3}(r + t)^3 - W_{\text{pc}} = 750^3/4 - 2 \times 375^3/3 - 52.4 \times 10^6 = 17.91 \times 10^6\,\text{mm}^3$$

From equation (C.8),

$$N_{\text{pm,Rd}} = A_{\text{c}}f_{\text{cd}} = 0.3632 \times 26.7 = \mathbf{9.70\,MN}$$

From equation (C.31),

$$h_{\text{n}} = \frac{N_{\text{pm,Rd}} - A_{\text{sn}}(2f_{\text{sd}} - f_{\text{cc}})}{2bf_{\text{cd}} + 4t(2f_{\text{yd}} - f_{\text{cc}})} = \frac{9.70 \times 10^6}{2 \times 750 \times 26.7 + 140(2 \times 355 - 26.7)} = 71.5\,\text{mm}$$

From equation (C.32),

$$W_{\text{pc,n}} = (b - 2t)h_{\text{n}}^2 = (750 - 70) \times 71.5^2 = 3.474 \times 10^6\,\text{mm}^3$$

From equation (C.33),

$$W_{\text{pa,n}} = bh_{\text{n}}^2 - W_{\text{pc,n}} = 750 \times 71.5^2 - 3.474 \times 10^6 = 0.358 \times 10^6\,\text{mm}^3$$

From equation (C.5),

$$M_{\text{max,Rd}} = W_{\text{pa}}f_{\text{yd}} + W_{\text{pc}}f_{\text{cd}}/2 = 17.91 \times 355 + 52.4 \times 26.7/2 = \mathbf{7057\,kNm}$$

From equation (C.7),

$$M_{n,Rd} = W_{pa,n}f_{yd} + W_{pc,n}f_{cd}/2 = 0.358 \times 355 + 3.474 \times 26.7/2 = 173 \, kNm$$

From equation (C.6),

$$\mathbf{M_{pl,Rd}} = M_{max,Rd} - M_{n,Rd} = 7057 - 173 = \mathbf{6884 \, kNm}$$

These results define the interaction polygon, shown in Fig. 6.47.

*Design maximum bending moment*
From *Table 6.4* with $r = 1$, $\beta = 1$, the equivalent first-order bending moment is:

$$\mathbf{M_{1st,Ed}} = 1350 \times 1.1 = \mathbf{1485 \, kNm}$$

From *Table 6.5*, the equivalent member imperfection is:

$$e_0 = L/300 = 12\,700/300 = 42.3 \, mm$$

For $N_{Ed} = 18 \, MN$, the imperfection moment is $18 \times 42.3 = \mathbf{761 \, kNm}$
To check whether second-order moments can be neglected, an effective value of $N_{cr}$ is required, to *clause 6.7.3.4(3)*. From *equation (6.42)*,

$$(EI)_{eff,II} = 0.9(E_aI_a + 0.5E_cI_c)$$

$$= 0.9 \times 10^6(210 \times 5036 + 0.5 \times 15.7 \times 10\,500) = 1.026 \times 10^{12} \, kN\,mm^2$$

Hence,

$$\mathbf{N_{cr,eff}} = 1026\pi^2/12.7^2 = \mathbf{62.8 \, MN}$$

This is less than $10N_{Ed}$, so second-order effects must be allowed for. *Table 6.4* gives $\beta = 1$ for the distribution of bending moment due to the initial bow imperfection of the member, so from *clause 6.7.3.4(5)*, the second-order factor is:

$$\frac{1}{1 - N_{Ed}/N_{cr,eff}} = \frac{1}{1 - 18/62.8} = 1.402$$

(The $\beta$ factor for the end moments was accounted for in $M_{1st,Ed}$.) Hence,

$$\mathbf{M_{max,Ed}} = 1.402(1485 + 761) = \mathbf{3149 \, kNm}$$

*Resistance of column*
From Fig. 6.47 with $N_{Ed} = 18 \, MN$, $M_{pl,N,Rd} = 4836 \, kNm$.
From *clause 6.7.3.6(1)*, the verification for uniaxial bending is:

$$M_{Ed}/M_{pl,N,Rd} \leq 0.9$$

Here, the ratio is $3149/4836 = \mathbf{0.65}$, so the column is strong enough.

*Shear connection and load introduction*
This column is within the scope of *clause 6.7.4.2(3)*, which permits shear connection to be omitted. The significance of this rule is now illustrated, using preceding results.
Creep increases shear transfer to the steel. Full-interaction elastic analysis with $n_L = n_0(1 + \psi_L\phi_t) = 17$ (*clause 5.4.2.2(2)*) finds the action effects on the steel to be:

$$N_{a,Ed} = 14.2 \, MN \quad and \quad M_{a,Ed} = \pm 1.2 \, MNm$$

based on $M_{Ed} = 1.35 \, MNm$ near an end of the column.
From the rules for shear connection, these transfers would require 90 25 mm studs for the axial force plus 28 for the bending moment, assuming it can act about any horizontal axis.
The significance of friction is illustrated by the following elastic analysis assuming that Poisson's ratio for concrete is 0.5. The bearing stress on the concrete from $N_{Ed} = 18 \, MN$

is 49.6 N/mm$^2$. Its resulting lateral expansion causes a hoop tensile stress in the steel of 225 N/mm$^2$ and a radial compression in the concrete of 23 N/mm$^2$ – Fig. 6.48. Assuming a coefficient of friction of 0.4, the vertical frictional stress is:

$$\tau_{Rd} = 23 \times 0.4 = 9.2 \, \text{N/mm}^2$$

The shear transfer reduces the compressive stress in the concrete. Using a guessed mean value of $\tau_{Rd} = 5 \, \text{N/mm}^2$ leads to a transfer length for 14.2 MN of 1.33 m. This is less than the introduction length of $2d (= 1.50 \, \text{m}$ here) permitted by *clause 6.7.4.2(2)*.

These figures serve only to illustrate the type of behaviour to be expected. In practice, it would be prudent to provide some shear connection; perhaps sufficient for the bending moment. Shrinkage effects are very small.

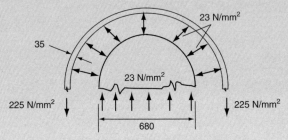

**Fig. 6.48.** Radial and hoop stresses near an end of a concrete-filled tube

## 6.8. Fatigue

### 6.8.1. General

The only complete set of provisions on fatigue in EN 1994-2 is for stud shear connectors. Fatigue in reinforcement, concrete and structural steel is covered mainly by cross-reference to EN 1992 and EN 1993. Commentary will be found in the guides to those codes.[3,4] Further cross-reference is necessary to EN 1993-1-9,[42] 'Fatigue', which gives supplementary guidance and fatigue detail classifications which are not specific to bridges.

The fatigue life of steel components subjected to varying levels of repetitive stress can be checked with the use of Miner's summation. This is a linear cumulative damage calculation for $n$ stress ranges:

$$\sum_{i=1}^{n} \frac{n_{Ei}}{N_{Ri}} \le 1.0 \tag{D6.32}$$

where $n_{Ei}$ is the number of loading cycles of a particular stress range and $N_{Ri}$ is the number of loading cycles to cause fatigue failure at that particular stress range. For most bridges, the above is a complex calculation because the stress in each steel component usually varies due to the random passage of vehicles from a spectrum. Details on a road or rail bridge can be assessed using the above procedure if the loading regime is known at design. This includes the weight and number of every type of vehicle that will use each lane or track of the bridge throughout its design life, and the correlation between loading in each lane or track. In general, this will produce a lengthy calculation.

As an alternative, clause 9.2 of EN 1993-2 allows the use of simplified Fatigue Load Models 3 and 71, from EN 1991-2, for road and rail bridges respectively. This reduces the complexity of the fatigue assessment calculation. It is assumed that the fictitious vehicle (or train) alone causes the fatigue damage. The calculated stress from the vehicle is then adjusted by factors to give a single stress range which, for $N^*$ cycles (2 million cycles for structural steel), causes the same damage as the actual traffic during the bridge's lifetime. This is called the 'damage equivalent stress range' and is discussed in section 6.8.4 below. Comments here are limited to the use of the damage equivalent stress method and, hence, a single stress range.

The term 'equivalent constant-amplitude stress range', defined in clause 1.2.2.11 of EN 1993-1-9, has the same meaning as 'damage equivalent stress range', used here and in clause 6.8.5 of EN 1992-1-1 and clause 9.4.1 of EN 1993-2.

Fatigue damage is related mainly to the number and amplitude of the stress ranges as seen in expression (D6.32). The peak of the stress range has a secondary influence that can be, and usually is, ignored in practice for peak stresses below about 60% of the characteristic strength. Ultimate loads are higher than peak fatigue loads, and the use of partial safety factors for ultimate-load design normally ensures that peak fatigue stresses are below this limit. This may not be the case for long-span bridges with a high percentage of dead load, so *clause 6.8.1(3)* specifies a limit to the longitudinal shear force per connector, with a recommended value $0.75P_{Rd}$, or $0.6P_{Rk}$ for $\gamma_V = 1.25$. As fatigue damage to studs may not be evident, some continental countries are understood to be specifying a lower limit, $0.6P_{Rd}$, in their national annexes. (For welded structural steel, the effect of peak stress is effectively covered in the detail classifications in EN 1993-1-9, where residual stresses from welding, typically reaching yield locally, are catered for in the detail categories.) *Clause 6.8.1(3)*

Most bridges will require a fatigue assessment. *Clauses 6.8.1(4)* and *(5)* refer to EN 1993-2 and EN 1992-2 for guidance on the types of bridges and bridge elements where fatigue assessment may not be required. Those relevant to composite bridge superstructures of steel and concrete include: *Clause 6.8.1(4)* *Clause 6.8.1(5)*

(i)   pedestrian footbridges not susceptible to pedestrian-induced vibration
(ii)  bridges carrying canals
(iii) bridges which are predominantly statically loaded
(iv)  parts of railway or road bridges that are neither stressed by traffic loads nor likely to be excited by wind loads
(v)   prestressing and reinforcing steel in regions where, under the frequent combination of actions and the characteristic prestress $P_k$, only compressive stresses occur at the extreme concrete fibres. (The strain and hence the stress range in the steel is typically small while the concrete remains in compression.)

Fatigue assessments are still required in the cases above (with the possible exception of (v)), if bridges are found to be susceptible to wind-induced excitation. The main cause of wind-induced fatigue, vortex shedding, is covered in EN 1991-1-4 and is not considered further here.

## 6.8.2. Partial factors for fatigue assessment of bridges

Resistance factors $\gamma_{Mf}$ may be given in National Annexes, so only the recommended values can be discussed here. For fatigue strength of concrete and reinforcement, *clause 6.8.2(1)* refers to EN 1992-1-1, which recommends the partial factors 1.5 and 1.15, respectively, for both persistent and transient design situations. For structural steel, EN 1993-1-9, Table 3.1 recommends values ranging from 1.0 to 1.35, depending on the design concept and consequence of failure. These apply, as appropriate, for a fatigue failure of a steel flange caused by a stud weld. The choice of design concept and the uncertainties covered by $\gamma_{Mf}$ are discussed in Ref. 4. *Clause 6.8.2(1)*

Fatigue failure of a stud shear connector, not involving the flange, is covered by EN 1994-2. The recommended value of $\gamma_{Mf,s}$ for fatigue of headed studs is given as 1.0 in a Note to clause 2.4.1.2(6) in the general rules of EN 1994. This is the value in EN 1993-1-9 for the 'damage tolerant' assessment method with 'low consequence of failure'. From clause 3(2) of EN 1993-1-9, the use of the damage tolerant method should be satisfactory, provided that 'a prescribed inspection and maintenance regime for detecting and correcting fatigue damage is implemented...'. A Note to this clause states that the damage tolerant method may be applied where 'in the event of fatigue damage occurring a load redistribution between components of structural elements can occur'.

The first condition does not apply to stud connectors, as lack of access prevents detection of small cracks by any simple method of inspection. For that situation, EN 1993-1-9 recommends use of the 'safe life' method, with $\gamma_{Mf} = 1.15$ for 'low consequence of failure'. The second condition does apply to stud connectors, and the value $\gamma_{Mf,s} = 1.0$ is considered to be appropriate for studs in bridges. Relevant considerations are as follows.

Fatigue failure results from a complex interaction between steel and concrete, commencing with powdering of the highly stressed concrete adjacent to the weld collar. This displaces upwards the line of action of the shear force, increasing the bending and shear in the shank just above the weld collar, and probably also altering the tension. Initial fatigue cracking further alters the relative stiffnesses and the local stresses. Research has found that the exponent that relates the cumulative damage to the stress range may be higher than the value, 5, for other welds in shear. The value chosen for EN 1994-2, 8, is controversial, as discussed later.

As may be expected from the involvement of a tiny volume of concrete, tests show a wide scatter in fatigue lives, which is allowed for in the design resistances. Studs are provided in large numbers, and are well able to redistribute shear between themselves.

One reason for not recommending a partial factor more conservative than 1.0 comes from experience with bridges, where stud connectors have been used for almost 50 years. Whenever occasion has arisen in print or at a conference, the second author has stated that there is no known instance of fatigue failure of a stud in a bridge, other than a few clearly attributable to errors in design. This has not been challenged. Research has identified, but not yet quantified, many reasons for this remarkable experience.[97,98] Most of them (e.g. slip, shear lag, permanent set, partial interaction, adventitious connection from bolt heads, friction) lead to predicted stress ranges on studs lower than those assumed in design. With an eighth-power law, a 10% reduction in stress range more than doubles the fatigue life.

### 6.8.3. Fatigue strength

*Clause 6.8.3(3)* The format of *clause 6.8.3(3)* for shear studs, as in EN 1993-1-9, uses a reference value of range of shear stress at 2 million cycles, $\Delta\tau_C = 90\,\text{N/mm}^2$. It defines the slope $m$ of the line through this point on the log-log plot of range of stress $\Delta\tau_R$ against number of *Clause 6.8.3(4)* constant-range stress cycles to failure, $N_R$, Fig. 6.25. *Clause 6.8.3(4)* modifies the expression slightly for lightweight-aggregate concrete.

It is a complex matter to deduce a value for $m$ from the mass of test data, which are often inconsistent. Many types of test specimen have been used, and the resulting scatter of results must be disentangled from that due to inherent variability. Values for $m$ recommended in the literature range from 5 to 12, mostly based on linear-regression analyses. The method of regression used ($x$ on $y$, or $y$ on $x$) can alter the value found by up to 3.[97]

The value 8, which was also used in BS 5400 Part 10, may be too high. In design for a loading spectrum, its practical effect is that the cumulative damage is governed by the highest-range components of the spectrum (e.g. by the small number of very heavy lorries in the traffic spectrum). A lower value, such as 5, would give more weight to the much higher number of average-weight vehicles. This is illustrated in Example 6.13.

While fatigue design methods for stud connectors continue to be conservative (for bridges and probably for buildings too) the precise value for $m$ is of academic interest. Any future proposals for more accurate methods for prediction of stress ranges should be associated with re-examination of the value for $m$. Annex C gives a different design rule for fatigue of lying studs, which is discussed in Chapter 10.

### 6.8.4. Internal forces and fatigue loadings

For fatigue assessment, it is necessary to find the range or ranges of stress in a given material at a chosen cross-section, caused by the passage of a vehicle along the bridge. Loading other than the vehicle influences the extent of cracking in the concrete, and hence, the stiffnesses of members and the calculated stresses. Cracking depends mainly on the heaviest previous *Clause 6.8.4(1)* loading, and so tends to increase with time. *Clause 6.8.4(1)* refers to clause 6.8.3 of EN 1992-1-1. This defines the non-cyclic loading assumed to coexist with the design value

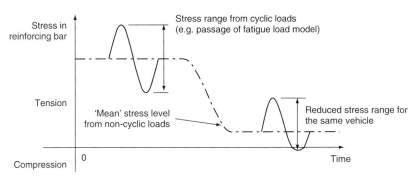

**Fig. 6.49.** Stress ranges for fatigue verification of reinforcement caused by the same cyclic action at different mean stress levels

of the cyclic load, $Q_{\text{fat}}$: it is the 'frequent' combination, represented by

$$\sum_{j \geq 1} G_{k,j} + P + \psi_{1,1} Q_{k,1} + \sum_{i > 1} \psi_{2,i} Q_{k,i}$$

where the $Q$'s are non-cyclic variable actions.

Traffic will usually be the leading non-cyclic action since the $\psi_2$ value for traffic recommended in Annex A2 of EN 1990 is zero. With traffic as the leading action, only thermal actions have a non-zero value of $\psi_2$ and therefore need to be considered.

The non-cyclic combination gives a mean stress level upon which the cyclic part of the action effect is superimposed. The importance of mean stress is illustrated in Fig. 6.49 for the calculation of stress range in reinforcement in concrete. It shows that the stress change in the reinforcement for any part of the loading cycle that induces compression in the concrete is much less than the stress change where the slab remains in tension throughout the cycle.

*Clause 6.8.4(2)* defines symbols that are used for bending moments in *clause 6.8.5.4*. The sign convention is evident from *Fig. 6.26*, which shows that $M_{\text{Ed,max,f}}$ is the bending moment that causes the greatest tension in the slab, and is positive. *Clause 6.8.4(2)* also refers to internal forces, but does not give symbols. Analogous use of calculated tensile forces in a concrete slab (e.g. $N_{\text{Ed,max,f}}$) may sometimes be necessary.

*Clause 6.8.4(3)* refers to Annex A.1 of EN 1993-1-9 for a general treatment of fatigue based on summing the damage from a loading spectrum. As discussed in section 6.8.1 above, this would be a lengthy and complex calculation for most bridges and therefore *clauses 6.8.4(4)* to *(6)* provide the option of using simpler load models from EN 1991-2. The damage equivalent stress method for road bridges is based on Fatigue Load Model 3 defined in EN 1991-2 clause 4.6.4, while for rail bridges it is based on Load Model 71. *Clause 6.8.4(5)* says that the additional factors given in EN 1992-2 clause NN.2.1 '*should*' be applied to Load Model 3 where a road bridge is prestressed by tendons or imposed deformations. As Annex NN is Informative, the situation is unclear in a country where the National Annex does not make it available.

The load models and their application are discussed in the other guides in this series.[2–4]

### 6.8.5. Stresses

*Clause 6.8.5.1(1)* refers to a list of action effects in *clause 7.2.1(1)P* to be taken into account 'where relevant'. They are all relevant, in theory, to the extent of cracking. However, this can usually be represented by the same simplified model, chosen from *clause 5.4.2.3*, that is used for other global analyses. They also influence the maximum value of the fatigue stress range, which is limited for each material (e.g. the limit for shear connectors in *clause 6.8.1(3)*).

The provisions for fatigue are based on the assumption that the stress range caused by a given fluctuation of loading, such as the passage of a vehicle of known weight, remains approximately constant after an initial shakedown period. 'Shakedown' here includes the

*Clause 6.8.4(2)*

*Clause 6.8.4(3)*

*Clauses 6.8.4 to (6)*

*Clause 6.8.5.1(1)*

changes due to cracking, shrinkage, and creep of concrete, that occur mainly within the first year or two.

For bridges, most fatigue cycles occur over very short durations as the stress ranges are produced either by the passage of vehicles or by wind-induced oscillations. Cycles of stress from thermal actions also occur but over greater durations. The magnitude and small number of these cycles do not generally cause any significant fatigue damage. The short-term modular ratio should therefore be used when finding stress ranges from the cyclic action $Q_{fat}$. Where a peak stress is being checked, creep from permanent loading should be allowed for, if it increases the relevant stress.

*Clause 6.8.5.1(2)P*
*Clause 6.8.5.1(3)*
The effect of tension stiffening on the calculation of stress in reinforcement, *clause 6.8.5.1(2)P* and *(3)*, is illustrated in Example 6.13 and discussed under *clause 6.8.5.4* below. It is not conservative to neglect tension stiffening in this calculation for a composite beam as the increased stiffness attracts more stress to the concrete slab and hence to the reinforcement between cracks. For stresses in structural steel, the effects of tension stiffening
*Clause 6.8.5.1(4)*
may be included or neglected in accordance with *clause 6.8.5.1(4)*. Tension stiffening here has a beneficial effect in reducing the stresses in the structural steel. Tension stiffening
*Clause 6.8.5.1(5)*
should also be considered in deriving stresses for prestressing steel – *clause 6.8.5.1(5)*.

For analysis, the linear-elastic method of *Section 5* is used, from *clause 6.8.4(1)*. *Clause 7.2.1(8)* requires consideration of local and global effects in deck slabs. This is also reflected in *clause 6.8.6.1(3)*. When checking fatigue, it is important to bear in mind that the most critical areas for fatigue may not be the same as those for other ultimate limit state calculations. For example, the critical section for shear connection may be near mid-span, since its provision is usually based on the static design, and the contribution to the static shear from dead load is zero there.

### Concrete

*Clause 6.8.5.2(1)*
For concrete, *clause 6.8.5.2(1)* refers to clause 6.8 of EN 1992-1-1, where clause 6.8.5(2) refers to EN 1992-2. EN 1992-2 clause 6.8.7(101) provides a damage equivalent stress range method presented as for a spectrum. The method of its Annex NN is not applicable to composite members. As a simpler alternative, EN 1992-1-1 clause 6.8.7(2) gives a conservative verification based on the non-cyclic loading used for the static design. It will usually be sufficient to apply this verification to composite bridges as it is unlikely to govern design other than possibly for short spans where most of the compressive force in concrete is produced by live load.

### Structural steel

*Clause 6.8.5.3(1)*
*Clause 6.8.5.3(1)* repeats, in effect, the concession in *clause 6.8.5.1(4)*. Where the words 'or only
*Clause 6.8.5.3(2)*
$M_{Ed,min,f}$' in *clause 6.8.5.3(2)* apply, $M_{Ed,max,f}$ causes tension in the slab. The use of the uncracked section for $M_{Ed,max,f}$ would then underestimate the stress ranges in steel flanges, so that cracked section properties should be used for the calculation of this part of the stress range.

### Reinforcement

For reinforcement, *clause 6.8.3(2)* refers to EN 1992-1-1, where clause 6.8.4 gives the verification procedure. Its recommended value $N^*$ for straight bars is $10^6$. This should not be confused with the corresponding value for structural steel in EN 1993-1-9, $2 \times 10^6$, denoted $N_C$, which is used also for shear connectors, *clause 6.8.6.2(1)*.

Using the $\gamma$ values recommended in EN 1992-1-1, its expression (6.71) for verification of reinforcement becomes:

$$\Delta\sigma_{E,equ}(N^*) \leq \Delta\sigma_{Rsk}(N^*)/1.15 \qquad (D.6.33)$$

with $\Delta\sigma_{Rsk} = 162.5\,\text{N/mm}^2$ for $N^* = 10^6$, from Table 6.3N.

Where a range $\Delta\sigma_E(N_E)$ has been determined, the resistance $\Delta\sigma_{Rsk}(N_E)$ can be found from the *S–N* curve for reinforcement, and the verification is:

$$\Delta\sigma_E(N_E) \leq \Delta\sigma_{Rsk}(N_E)/1.15 \qquad (D6.34)$$

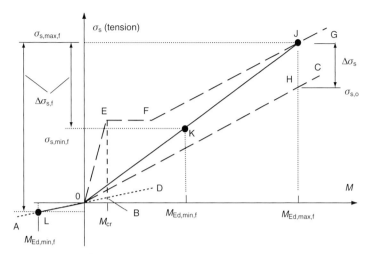

**Fig. 6.50.** Stress ranges in reinforcement in cracked regions

*Clause 6.8.5.4(1)* permits the use of the approximation to the effects of tension stiffening that is used for other limit states. It consists of adding to the maximum tensile stress in the 'fully cracked' section, $\sigma_{s,o}$, an amount $\Delta\sigma_s$ that is independent of $\sigma_{s,o}$. The value of $\Delta\sigma_s$ for fatigue verification is modified by replacing the factor of 0.4 in *equation (7.5)* by 0.2. This is to allow for the reduction in tension stiffening caused by repeated cycles of tensile stress.[99]

*Clauses 6.8.5.4(2)* and *(3)* give simplified rules for calculating stresses, with reference to *Fig. 6.26*, which is discussed using Fig. 6.50. This has the same axes, and also shows a minimum bending moment that causes compression in the slab. A calculated value for the stress $\sigma_s$ in reinforcement, that assumes concrete to be effective, would lie on line A0D. On initial cracking, the stress $\sigma_s$ jumps from B to point E. Lines 0BE are not shown in *Fig. 6.26* because *clause 7.2.1(5)P* requires the tensile strength of concrete to be neglected in calculations for $\sigma_s$. This gives line 0E. For moments exceeding $M_{cr}$, the stress $\sigma_s$ follows route EFG on first loading. Calculation of $\sigma_s$ using section property $I_2$ gives line 0C. At bending moment $M_{Ed,max,f}$ the stress $\sigma_{s,o}$ thus found is increased by $\Delta\sigma_s$, from *equation (7.5)*, as shown by line HJ.

*Clause 6.8.5.4* defines the unloading route from point J as J0A, on which the stress $\sigma_{s,min,f}$ lies. Points K and L give two examples, for $M_{Ed,min,f}$ causing tension and compression, respectively, in the slab. The fatigue stress ranges $\Delta\sigma_{s,f}$ for these two cases are shown.

*Shear connection*
The interpretation of *clause 6.8.5.5(1)P* is complex when tension stiffening is allowed for. Spacing of shear connectors near internal supports is unlikely to be governed by fatigue, so it is simplest to use uncracked section properties when calculating range of shear flow from range of vertical shear, *clause 6.8.5.5(2)*. These points are illustrated in Example 6.13.

*Reinforcement and prestressing steel in members prestressed by bonded tendons*
Where bonded prestress is present, stresses should be determined in a similar manner to the above for reinforcement alone, but account needs to be taken of the difference of bond behaviour between prestressing steel and reinforcement – *clause 6.8.5.6(1)*. *Clause 6.8.5.6(2)* makes reference to *clause 7.4.3(4)* which in turn refers to clause 7.3 of EN 1992-1-1 for the calculation of stresses '$\sigma_s$'. This is a generic symbol here, and so applies to the stress $\sigma_{s,max,f}$ referred to in *clause 6.8.5.6(2)*.

### 6.8.6. Stress ranges
*Clause 6.8.6.1* is most relevant to the damage equivalent stress method where the complex cyclic loadings from a spectrum of vehicles are condensed into one single stress range which, for $N^*$ cycles, is intended to give the same damage during the bridge's lifetime as

*Clause 6.8.5.4(1)*

*Clause 6.8.5.4(2)*
*Clause 6.8.5.4(3)*

*Clause 6.8.5.5(1)P*

*Clause 6.8.5.5(2)*

*Clause 6.8.5.6(1)*
*Clause 6.8.5.6(2)*

*Clause 6.8.6.1*

the real traffic. This stress range is determined by applying the relevant fatigue load model
discussed in section 6.8.4 and by multiplying it by the damage equivalent factor $\lambda$, according
*Clause 6.8.6.1(2)*  to *clause 6.8.6.1(2)*. The factor $\lambda$ is a property of the spectrum and the exponent $m$, which is
the slope of the fatigue curve as noted in *clause 6.8.6.1(4)*.

Deck slabs of composite bridge beams are usually subjected to combined global and local
fatigue loading events, due to the presence of local wheel loads. The effects of local and
global loading are particularly significant in reinforcement design in slabs adjacent to
cross-beams supporting the deck slab, in zones where the slab is in global tension. Here,
*Clause 6.8.6.1(3)*  wheel loads cause additional local hogging moments. *Clause 6.8.6.1(3)* provides a conservative interaction where the damage equivalent stress range is determined separately for the
global and local actions and then summed to give an overall damage equivalent stress range.

In combining the stress ranges in *clause 6.8.6.1(3)*, it is important to consider the actual
transverse location being checked within the slab. The peak local effect usually occurs
some distance from the web of a main beam, while the global direct stress reduces away
from the web due to shear lag. The reduction may be determined using *clause 5.4.1.2(8)*,
even though that clause refers to EN 1993-1-5, which is for steel flanges.

*Clause 6.8.6.2(1)*  A similar damage equivalent factor, $\lambda_v$, is used in *clause 6.8.6.2(1)* to convert the shear
stress range in the studs from the fatigue load model into a damage equivalent stress range.

*Clause 6.8.6.2(2)*  For other types of shear connection *clause 6.8.6.2(2)* refers to Section 6 of EN 1993-1-9.
This requires the damage equivalent stress to be determined from its Annex A using the
actual traffic spectrum and Miner's summation. This approach could also be used for
shear studs as an alternative, provided that $m$ is taken as 8, rather than 3.

For connectors other than studs, the authors recommend that the method of Annex A be
used only where the following conditions are satisfied:

- the connectors are attached to the steel flange by welds that are within the scope of
  EN 1993-1-9
- the fatigue stress ranges in the welds can be determined realistically
- the stresses applied to concrete by the connectors are not high enough for fatigue failure
  of the concrete to influence the fatigue life.

The exponent $m$ should then have the value given in EN 1993-1-9; $m = 8$ should not be used.

In other situations, fatigue damage to concrete could influence the value of $m$. The
National Annex may refer to guidance, as permitted by the Note to *clause 1.1.3(3)*.
*Clauses 6.8.6.2(3)*  *Clauses 6.8.6.2(3)* to *(5)* provide a method of calculating the damage equivalent factors
*to (5)*  for studs. With the exception of $\lambda_{v,1}$, those for road bridges are based on those in EN 1993-2
clause 9.5.2, but with the exponents modified to 8 or $\frac{1}{8}$ as discussed in section 6.8.3.

In EN 1993-2, an upper limit to $\lambda$ is defined in clause 9.5.2, in paragraphs that EN 1994-2
does not refer to. This is because the upper limit is not required for stud shear connectors.

## 6.8.7. Fatigue assessment based on nominal stress ranges

*Clause 6.8.7.1*  Comment on the methods referred to from *clause 6.8.7.1* will be found in other guides in this
series. The term 'nominal stress range' in the heading of *clause 6.8.7* is defined in Section 6 of
EN 1993-1-9 for structural steel. It is the stress range that can be compared directly with the
detail categories in EN 1993-1-9. It is not the stress range before the damage equivalent
factors are applied. It is intended to allow for all stress concentration factors implicit
within the particular detail category selected. If additional stress concentrating details
exist adjacent to the detail to be checked which are not present in the detail category selected
(e.g. a hole), these additional effects need to be included via an appropriate stress concentration factor. This factored stress range then becomes a 'modified nominal stress range' as
defined in clause 6.3 of EN 1993-1-9.

*Clause 6.8.7.2(1)*  For shear connectors, *clause 6.8.7.2(1)* introduces the partial factors. The recommended
value of $\gamma_{Mf,s}$ is 1.0 (*clause 2.4.1.2(6)*). For $\gamma_{Ff}$, EN 1990 refers to the other Eurocodes. The
recommended value in EN 1992-1-1, clause 6.8.4(1), is 1.0. Clause 9.3(1) of EN 1993-2
recommends 1.0 for steel bridges.

*Clause 6.8.7.2(2)* covers interaction between the fatigue failures of a stud and of the steel flange to which it is welded, where the flange is in tension. The first of *expressions (6.57)* is the verification for the flange, from clause 8(2) of EN 1993-1-9, and the second is for the stud, copied from *equation (6.55)*. The linear interaction condition is given in *expression (6.56)*.

It is necessary to calculate the longitudinal stress range in the steel flange that coexists with the stress range for the connectors. The load cycle that gives the maximum value of $\Delta\sigma_{E,2}$ in the flange will not, in general, be that which gives the maximum value of $\Delta\tau_{E,2}$ in a shear connector, because the first is caused by flexure and the second by shear. Also, both $\Delta\sigma_{E,2}$ and $\Delta\tau_{E,2}$ may be influenced by whether the concrete is cracked, or not.

It thus appears that *expression (6.56)* may have to be checked four times. In practice, it is best to check first the conditions in *expression (6.57)*. It should be obvious, for these, whether the 'cracked' or the 'uncracked' model is the more adverse. Usually, one or both of the left-hand sides is so far below 1.0 that no check to *expression (6.56)* is needed.

### Example 6.13: fatigue verification of studs and reinforcement

The bridge shown in Fig. 6.22 is checked for fatigue of the shear studs at an abutment and of the top slab reinforcement at an internal support. The Client requires a design life of 120 years. Fatigue Load Model 3 of EN 1991-2 is used. The bridge will carry a road in Traffic Category 2 of Table 4.5(n) of EN 1991-2, 'roads with medium flow rates of lorries'. The table gives the 'indicative number of heavy vehicles expected per year and per slow lane' as 500 000, and this value is used. The 'safe life' method (defined in clause 3(7)(b) of EN 1993-1-9) is used, as this is likely to be recommended by the UK's National Annex.

*Studs at an abutment*
The cross-section of an inner beam at the abutments is as shown for length DE in Fig. 6.22. Groups of three 19 mm studs are provided, Fig. 6.41, at 150 mm spacing. The 'special vehicle' of Load Model 3 is defined in clause 4.6.4 of EN 1991-2. For this cross-section its passage produces maximum and minimum unfactored vertical shears of +235 kN and −19 kN. Since the detail is adjacent to an expansion joint, these values should be increased by a factor of 1.3 in accordance with EN 1991-2 Fig. 4.7, so the shear range becomes $1.3 \times (235 + 19) = 330$ kN.

The short-term uncracked properties of the composite beam are used for the calculation of shear flow. From Table 6.3 in Example 6.10, $A\bar{z}/I = 0.810\,\text{m}^{-1}$. The range of shear force per connector is:

$$0.810 \times 330 \times 0.150/3 = 13.4\,\text{kN}$$

The shear stress range for the connector is:

$$\Delta\tau = \frac{13.4 \times 10^3}{\pi \times 19^2/4} = 47.1\,\text{N/mm}^2$$

To determine the damage equivalent stress range, the factor

$$\lambda_v = \lambda_{v,1} \times \lambda_{v,2} \times \lambda_{v,3} \times \lambda_{v,4}$$

should be calculated in accordance with *clause 6.8.6.2(3)*. From *clause 6.8.6.2(4)*, $\lambda_{v,1} = 1.55$. The remaining factors are calculated from EN 1993-2 clause 9.5.2 using exponents 8 and $\frac{1}{8}$ in place of those given.

For $\lambda_{v,2}$ it would be possible to use the recommended data for Load Model 4 in Tables 4.7 and 4.8 of EN 1991-2. However, the UK's National Annex to EN 1991-2 is likely to replace these with the BS 5400 Part 10 data, which are given in Table 6.5. From clause 9.5.2(3) of EN 1993-2:

$$Q_{m1} = \left(\frac{\sum n_i Q_i^5}{\sum n_i}\right)^{1/5} = \left(\frac{8.051 \times 10^{18}}{1.000 \times 10^6}\right)^{1/5} = 381.2\,\text{kN for checks on structural steel}$$

$$Q_{m1} = \left(\frac{\sum n_i Q_i^8}{\sum n_i}\right)^{1/8} = \left(\frac{3.384 \times 10^{29}}{1.000 \times 10^6}\right)^{1/8} = 873.3\,\text{kN for checks on shear studs}$$

It can be seen from the above that the contribution of the small number of very heavy vehicles is much more significant when the exponent 8 is used.

**Table 6.5.** Vehicle spectrum for fatigue verifications

| Vehicle ref. | Weight (kN) $(Q_i)$ | No. per million vehicles $(n_i)$ | $(n_i Q_i^5)$ | $(n_i Q_i^8)$ |
|---|---|---|---|---|
| 18GTH | 3680 | 10 | $6.749 \times 10^{18}$ | $3.363 \times 10^{29}$ |
| 18GTM | 1520 | 30 | $2.434 \times 10^{17}$ | $8.548 \times 10^{26}$ |
| 9TT-H | 1610 | 20 | $2.164 \times 10^{17}$ | $9.029 \times 10^{26}$ |
| 9TT-M | 750 | 40 | $9.492 \times 10^{15}$ | $4.005 \times 10^{24}$ |
| 7GT-H | 1310 | 30 | $1.157 \times 10^{17}$ | $2.602 \times 10^{26}$ |
| 7GT-M | 680 | 70 | $1.018 \times 10^{16}$ | $3.200 \times 10^{24}$ |
| 7A-H | 790 | 20 | $6.154 \times 10^{15}$ | $3.034 \times 10^{24}$ |
| 5A-H | 630 | 280 | $2.779 \times 10^{16}$ | $6.948 \times 10^{24}$ |
| 5A-M | 360 | 14 500 | $8.768 \times 10^{16}$ | $4.091 \times 10^{24}$ |
| 5A-L | 250 | 15 000 | $1.465 \times 10^{16}$ | $2.289 \times 10^{23}$ |
| 4A-H | 335 | 90 000 | $3.797 \times 10^{17}$ | $1.428 \times 10^{25}$ |
| 4A-M | 260 | 90 000 | $1.069 \times 10^{17}$ | $1.879 \times 10^{24}$ |
| 4A-L | 145 | 90 000 | $5.769 \times 10^{15}$ | $1.759 \times 10^{22}$ |
| 4R-H | 280 | 15 000 | $2.582 \times 10^{16}$ | $5.667 \times 10^{23}$ |
| 4R-M | 240 | 15 000 | $1.194 \times 10^{16}$ | $1.651 \times 10^{23}$ |
| 4R-L | 120 | 15 000 | $3.732 \times 10^{14}$ | $6.450 \times 10^{20}$ |
| 3A-H | 215 | 30 000 | $1.378 \times 10^{16}$ | $1.370 \times 10^{23}$ |
| 3A-M | 140 | 30 000 | $1.613 \times 10^{15}$ | $4.427 \times 10^{21}$ |
| 3A-L | 90 | 30 000 | $1.771 \times 10^{14}$ | $1.291 \times 10^{20}$ |
| 3R-H | 240 | 15 000 | $1.194 \times 10^{16}$ | $1.651 \times 10^{23}$ |
| 3R-M | 195 | 15 000 | $4.229 \times 10^{15}$ | $3.136 \times 10^{22}$ |
| 3R-L | 120 | 15 000 | $3.732 \times 10^{14}$ | $6.450 \times 10^{20}$ |
| 2R-H | 135 | 170 000 | $7.623 \times 10^{15}$ | $1.876 \times 10^{22}$ |
| 2R-M | 65 | 170 000 | $1.972 \times 10^{14}$ | $5.417 \times 10^{19}$ |
| 2R-L | 30 | 180 000 | $4.374 \times 10^{12}$ | $1.181 \times 10^{17}$ |
| Totals | | $1.000 \times 10^6$ | $8.051 \times 10^{18}$ | $3.384 \times 10^{29}$ |

For a two-lane road, traffic category 2, $N_{\text{Obs}} = 0.5 \times 10^6$. (The UK's National Annex to EN 1991-2 may modify this value.)

Also from clause 9.5.2(3), $N_0 = 0.5 \times 10^6$
$Q_0 = 480\,\text{kN}$ (weight of vehicle for Fatigue Load Model 3)

Therefore

$$\lambda_{v,2} = \frac{Q_{m1}}{Q_0}\left(\frac{N_{\text{Obs}}}{N_0}\right)^{1/8} = \frac{873.3}{480}\left(\frac{0.5 \times 10^6}{0.5 \times 10^6}\right)^{1/8} = 1.819$$

From clause 9.5.2(5) of EN 1993-2:

$\lambda_{v,3} = (t_{\text{Ld}}/100)^{1/8} = 1.023$ for the 120-year design life.

From clause 9.5.2(6) of EN 1993-2:

$$\lambda_{v,4} = \left[1 + \frac{N_2}{N_1}\left(\frac{\eta_2 Q_{m2}}{\eta_1 Q_{m1}}\right)^8 + \frac{N_3}{N_1}\left(\frac{\eta_3 Q_{m3}}{\eta_1 Q_{m1}}\right)^8 + \cdots + \frac{N_k}{N_1}\left(\frac{\eta_k Q_{mk}}{\eta_1 Q_{m1}}\right)^8\right]^{1/8}$$

The influence coefficient from lane 2 is approximately 75% of that from lane 1. As both lanes are slow lanes with $N = 0.5 \times 10^6$ vehicles per year,

$$\lambda_{v,4} = \left[1 + \frac{N_2}{N_1}\left(\frac{\eta_2 Q_{m2}}{\eta_1 Q_{m1}}\right)^8\right]^{1/8} = \left[1 + \frac{0.5 \times 10^6}{0.5 \times 10^6}\left(\frac{0.75}{1.0}\right)^8\right]^{1/8} = 1.012$$

$$\lambda_v = \lambda_{v,1} \times \lambda_{v,2} \times \lambda_{v,3} \times \lambda_{v,4} = 1.55 \times 1.819 \times 1.023 \times 1.012 = 2.92$$

From *clause 6.8.6.2(1)*, $\Delta\tau_{E,2} = \lambda_v\Delta\tau = 2.92 \times 47.1 = 138\,\text{N/mm}^2$

From *clause 6.8.7.2(1)*, $\gamma_{Ff}\Delta\tau_{E,2} = 1.0 \times 138 = 138\,\text{N/mm}^2$

From *clause 6.8.3(3)*, $\Delta\tau_c = 90\,\text{N/mm}^2$, so the fatigue resistance is:

$$\Delta\tau_c/\gamma_{Mf,s} = 90/1.0 = 90\,\text{N/mm}^2$$

The shear studs are therefore not adequate and would need to be increased. There is no need to check the interaction in *clause 6.8.7.2(2)* as the stress in the steel flange is small and compressive at an abutment.

*Fatigue of reinforcement, global effects*
*Note*: throughout this Example, all cross-references commencing 'NN' are to Annex NN of EN 1992-2, 'Damage equivalent stresses for fatigue verification'.

The cross-section at an intermediate support is shown in Fig. 6.22. For these cross-sections, the axle loads of Fatigue Load Model 3 should be multiplied by 1.75 according to clause NN.2.1(101). The maximum hogging moment from the fatigue vehicle was $1.75 \times 593 = 1038\,\text{kNm}$ and the minimum was $1.75 \times (-47) = -82\,\text{kNm}$.

In this calculation, the maximum and minimum moments occurred with the vehicle in the same lane. Previous practice in the UK has been to calculate the stress range by allowing the maximum and minimum effects from the vehicle to come from different lanes. Clause 4.6.4(2) of EN 1991-2 however implies that the maximum stress range should be calculated as the greatest stress range produced by the passage of the vehicle along any one lane. The UK's draft National Annex currently requires the former interpretation (the safer of the two) to be used, but there is no national provision in EN 1991-2 for this to be done.

The maximum hogging moment on the composite section from the frequent combination was found to be 3607 kNm. This includes the effects of superimposed dead load, secondary effects of shrinkage, settlement, thermal actions and traffic load (load group 1a). Traffic was taken as the leading variable action and hence the combination factors applied were $\psi_1$ for traffic loading and $\psi_2$ for thermal actions. Wind was not considered, as the recommended value of $\psi_2$ is zero from EN 1990 Table A2.1.

From *clause 6.8.4(1)*, the minimum moment from the cyclic + non-cyclic loading is:

$$M_{Ed,min,f} = 3607 - 82 = 3525\,\text{kNm}$$

and the maximum is:

$$M_{Ed,max,f} = 3607 + 1038 = 4645\,\text{kNm}$$

From *clause 7.4.3(3)* as modified by *clause 6.8.5.4(1)*, the increase in stress in the reinforcement, due to tension stiffening, above that calculated using a fully cracked analysis is:

$$\Delta\sigma_s = \frac{0.2f_{ctm}}{\alpha_{st}\rho_s} \quad \text{where} \quad \alpha_{st} = \frac{AI}{A_a I_a} = \frac{74\,478 \times 22\,660}{55\,000 \times 12\,280} = 2.50$$

The reinforcement ratio $\rho_s = 0.025$ and $f_{ctm} = 2.9\,\text{N/mm}^2$ and thus $\Delta\sigma_s = 9.3\,\text{N/mm}^2$.

From Example 6.6, the section modulus for the top layer of reinforcement is $34.05 \times 10^6\,\text{mm}^3$. Therefore the stress due to $M_{Ed,max,f}$ ignoring tension stiffening is:

$$\sigma_{s,o} = 4645/34.05 = 136.4\,\text{N/mm}^2$$

From *equation (7.4)*, the stress including allowance for tension stiffening is:

$$\sigma_{s,max,f} = 136.4 + 9.3 = 146\,\text{N/mm}^2$$

From *clause 6.8.5.4(2)*,

$$\sigma_{s,min,f} = 136.4 \times 3525/4645 + 9.3 = 113\,\text{N/mm}^2$$

The damage equivalent parameters are next calculated from Annex NN. Figure NN.1 refers to the 'length of the influence line'. This length is intended to be the length of the lobe creating the greatest stress range. EN 1993-2 clause 9.5.2 provides definitions of the critical length of the influence line for different situations and these can be referred to. For bending moment at an internal support, the average length of the two adjacent spans may be used, but here the length of the main span has been conservatively used. From Fig. NN.1 for straight reinforcing bars (curve 3) and critical length of the influence line of 31 m, $\lambda_{s,1} = 0.98$.

From equation (NN.103):

$$\lambda_{s,2} = \bar{Q} \times \sqrt[k_2]{N_{obs}/2.0} \text{ with } N_{obs} \text{ in millions (which is not stated)}$$

From Table 4.5(n) of EN 1991-2, $N_{obs} = 0.5 \times 10^6$.
From EN 1992-1-1/Table 6.3N, $k_2 = 9$ for straight bars.
The factor for traffic type, $\bar{Q}$, is given in Table NN.1, but no guidance is given on its selection. 'Traffic type' is defined in Note 3 of EN 1991-2 clause 4.6.5(1). The definitions given are not particularly helpful:

- 'long distance' means hundreds of kilometres
- 'medium distance' means 50–100 km
- 'local traffic' means distances less than 50 km.

'Long distance' will typically apply to motorways and trunk roads. The use of either of the lower categories should be agreed with the Client as the traffic using a road may not be represented by a typical length of journey. 'Long distance' traffic is conservatively used here, so from Table NN.1, $\bar{Q} = 1.0$. Thus,

$$\lambda_{s,2} = 1.0 \times \sqrt[9]{0.5/2.0} = 0.86$$

From equation (NN.104): $\lambda_{s,3} = \sqrt[k_2]{N_{Years}/100} = \sqrt[9]{120/100} = 1.02$

From equation (NN.105): $\lambda_{s,4} = \sqrt[k_2]{\dfrac{\sum N_{obs,i}}{N_{obs,1}}}$.

Since both lanes are slow lanes, from Table 4.5 of EN 1991-2,

$$N_{obs,1} = N_{obs,2} = 0.5 \times 10^6$$

and therefore

$$\lambda_{s,4} = \sqrt[9]{\dfrac{0.5 + 0.5}{0.5}} = 1.08$$

From clause NN.2.1(108) and then EN 1991-2, Annex B, the damage equivalent impact factor for surfaces of good roughness (i.e. regularly maintained surfaces) is $\varphi_{fat} = 1.2$.
From equation (NN.102):

$$\lambda_s = \varphi_{fat}\lambda_{s,1}\lambda_{s,2}\lambda_{s,3}\lambda_{s,4} = 1.20 \times 0.98 \times 0.86 \times 1.02 \times 1.08 = 1.11$$

From *clause 6.8.6.1(2)* and *(7)*:

$$\Delta\sigma_E = \lambda\phi(\sigma_{max,f} - \sigma_{min,f}) = 1.11 \times 1.0 \times (146 - 113) = 37\,\text{N/mm}^2$$

There is an inconsistency here between EN 1992-2, where $\lambda_s$ includes the impact factor $\varphi_{fat}$ and EN 1994-2 where $\lambda$ excludes this factor, which is written as $\phi$.

From Table 6.3N of EN 1992-1-1, for straight bars, $N^* = 10^6$ and $\Delta\sigma_{Rsk}(10^6) = 162.5\,\text{N/mm}^2$.

The verification is carried out using expression (6.71) of EN 1992-1-1, taking $\Delta\sigma_{s,equ}(N^*) = \Delta\sigma_E$ above:

$$\gamma_{F,fat}\Delta\sigma_{s,equ}(N^*) = 1.0 \times 37 = 37\,\text{N/mm}^2 \leq \frac{\Delta\sigma_{Rsk}(N^*)}{\gamma_{s,fat}} = 162.5/1.15 = 141\,\text{N/mm}^2$$

The reinforcement has adequate fatigue life under global loading.

### Fatigue of reinforcement, local effects

Local bending moments are caused by hogging of the deck slab over the pier diaphragm. The worst local effects are here conservatively added to the global effects according to *expression (6.53)*. A stress range of $44\,\text{N/mm}^2$ in the reinforcement was determined from the maximum hogging moment caused by the passage of the factored fatigue vehicle of EN 1992-2 Annex NN. (The moments were found using Pucher's influence surfaces.[100]) Cracked section properties were used for the slab in accordance with clause 6.8.2(1)P of EN 1992-1-1 since the slab remains in tension when the local effect is added under the 'basic combination plus the cyclic action' as defined in clause 6.8.3(3) of EN 1992-1-1.

The damage equivalent factors from EN 1992-2 Annex NN are the same as above with the exception of $\lambda_{s,1}$. For local load, the critical length of the influence line is the length causing hogging moment each side of the pier diaphragm. From the Pucher chart used to determine the local moment, the influence of loads applied more than 6 m from the pier diaphragm is approximately zero so the total influence line length to consider is approximately 12 m. From Fig. NN.1, $\lambda_{s,1} = 0.91$.

From equation (NN.102):

$$\lambda_s = \phi_{fat}\lambda_{s,1}\lambda_{s,2}\lambda_{s,3}\lambda_{s,4} = 1.20 \times 0.91 \times 0.86 \times 1.02 \times 1.08 = 1.03$$

From *clause 6.8.6.1(2)* and *(7)*:

$$\Delta\sigma_E = \lambda\phi(\sigma_{max,f} - \sigma_{min,f}) = 1.03 \times 1.0 \times (44) = 45\,\text{N/mm}^2$$

Verifying as for the global loading:

$$\gamma_{F,fat}\Delta\sigma_{s,equ}(N^*) = 1.0 \times 45 = 45\,\text{N/mm}^2 \leq \frac{\Delta\sigma_{Rsk}(N^*)}{\gamma_{s,fat}} = 162.5/1.15 = 141\,\text{N/mm}^2$$

The reinforcement has adequate fatigue life under local loading.

### Fatigue of reinforcement, combined global and local effects

The simple interaction method of *clause 6.8.6.1(3)* is used. This entails summing the damage equivalent stresses from the local and global loading, so that the total damage equivalent stress $\Delta\sigma_E = 37 + 45 = 82\,\text{N/mm}^2$. In this case, the locations of peak global stress in the reinforcement and peak local stress do coexist because there was no reduction to the slab width for shear lag. The verification is now:

$$82\,\text{N/mm}^2 \leq 141\,\text{N/mm}^2$$

The reinforcement has adequate fatigue life under the combined loading.

## 6.9. Tension members in composite bridges

The terms 'concrete tension member' and 'composite tension member' used in this clause are defined in *clause 5.4.2.8*. Global analysis for action effects in these members and determination of longitudinal shear is discussed in comments on that clause.

*Clause 6.9(1)* concerns members that have tensile force introduced only near their ends. It refers to their design to EN 1992, as does *clause 6.9(2)*, with reference to simplifications

*Clause 6.9(1)*
*Clause 6.9(2)*

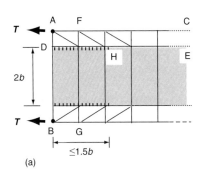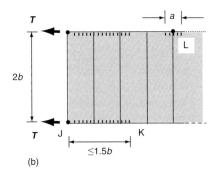

**Fig. 6.51.** Shear connection to the deck of a bowstring arch bridge

given in *clause 5.4.2.8*. *Clause 6.9(2)* applies also to composite tension members, which have shear connectors throughout their length. The subsequent paragraphs concern the distribution of the connectors along the member.

A plan of the steel members at deck level near one end of a bowstring arch bridge is shown in Fig. 6.51(a). The arch applies concentrated forces $T$ at points A and B. The force at A is shared between the steel tie AC and the composite deck, shown shaded. The deck has steel edge members such as DE, and spans longitudinally between composite cross-beams FG, etc. The proportion of each force $T$ that is resisted by the deck structure, $T_d$ say, depends on the extent to which its stiffness is reduced by cracking of the concrete. The force $T_d$ is applied to the deck by diagonal members such as FH. The stiffness of these members also influences the magnitude of $T_d$. Details of bridges of this type are available elsewhere.[101]

*Clause 6.9(3)*

In some bridges, the deck is shear-connected directly to the main tie member, as shown in Fig. 6.51(b). *Clause 6.9(3)* requires the shear connection for the force $T_d$ to be provided within the lengths $1.5b$ shown.

The precise distribution of the connectors along a length such as JK has been studied, using the rules of EN 1994-2 for tension stiffening.[102] In this bridge, Newark Dyke, the arch is the top chord of a truss of span 77 m with diagonals that apply longitudinal force also at points such as L in Fig. 6.51(b). Neither *paragraph (3)* nor *(6)* defines the length $a$ over which shear connection near point L should be provided, but *clause 6.6.2.3* provides guidance.

The number of connectors to be provided over a length such as JK can be conservatively found by assuming the deck to be uncracked. In this bridge, the design ultimate force $T$ was about 18 MN, and 'uncracked' analysis gave $T_d \approx 9$ MN at mid-span. Fully cracked analysis gave this force as about 5 MN. Accurate analysis found the deck to be in a state of single cracking (explained in comments on *clause 5.4.2.8(6)*), with a tensile force of about 8 MN.

Lower levels of shear connection are, of course, required along the whole length of the deck for other combinations and arrangements of variable actions.

*Clause 6.9(4)P*

*Clause 6.9(5)*

*Clause 6.9(4)P*, a principle that corresponds to *clause 6.7.4.1(1)P* for compression members, is followed by application rules. For laterally loaded tension members, shear connection within the length is related to the transverse shear in *clause 6.9(5)*, exactly as for composite beams.

Where axial tension is applied to the ends of a member through only one material, steel or concrete, the length over which part of the tension should be transferred to the other material (typically by shear connection), is limited by *clause 6.9(6)*. This corresponds to *clause 6.7.4.2(2)* for compression members. Other provisions of *clause 6.7.4.2* may be relevant here.

*Clause 6.9(6)*

# CHAPTER 7

# Serviceability limit states

This chapter corresponds to *Section 7* of EN 1994-2, which has the following clauses:

## 7.1. General

*Section 7* of EN 1994-2 is limited to provisions on serviceability that are specific to composite structures and are not in *Sections 1, 2, 4* or *5* (for global analysis), or in Eurocodes 1990, 1991, 1992 or 1993. Some of these other provisions are briefly referred to here. Further comments on them are in other chapters of this book, or in other guides in this series.

The initial concept for a composite bridge is mainly influenced by the intended method of construction, durability, ease of maintenance, and the requirements for ultimate limit states. Serviceability criteria that should be considered at an early stage are stress limits in cross-sections in Class 1 or 2 and susceptibility to excessive vibration. It should not however be assumed that Class 3 and 4 cross-sections require no checks of stress limits at serviceability. For example, if torsional warping or St Venant torsional effects have been neglected at ultimate limit state (ULS), as allowed by a reference in clause 6.2.7.2(1) of EN 1993-2, then the serviceability limit state (SLS) stresses should be checked taking these torsional effects into account. Considerations of shear lag at SLS may also cause unacceptable yielding as the effective widths of steel elements are greater at ULS.

Control of crack width can usually be achieved by appropriate detailing of reinforcement. Provision of fire resistance and limiting of deformations have less influence at this stage than in structures for buildings. The important deformations are those caused by imposed load. Limits to these influence the design of railway bridges, but generally, stiffness is governed more by vibration criteria than by limits to deflection.

The drafting of the serviceability provisions in the Eurocodes is less prescriptive than for other limit states. It is intended to give designers and clients greater freedom to take account of factors specific to the project.

The content of *Section 7* was also influenced by the need to minimize calculations. Results already obtained for ultimate limit states are scaled or reused wherever possible. Experienced designers know that many structural elements satisfy serviceability criteria by wide margins. For these, design checks should be simple, and it does not matter if they are conservative. For other elements, a longer but more accurate calculation may be justified. Some application rules therefore include alternative methods.

Clause 7.1(1)P
Clause 7.1(2)
***Clause 7.1(1)P*** and *(2)* refer to clause 3.4 of EN 1990. This gives criteria for placing a limit state within the 'serviceability' group, with reference to deformations (including vibration), durability, and the functioning of the structure. The relevance of EN 1990 is not limited to the clauses referred to, because *clause 2.1(1)P* requires design to be in accordance with the general rules of EN 1990. This means all of it except annexes that are either informative or not for bridges.

### Serviceability verification and criteria

The requirement for a serviceability verification is given in clause 6.5.1(1)P of EN 1990 as:

$$E_d \leq C_d$$

where $E_d$ is the design value of the effects of the specified actions and the 'relevant' combination, and $C_d$ is the limiting design value of the 'relevant' criterion.

From clause 6.5.3 of EN 1990, the relevant combination is 'normally' the characteristic, frequent, or quasi-permanent combination, for serviceability limit states that are respectively irreversible, reversible, or a consequence of long-term effects. The quasi-permanent combination is also relevant for the appearance of the structure.

For bridges, rules on combinations of actions are given in clause A2.2 of EN 1990. Its clause A2.2.2(1) defines a fourth combination, 'infrequent', for use for concrete bridges. It is not used in EN 1994-2, but may be invoked by a reference to EN 1992, or found in a National Annex.

Clause 7.1(3)
***Clause 7.1(3)*** refers to 'environmental classes'. These are the 'exposure classes' of EN 1992, and are discussed in Chapter 4. The exposure class influences the cover to reinforcing bars, and the choice of concrete grade and hence the stress limits.

Clause 7.1(4)
***Clause 7.1(4)*** on serviceability verification gives no detailed guidance on the extent to which construction phases should be checked. The avoidance of excessive stress is one example. Yielding of steel can cause irreversible deformation, and handling of precast components can cause yielding of reinforcement or excessive crack width. Bridges can also be more susceptible to aerodynamic oscillation during erection. In extreme cases, this can lead to achievement of an ultimate limit state.

Clause 7.1(5)
***Clause 7.1(5)*** refers to the eight-page clause A2.4 of EN 1990. It covers partial factors, serviceability criteria, design situations, comfort criteria, deformations of railway bridges and criteria for the safety of rail traffic. Few of its provisions are quantified. Recommended values are given in Notes, as guidance for National Annexes.

Clause 7.1(6)
The meaning of ***clause 7.1(6)*** on composite plates is that account should be taken of *Section 9* when applying *Section 7*. There are no serviceability provisions in *Section 9*.

No serviceability limit state of 'excessive slip of shear connection' is defined. Generally, it is assumed that *clause 6.8.1(3)*, which limits the shear force per connector under the characteristic combination, and other rules for ultimate limit states, will ensure satisfactory performance in service.

No serviceability criteria are specified for composite columns, so from here on, this chapter is referring to composite beams or plates or, in a few places, to composite frames.

## 7.2. Stresses

Excessive stress is not itself a serviceability limit state. Stresses in bridges are limited to ensure that under normal conditions of use, assumptions made in design models (e.g. linear-elastic behaviour) remain valid, and to avoid deterioration such as the spalling of concrete or disruption of the corrosion protection system.

The stress ranges in a composite structure caused by a particular level of imposed loading take years to stabilise, mainly because of the cracking, shrinkage and creep of concrete. Stress limits are also intended to ensure that after this initial period, live-load behaviour is reversible.

For the calculation of stresses, the principle of *clause 7.2.1(1)P* says, in effect, 'take account of everything that is relevant'. It is thus open to interpretation, subject to the guidance in the rest of *clause 7.2.1*. Four of its paragraphs are worded 'may'.

*Clause 7.2.1(1)P*

For persistent design situations, it is usual to check stresses soon after the opening of the bridge to traffic, ignoring creep, and also at a time when further effects of creep and shrinkage have become negligible. Their values are usually found by letting $t \to \infty$ when applying the data on creep and shrinkage in clause 3.1.4 and Annex B of EN 1992-1-1. Assuming that $t = 10$ years, for example, gives only about 90% of the long-term shrinkage strain and creep coefficient. It may be necessary to include part of the long-term shrinkage effects in the first check, because up to half of the long-term shrinkage can occur in the first three months after the end of curing of the concrete.

*Clause 7.2.1(4)* refers to the primary effects of shrinkage. These are calculated for uncracked cross-sections (Example 5.3). After cracking, these effects remain in the concrete between cracks, but have negligible influence on stresses at the cracked cross-sections, at which stresses are verified.

*Clause 7.2.1(4)*

*Clauses 7.2.1(6)* and *(7)* refer to tension stiffening. At a cross-section analysed as cracked, its effect is to increase the tensile stress in the reinforcement, as discussed under *clause 7.4.3*. It has negligible effect on the stress in the steel flange adjacent to the slab, and slightly reduces the compressive stress in the other steel flange.

*Clause 7.2.1(6)*
*Clause 7.2.1(7)*

*Clause 7.2.1(8)* refers to the effects of local actions on the concrete slab, presumably a deck slab. In highway bridges, these effects are mainly the sagging and hogging moments caused by a single wheel, a pair of wheels, or a four-wheel tandem system, whichever is the most adverse. In Load Model 1 these are combined with the effects of distributed loading and the global effects in the plane of the slab. This combination is more adverse where the slab spans longitudinally between cross-beams than for transverse spanning. Longitudinal spanning can also occur at intermediate supports at the face of diaphragms. In combining the stress ranges, it is important to consider the actual transverse location being checked within the slab. The peak local effect usually occurs some distance from the web of a main beam, while the global direct stress reduces away from the web due to shear lag. The global stress distribution allowing for shear lag may be determined using *clause 5.4.1.2(8)*, even though this refers to EN 1993-1-5 which is for steel flanges.

*Clause 7.2.1(8)*

For serviceability stress limits, *clause 7.2.2* refers to EN 1992 and EN 1993. Both codes allow choice in the National Annex. EN 1992 does so by means of coefficients $k_j$, whereas EN 1993 permits national values for a partial factor $\gamma_{M,ser}$. If any National Annex uses other than the recommended value, 1.0, this could be a source of error in practice, because partial factors for serviceability checks are almost invariably 1.0, and so tend to be forgotten.

*Clause 7.2.2*

### Combinations of actions for serviceability checks

*Clause 7.2* defines these combinations only by cross-reference, so the following summary is given. The limiting stresses can be altered by National Annexes.

*Clause 7.2.2(2)* leads to the following recommendations for concrete.

*Clause 7.2.2(2)*

- Where creep coefficients are based on clause 3.1.4(2) of EN 1992-1-1, as is usual, its clause 7.2(3) gives the stress limit for the quasi-permanent combination as $0.45f_{ck}$.
- In areas where the exposure class is XD, XF or XS, clause 7.2(102) of EN 1992-2 gives the stress limit for the characteristic combination as $0.60f_{ck}$. Comment on *clause 4.1(1)* refers to the XD class in bridges.

From *clause 7.2.2(4)*, the recommended limit for reinforcement is $0.8f_{sk}$ under the characteristic combination, increased to $1.0f_{sk}$ for imposed deformations.

*Clause 7.2.2(4)*

*Clause 7.2.2(5)* refers to clause 7.3 of EN 1993-2, where the stress limits for structural steel and the force limits for bolts are based on the characteristic combination, with a limit on stress range under the frequent combination.

*Clause 7.2.2(5)*

For service loading of shear connectors generally, *clause 7.2.2(6)* refers to *clause 6.8.1(3)*. That clause refers only to stud connectors under the characteristic combination, and uses a

*Clause 7.2.2(6)*

factor $k$ that can be chosen nationally. EN 1994-2 envisages the use of other types of connector (for example, in *clause 6.6.1.1(6)P*). Rules for the use of these, which may be given in a National Annex, from *clause 1.1.3(3)*, should include a service load limit.

To sum up, most stress checks are based on characteristic combinations, as are the determination of cracked regions, *clause 5.4.2.3(2)*, and the provision of minimum reinforcement, *clause 7.4.2(5)*. However, limiting crack widths are given, in clause 7.3.1(105) of EN 1992-2, for the quasi-permanent combination.

### Web breathing
*Clause 7.2.3(1)*

*Clause 7.2.3(1)* refers to EN 1993-2 for 'breathing' of slender steel web plates. The effect on a slender plate of in-plane shear or compressive stress is to magnify its initial out-of-plane imperfection. This induces cyclic bending moments at its welded edges about axes parallel to the welds. If excessive, it can lead to fatigue failure in these regions. Further comment is given in the Guide to EN 1993-2.[4]

## 7.3. Deformations in bridges
### 7.3.1. Deflections
*Clause 7.3.1(1)*

*Clause 7.3.1(1)* refers to clauses in EN 1993-2 that cover clearances, visual impression, precambering, slip at connections, performance criteria and drainage. For precambering, 'the effects of shear deformation ... should be considered'. This applies to vertical shear in steel webs, not to the shear connection.

*Clause 7.3.1(2)*

*Clause 7.3.1(2)* refers to *Section 5* for calculation of deflections. Rules for the effects of slip are given in *clause 5.4.1.1*. They permit deformations caused by slip of shear connection to be neglected, except in non-linear analysis. *Clause 5.4.2.1(1)* refers to the sequence of construction, which affects deflections. When the sequence is unknown, an estimate on the high side can be obtained by assuming unpropped construction and that the adverse areas of the influence line, with respect to deflection at the point being considered, are concreted first, followed by the relieving areas. Sufficient accuracy should usually be obtained by assuming that the whole of the concrete deck is cast at one time, on unpropped steelwork.

The casting of an area of deck slab may increase the curvature of adjacent beams where the shear connectors are surrounded by concrete that is too young for full composite action to occur. It is possible that subsequent performance of these connectors could be impaired by what is, in effect, an imposed slip. *Clause 7.3.1(3)* refers to this, but not to the detailed guidance given in *clause 6.6.5.2(3)*, which follows.

*Clause 7.3.1(3)*

'*Wherever possible, deformation should not be imposed on a shear connection until the concrete has reached a cylinder strength of at least 20 N/mm².*'

The words 'Wherever possible' are necessary because shrinkage effects apply force to shear connection from a very early age without, so far as is known, any adverse effect.

### 7.3.2. Vibrations
*Clause 7.3.2(1)*

The limit state of vibration is covered in *clause 7.3.2(1)* by reference to other Eurocodes. Composite bridges are referred to only in clause 6.4.6.3.1(3) of EN 1991-2, which covers resonance under railway loading. This gives 'lower bound' values for damping that are the same for composite bridges as for steel bridges, except that those for filler-beam decks are much higher, and the same as for concrete bridges. Alternative values may be given in the National Annex. The specialized literature generally gives damping values for composite floor or deck systems that are between those for steel and for concrete members, as would be expected. In railway bridges, the presence or absence of ballast is a relevant factor.

The reference to EN 1993-2 requires consideration of pedestrian discomfort and fatigue under wind-induced motion, usually vortex shedding. The relevant reference is then to EN 1991-1-4.[103] Its Annex E provides guidance on the calculation of amplitudes of oscillation while its Annex F provides guidance on the determination of natural frequencies and damping. The damping values for steel-composite bridges in its Table F.2 this time do lie between the values for steel bridges and reinforced concrete bridges.

# 7.4. Cracking of concrete
## 7.4.1. General

In the early 1980s it was found[64,104] that for composite beams in hogging bending, the long-established British methods for control of crack width were unreliable for initial cracks, which were wider than predicted. Before this, it had been found for reinforced concrete that the appropriate theoretical model for cracking caused by restraint of imposed deformation was different from that for cracking caused by applied loading. This has led to the presentation of design rules for control of cracking as two distinct procedures:

- for minimum reinforcement, in *clause 7.4.2*, for all cross-sections that could be subjected to significant tension by imposed deformations (e.g. by effects of shrinkage, which cause higher stresses than in reinforced concrete, because of restraint from the steel beam)
- for reinforcement to control cracking due to direct loading, *clause 7.4.3*.

The rules given in EN 1994-2 are based on an extensive and quite complex theory, supported by testing on hogging regions of composite beams.[104,105] Much of the original literature is either in German or not widely available[106] so a detailed account of the theory has been published in English,[107] with comparisons with results of tests on composite beams, additional to those used originally. The paper includes derivations of the equations given in *clause 7.4*, comments on their scope and underlying assumptions, and procedures for estimating the mean width and spacing of cracks. These are tedious, and so are not in EN 1994-2. Its methods are simple: *Tables 7.1* and *7.2* give maximum diameters and spacings of reinforcing bars for three design crack widths: 0.2, 0.3 and 0.4 mm.

These tables are for 'high-bond' bars only. This means ribbed bars with properties referred to in clause 3.2.2(2)P of EN 1992-1-1. The use of reinforcement other than ribbed is outside the scope of the Eurocodes.

The references to EN 1992 in *clause 7.4.1(1)* give the surface crack-width limits required for design. Typical exposure classes for composite bridge decks are discussed in section 4.1 of this guide. *Clause 7.4.1(1)*

*Clause 7.4.1(2)* refers to 'estimation' of crack width, using EN 1992-1-1. This rather long procedure is rarely needed, and does not take full account of the following differences between the behaviours of composite beams and reinforced concrete T-beams. The steel member in a composite beam does not shrink or creep and has much greater flexural stiffness than the reinforcement in a concrete beam. Also, the steel member is attached to the concrete flange only by discrete connectors that are not effective until there is longitudinal slip, whereas in reinforced concrete there is monolithic connection. There is no need here for a reference to EN 1992-2. *Clause 7.4.1(2)*

*Clause 7.4.1(3)* refers to the methods developed for composite members, which are easier to apply than the methods for reinforced concrete members. *Clause 7.4.1(3)*

*Clause 7.4.1(4)* refers to limiting calculated crack widths $w_k$, with a Note on recommended values. Those for all XC, XD and XS exposure classes are given in a Note to clause 7.3.1(105) of EN 1992-2 as 0.3 mm. This is for the quasi-permanent load combination, and excludes prestressed members with bonded tendons. Both the crack width and the load combination may be changed in the National Annex. It is expected that the UK's National Annex to EN 1992-2 will confirm these recommendations and give further guidance for combinations that include temperature difference. *Clause 7.4.1(4)*

*Clause 7.4.1(5)* and *(6)* draws attention to the need to control cracking caused by early thermal shrinkage. The problem is that the heat of hydration causes expansion of the concrete before it is stiff enough for restraint from steel to cause much compressive stress in it. When it cools, it is stiffer, so tension develops. This can occur in regions that *Clause 7.4.1(5)* *Clause 7.4.1(6)* are in permanent compression in the finished bridge. They may require crack-control reinforcement for this phase only.

The check is made assuming that the temperatures of the steel and the concrete are both uniform. The concrete is colder, to an extent that may be given in the National Annex. This causes tension, and possibly cracking. Further comment is given in Example 7.1.

### 7.4.2. Minimum reinforcement

The only data needed when using *Tables 7.1* and *7.2* are the design crack width and the tensile stress in the reinforcement, $\sigma_s$. For minimum reinforcement, $\sigma_s$ is the stress immediately after initial cracking. It is assumed that cracking does not change the curvature of the steel beam, so all of the tensile force in the concrete just before cracking is transferred to the reinforce-

*Clause 7.4.2(1)* ment, of area $A_s$. If the slab were in uniform tension, *equation (7.1)* in *clause 7.4.2(1)* would be:

$$A_s \sigma_s = A_{ct} f_{ct,eff}$$

where $f_{ct,eff}$ is an estimate of the mean tensile strength of the concrete at the time of cracking.

The three correction factors in *equation (7.1)* are based on calibration work.[106] These allow for the non-uniform stress distribution in the area $A_{ct}$ of concrete assumed to crack. 'Non-uniform self-equilibrating stresses' arise from primary shrinkage and temperature effects, which cause curvature of the composite member. Slip of the shear connection also causes curvature and reduces the tensile force in the slab.

The magnitude of these effects depends on the geometry of the uncracked composite section, as given by *equation (7.2)*. With experience, calculation of $k_c$ can often be omitted, because it is less than 1.0 only where $z_0 < 1.2h_c$. (These symbols are shown in Fig. 7.5.) The depth of the 'uncracked' neutral axis below the bottom of the slab normally exceeds about 70% of the slab thickness, and then, $k_c = 1$.

The method of *clause 7.4.2(1)* is not intended for the control of early thermal cracking, which can occur in concrete a few days old, if the temperature rise caused by heat of hydration is excessive. The flanges of composite beams are usually too thin for this to occur. It would not be correct, therefore, to assume a very low value for $f_{ct,eff}$.

The suggested value of $f_{ct,eff}$, $3\,\text{N/mm}^2$, was probably rounded from the mean 28-day tensile strength of grade C30/37 concrete, given in EN 1992-1-1 as $2.9\,\text{N/mm}^2$ – the value

*Clause 7.4.2(2)* used as the basis for the optional correction given in *clause 7.4.2(2)*. The maximum bar diameter may be increased for stronger concrete because the higher bond strength of the concrete compensates for the lower total perimeter of a set of bars with given area per unit width of slab. The difference between 2.9 and 3.0 is obviously negligible. It may be an error in drafting, because in EN 1992, the value $2.9\,\text{N/mm}^2$ is used in both places.

If there is good reason to assume a value for $f_{ct,eff}$ such that the correction is not negligible, a suitable procedure is to assume a standard bar diameter, $\phi$, calculate $\phi^*$, and then find $\sigma_s$ by interpolation in *Table 7.1*.

The reinforcement in a deck slab will usually be in two layers in each direction, with at least

*Clause 7.4.2(3)* half of it adjacent to the surface of greater tensile strain. The relevant rule, in *clause 7.4.2(3)*, refers not to the actual reinforcement, but to the minimum required. The reference to '*local*

*Clause 7.4.2(4)* *depth*' in *clause 7.4.2(4)* means the depth at the cross-section considered.

*Clause 7.4.2(5)* The rule of *clause 7.4.2(5)* on placing of minimum reinforcement refers to its horizontal extent, not to its depth within the slab. Analysis of the structure for ultimate load combinations of variable actions will normally find regions in tension that are more extensive than those for the characteristic combination specified here. The regions so found may need to be extended for early thermal effects (*clause 7.4.1(5)*).

#### Design of minimum reinforcement for a concrete slab

For design, the design crack width and thickness of the slab, $h_c$, will be known. For a chosen bar diameter $\phi$, *Table 7.1* gives $\sigma_s$, the maximum permitted stress in the reinforcement, and *equation (7.1)* allows the bar spacing to be determined. If this is too high or low, $\phi$ is changed.

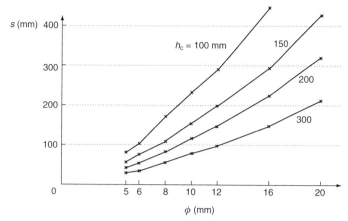

**Fig. 7.1.** Bar diameter and spacing for minimum reinforcement in two equal layers, for $w_k = 0.3$ mm and $f_{ct,eff} = 3.0 \, \text{N/mm}^2$

A typical relationship between slab thickness $h_c$, bar spacing $s$ and bar diameter $\phi$ is shown in Fig. 7.1. It is for two similar layers of bars, with $k_c = 1$ and $f_{ct,eff} = 3.0 \, \text{N/mm}^2$. *Equation (7.1)* then gives, for a fully cracked slab of breadth $b$:

$$(\pi\phi^2/4)(2b/s) = 0.72 \times 3bh_c/\sigma_s$$

Hence,

$$h_c s = 0.727\phi^2\sigma_s \text{ (with } \sigma_s \text{ in N/mm}^2 \text{ units)} \tag{D7.1}$$

For each bar diameter and a given crack width, *Table 7.1* gives $\phi^2\sigma_s$, so the product $h_c s$ is known. This is plotted in Fig. 7.1, for $w_k = 0.3$ mm, as curves of bar spacing for four given slab thicknesses, which can of course also be read as maximum slab thickness size and for bar spacing. The shape of the curves results partly from the use of rounded values of $\sigma_s$ in *Table 7.1*. The correction to minimum reinforcement given in *clause 7.4.2(2)* is negligible here, and has not been made.

The weight of minimum reinforcement, per unit area of slab, is proportional to $\phi^2/s$, which is proportional to $\sigma_s^{-1}$, from equation (D7.1). The value of $\sigma_s^{-1}$ increases with bar diameter, from *Table 7.1*, so the use of smaller bars reduces the weight of minimum reinforcement. This is because their greater surface area provides more bond strength.

### 7.4.3. Control of cracking due to direct loading

*Clause 7.4.3(2)* specifies elastic global analysis to *Section 5*, allowing for the effects of cracking. The preceding comments on global analysis for deformations apply also to this analysis for bending moments in regions with concrete in tension.

*Clause 7.4.3(2)*

From *clause 7.4.1(4)*, the combination of actions will be given in the National Annex. There is no need to reduce the extent of the cracked regions below that assumed for global analysis for ultimate limit states, so the new bending moments for the composite members can be found by scaling values found previously. At each cross-section, the area of reinforcement will already be known: that required for ultimate loading or the specified minimum, if greater; so the stresses $\sigma_{s,o}$, *clause 7.4.3(3)*, can be found.

*Clause 7.4.3(3)*

*Tension stiffening*
A correction for tension stiffening is now required. At one time, these effects were not well understood. It was thought that, for a given tensile strain at the level of the reinforcement, the total extension must be the extension of the concrete plus the width of the cracks, so that allowing for the former reduced the latter. The true behaviour is more complex.

The upper part of Fig. 7.2 shows a single crack in a concrete member with a central reinforcing bar. At the crack, the external tensile force $N$ causes strain $\varepsilon_{s2} = N/A_s E_a$ in the bar, and the strain in the concrete is the free shrinkage strain $\varepsilon_{cs}$, which is shown as

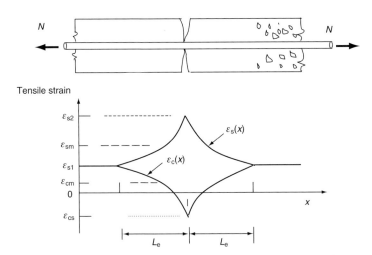

**Fig. 7.2.** Strain distributions near a crack in a reinforced concrete tension member

negative here. There is a transmission length $L_e$ each side of the crack, within which there is transfer of shear between the bar and the concrete. Outside this length, the strain in both the steel and the concrete is $\varepsilon_{s1}$, and the stress in the concrete is fractionally below its tensile strength. Within the length $2L_e$, the curves $\varepsilon_s(x)$ and $\varepsilon_c(x)$ give the strains in the two materials, with mean strains $\varepsilon_{sm}$ in the bar and $\varepsilon_{cm}$ in the concrete.

It is now supposed that the graph represents the typical behaviour of a reinforcing bar in a cracked concrete flange of a composite beam, in a region of constant bending moment such that the crack spacing is $2L_e$. The curvature of the steel beam is determined by the mean stiffness of the slab, not the fully cracked stiffness, and is compatible with the mean longitudinal strain in the reinforcement, $\varepsilon_{sm}$.

Midway between the cracks, the strain is the cracking strain of the concrete, corresponding to a stress less than $30\,\text{N/mm}^2$ in the bar. Its peak strain, at the crack, is much greater than $\varepsilon_{sm}$, but less than the yield strain of the reinforcement, if crack widths are not to exceed 0.3 mm. The crack width corresponds to this higher strain, not to the strain $\varepsilon_{sm}$ that is compatible with the curvature, so a correction to the strain is needed. It is presented in *clause 7.4.3(3)* as a correction to the stress $\sigma_{s,o}$ because that is easily calculated, and *Tables 7.1* and *7.2* are based on stress. The strain correction cannot be shown in Fig. 7.2 because the stress $\sigma_{s,o}$ is calculated using the 'fully cracked' stiffness, and so relates to a curvature greater than the true curvature. The derivation of the correction[107] takes account of crack spacings less than $2L_e$, the bond properties of reinforcement, and other factors omitted from this simplified outline.

The section properties needed for the calculation of the correction $\Delta\sigma_s$ will usually be known. For the cracked composite cross-section, the transformed area $A$ is needed to find $I$, which is used in calculating $\sigma_{s,o}$, and $A_a$ and $I_a$ are standard properties of the steel section. The result is independent of the modular ratio. For simplicity, $\alpha_{st}$ may conservatively be taken as 1.0, because $AI > A_aI_a$.

When the stress $\sigma_s$ at a crack has been found, the maximum bar diameter or the maximum spacing are found from *Tables 7.1* and *7.2*. Only one of these is needed, as the known area of reinforcement then gives the other. The correction of *clause 7.4.2(2)* does not apply.

## General comments on *clause 7.4*, and flow charts

The design actions for checking cracking will always be less than those for the ultimate limit state due to the use of lower load factors. The difference is greatest where unpropped construction is used for a continuous beam with hogging regions in Class 1 or 2 and with lateral–torsional buckling prevented. This is because the entire design hogging moment is carried by the composite section for Class 1 and 2 composite sections at ULS, but at SLS, reinforcement stresses are derived only from actions applied to the composite section in the construction sequence. It is also permissible in such cases to neglect the effects of indirect actions at ULS. The quantity of reinforcement provided for resistance to load should be

See the Notes in the section 'Flow charts for crack-width control'

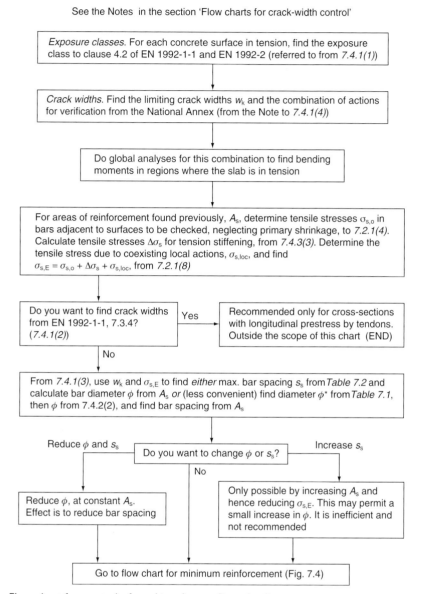

**Fig. 7.3.** Flow chart for control of cracking due to direct loading

sufficient to control cracking. The main use of *clause 7.4.3* is then to check that the spacing of the bars is not excessive.

Where propped construction is used, the disparity between the design loadings for the two limit states is smaller. A check to *clause 7.4.3* is then more likely to influence the reinforcement required.

### Flow charts for crack-width control

The check to *clause 7.4.3* is likely to be done first, so its flow chart, Fig. 7.3, precedes Fig. 7.4 for minimum reinforcement, to *clause 7.4.2*. The regions where the slab is in tension depend on the load combination, and three may be relevant, as follows.

- Most reinforcement areas are found initially for the ultimate combination.
- Load-induced cracking is checked for a combination to be specified in the National Annex, to *clause 7.4.1(4)*. It may be the quasi-permanent or frequent combination.
- Minimum reinforcement is required in regions in tension under the characteristic combination, *clause 7.4.2(5)*.

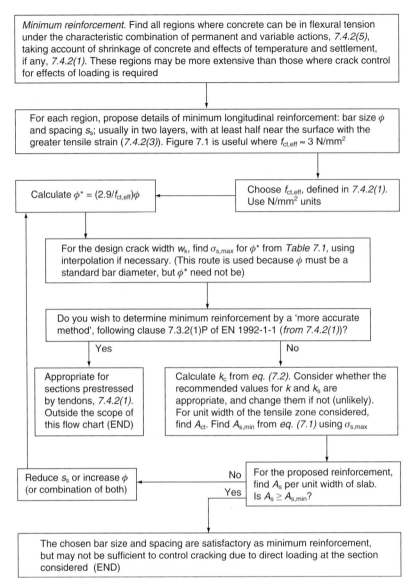

**Fig. 7.4.** Flow chart for minimum reinforcement for control of cracking

The following notes apply to these charts.

*Note 1.* Creep and shrinkage of concrete both increase stress in reinforcement at internal supports of beams, so crack widths are usually verified using the long-term modular ratio for permanent actions. This is assumed here.

*Note 2.* The flow charts apply to a tension flange of a continuous longitudinal beam. It is assumed (for brevity) that:

- areas of reinforcement required for ultimate limit states have been found
- the flexural stiffnesses $E_a I_1$ are known for the uncracked cross-sections, using relevant modular ratios (inclusion of reinforcement optional)
- the cracked flexural stiffnesses $E_a I_2$ are known. For these, modular ratios are usually irrelevant, unless double composite action is being used
- the deck slab is above the steel beam, and at cross-sections considered, maximum tensile strain occurs at the top surface of the slab
- there is no double composite action
- early thermal cracking does not govern
- the symbols $A_s$ (area of reinforcement) are for a unit width of slab.

*Note 3.* A second subscript, *l* for loading, is used in this note to indicate quantities found in the check to *clause 7.4.3*. Area $A_{s,l}$ is usually that required for resistance to ultimate loads. It is assumed, for simplicity, that minimum reinforcement consists of two identical layers of bars, one near each surface of the slab. Area $A_{s,l}$ should be compared with the minimum reinforcement area $A_s$ required when bars of diameter $\phi_l$ are used. If $A_{s,l} < A_s$, minimum reinforcement governs.

## 7.5. Filler beam decks

This clause is applicable to simply-supported or continuous decks of the type shown in *Fig. 6.8*, spanning longitudinally. The Note to *clause 6.3.1(1)* permits the use of transverse filler beams according to the National Annex, which should refer also to serviceability requirements, if any.

From **clause 7.5.1(1)**, the methods of global analysis for serviceability limit states are the same as for ultimate limit states, *clause 5.4.2.9*, except that no redistribution of moments is permitted. *Clause 7.5.1(1)*

The word '*considered*' is used in **clause 7.5.2(1)** because some of the clauses may not be applicable. For example, the thickness of the concrete in a filler-beam deck will exceed that in a conventional composite beam, so the effects of heat of hydration will be greater. The temperature difference recommended in the Note to *clause 7.4.1(6)* may not be appropriate. Tension stiffening is also different (*clause 7.5.4(2)*). *Clause 7.5.2(1)*

The objective of **clause 7.5.3(1)** is to ensure that cracking of concrete does not cause its reinforcement to yield. It applies above an internal support of a continuous filler-beam deck, and can be illustrated as follows. *Clause 7.5.3(1)*

It is assumed that all the concrete above the top flanges of the steel beams reaches its mean tensile strength, $f_{ctm}$, and then cracks. This releases a tensile force of $A_{c,eff}f_{ctm}$ per beam, where $A_{c,eff} = s_w c_{st}$, as in *clause 7.5.3(1)*. The notation is shown in *Fig. 6.8*.

The required condition, with partial factors $\gamma_M$ taken as 1.0, is:

$$A_{s,min}f_{sk} \geq A_{c,eff}f_{ctm} \tag{D7.2}$$

For concretes permitted by *clause 3.1(2)*, $f_{ctm} \leq 4.4\,N/mm^2$.

If, to satisfy *expression (7.7)*, $A_{s,min} > 0.01A_{c,eff}$, then expression (D7.2) is satisfied if $f_{sk} > 440\,N/mm^2$. In design to EN 1994, normally $f_{sk} = 500\,N/mm^2$, so the objective is met.

**Clause 7.5.4(1)** applies to longitudinal bottom reinforcement in mid-span regions. Widths of cracks in the concrete soffit between the steel beams should be controlled unless the formwork used (shown in *Fig. 6.8*) provides permanent protection. Otherwise, wide transverse cracks could form under the bottom transverse bars specified in *clause 6.3.1(4)*, putting them at risk of corrosion. *Clause 7.5.4(1)*

**Clause 7.5.4(2)** says, in effect, that the stress in the reinforcement may be taken as $\sigma_{s,o}$, defined in *clause 7.4.3(3)*. Thus, there is no need to consider tension stiffening in filler-beam decks. *Clause 7.5.4(2)*

### Example 7.1: checks on serviceability stresses, and control of cracking
The following serviceability checks are performed for the internal girders of the bridge in Figs 5.6 and 6.22:

- tensile stress in reinforcement and crack control at an intermediate support
- minimum longitudinal reinforcement for regions in hogging bending
- stresses in structural steel at an intermediate support
- compressive stress in concrete at mid-span of the main span.

*Tensile stress in reinforcement*
The cross-section at an intermediate support is shown in Fig. 7.5. All reinforcement has $f_{sk} = 500\,N/mm^2$.

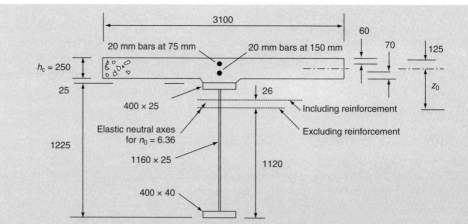

**Fig. 7.5.** Elastic neutral axes of uncracked cross-section at internal support

From *clause 7.2.1(8)*, stresses in reinforcement caused by simultaneous global and local actions should be added. Load Model 1 is considered here. The tandem system (TS) and UDL produce a smaller local effect than does Load Model 2, but Load Model 1 produces the greatest combined local plus global effect. Local moments are caused here by hogging of the deck slab over the pier diaphragm. Full local effects do not coexist with full global effects since, for maximum global hogging moment, the axles are further from the pier. The maximum local and global effects are here calculated independently and then combined. A less conservative approach, if permitted by the National Annex, is to use the combination rule in Annex E of EN 1993-2 as noted below *clause 5.4.4(1)*. This enables the maximum global effect to be combined with a reduced local effect and vice versa.

The maximum global hogging moment acting on the composite section under the characteristic combination was found to be 4400 kNm. *Clause 7.2.1(4)* allows the primary effects of shrinkage to be ignored for cracked sections, but not the secondary effects which are unfavourable here.

From Table 6.2 in Example 6.6, the section modulus for the top layer of reinforcement in the cracked composite section is $34.05 \times 10^6 \text{ mm}^3$. The stress due to global effects in this reinforcement, ignoring tension stiffening, is:

$$\sigma_{s,o} = 4400/34.05 = 129 \text{ N/mm}^2$$

From *clause 7.2.1(6)*, the calculation of reinforcement stress should include the effects of tension stiffening. From *clause 7.4.3(3)*, the increase in stress in the reinforcement, due to tension stiffening, from that calculated using a fully cracked analysis is:

$$\Delta\sigma_s = \frac{0.4f_{ctm}}{\alpha_{st}\rho_s} \quad \text{where} \quad \alpha_{st} = \frac{AI}{A_a I_a} = \frac{74\,478 \times 2.266 \times 10^{10}}{55\,000 \times 1.228 \times 10^{10}} = 2.50$$

The reinforcement ratio $\rho_s = 0.025$ and $f_{ctm} = 2.9 \text{ N/mm}^2$ and thus:

$$\Delta\sigma_s = \frac{0.4 \times 2.9}{2.50 \times 0.025} = 19 \text{ N/mm}^2$$

The stress in the reinforcement from global effects is therefore:

$$129 + 19 = 148 \text{ N/mm}^2$$

The stress in the reinforcement due to local load was found by determining the local moment from an analysis using the appropriate Pucher chart.[100] This bending moment, 12.2 kNm/m hogging, is not sufficient to cause compression in the slab, so it is resisted solely by the two layers of reinforcement, and causes a tensile stress of 73 N/mm² in the top layer. The total stress from global plus local effects is therefore:

$$\sigma_s = 148 + 73 = 221 \text{ N/mm}^2$$

From *clause 7.2.2(4)* and from EN 1992-1-1 clause 7.2(5), the tensile stress in the reinforcement should not exceed $k_3 f_{sk} = 400\,\text{N/mm}^2$ (recommended $k_3 = 0.8$, and $f_{sk} = 500\,\text{N/mm}^2$) so this check is satisfied.

Where the global tension is such that local effects cause net compression at one face of the slab, iterative calculation can be avoided by taking the lever arm for local bending as the lesser of the distance between the two layers of reinforcement and that derived from considering the cracked section in flexure alone.

### Control of cracking due to direct loading – persistent design situation
Creep of concrete in sagging regions causes hogging moments to increase, so this check is done at $t \to \infty$. Cracking during construction is considered later.

For concrete protected by waterproofing, EN 1992-2 clause 4.2(105) recommends an exposure class of XC3 for which Table 7.101N of EN 1992-2 recommends a limiting crack width of 0.3 mm under the quasi-permanent load combination.

Crack widths are checked under this load combination for which the maximum hogging moment acting on the composite section was found to be 2500 kNm. The secondary effects of shrinkage were unfavourable here. The primary effects can be ignored because the derivation of the simplified method (*Tables 7.1* and *7.2*) takes account of a typical amount of shrinkage.[107]

Using a section modulus from Table 6.2, the stress due to global effects in the top layer of reinforcement, ignoring tension stiffening, is:

$$\sigma_{s,o} = 2500/34.05 = 73\,\text{N/mm}^2$$

The increase in stress in the reinforcement due to tension stiffening is $19\,\text{N/mm}^2$ as found above. From *equation (7.4)*, the reinforcement stress is:

$$\sigma_s = 73 + 19 = 92\,\text{N/mm}^2$$

For this stress, *Table 7.1* gives a bar diameter above 32 mm, and *Table 7.2* gives a bar spacing exceeding 300 mm, so there is sufficient crack control from the reinforcement provided, 20 mm bars at 75 mm spacing.

### Control of cracking during construction
Construction is unpropped, so *clause 7.4.1(5)* is applicable. Effects of heat of hydration of cement should be analysed '*to define areas where tension is expected*'. These areas require at least minimum reinforcement, from *clause 7.4.2*. The curvatures for determining secondary effects should be based initially on uncracked cross-sections.

*Clause 7.4.1(6)* requires account to be taken of the effects of heat of hydration for limitation of crack width '*unless specific measures are taken*' to limit its effects. The National Annex may refer to specific measures.

Assuming that no specific measures have been taken, *clause 7.4.1(6)* applies. Its Note recommends that the concrete slab should be assumed to be 20 K colder than the steel member, and that the short-term modular ratio $n_0$ should be used. It is expected that the National Annex for the UK will replace 20 K by 25 K, the value used here.

Referring to Fig. 5.6, it is assumed that the whole of the deck slab has been concreted except for lengths such as CD, which extend for 6 m each side of each internal support. These two 12 m lengths are now cast, over the whole width of the deck. When they harden, it is assumed that the only longitudinal stress in their concrete arises from shrinkage and the temperature difference. The primary effects are uniform over the whole 12 m length. The secondary effects are a hogging bending moment over the whole length of the bridge, which is a maximum at the internal supports, and associated shear forces.

It is reasonable to assume that the 12 m lengths are either cracked throughout, or uncracked. In calculating secondary effects, primary effects due to shrinkage can be neglected in cracked regions, from *clause 5.4.2.2(8)*, so only effects of heat of hydration need be considered. A similar conclusion is reached if the method of *clause 5.4.2.3(3)*, '15% of the span cracked', is used. In any case, shrinkage is a minor effect, as shown below.

From Example 5.3, the autogenous and long-term shrinkage strains are $\varepsilon_{ca} = 50 \times 10^{-6}$ and $\varepsilon_{cd} = 282 \times 10^{-6}$ respectively. From clause 3.1.4(6) of EN 1992-1-1, drying shrinkage may be assumed to commence at the end of curing.

Autogenous shrinkage is a function of the age of the concrete, $t$ in days:

$$\varepsilon_{ca}(t) = [1 - \exp(0.2t^{0.5})]\varepsilon_{ca}(\infty)$$

Here, the temperature difference is assumed to reach its peak at age seven days, and curing is conservatively assumed to have ended at age three days. From EN 1992-1-1, less than 1% of the long-term drying shrinkage will have occurred in the next four days, so it is neglected.

From the equation above,

$$\varepsilon_{ca}(7) = [1 - \exp(-0.53)] \times 50 \times 10^{-6} = 21 \times 10^{-6}$$

For temperature, clause 3.1.3(5) of EN 1992-1-1 gives the thermal coefficient for concrete as $10 \times 10^{-6}$, so a difference of 25 K causes a strain of $250 \times 10^{-6}$.

The resulting sagging curvature of each 12 m length of deck is found by analysis of the uncracked composite section with $n_0 = 6.36$ from Example 5.2. To find whether cracking occurs, the secondary effects are found from these curvatures by global analysis using uncracked stiffnesses.

The definition of 'regions in tension' is based on the characteristic combination, from *clause 5.4.2.3(2)*. It is suggested here that heat of hydration should be treated as a permanent action, as shrinkage is. The leading variable action is likely to be construction load elsewhere on the deck, in association with either temperature or wind. The permanent actions are dead load and any drying shrinkage in the rest of the deck. The action effects so found from 'uncracked' analysis are added to the secondary effects, above, to determine the regions in tension, in which at least minimum reinforcement (to *clause 7.4.2*) should be provided. If tensile stresses in concrete are such that it cracks, reanalysis using cracked sections and ignoring primary effects gives the tensile stresses in reinforcement needed for crack-width control. Minimum reinforcement will not be sufficient at the internal supports, where reinforcement will have been designed both for resistance to ultimate direct loading and for long-term crack-width control. The seven-day situation studied here is unlikely to be more adverse.

*Minimum reinforcement*

The minimum reinforcement required by *clause 7.4.2* is usually far less than that required at an internal support. The rules apply to any region subjected to significant tension and can govern where the main longitudinal reinforcement is curtailed, or near a point of contraflexure.

Figure 7.1 gives the minimum reinforcement for this 250 mm slab as 20 mm bars at 260 mm spacing, top and bottom. The top layer has a cross-section only 29% of that of the top layer provided at the pier. This result is now checked. From *clause 7.4.2(1)*:

$$A_{s,min} = k_s k_c k f_{ct,eff} A_{ct}/\sigma_s \qquad (7.1)$$

with $k_s = 0.9$ and $k = 0.8$.

Assuming that the age of the concrete at cracking is likely to exceed 28 days,

$$f_{ct,eff} = 3.0 \, \text{N/mm}^2$$

The only term in *equation (7.1)* that depends on the steel cross-section is $k_c$, given by:

$$k_c = \frac{1}{1 + h_c/(2z_0)} + 0.3 \leq 1.0 \qquad (7.2)$$

where $h_c$ is the flange thickness (250 mm) and $z_0$ is the distance between the centres of area of the uncracked composite section and the uncracked concrete flange, with modular ratio $n_0$ (6.36 here). It makes little difference whether reinforcement is included or not. Excluding it (for simplicity) and ignoring the haunch, then from Fig. 7.5:

$$z_0 = 1500 - 1120 - 125 = 255 \, \text{mm}$$

and

$$k_c = 1/(1 + 250/510) + 0.3 = 0.97$$

If the area of longitudinal reinforcement at the internal support is included, $k_c$ is reduced by only 0.02.

Ignoring the difference between 2.9 and 3.0 N/mm², *Table 7.1* gives the maximum stress for 20 mm bars as 220 N/mm² for a limiting crack width of 0.3 mm.

For a 1 m width of flange, from *equation (7.1)*:

$$A_{s,\text{min}} = 0.9 \times 0.97 \times 0.8 \times 3.0 \times 1000 \times 250/220 = 2380 \, \text{mm}^2/\text{m}$$

*Clause 7.4.2(3)* requires at least half of this reinforcement to be placed in the upper layer. This gives **20 mm bars** at **264 mm** spacing; probably 250 mm in practice. A similar calculation for 16 mm bars gives their spacing as 184 mm.

### Stress limits for structural steel

The hogging moments under the characteristic load combination are found to be 1600 kNm acting on the steel beam and 4400 kNm acting on the composite section. The relevant section moduli are given in Table 6.2 in Example 6.6. The stress in the bottom flange was found to be critical, for which:

$$\sigma_{\text{Ed,ser}} = \frac{1600}{22.20} + \frac{4400}{29.25} = 222 \, \text{N/mm}^2$$

The coexisting shear force acting on the section was found to be 1900 kN, so:

$$\tau_{\text{Ed,ser}} = \frac{1900 \times 10^3}{25 \times 1160} = 66 \, \text{N/mm}^2$$

if buckling is neglected at SLS.

From *clause 7.2.2(5)* and EC3-2 clause 7.3, stresses should be limited as follows:

$$\sigma_{\text{Ed,ser}} = 222 \leq \frac{f_y}{\gamma_{\text{M,ser}}} = 345 \, \text{N/mm}^2$$

$$\tau_{\text{Ed,ser}} = 66 \leq \frac{f_y}{\sqrt{3}\gamma_{\text{M,ser}}} = 199 \, \text{N/mm}^2$$

$$\sqrt{\sigma_{\text{Ed,ser}}^2 + 3\tau_{\text{Ed,ser}}^2} = 250 \leq \frac{f_y}{\gamma_{\text{M,ser}}} = 345 \, \text{N/mm}^2$$

where $\gamma_{\text{M,ser}} = 1.00$. The stresses in structural steel are all satisfactory.

### Compressive stress in concrete

The cross-section at mid-span is shown in Fig. 6.2. The compressive stress in the slab is checked under simultaneous global and local actions. Both the primary and secondary effects of shrinkage are favourable and are conservatively ignored. The concrete is checked shortly after opening the bridge, ignoring creep, as this produces the greatest concrete compressive stress here, so the short-term modular ratio is used. The sagging moment on the composite section from the characteristic combination was found to be 3500 kNm.

The section modulus for the top of the concrete slab is $575.9 \times 10^6 \, \text{mm}^3$ from Table 6.4 in Example 6.10. The compressive stress at the top of the slab is:

$$\sigma_c = 3500/575.9 = 6.1 \, \text{N/mm}^2$$

The maximum longitudinal sagging moment from local loading was found to be $20\,\text{kNm/m}$. The short-term section modulus for the top surface of the uncracked reinforced slab is $W_{c,top} = 10.7 \times 10^6\,\text{mm}^4/\text{m}$ in 'concrete' units, so the compressive stress from local load is $\sigma_{c,loc} = 20/10.7 = 1.9\,\text{N/mm}^2$.

The total concrete stress, fully combining global and local effects, is:

$$\sigma_c = 6.1 + 1.9 = 8.0\,\text{N/mm}^2$$

The global stress is sufficient to keep the whole depth of the slab in compression so this calculation of stresses from local moment using gross properties for the slab is appropriate. If the local moment caused tension in the slab, this would no longer be adequate. Either the stress from local moment could conservatively be calculated from a cracked section analysis considering the local moment acting alone, or an iterative calculation considering the local moment and axial force acting together would be required. In this case, application of the combination rule of EN 1993-2 Annex E would underestimate the combined effect as the global and local loading cases are the same.

From *clause 7.2.2(2)* and from EN 1992-1-1 clause 7.2 with the recommended value for $k_1$, concrete stresses should be limited to $k_1 f_{ck} = 0.6 \times 30 = 18\,\text{N/mm}^2$ so the concrete stress is acceptable.

# CHAPTER 8

# Precast concrete slabs in composite bridges

This chapter corresponds to *Section 8* in EN 1994-2, which has the following clauses:

- General — *Clause 8.1*
- Actions — *Clause 8.2*
- Design, analysis and detailing of the bridge slab — *Clause 8.3*
- Interface between steel beam and concrete slab — *Clause 8.4*

## 8.1. General

***Clause 8.1(1)*** states the scope of *Section 8*: precast deck slabs of reinforced or prestressed concrete which are either:

- partial thickness, acting as permanent participating formwork to the *in-situ* concrete topping, or
- full thickness, where only a small quantity of concrete needs to be cast *in situ* to join the precast units together. Figure 8.1 illustrates a typical deck of this type.

Precast slabs within the scope of *Section 8* should be fully composite with the steel beam – ***clause 8.1(2)***. Non-participating permanent formwork is not covered, for it is difficult both to prevent such formwork from being stressed by imposed loading, and to ensure its durability.

*Clause 8.1(1)*

*Clause 8.1(2)*

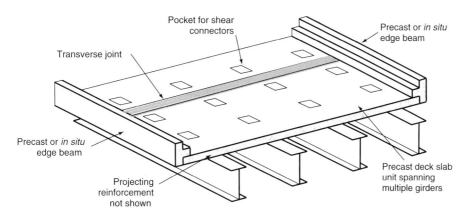

**Fig. 8.1.** Typical full-thickness precast concrete deck

*Clause 8.1(3)*    ***Clause 8.1(3)*** is a reminder that the designer should check the sensitivity of the detailing to tolerances and specify stricter values than those required by EN 1992 (through EN 13670) if necessary. Key issues to consider include:

- detailing of the precast slabs at pockets to ensure that each pocket is correctly located over the steel beam, that projecting transverse reinforcement will not clash with the shear connection, and that there is sufficient space for concreting (*clause 8.4.3(2)*)
- detailing of stitch reinforcement between adjacent precast slabs to ensure that bars do not clash and to satisfy *clause 8.3(1)* on continuity
- tolerances on overall geometry of each precast unit so that, where required, abutting units are sufficiently parallel to each other to avoid the need for additional sealing from underneath. The tolerances for steelwork are also important, and are referred to in *clause 8.4.1*.

## 8.2. Actions

*Clause 8.2(1)*    ***Clause 8.2(1)*** warns that the design of precast deck slabs should consider the actions arising from the proposed construction method as well as the actions given in EN 1991-1-6.[30]

## 8.3. Design, analysis and detailing of the bridge slab

Even where full-thickness slabs are used, some interaction with *in-situ* concrete occurs at
*Clause 8.3(1)*    joints, so ***clause 8.3(1)*** is relevant to both types of precast concrete slab. Its requirement for the deck to be designed as continuous in both directions applies to the finished structure. It does not mean that the reinforcement in partial-thickness precast slabs or planks must be continuous. That would exclude the use of 'Omnia'-type planks, shown in Fig. 8.2. Precast planks of this sort span simply-supported between adjacent steel beams and are joined with *in-situ* concrete over the tops of the beams. The main reinforcement in the planks is not continuous across these joints, but the reinforcement in the *in-situ* concrete is. In the other direction, the planks abut as shown, so that only a small part of the thickness of the slab is discontinuous in compression. Continuity of reinforcement is again achieved in the slab but not in the planks. The resulting slab (part precast, part *in situ*) is continuous in both directions.

EN 1992-1-1 clause 6.2.5 is relevant for the horizontal interface between the precast and in situ concrete. Examples of bridges of this type are given in Ref. 108.

To allow precast slab units to be laid continuously across the steel beams, shear connection usually needs to be concentrated in groups with appropriate positioning of pockets in the
*Clause 8.3(2)*    precast slab as illustrated in Fig. 8.1. ***Clause 8.3(2)*** therefore refers to *clause 6.6.5.5(4)*
*Clause 8.3(3)*    for the use of stud connectors in groups. ***Clause 8.3(3)*** makes reference to *clause 6.6.1.2*. This allows some degree of averaging of the shear flow over a length, which facilitates standardisation of the details of the shear connection and the pockets.

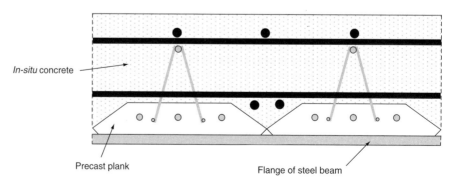

**Fig. 8.2.** Typical partial-thickness precast concrete planks

## 8.4. Interface between steel beam and concrete slab

*Clause 8.4.1(1)* refers to bedding, such as the placing of the slabs on a layer of mortar. Sealing of the interface between steel beam and precast beam is needed both to protect the steel flange from corrosion and to prevent leakage of grout when the pockets are concreted. Where a precast unit is supported by more than two beams, bedding may also be needed to ensure that load is shared between the beams as intended.

'Bedding' in *clause 8.4.1(1)* appears to mean a gap-filling material capable of transferring vertical compression. Where it is intended not to use it, the clause requires special tolerances to be specified for the steelwork to minimise the effects of uneven contact between slab and steel flange.

This does not solve the problems of corrosion and grout leakage, for which a compressible sealing strip could be applied to the edges of the flange and around the pocket. There would then still be no direct protection of the top flange by *in-situ* concrete (other than at a pocket) and so *clause 8.4.2(1)* requires that a top flange without bedding be given the same corrosion protection as the rest of the beam, apart from the site-applied top coat.

If a non-loadbearing anti-corrosion bedding is provided, then the slab should be designed for the transfer of vertical loads only at the positions of the pockets. It would be prudent also to assume that *clause 8.4.1(1)* on special tolerances still applies.

*Clause 8.4.3* gives provisions for the shear connection and transverse reinforcement, supplementing *Sections 6* and *7*. *Clause 8.4.3(2)* emphasises the need for both suitable concrete mix design and appropriate clearance between shear connectors and precast concrete, allowing for tolerances, in order to enable *in-situ* concrete to be fully compacted. *Clause 8.4.3(3)* highlights the need to detail reinforcement appropriately adjacent to groups of connectors. This is discussed with the comments on *clause 6.6.5.5(4)*.

EN 1994-2 gives no specific guidance on the detailing of the transverse and longitudinal joints between precast deck units. Transverse joints between full-depth precast slabs at the intermediate supports of continuous bridges are particularly critical. Here, the slab reinforcement must transmit the tension caused by both global hogging moments and the bending moment from local loading. To allow for full laps in the reinforcement, a clear gap between units would need to be large and a problem arises as to how to form the soffit to the joint. One potential solution is to reduce the gap by using interlocking looped bars protruding from each end of adjoining slab units. Such a splicing detail is not covered in EN 1992-2, other than in the strut-and-tie rules. Experience has shown that even if satisfactory ultimate performance can be established by calculation, tests may be required to demonstrate acceptable performance at the serviceability limit state and under fatigue loading.

The publication *Precast Concrete Decks for Composite Highway Bridges*[109] gives further guidance on the detailing of longitudinal and transverse joints for a variety of bridge types.

*Clause 8.4.1(1)*

*Clause 8.4.2(1)*

*Clause 8.4.3*
*Clause 8.4.3(2)*

*Clause 8.4.3(3)*

# CHAPTER 9

# Composite plates in bridges

This chapter corresponds to *Section 9* of EN 1994-2, which has the following clauses:

- General                                                    *Clause 9.1*
- Design for local effects                         *Clause 9.2*
- Design for global effects                      *Clause 9.3*
- Design of shear connectors                 *Clause 9.4*

## 9.1. General

A composite plate comprises a steel plate acting compositely with a concrete slab in both longitudinal and transverse directions. The requirements of *Section 9* apply to composite top flanges of box girders, which resist local wheel loads in addition to performing the function of a flange in the global system. ***Clause 9.1(1)*** clarifies that this section of EN 1994-2 does not cover composite plates with shear connectors other than headed studs, or sandwich construction where the concrete is enclosed by a top and bottom steel plate. Composite plates can also be used as bottom flanges of box girders in hogging zones. This reduces the amount of stiffening required to prevent buckling. Composite bottom flanges have been used both in new bridges[110,111] and for strengthening older structures. *Clause 9.1(1)*

    ***Clause 9.1(2)*** imposes a deflection limit on the steel flange under the weight of wet concrete, unless the additional weight of concrete due to the deflection is included in the calculation. In most bridges where this deflection limit would be approached, the steel top plate would probably require stiffening to resist the global compression during construction. *Clause 9.1(2)*

    ***Clause 9.1(3)*** gives a modified definition for $b_0$ in *clause 5.4.1.2* on shear lag. Its effect is that where the composite plate has no projection beyond an outer web, the value of $b_0$ for that web is zero. For global analysis, the effects of staged construction, cracking, creep and shrinkage, and shear lag all apply. ***Clause 9.1(4)*** therefore makes reference to *clause 5.4*, together with *clause 5.1* on structural modelling. *Clause 9.1(3)*

*Clause 9.1(4)*

## 9.2. Design for local effects

Local effects arise from vertical loading, usually from wheels or ballast, acting on the composite plate. For flanges without longitudinal stiffeners, most of the load is usually carried by transverse spanning between webs, but longitudinal spanning also occurs in the vicinity of any cross-beams and diaphragms. For flanges with longitudinal stiffeners, the direction of spanning depends on the flange geometry and the relative stiffnesses of the various components. It is important to consider local loading for the fatigue check of the studs as the longitudinal shear from wheel loads can be as significant as that from global loading in low-shear regions of the main member.

**Clause 9.2(1)** permits the local analysis to be carried out using elastic analysis with uncracked concrete properties throughout. This is reasonable because the concrete is likely to be cracked in flexure regardless of the sign of the bending moment. There is therefore no need to distinguish between uncracked and cracked behaviour, although where the steel flange is in tension, the cracked stiffness is likely to be significantly higher for sagging moments than for hogging moments. The same assumption is made in the design of reinforced concrete and is justified at ultimate limit states by the lower-bound theorem of plasticity. *Clause 9.2(1)* also clarifies that the provisions of *Section 9* need not be applied to the composite flange of a discrete steel I-girder, since the flange will not usually be wide enough for significant composite action to develop across its width.

A small amount of slip can be expected between the steel plate and concrete slab, as discussed in the comments under *clause 9.4(4)*, but as in beams its effect on composite action is small. **Clause 9.2(2)** therefore allows slip to be ignored when determining resistances. Excessive slip could however cause premature failure. This needs to be prevented by following the applicable provisions of *clause 6.6* on shear connection in conjunction with *clause 9.4*.

Providing the shear studs are designed as above, the steel deck plate may be taken to act fully compositely with the slab. **Clause 9.2(3)** then permits the section to be designed for flexure as if the steel flange plate were reinforcement. The requirements of EN 1992-2 clause 6.1 should then be followed. The shear resistance may similarly be derived by treating the composite plate as a reinforced concrete section without links according to EN 1992-2 clause 6.2.2 (as modified by *clause 6.2.2.5(3)*), provided that the spacing of the studs transversely and longitudinally is less than three times the thickness of the composite plate. The studs should also be designed for the longitudinal shear flow from local loading for ultimate limit states, other than fatigue, and for the shear flow from combined global and local effects at serviceability and fatigue limit states.

Both punching and flexural shear should be checked. Checks on flexural shear for unstiffened parts of the composite plate should follow the usual procedures for reinforced concrete design. An effective width of slab, similar to that shown below in Fig. 9.1, could be assumed when determining the width of slab resisting flexural shear. Checks on punching shear could consider any support provided by longitudinal stiffeners, although this could conservatively be ignored.

## 9.3. Design for global effects

**Clause 9.3(1)** requires the composite plate to be designed for the effects induced in it by axial force, bending moment and torsion acting on the main girder. In the longitudinal direction, the composite plate will therefore resist direct compression or tension. Most bridge box girders will be in Class 3 or Class 4 and therefore the elastic stresses derived in the concrete and steel elements should be limited to the values in *clause 6.2.1.5* for ultimate limit states.

Torsion acting on the box will induce in-plane shear in both steel and concrete elements of the flange. These shear flows can be determined using a transformed section for the concrete as given in *clauses 5.4.2.2(11)* and *5.4.2.3(6)*. Checks of the steel flange under combined direct stress and in-plane shear are discussed under the comments on *clause 6.2.2.4(3)*. The concrete flange should be checked for in-plane shear in accordance with EN 1992-2 clause 6.2.

Distortion of a box girder will cause warping of the box walls, and thus in-plane bending in the composite plate. The direct stresses from warping will need to be added to those from global bending and axial force. Distortion will also cause transverse bending of the composite plate.

Once a steel flange in compression is connected to the concrete slab, it is usually assumed that the steel flange panels are prevented from buckling (providing the shear studs are spaced sufficiently closely – *clause 9.4(7)* refers). It is still possible, although very unlikely, that the composite plate might buckle as a whole. **Clause 9.3(2)** acknowledges this possibility and requires reference to be made to clause 5.8 of EN 1992-1-1 for the calculation of the second-order effects. None of the simple methods of accounting for second-order effects in this clause apply to plates so a general second-order non-linear analysis with imperfections would be required in accordance with EN 1992-1-1 clause 5.8.6. No guidance is given in EN 1992-1-1 on imperfections in plate elements. The imperfection shape could be based on the elastic critical buckling mode shape for the composite plate. The magnitude of imperfection could be estimated as the sum of the plate imperfection given in EN 1090 and the deflection caused by wet concrete, less any specified camber of the plate.

EN 1992-1-1 clause 5.8.2(6) provides a criterion for ignoring second-order effects which requires them first be calculated. This is unhelpful. A simpler alternative would be to use the criterion in *clause 5.2.1(3)* based on an elastic critical buckling analysis of the composite plate.

Where account should be taken of significant shear force acting on the studs in both longitudinal and transverse directions simultaneously, *clause 9.3(4)* requires the force on the connectors to be based on the vector sum. Hence,

*Clause 9.3(4)*

$$P_{Ed} = \sqrt{P_{l,Ed}^2 + P_{t,Ed}^2}$$

where $P_{l,Ed}$ and $P_{t,Ed}$ are the shear forces per stud in the longitudinal and transverse directions respectively. This can influence the spacing of the studs nearest to the webs because they are the most heavily stressed from global effects (see section 9.4 below) and also tend to be the most heavily loaded from local effects in the transverse direction.

## 9.4. Design of shear connectors

The effect of *clause 9.4(1)* and *clause 9.3(4)* is that local and global effects need only be combined in calculations for serviceability and fatigue limit states, but not for other ultimate limit states. Several justifications can be made for this concession. The main ones are as follows.

*Clause 9.4(1)*

- The effects of local loading are usually high only over a relatively small width compared with the total width providing the global resistance.
- The composite plate will have significant reserves in local bending resistance above that obtained from elastic analysis.
- Complete failure requires the deformation of a mechanism of yield lines, which is resisted by arching action. This action can be developed almost everywhere in the longitudinal direction and in many areas in the transverse direction also.

There is no similar relaxation in EN 1993-2 for bare steel flanges so a steel flange should, in principle, be checked for any local loading in combination with global loading. It will not normally be difficult to satisfy this check, even using elastic analysis.

For serviceability calculations, elastic analysis is appropriate. This greatly simplifies the addition of global and local effects. For the serviceability limit state, the relevant limiting force per connector is that in *clause 6.8.1(3)*, referred to from *clause 7.2.2(6)*. The force per connector should be derived according to *clause 9.3(4)*. When checking the Von Mises equivalent stress in the steel flange plate, the weight of wet concrete carried by it should be included.

No guidance is given on the calculation of stud shear flow from local wheel loads, other than that in *clause 9.2(1)*. Longitudinally stiffened parts of composite plates can be designed as beams spanning between transverse members, where present. The rules for effective width of *clause 5.4.1.2* would apply in determining the parts of the composite plate acting with each longitudinal stiffener. For unstiffened parts of the composite plate, spanning transversely between webs or longitudinally between cross-beams, a simplified calculation of shear flow could be based on an equivalent simply-supported beam. A reasonable assumption for beam width, as recommended in Ref. 112, would be the width of the load, $w$, plus four-thirds of the distance to the nearest support, $x$, as shown in Fig. 9.1.

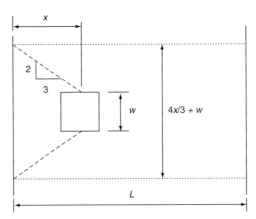

**Fig. 9.1.** Effective beam width for the determination of shear flow in a composite plate

At cross-sections where there is an abrupt change from composite plate to reinforced concrete section, such as at the web of the box in Fig. 9.2, the method of *clause 6.6.2.4* can be used to determine the transverse shear on the studs near the edge of the plate.

Although the composite section formed by a steel flange and concrete slab might provide adequate strength against local sagging moments without additional transverse reinforcement, transverse reinforcement is still required in the bottom of the slab to control cracking and prevent splitting of the concrete ahead of the studs. ***Clause 9.4(2)*** requires a fairly *Clause 9.4(2)* modest quantity of bottom reinforcement to be provided in two orthogonal directions. It implies that in the absence of such reinforcement, the static design resistances of studs given in *clause 6.6.3.1(1)* cannot be used as they assume that splitting is prevented. The limiting fatigue stress range for studs provided in *clause 6.8.3* is also inappropriate without some transverse reinforcement as splitting will increase the flexural stresses in the stud.

*Clause 9.4(3)* ***Clause 9.4(3)*** refers to the detailing rules of *clause 6.6.5*. The minimum steel flange thickness in *clause 6.6.5.7(3)* is only likely to become relevant where the top flange is heavily stiffened as discussed in the comments on that clause.

The force on shear connectors in wide composite flanges is influenced both by shear lag in the concrete and steel flanges and also slip of the shear connection. At the serviceability limit state, these lead to a non-uniform distribution of connector force across the flange width. *Clause 9.4(4)* This distribution can be approximated by *equation (9.1)* in ***clause 9.4(4)***:

$$P_{Ed} = \frac{v_{L,Ed}}{n_{tot}}\left[\left(3.85\left(\frac{n_w}{n_{tot}}\right)^{-0.17} - 3\right)\left(1 - \frac{x}{b}\right)^2 + 0.15\right] \qquad (9.1)$$

*Equation (9.1)* was derived from a finite-element study by Moffat and Dowling.[113] The study considered only simply-supported beams with ratios of flange half-breadth between webs (*b* in *equation (9.1)*) to span in the range 0.05 and 0.20. The stud stiffness was taken as 400 kN/mm.

The studs nearest the web can pick up a significantly greater force than that obtained by dividing the total longitudinal shear by the total number of connectors. This is illustrated in Example 9.1 and in Ref. 74. Connectors within a distance of the greater of $10t_f$ and 200 mm are assumed to carry the same shear force. This result is obtained by using $x = 0$ in *equation (9.1)* when calculating the stud force and it is necessary to avoid underestimating the force, compared to the finite-element results, in the studs nearest the web. The rule is consistent with practice for flanges of plate girders, where all shear connectors at a cross-section are assumed to be equally loaded.

The assumed value of stud stiffness has a significant effect on the transverse distribution of stud force as greater slip leads to a more uniform distribution. Recent studies, such as that in Ref. 98, have concluded that stud stiffnesses are significantly lower than 400 kN/mm. The same value of stiffness is probably not appropriate for both fatigue calculation and serviceability calculations under the characteristic load combination, due to the greater slip, and therefore flexibility, possible in the latter case. Nevertheless, the assumed stiffness of 400 kN/mm is an upper bound and therefore the transverse distribution is conservative.

*Clause 9.4(5)* permits a relaxation of the requirements of *clause 9.4(4)* for composite bottom flanges of box girders, provided that at least half of the shear connectors required are concentrated near the web–flange junction. 'Near' means either on the web or within the defined adjacent width $b_f$ of the flange. The rule is based on extensive practice in Germany, and assumes that there is no significant local loading.

*Clause 9.4(5)*

At the ultimate limit state, plasticity in the flange and increased slip lead to a much more uniform distribution of stud forces across the box, which is allowed for in *clause 9.4(6)*.

*Clause 9.4(6)*

To prevent buckling of the steel compression flange in half waves between studs, *clause 9.4(7)* refers to *Table 9.1* for limiting stud spacings in both longitudinal and transverse directions. These could, in principle, be relaxed if account is taken of any longitudinal stiffening provided to stabilise the compression flange prior to hardening of the concrete. Most bridge box girders will have webs in Class 3 or Class 4, so it will usually only be necessary to comply with the stud spacings for a Class 3 flange; there is however little difference between the spacing requirements for Class 2 and Class 3.

*Clause 9.4(7)*

### Example 9.1: design of shear connection for global effects at the serviceability limit state

The shear connection for the box girder shown in Fig. 9.2 is to be designed using 19 mm stud connectors. For reasons to be explained, it may be governed by serviceability, for which the longitudinal shear per web at SLS (determined from elastic analysis of the cross-section making allowance for shear lag) was found to be 800 kN/m.

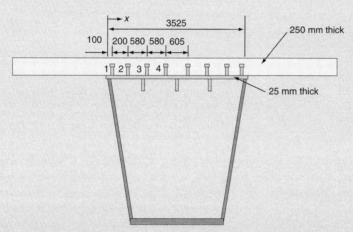

**Fig. 9.2.** Box girder for Example 9.1

From *clause 6.8.1(3)* the force per connector at SLS is limited to $0.75P_{Rd}$. From Example 6.10, this limit is $0.75 \times 83.3 = 62.5$ kN.

It will be found that longitudinal shear forces per stud decrease rapidly with distance from the web. This leaves spare resistance for the transverse shear force and local effects (e.g. from wheel loads), both of which can usually be neglected adjacent to the web, but increase with distance from it.[113] The following method is further explained in Ref. 74. It is based on finite-element analyses that included shear lag, and so is applied to the whole width of composite plate associated with the web concerned, not just to the effective width. In this case, both widths are $3525/2 = 1762$ mm, denoted $b$ in *Fig. 9.1* in EN 1994-2.

From *clause 9.4(4)*, $n_w$ is the number of connectors within 250 mm of the web, because $10t_f > 200$ mm. The method is slightly iterative, as the first step is to estimate the ratio $n_w/n_{tot}$, here taken as 0.25. The longitudinal spacing of the studs is assumed to be 0.15 m, so the design shear per transverse row is $v_{L,Rd} = 800 \times 0.15 = 120$ kN.

If all the studs were within 250 mm of the web, their $x$-coordinate in *equation (9.1)* would be zero. The number of studs required is found from this equation by putting $P_{Ed} = 0.75P_{Rd} = 62.5$ kN and $x = 0$:

$$6.25 = \frac{120}{n_{tot}}[(3.85(0.25)^{-0.17} - 3) + 0.15]$$

whence $n_{tot} = 3.88$. Design is therefore based on four studs per transverse row, of which one will be within 250 mm of the web. To conform to the assumptions made in deriving *equation (9.1)*, the other studs will be equally spaced over the whole width $b$, not the width $b - 250$ mm. (This distinction only matters where $n_{tot}$ is low, as it is here.) In a wider box, non-uniform lateral spacing may be more convenient, subject to the condition given in the definition of $n_{tot}$ in *clause 9.4(4)*.

For these studs, uniform spacing means locations at $x = b/6$, $b/2$ and $5b/6$ – that is, at $x = 294$, 881 and 1468 mm. These are rounded to $x = 300$, 880 and 1460 mm. The maximum lateral spacing is midway between the webs: $3525 - 2 \times 1460 = 605$ mm. This spacing satisfies the provisions on spacing of *clause 9.2(3)* (i.e. $<3 \times 275 = 825$ mm) and also those of *Table 9.1* for Class 3 behaviour. It would not be necessary to comply with the latter if the longitudinal stiffeners were close enough to ensure that there is no reduction to the effective width of the plate for local sub-panel buckling; this is not the case here.

The shear force $P_{Ed}$ per stud is found from *equation (9.1)*, which is:

$$P_{Ed} = \frac{120}{4}\left[(3.85(0.25)^{-0.17} - 3)\left(1 - \frac{x}{1762}\right)^2 + 0.15\right]$$

Results are given in Table 9.1.

**Table 9.1.** Forces in studs from global effects

| Stud No. | 1 | 2 | 3 | 4 | Total |
|---|---|---|---|---|---|
| $x$ (mm) | 100 | 300 | 880 | 1460 | — |
| $P_{Ed}$ (kN) | 60.7 | 43.2 | 18.6 | 6.2 | 129 |

The shear resisted by the four studs, 129 kN, exceeds 120 kN, and no stud is overloaded, so the spacing is satisfactory. The result, 129 kN, differs from 120 kN because *equation (9.1)* is an approximation. This ratio, 129/120, is a function, given in a graph in Ref. 74, of $n_w/n_{tot}$ and of the effective-width ratio $b_{eff}/b$. Where the lateral spacing of the $n_{tot}-n_w$ studs is uniform, as here, the ratio exceeds 1.0 provided that $n_w/n_{tot} < 0.5$ and $b_{eff}/b > 0.7$. Its minimum value is about 0.93. If the design needs to be modified, revision of the longitudinal spacing is a simple method, as the ratios between the forces per stud do not then change.

From *clause 9.4(6)*, at ULS the studs may be assumed to be equally loaded. Here, their design resistance is:

$$(n_{tot}/0.15)(P_{Rd}/\gamma_V) = (4/0.15)(83.3/1.25) = 1777 \text{ kN/m}$$

This is more than twice the design shear for SLS, so ULS is unlikely to govern. Table 9.1 shows that for SLS, studs 2 to 4 have a reserve of resistance (cf. 62.5 kN) that should be sufficient for transverse shear and local effects.

# CHAPTER 10

# Annex C (Informative). Headed studs that cause splitting forces in the direction of the slab thickness

This chapter corresponds to Annex C of EN 1994-2, which has the following clauses:

- Design resistance and detailing            *Clause C.1*
- Fatigue strength            *Clause C.2*

Annex A of EN 1994-1-1 is for buildings only. Annex B of EN 1994-1-1, 'Standard tests', for shear connectors and composite floor slabs, is not repeated in EN 1994-2. Comment on these annexes is given in Ref. 5.

*Annex C* gives a set of design rules for the detailing and resistance of shear studs that are embedded in an edge of a concrete slab, as shown in *Figs 6.13* and *C.1* of EN 1994-2 and in Fig. 6.35. Details of this type can occur at an edge of a composite deck in a tied arch or half-through bridge, or where double composite action is used in a box girder. The same problem, premature splitting, could occur in a steep-sided narrow haunch. The use of such haunches is now discouraged by the 45° rule in *clause 6.6.5.4(1)*.

The rules in *Annex C* were developed from research at the University of Stuttgart that has been available in English only since 2001.[82,114,115] These extensive push tests and finite-element analyses showed that to avoid premature failure by splitting of the slab and to ensure ductile behaviour, special detailing rules are needed. *Clause 6.6.3.1(3)* therefore warns that the usual rules for resistance of studs do not apply. The new rules, in *Annex C*, are necessarily of limited scope, because there are so many relevant parameters. The rules are partly based on elaborate strut-and-tie modelling. It was not possible to find rules that are dimensionally consistent, so the units to be used are specified – the only occasion in EN 1994 Parts 1-1 and 2 where this has been necessary. For these reasons, *Annex C* is Informative, even though its guidance is the best available. The simplified and generally more conservative rules given in *clause 6.6.4* do not cover interaction with transverse (e.g. vertical) shear or resistance to fatigue.

It will be found that these 'lying studs' have to be much longer than usual, and that the minimum slab thickness to avoid a reduction in the shear resistance per stud can exceed 250 mm. The comments that follow are illustrated in Example 10.1, and in Fig. 10.1 where the longitudinal shear acts normal to the plane of the figure and vertical shear acts downwards from the slab to the steel web.

## C.1. Design resistance and detailing

*Clause C.1(1)*

*Clause C.1(1)* gives the static resistance of a stud to longitudinal shear in the absence of vertical shear, which should not be taken as greater than that from *clause 6.6.3.1(1)*. The minimum length $h$ of the stud and the reinforcement details are intended to be such that splitting of the slab is followed by fracture or pulling out of the stud, giving a ductile mode of failure. The important dimensions are $a'_{\text{r,o}}$ and $v$, from the stud to the centre-lines of the stirrup reinforcement, as shown in Fig. 10.1.

*Equation (C.1)*, repeated in the Example, uses factor $k_\text{v}$ to distinguish between two situations. The more favourable, where $k_\text{v} = 1.14$, applies where the slab is connected to both sides of the web and resists hogging bending – a 'middle position'. This requires reinforcement to pass continuously above the web, as shown in *Fig. C.1*. Some shear is then transferred by friction at the face of the web. Where this does not occur, an 'edge position', $k_\text{v}$ has the lower value 1.0. Details in bridge decks are usually edge positions, so further comment is limited to these. The geometries considered in the Stuttgart tests, however, covered composite girders where the steel top flange was omitted altogether, with the web projecting into the slab.

The general symbol for distance from a stud to the nearest free surface is $a_\text{r}$, but notation $a_{\text{r,o}}$ is used for the upper surface, from the German *oben*, 'above'. Its use is relevant where there is vertical shear, acting downwards from the slab to the studs. Allowing for cover and the stirrups, the important dimension is:

$$a'_{\text{r,o}} = a_{\text{r,o}} - c_\text{v} - \phi_\text{s}/2$$

If the lower free surface is closer to the stud, its dimension $a'_\text{r}$ should be used in place of $a'_{\text{r,o}}$.

*Clause 6.6.4* appears to cover only this 'edge position' layout, and uses the symbol $e_\text{v}$ in place of $a'_{\text{r,o}}$ or $a'_\text{r}$.

Although $f_{\text{ck}}$ in *equation (C.1)* is defined as the strength 'at the age considered', the specified 28-day value should be used, unless a check is being made at a younger age.

The longitudinal spacing of the stirrups, $s$, should be related to that of the studs, $a$, and should ideally be uniform.

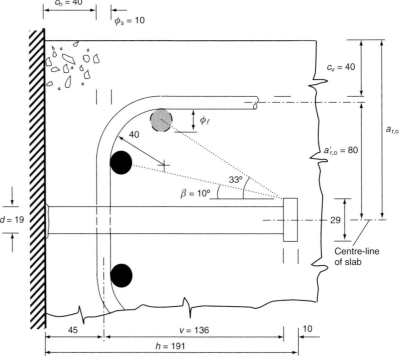

**Fig. 10.1.** Notation and dimensions for lying studs in Example 10.1

For concretes of grade C35/45 and above, the resistance $P_{Rd}$ from *clause 6.6.3.1* is independent of the concrete grade. Then, *equation (C.1)* can be used to find a minimum value for $a'_r$ such that $P_{Rd,L} \geq P_{Rd}$.

For example, let $a = s$, $d = 19\,mm$, $f_{ck} = 35\,N/mm^2$, $k_v = 1$, and $\gamma_V = 1.25$. Then, $P_{Rd} = 90.7\,kN$ from *equation (6.18)* and $P_{Rd,L}$ from *equation (C.1)* does not govern unless $a'_r < 89\,mm$, say 90 mm. With 40 mm cover and 10 mm stirrups, the minimum slab thickness is then $2(90 + 40 + 5) = 270\,mm$ if the studs are centrally placed, but greater if they are off centre. If a thinner slab is required, the ratio $a/s$ can be increased or more studs provided, to compensate for a value $P_{Rd,L} < P_{Rd}$.

The limits on $v$ in **clause C.1(2)** are more convenient for use in practice than the limits on $\beta$, because the angle $\beta$ is defined by the position of the longitudinal corner bar within the bend of the stirrup (Fig. 10.1), which is difficult to control on site. *Clause C.1(2)*

It follows from **clause C.1(3)** that the minimum stirrup diameter $\phi_s$ is roughly proportional to the stud diameter $d$. Where $a/s = 1.0$, $\phi_s \approx d/2$. *Clause C.1(3)*

The expression for interaction between longitudinal and vertical shear, **clause C.1(4)**, is only slightly convex. The vertical shear resistance given in Example 10.1, *equation (C.4)*, is typically less than 40% of the longitudinal shear resistance, being governed mainly by the upper edge distance $a_{r,o}$. Application of vertical shear to lying studs is best avoided, and can be minimized by spanning the concrete slab longitudinally between cross-beams. *Clause C.1(4)*

## C.2. Fatigue strength

*Equation (C.5)* in **clause C.2(1)**, $(\Delta P_R)^m N = (\Delta P_c)^m N_c$, differs from *equation (6.50)* in *clause 6.8.3(3)* (for the fatigue strength of studs in a non-lying position) only in that symbols $\Delta P$ in *equation (C.5)* appear as $\Delta \tau$ in *equation (6.50)*. Both methods use $m = 8$. *Clause C.2(1)*

In *Annex C*, $\Delta P_c$ is a function of dimension $a'_r$ (*Fig. C.1*, Fig. 10.1), and is 35.6 kN at 2 million cycles, for $a'_r \geq 100\,mm$. With typical covers to reinforcement, this corresponds to a lying stud at mid-depth of a slab at least 280 mm thick, where the splitting effect is probably minimal. This value 35.6 kN should therefore correspond to the value given in *clause 6.8.3* for $\Delta \tau$ at 2 million cycles, $90\,N/mm^2$. It does so when the stud diameter is 22.4 mm. This is as expected, because in the fatigue tests, only 22 mm diameter studs were used. However, the method of *Annex C* is provided for studs of diameter 19 mm to 25 mm, for which: 'numerous FE-calculations show, that the fatigue strength curve should be based on the absolute range of shear force per stud rather than on the range of shear stress' (p. 9 of Ref. 115).

The value of $\Delta P_R$ given by the rule in *clause 6.8.3* is proportional to the square of the shank diameter of the stud. For 19 mm studs, it is only 25.6 kN at $2 \times 10^6$ cycles, which is only 72% of the resistance 35.6 kN given in *Table C.1*. This is why *clause C.2(1)* requires the lower of the two values from *clause 6.8.3* and *Annex C* to be used.

**Clause C.2(2)** refers to the recommended upper limit for the longitudinal shear force per connector, which is $0.75 P_{Rd}$. The word '*longitudinal*' reveals that the rule for fatigue resistance does not apply where vertical shear is present, which is not clear in *clause C.2(1)*. There were no fatigue tests in combined longitudinal and vertical shear – another reason why application of vertical shear to lying studs is best avoided. *Clause C.2(2)*

## Applicability of *Annex C*

The definition of a 'lying stud', given in the titles of *clause 6.6.4* and *Annex C*, does not state how far from a free surface a stud must be, for the normal rules for its resistance and the detailing to apply.

*Clause 6.6.5.3* refers to a '*longitudinal edge*', not a top surface, but appears to deal with the same problem of splitting parallel to a free surface nearby. Where the edge distance (i.e. $a_{r,o}$ in Fig. 10.1) is less than 300 mm, it specifies 'U-bars' (i.e. stirrups) of diameter $\phi_s \geq 0.5d$ and an edge distance $a_r \geq 6d$. These limits correspond closely with the results of

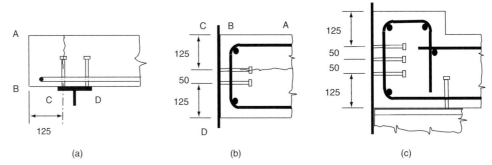

**Fig. 10.2.** Cross-sections at an edge of a slab: (a) edge studs; (b) lying studs in an edge position; and (c) three rows of lying studs

Example 10.1, $\phi_s = 0.53d$ and $a_r = 6.6d$, but the stirrups are required to pass around the studs, whereas in *Annex C* they pass between them. The difference is that the surface parallel to the plane of splitting, AB in Fig. 10.2, is normal to the plane of the slab in one case, not in the other. The minimum height of the stud, about 90 mm to *clause 6.6.5.1(1)* and 191 mm in Example 10.1, is less significant in the detail in Fig. 10.2(a) than in detail (b). Details may occur where *clause 6.6.5.3* is also applicable, but it does not clarify the scope of *Annex C*.

Let us consider the options, as the local thickness $h_c$ of the slab in Fig. 10.1 is increased (e.g. by the addition of an upstand haunch) without change to other details. If the top cover is maintained, length $a'_{r,o}$ must increase, so from *clause C.1(2)* for $v$, the studs have to be longer. An alternative is to keep $a'_{r,o}$ and $v$ unchanged, by increasing the cover to the legs of the stirrups. When $h_c$ exceeds 300 mm (using data from Example 10.1), two rows of studs are possible, Fig. 10.2(b), because the minimum vertical spacing of studs is $2.5d$, from *clause 6.6.5.7(4)*. In the absence of vertical shear, the shear resistance is doubled, as is the potential splitting force. For two rows of lying studs, the force $T_d$ given by *equation (C.2)* should be 0.3 times the sum of their resistances.

Limits to the applicability of *Annex C* are further discussed at the end of Example 10.1.

### Example 10.1: design of lying studs
A bridge deck slab 250 mm thick is to be connected along its sides to steel webs. The final detail is shown to scale in Fig. 10.1. The design ultimate longitudinal shear at each edge is $V_{L,Ed} = 600$ kN/m. The vertical shear is at first assumed to be negligible. The effect of adding $V_{V,Ed} = 60$ kN/m is then found. The strengths of the materials are: $f_{yd} = 500/1.15 = 435$ N/mm$^2$, $f_u = 500$ N/mm$^2$ and $f_{ck} = 40$ N/mm$^2$. Resistances in *Annex C* are given in terms of $f_{ck}$, not $f_{cd}$, because the partial factor $\gamma_V$ allows for both the stud material and the concrete. The minimum cover is 40 mm.

There is space only for a single row of studs at mid-depth, and 19 mm studs are preferred. Assuming the studs have a height greater than four times their shank diameter, their shear resistance to *equation (6.19)* is:

$$P_{Rd} = 0.29 \times 19^2\sqrt{40 \times 35\,000}/(1.25 \times 1000) = \textbf{99.1 kN/stud} \tag{D10.1}$$

and to *equation (6.18)* is:

$$P_{Rd} = 0.8 \times 500 \times \pi \times 19^2/(4 \times 1.25) = \textbf{90.7 kN/stud} \tag{D10.2}$$

so *equation (6.18)* governs.

This gives a spacing of $90.7/600 = 0.151$ m, so a spacing $a = 150$ mm is assumed, with stirrups also at 150 mm. Their required diameter $\phi_s$ can be estimated from *clause C.1(3)*, *equation (C.2)*:

$$T_d = 0.3P_{Rd,L}$$

Using $P_{Ed,L}$ as an approximation to $P_{Rd,L}$:

$$T_d = (\pi\phi_s^2/4) \times 500/1.15 \geq 0.3 \times 600 \times 1000 \times 0.15$$

This gives $\phi_s \geq 8.9$ mm, so 10 mm stirrups are assumed for finding $d'_{r,o}$.

With cover of 40 mm,

$$d'_{r,o} = [250 - 2(40 + 5)]/2 = 80 \text{ mm}$$

From *equation (C.1)* with $k_v = 1.0$ for an edge position and $a = s$,

$$\boldsymbol{P_{Rd,L}} = 1.4k_v(f_{ck}dd'_r)^{0.4}(a/s)^{0.3}/\gamma_V = 1.4(40 \times 19 \times 80)^{0.4}/1.25 = \boldsymbol{91.7 \text{ kN/stud}} \quad (C.1)$$

This is greater than result (D10.2), so the shear resistance is governed by *equation (6.18)*. Where this occurs, the term $P_{Rd,L}$ in *equations (C.2)* and *(C.3)* should be replaced by the governing shear resistance.

For studs at 0.15 m spacing, $V_{Rd,L} = 90.7/0.15 = 605$ kN/m which is sufficient. This result requires the diameter of the stirrups to be increased to $8.9 \times 605/600 = 9.0$ mm, so 10 mm is still sufficient. The length of the studs is governed by $d'_r$. From *clause C.1(2)*:

- for uncracked concrete,   $v \geq \max\{110, 1.7 \times 80, 1.7 \times 75\} = 136$ mm
- for cracked concrete,   $v \geq \max\{160, 2.4 \times 80, 2.4 \times 75\} = 192$ mm

To these lengths must be added $c_h + \phi_s/2$ (i.e. 45 mm) plus the thickness of the head of the stud, 10 mm, giving lengths $h$ after welding of 191 mm and 247 mm respectively. In practice, these would be rounded up. Here, $h$ is taken as 191 mm. Figure 10.1 shows that the angle $\beta$ can then be anywhere between $10°$ and $33°$. This is roughly consistent with the alternative rule in *clause C.1(2)*, $\beta \leq 30°$.

The simpler rules of *clause 6.6.4* would require $d'_{r,o}$ to be increased from 80 mm to $6 \times 19 = 114$ mm. It would then be necessary for the slab thickness to be increased locally from 250 mm to at least 318 mm. Dimension $v$ would be increased from 136 or 192 mm to 266 mm, requiring much longer studs.

In the absence of vertical shear, a check on fatigue to *clause C.2(1)* is straightforward.

### Interaction with vertical shear

The design vertical shear is $F_{d,V} = 0.15 \times 60 = 9$ kN/stud.

*Clause C.1(4)* requires longitudinal reinforcement with $\phi_l \leq 16$ mm, so this value is used. From *equation (C.4)* with $k_v = 1.0$ and $a = s$,

$$\boldsymbol{P_{Rd,V}} = 0.012(f_{ck}\phi_l)^{0.5}(da/s)^{0.4}(\phi_s)^{0.3}(d'_{r,o})^{0.7}k_v/\gamma_V \qquad (C.4)$$

$$= 0.012(40 \times 16)^{0.5}(19)^{0.4}(10)^{0.3}(80)^{0.7} \times 1.0/1.25 = \boldsymbol{33.8 \text{ kN/stud}}$$

From interaction *expression (C.3)*:

$$(600 \times 0.15/90.7)^{1.2} + (9/33.8)^{1.2} = 1.20 \text{ (but } \leq 1.0)$$

which is too large. Changing the spacing of the studs and stirrups from 150 mm to 125 mm would reduce result 1.20 to 0.96.

### Two or more rows of lying studs

The detail shown in Fig. 10(c) is now considered, with materials and studs as before. The deck spans longitudinally, so it can be assumed that no vertical shear is applied to the three rows of lying studs. The preceding calculations apply to the top and bottom rows. For the middle row, $d'_r$ increases from 80 mm to 130 mm. From *equation (C.1)* the resistance of its studs increases from 91.7 kN to 111 kN, so result (D10.2), 90.7 kN, still governs. Assuming uncracked concrete, the minimum height of these studs increases by 1.7 times the change in $d'_r$, from *clause C.1(2)*; that is, from 191 mm to 276 mm. This situation was not researched, and the increase may not be necessary; but the stirrups should be designed for a force

$$T_d = 0.3(3 \times 90.7) = 82 \text{ kN per 150 mm length of beam,}$$

if the full shear resistance of the studs is needed.

# References

European Standards listed as EN... are being published in each Member State of the Comité Européen de Normalisation (CEN) by its National Standards organisation between 2002 and 2007. In the UK, publication is by the British Standards Institution, London, as BS EN....

The Eurocodes, EN 1990 to EN 1999, are accompanied by National Annexes. These annexes for the UK are expected to be completed by the end of 2007.

1. Gulvanessian, H., Calgaro, J.-A. and Holický, M. (2002) *Designers' Guide to EN 1990. Eurocode: Basis of Structural Design.* Thomas Telford, London.
2. Calgaro, J.-A., Tschumi, M., Gulvanessian, H. and Shetty, N. *Designers' Guide to EN 1991-1-1, 1991-1-3, 1991-1-5 to 1-7 and 1991-2, Eurocode 1: Actions on Structures. (Traffic loads and other actions on bridges).* Thomas Telford, London (in preparation).
3. Smith, D. and Hendy, C. R. *Designers' Guide to EN 1992-2. Eurocode 2: Design of Concrete Structures. Part 2: Bridges.* Thomas Telford, London (in preparation).
4. Murphy, C. J. M. and Hendy, C. R. *Designers' Guide to EN 1993-2. Eurocode 3: Design of Steel Structures. Part 2: Bridges.* Thomas Telford, London (to be published, 2007).
5. Johnson, R. P. and Anderson, D. (2004) *Designers' Guide to EN 1994-1-1. Eurocode 4: Design of Composite Steel and Concrete Structures. Part 1-1: General Rules and Rules for Buildings.* Thomas Telford, London.
6. Beeby, A. W. and Narayanan, R. S. (2005) *Designers' Guide to EN 1992. Eurocode 2, Design of Concrete Structures. Part 1-1: General Rules and Rules for Buildings.* Thomas Telford, London.
7. Gardner, L. and Nethercot, D. (2005) *Designers' Guide to EN 1993. Eurocode 3, Design of Steel Structures. Part 1-1: General Rules and Rules for Buildings.* Thomas Telford, London.
8. British Standards Institution. *Design of Composite Steel and Concrete Structures. Part 1-1: General Rules and Rules for Buildings.* BSI, London, EN 1994.
9. British Standards Institution. *Design of Composite Steel and Concrete Structures. Part 2: General Rules and Rules for Bridges.* BSI, London, EN 1994.
10. The European Commission (2002) *Guidance Paper L (Concerning the Construction Products Directive – 89/106/EEC). Application and Use of Eurocodes.* EC, Brussels.
11. British Standards Institution. *Steel, Concrete and Composite Bridges.* (In many Parts.) BSI, London, BS 5400.
12. Hanswille, G. (2006) The new German design code for composite bridges. In: Leon, R. T. and Lange, J. (eds), *Composite Construction in Steel and Concrete V.* American Society of Civil Engineers, New York, pp. 13–24.
13. British Standards Institution. *Eurocode: Basis of Structural Design.* (Including Annexes for Buildings, Bridges, etc.). BSI, London, EN 1990.

14. British Standards Institution. *Actions on Structures*. BSI, London, EN 1991. (In many Parts.) See also Refs 26, 30, 53 and 103.
15. British Standards Institution. *Design of Concrete Structures*. BSI, London, EN 1992. (In several Parts.) See also Ref. 27.
16. British Standards Institution. *Design of Steel Structures*. BSI, London, EN 1993. (In many Parts.) See also Refs 19, 28, 38, 41, and 42.
17. British Standards Institution. *Design of Structures for Earthquake Resistance*. BSI, London, EN 1998. (In several Parts.)
18. Niehaus, H. and Jerling, W. (2006) The Nelson Mandela bridge as an example of the use of composite materials in bridge construction in South Africa. In: Leon, R. T. and Lange, J. (eds), *Composite Construction in Steel and Concrete V*. American Society of Civil Engineers, New York, pp. 487–500.
19. British Standards Institution. *Design of Steel Structures. Part 1-8: Design of Joints*. BSI, London, EN 1993.
20. British Standards Institution (1994) *Design of Composite Steel and Concrete Structures. Part 1-1, General Rules and Rules for Buildings*. BSI, London, BS DD ENV 1994.
21. Hosain, M. U. and Pashan, A. (2006) Channel shear connectors in composite beams: push-out tests. In: Leon, R. T. and Lange, J. (eds), *Composite Construction in Steel and Concrete V*. American Society of Civil Engineers, New York, pp. 501–510.
22. Veljkovic, M. and Johansson, B. (2006) Residual static resistance of welded stud shear connectors. In: Leon, R. T. and Lange, J. (eds), *Composite Construction in Steel and Concrete V*. American Society of Civil Engineers, New York, pp. 524–533.
23. Andrä, H.-P. (1990) Economical shear connection with high fatigue strength. *Proceedings of a Symposium on Mixed Structures, including New Materials*, Brussels. IABSE, Zurich. *Reports* **60**, 167–172.
24. Marecek, J., Samec, J. and Studnicka, J. (2005) Perfobond shear connector behaviour. In: Hoffmeister, B. and Hechler, O. (eds), *Eurosteel 2005, vol. B*. Druck und Verlagshaus Mainz, Aachen, pp. 4.3-1 to 4.3-8.
25. Hauke, B. (2005) Shear connectors for composite members of high strength materials. In: Hoffmeister, B. and Hechler, O. (eds), *Eurosteel 2005, vol. B*. Druck und Verlagshaus Mainz, Aachen, pp. 4.2-57 to 4.2-64.
26. British Standards Institution. *Actions on Structures. Part 2: Traffic Loads on Bridges*. BSI, London, EN 1991.
27. British Standards Institution. *Design of Concrete Structures. Part 2: Bridges*. BSI, London, EN 1992.
28. British Standards Institution. *Design of Steel Structures. Part 2: Bridges*. BSI, London, EN 1993.
29. International Organisation for Standardization (1997) *Basis of Design for Structures – Notation – General Symbols*. ISO, Geneva, ISO 3898.
30. British Standards Institution. *Actions on Structures. Part 1-6: Actions during Execution*. BSI, London, EN 1991.
31. The European Commission (1989) *Construction Products Directive 89/106/EEC*, OJEC No. L40 of 11 February. EC, Brussels.
32. British Standards Institution. *Geotechnical Design*. BSI, London, EN 1997. (In several Parts.)
33. Anderson, D., Aribert, J.-M., Bode, H. and Kronenburger, H. J. (2000) Design rotation capacity of composite joints. *Structural Engineer*, **78**, No. 6, 25–29.
34. Working Commission 2 (2005) Use and application of high-performance steels for steel structures. *Structural Engineering Documents 8*, IABSE, Zurich.
35. Morino, S. (2002) Recent developments on concrete-filled steel tube members in Japan. In: Hajjar, J. F., Hosain, M., Easterling, W. S. and Shahrooz, B. M. (eds), *Composite Construction in Steel and Concrete IV*. American Society of Civil Engineers, New York, pp. 644–655.

36. Hegger, J. and Döinghaus, P. (2002) High performance steel and high performance concrete in composite structures. In: Hajjar, J. F., Hosain, M., Easterling, W. S. and Shahrooz, B. M. (eds), *Composite Construction in Steel and Concrete IV*. American Society of Civil Engineers, New York, pp. 891–902.

37. Hoffmeister, B., Sedlacek, G., Müller, C. and Kühn, B. (2002) High strength materials in composite structures. In: Hajjar, J. F., Hosain, M., Easterling, W. S. and Shahrooz, B. M. (eds), *Composite Construction in Steel and Concrete IV*. American Society of Civil Engineers, New York, pp. 903–914.

38. British Standards Institution. *Design of Steel Structures. Part 1-3: Cold Formed Thin Gauge Members and Sheeting*. BSI, London, EN 1993.

39. Sedlacek, G. and Trumpf, H. (2006) Composite design for small and medium spans. In: Leon, R. T. and Lange, J. (eds), *Composite Construction in Steel and Concrete V*. American Society of Civil Engineers, New York, pp. 105–113.

40. British Standards Institution. (1998) *Welding – Studs and Ceramic Ferrules for Arc Stud Welding*. BSI, London, EN 13918.

41. British Standards Institution. *Design of Steel Structures. Part 1-5: Plated Structural Elements*. BSI, London, EN 1993.

42. British Standards Institution. *Design of Steel Structures. Part 1-9: Fatigue Strength of Steel Structures*. BSI, London, EN 1993.

43. Trahair, N. S., Bradford, M. A. and Nethercot, D. A. (2001) *The Behaviour and Design of Steel Structures to BS 5950*, 3rd edn. Spon, London.

44. Johnson, R. P. and Cafolla, J. (1977) Stiffness and strength of lateral restraints to compressed flanges. *Journal of Constructional Steel Research*, **42**, No. 2, 73–93.

45. Johnson, R. P. and Chen, S. (1991) Local buckling and moment redistribution in Class 2 composite beams. *Structural Engineering International*, **1**, No. 4, 27–34.

46. Johnson, R. P. and Fan, C. K. R. (1988) Strength of continuous beams designed to Eurocode 4. *Proceedings of IABSE, Periodica 2/88, P-125/88*, May, pp. 33–44.

47. Johnson, R. P. and Huang, D. J. (1995) Composite bridge beams of mixed-class cross-section. *Structural Engineering International*, **5**, No. 2, 96–101.

48. British Standards Institution (1990) *Code of Practice for Design of Simple and Continuous Composite Beams*. BSI, London, BS 5950-3-1.

49. Haensel, J. (1975) *Effects of Creep and Shrinkage in Composite Construction*. Institute for Structural Engineering, Ruhr-Universität, Bochum, Report 75-12.

50. Johnson, R. P. and Hanswille, G. (1998) Analyses for creep of continuous steel and composite bridge beams, according to EC4:Part 2. *Structural Engineer*, **76**, No. 15, 294–298.

51. Johnson, R. P. (1987) Shrinkage-induced curvature in cracked concrete flanges of composite beams. *Structural Engineer*, **65B**, Dec., 72–77.

52. Guezouli, S. and Aribert, J.-M. (2006) Numerical investigation of moment redistribution in continuous beams of composite bridges. In: Leon, R. T. and Lange, J. (eds), *Composite Construction in Steel and Concrete V*. American Society of Civil Engineers, New York, pp. 47–56.

53. British Standards Institution. *Actions on Structures. Part 1-5: Thermal Actions*. BSI, London, EN 1991.

54. British Standards Institution (1997) *Design of Composite Structures of Steel and Concrete. Part 2: Bridges*. BSI, London, BS DD ENV 1994.

55. Johnson, R. P. (2003) Cracking in concrete tension flanges of composite T-beams – tests and Eurocode 4. *Structural Engineer*, **81**, No. 4, Feb., 29–34.

56. Johnson, R. P. (2003) Analyses of a composite bowstring truss with tension stiffening. *Proceedings of the Institution of Civil Engineers, Bridge Engineering*, **156**, June, 63–70.

57. Way, J. A. and Biddle, A. R. (1998) *Integral Steel Bridges: Design of a Multi-span Bridge – Worked Example*. Steel Construction Institute, Ascot, Publication 180.

58. Lawson, R. M. (1987) *Design for Openings in the Webs of Composite Beams*. Steel Construction Institute, Ascot, Publication 068.

197

59. Lawson, R. M., Chung, K. F. and Price, A. M. (1992) Tests on composite beams with large web openings. *Structural Engineer*, **70**, Jan., 1–7.

60. Johnson, R. P. and Huang, D. J. (1994) Calibration of safety factors $\gamma_M$ for composite steel and concrete beams in bending. *Proceedings of the Institution of Civil Engineers, Structures and Buildings*, **104**, May, 193–203.

61. Johnson, R. P. and Huang, D. J. (1997) Statistical calibration of safety factors for encased composite columns. In: Buckner, C. D. and Sharooz, B. M. (eds), *Composite Construction in Steel and Concrete III*, American Society of Civil Engineers, New York, pp. 380–391.

62. British Standards Institution (1997) *Structural Use of Concrete. Part 1: Code of Practice for Design and Construction.* BSI, London, BS 8110.

63. Stark, J. W. B. (1984) *Rectangular Stress Block for Concrete.* Technical paper S16, June. Drafting Committee for Eurocode 4 (unpublished).

64. Johnson, R. P. and Anderson, D. (1993) *Designers' Handbook to Eurocode 4.* Thomas Telford, London. [This handbook is for ENV 1994-1-1.]

65. Lääne, A. and Lebet, J.-P. (2005) Available rotation capacity of composite bridge plate girders with negative moment and shear. *Journal of Constructional Steelwork Research*, **61**, 305–327.

66. Johnson, R. P. and Willmington, R. T. (1972) Vertical shear in continuous composite beams. *Proceedings of the Institution of Civil Engineers*, **53**, Sept., 189–205.

67. Allison, R. W., Johnson, R. P. and May, I. M. (1982) Tension-field action in composite plate girders. *Proceedings of the Institution of Civil Engineers, Part 2, Research and Theory*, **73**, June, 255–276.

68. Veljkovic, M. and Johansson, B. (2001) Design for buckling of plates due to direct stress. In: Mäkeläinen, P., Kesti, J., Jutila, A. and Kaitila, O. (eds) *Proceedings of the 9th Nordic Steel Conference, Helsinki*, 721–729.

69. Lebet, J.-P. and Lääne, A. (2005) Comparison of shear resistance models with slender composite beam test results. In: Hoffmeister, B. and Hechler, O. (eds), *Eurosteel 2005, vol. B.* Druck und Verlagshaus Mainz, Aachen, pp. 4.3-33 to 4.3-40.

70. Ehmann, J. and Kuhlmann, U. (2006) Shear resistance of concrete bridge decks in tension. In: Leon, R. T. and Lange, J. (eds), *Composite Construction in Steel and Concrete V.* American Society of Civil Engineers, New York, pp. 67–76.

71. Johnson, R. P. and Fan, C. K. R. (1991) Distortional lateral buckling of continuous composite beams. *Proceedings of the Institution of Civil Engineers, Part 2*, **91**, Mar., 131–161.

72. Johnson, R. P. and Molenstra, N. (1990) Strength and stiffness of shear connections for discrete U-frame action in composite plate girders. *Structural Engineer*, **68**, Oct., 386–392.

73. Trahair, N. S. (1993) *Flexural Torsional Buckling of Structures.* E & FN Spon, London.

74. Johnson, R. P. and Buckby, R. J. (1986) *Composite Structures of Steel and Concrete, Vol. 2, Bridges*, 2nd edn. Collins, London.

75. Johnson, R. P. and Molenstra, N. (1991) Partial shear connection in composite beams for buildings. *Proceedings of the Institution of Civil Engineers, Part 2, Research and Theory*, **91**, 679–704.

76. Johnson, R. P. and Oehlers, D. J. (1981) Analysis and design for longitudinal shear in composite T-beams. *Proceedings of the Institution of Civil Engineers, Part 2, Research and Theory*, **71**, Dec., 989–1021.

77. Menzies, J. B. (1971) CP 117 and shear connectors in steel–concrete composite beams. *Structural Engineer*, **49**, March, 137–153.

78. Johnson, R. P. and Ivanov, R. I. (2001) Local effects of concentrated longitudinal shear in composite bridge beams. *Structural Engineer*, **79**, No. 5, 19–23.

79. Oehlers, D. J. and Johnson, R. P. (1987) The strength of stud shear connections in composite beams. *Structural Engineer*, **65B**, June, 44–48.

80. Roik, K., Hanswille, G. and Cunze-O. Lanna, A. (1989) *Eurocode 4, Clause 6.3.2: Stud Connectors.* University of Bochum, Report EC4/8/88, March.

81. Stark, J. W. B. and van Hove, B. W. E. M. (1991) *Statistical Analysis of Pushout Tests on Stud Connectors in Composite Steel and Concrete Structures.* TNO Building and Construction Research, Delft, Report BI-91-163, Sept.

82. Kuhlmann, U. and Breuninger, U. (2002) Behaviour of horizontally lying studs with longitudinal shear force. In: Hajjar, J. F., Hosain, M., Easterling, W. S. and Shahrooz, B. M. (eds), *Composite Construction in Steel and Concrete IV.* American Society of Civil Engineers, New York, pp. 438–449.

83. Bridge, R. Q., Ernst, S., Patrick, M. and Wheeler, A. T. (2006) The behaviour and design of haunches in composite beams and their reinforcement. In: Leon, R. T. and Lange, J. (eds), *Composite Construction in Steel and Concrete V.* American Society of Civil Engineers, New York, pp. 282–292.

84. Johnson, R. P. and Oehlers, D. J. (1982) Design for longitudinal shear in composite L-beams. *Proceedings of the Institution of Civil Engineers, Part 2, Research and Theory*, **73**, March, 147–170.

85. Johnson, R. P. (2004) *Composite Structures of Steel and Concrete*, 3rd edn. Blackwell, Oxford.

86. Bulson, P. S. (1970) *The Stability of Flat Plates.* Chatto & Windus, London.

87. Roik, K. and Bergmann, R. (1990) Design methods for composite columns with unsymmetrical cross-sections. *Journal of Constructional Steelwork Research*, **15**, 153–168.

88. Wheeler, A. T. and Bridge, R. Q. (2002) Thin-walled steel tubes filled with high strength concrete in bending. In: Hajjar, J. F., Hosain, M., Easterling, W. S. and Shahrooz, B. M. (eds), *Composite Construction in Steel and Concrete IV.* American Society of Civil Engineers, New York, pp. 584–595.

89. Kilpatrick, A. and Rangan, V. (1999) Tests on high-strength concrete-filled tubular steel columns. *ACI Structural Journal*, Mar.–Apr., Title No. 96-S29, 268–274. American Concrete Institute, Detroit.

90. May, I. M. and Johnson, R. P. (1978) Inelastic analysis of biaxially restrained columns. *Proceedings of the Institution of Civil Engineers, Part 2, Research and Theory*, **65**, June, 323–337.

91. Roik, K. and Bergmann, R. (1992) Composite columns. In: Dowling, P. J., Harding, J. L. and Bjorhovde, R. (eds), *Constructional Steel Design – an International Guide.* Elsevier, London and New York, pp. 443–469.

92. Bergmann, R. and Hanswille, G. (2006) New design method for composite columns including high strength steel. In: Leon, R. T. and Lange, J. (eds), *Composite Construction in Steel and Concrete V.* American Society of Civil Engineers, New York, pp. 381–389.

93. Chen, W. F. and Lui, E. M. (1991) *Stability Design of Steel Frames.* CRC Press, Boca Raton, Florida.

94. Bondale, D. S. and Clark, P. J. (1967) Composite construction in the Almondsbury interchange. *Proceedings of a Conference on Structural Steelwork*, British Constructional Steelwork Association, London, pp. 91–100.

95. Virdi, K. S. and Dowling, P. J. (1980) Bond strength in concrete-filled tubes. *Proceedings of IABSE, Periodica 3/80, P-33/80*, Aug., 125–139.

96. Kerensky, O. A. and Dallard, N. J. (1968) The four-level interchange between M4 and M5 motorways at Almondsbury. *Proceedings of the Institution of Civil Engineers*, **40**, 295–321.

97. Johnson, R. P. (2000) Resistance of stud shear connectors to fatigue. *Journal of Constructional Steel Research*, **56**, 101–116.

98. Oehlers, D. J. and Bradford, M. (1995) *Composite Steel and Concrete Structural Members – Fundamental Behaviour.* Elsevier Science, Oxford.

99. Gomez Navarro, M. (2002) Influence of concrete cracking on the serviceability limit state design of steel-reinforced concrete composite bridges: tests and models. In: J. Martinez Calzon (ed.), *Composite Bridges – Proceedings of the 3rd International Meeting*, Spanish Society of Civil Engineers, Madrid, pp. 261–278.

100. Pucher, A. (1977) *Influence Surfaces of Elastic Plates.* Springer-Verlag Wien, New York.
101. Kuhlmann, U. (1997) Design, calculation and details of tied-arch bridges in composite constructions. In: Buckner, C. D. and Sharooz, B. M. (eds), *Composite Construction in Steel and Concrete III*, American Society of Civil Engineers, New York, pp. 359–369.
102. Monnickendam, A. (2003) The design, construction and performance of Newark Dyke railway bridge. *Proceedings of a Symposium on Structures for High-speed Railway Transportation*, Antwerp. IABSE, Zurich. Reports, **87**, 42–43.
103. British Standards Institution. *Actions on Structures. Part 1-4: General Actions – Wind actions.* BSI, London, EN 1991.
104. Randl, E. and Johnson, R. P. (1982) Widths of initial cracks in concrete tension flanges of composite beams. *Proceedings of IABSE, Periodica 4/82, P-54/82*, Nov., 69–80.
105. Johnson, R. P. and Allison, R. W. (1983) Cracking in concrete tension flanges of composite T-beams. *Structural Engineer*, **61B**, Mar., 9–16.
106. Roik, K., Hanswille, G. and Cunze-O. Lanna, A. (1989) *Report on Eurocode 4, Clause 5.3, Cracking of Concrete.* University of Bochum, Report EC4/4/88.
107. Johnson, R. P. (2003) Cracking in concrete flanges of composite T-beams – tests and Eurocode 4. *Structural Engineer*, **81**, No. 4, 29–34.
108. Schmitt, V., Seidl, G. and Hever, M. (2005) Composite bridges with VFT-WIB construction method. In: Hoffmeister, B. and Hechler, O. (eds), *Eurosteel 2005, vol. B.* Druck und Verlagshaus Mainz, Aachen, pp. 4.6-79 to 4.6-83.
109. Yandzio, E. and Iles, D. C. (2004) *Precast Concrete Decks for Composite Highway Bridges.* Steel Construction Institute, Ascot, Publication 316.
110. Calzon, J. M. (2005). Practice in present-day steel and composite structures. In: Hoffmeister, B. and Hechler, O. (eds), *Eurosteel 2005, vol. A.* Druck und Verlagshaus Mainz, Aachen, pp. 0-11 to 0-18.
111. Doeinghaus, P., Dudek, M. and Sprinke, P. (2004) Innovative hybrid double-composite bridge with prestressing. In: Pre-Conference Proceedings, *Composite Construction in Steel and Concrete V*, United Engineering Foundation, New York, Session E4, paper 1.
112. Department of Transport (now Highways Agency) DoT (1987) *Use of BS 5400:Part 5:1979.* London, Departmental Standard BD 16/82.
113. Moffat, K. R. and Dowling, P. J. (1978) The longitudinal bending behaviour of composite box girder bridges having incomplete interaction. *Structural Engineer*, **56B**, No. 3, 53–60.
114. Kuhlmann, U. and Kürschner, K. (2001) Behavior of lying shear studs in reinforced concrete slabs. In: Eligehausen, R. (ed.), *Connections between Steel and Concrete.* RILEM Publications S.A.R.L., Bagneux, France, pp. 1076–1085.
115. Kuhlmann, U. and Kürschner, K. (2006) Structural behavior of horizontally lying shear studs. In: Leon, R. T. and Lange, J. (eds), *Composite Construction in Steel and Concrete V.* American Society of Civil Engineers, New York, pp. 534–543.

# Index

Notes: references to 'beams' and to 'columns' are to composite members; cross-references to EN 1992 and EN 1993 are too numerous to be indexed